Published in 1977 by
Arms and Armour Press,
Lionel Leventhal Ltd.,
2–6 Hampstead High St.,
London NW3 1QQ.

First German-language
edition: *Von Salamis bis
Okinawa,* published 1975,
© J. F. Lehmanns Verlag,
1975.
First English-language
edition, fully revised,
© Lionel Leventhal Ltd.,
1977.

BRITISH LIBRARY CATA-
LOGUING IN PUBLICATION
DATA:
Pemsel, Helmut
Atlas of Naval Warfare
1. Naval history—maps.
I. Title   II. Smith,
Digby G.
911 G1030
ISBN 0-85368-351-4

The publishers wish to
express their especial
thanks to Colin Duffield,
who provided much useful
advice on the revisions
necessary for the
production of this English-
language edition. Cartography
by Helmut Fechter;
edited and designed by
David Gibbons; indexed by
Tessa Rose; printed and
bound by Billing & Sons
Ltd., Guildford, Surrey,
England.

ATLAS OF NAVAL WARFARE

An atlas and chronology of conflict at sea
from earliest times to the present day

Helmut Pemsel

Translated by Major i.G. D. G. Smith

ARMS AND ARMOUR PRESS

London — Melbourne

List of contents

Chronological Summary

* Numbers in parentheses refer to the points table on page 155.

DATE	WARS	BATTLES*	COMMANDERS	SHIPS/TECHNOLOGY
500BC	Persian Wars	Salamis (7)	Themistocles	
	Peloponnesian Wars	Syracuse (5)		
400BC		Aegospotami (4)		
300BC	First Punic War	Ecnomus (6)		Boarding ramps
200BC		Aegates Islands (7)		
100BC	Pirate Wars		Sextus Pompey	
—	Roman Civil War	Actium (7)	Agrippa	
AD100	Roman Empire			
200				
300		Hellespont (3)		
400	Barbarian Migrations begin			
500				
600	Spread of Islam			
700		'Battle of the Masts' (3)		'Greek Fire'
	Byzantine Empire	Constantinople (4)		
800	Depredations of 'Norsemen'			'Long ships'
900	Normandy founded			
	Arabs conquer Sicily			
1000	Norsemen in America and Sicily			
	Norman invasion of England			
1100	Crusades			
1200				
1300	Venetian-Genoese rivalry			'Mature' sailing ship design
	Hundred Years War	Sluys (5)		Fixed rudders
1400	Hanseatic League	Chioggia (3)		The compass
				Cannon

DATE	WARS	BATTLES	COMMANDERS	SHIPS/TECHNOLOGY
1500	Ottoman Turks		Andrea Doria Barbarossa	*Great Harry*
1550		Lepanto (6) Armada (6)	Howard, Drake	Fire-ships
	Dutch War of Independence			
1600			Yi Sun-sin	
1650	First Anglo-Dutch War Swedish-Danish War Second Anglo-Dutch War Third Anglo-Dutch War Scanian War	The Downs (4) Portland (5) The Sound (4) Gabbard Bank (5) Four Days Fight (5) Texel (6) Kjöje Bay (4) Beachy Head (5)	Van Tromp Blake De Ruyter Niels Juel	*Sovereign of the Seas* 'Rating' of warships *Fighting Instructions* *Soleil Royal*
1700	League of Augsburg War of the Spanish Succession Great Northern War	La Hogue (7) Malaga (4) Cape Passaro (4)	Tourville Russell	Steering wheel Commerce warfare
1750	Seven Years War American Revolution	Quiberon Bay (6) Chesapeake Bay (5) The Saints (6)	Hawke Suffren Rodney	Ships of the line and frigates Blockade warfare League of Armed Neutrality Flintlock cannon mechanisms Improved signalling
1800	French Revolutionary War	Glorious First of June (5) The Nile (6) Trafalgar (7) Navarino Bay (5)	Howe Nelson	First iron steam ship Screw-driven steamers

1850	Crimean War
	American Civil War
	Austro-Italian War
	Sino-Japanese War
	Spanish-American War
		Bombardment of Kinburn
		Chesapeake Bay (first
		  action between armoured
		  ships) Lissa (4)
			Tegetthoff	Mine warfare, rams, *Duillo*
				Steam replaces sail.
				Torpedo-boats, submarines.
				Gunfire at 5,000 yards.
				Radio telegraphy

1900	Russo-Japanese War First World War Washington Naval Treaty	Tsushima (6) Jutland (7)	Togo Jellicoe Scheer Beatty	*Dreadnought* Submarine warfare Aircraft
1950	Second World War Korean War Vietnam	Pearl Harbor (6) Midway Island (6) Leyte Gulf (8)	Yamamoto Nimitz	Radar, Rockets Nuclear propulsion Man on the Moon

Foreword

by Professor Jürgen Rohwer
President of the Society of Defence Research, Stuttgart

P   Flagship
+   Sinking
⊕   Badly damaged
⊘   Damaged
○   Lightly damaged
P   Prize (captured)
⌐   Sea-borne landing
⊗   Naval battle
X   Naval action/land battle
⚓   Shipwreck
▲▲▲   Blockade
⚓   Anchorage
⌐   Radio message

○   England, Great Britain,
    USA, Austria, China,
    Sweden, Venice
●   France, Denmark,
    Italy, Japan,
    Germany, Confederacy
◑   Spain
◔   Netherlands, Russia
◕   Turkey

AUS Australia
DK Denmark
E   England
GB Great Britain
F   France
NL Netherlands

Within these pages, Helmut Pemsel has ably succeeded in presenting a concise chronicle of more than three thousand years of naval warfare.

The wars and battles normally found in naval histories are all here. But great effort has also been made to include actions and events less well known to Western readers—seldom-heard-of battles (which have generally received far less attention than their places in history would warrant) in the Mediterranean, the Baltic, the Black Sea, the Indian Ocean and the Far East.

Such an enlarged geographical scope has made a strict selection process vital, in order to keep the book to a reasonable size, and Helmut Pemsel has taken considerable pains to ensure that the reader really can 'see the wood from the trees'.

Thus, his principal criterion has been the inclusion of fleet engagements, at the expense of less important single ship actions.

A brief résumé of the political background to the wars and campaigns accompanies the wealth of detailed information on the battles themselves, and a parallel running commentary places the evolution of warships and weapons in their proper historical perspective. All of this is both complemented and illuminated by Helmut Fechter's fine maps.

This book has brought a very great number of geographically and chronologically diverse events into a clear and comprehensible form. I trust that it will attain the readership that it so richly deserves.

Jürgen Rohwer

Introduction

My intention in writing this book was to provide an easily accessible chronicle of all significant armed conflicts at sea from the time of the Persian Wars to the present day. In compiling it, the aim has always been to approach the subject from an objectively international aspect, favouring the history of no one nation above the others.

A particular concern was to cover the 'Dark Ages' of maritime history (especially the wars in the Mediterranean between Actium and the mid-16th century) as far as they could be adequately researched. But to include all the battles that ever took place would have inflated the book out of all proportion, so it is generally the activities of 'ships of the line' and fleets that are recorded here—without, however, the exclusion of those few cases (such as the action between *Monitor* and *Virginia*) where a technological innovation is apparent. For coverage of the World Wars, a correct balance would have been impossible without including the many naval-air battles, convoy operations and sea-borne landings.

For the names of both places and people, contradictions abound in the many reference books available to the reader; so, where a choice seems to exist, the most generally accepted spelling has been used. Similarly, there is conflict between sources due to the staggered introduction of the Gregorian Calendar. I have tried, where possible, to eliminate such differences, and from 1582 onwards, have consistently quoted the new calendar.

The ship profiles, which are intended to demonstrate the gradual changes in ship construction and armament, are drawn at a scale of 1:1,000 up to page 88, and 1:1,200 from there on. The transition between the two scales is illustrated by *Victoria*, on page 88, which is shown in both scales. These profiles were gathered from many sources, including the

following: S. Breyer, Hanau; C. Canby, *Geschichte der Schiffahrt*; B. Grabner, Vienna; E. Gröner, *Die deutschen Kriegsschiffe, 1815–1945*; E. Groner, D. Jung and Martin Maass, *Die Schiffe der deutschen Kriegsmarine und Luftwaffe 1939-45 und ihr Verblieb*; H. Jentschura, D. Jung and P. Mickel, *Die Japanischen Kriegsschiffe, 1869-1945*; Weyer, *Taschenbuch der Kriegsflotten* and *Flottentaschenbuch*.

To the many people who have helped me in making possible the publication of this book I should like to express my appreciation. Professor Jürgen Rohwer read the manuscript and recommended the publisher and, at J.F.Lehmanns Verlag, Herr V. Schwartz has always had an open ear for me. I also owe the greatest thanks to Herr Wolf Kaliebe, who carried out the tiresome and time-consuming task of editing the original text and the maps, besides solving many technical questions. My special thanks go to Herr Fechter, who made a major contribution to the clarity of this book: based on my preliminary sketches (which were not always easy to interpret), he laboured for two years to produce the finished maps exactly according to my ideas.

I am also grateful to the naval museums and archives who so quickly and helpfully processed my queries.

My colleagues in the Arbeitsgemeinschaft für österreichische Marinegeschichte (Society for Austrian Naval History) and Dr. Reisch in Kitzbühel, with his rich English-language naval library, were also of great assistance to me. And, finally, I would like to thank Dr. Hertha Ladenbauer of the Federal Austrian Office of Monuments for her encouragement and for her wealth of experience in the publication of scientific works which she shared with me.

Helmut Pemsel

The Age of Galleys

Illustration by Geoff Hunt

In ancient times, travel by sea was restricted to coastal waters, and made doubly dangerous by the small size of the early vessels and the absence of navigational instruments. Voyages were undertaken only during daylight, and the vessels were anchored each night, or run up on to the beach. Although trade and war often went hand in hand, two distinct types of vessels gradually evolved: the broad-beamed 'freighter', propelled by sail; and the ship of war, narrower in the beam, designed to be rowed, and thus having but an auxiliary sail, which, in preparation for combat, would have been furled, and the mast unstepped. The only guides to navigation were the plumb line, to determine the depth of the water; such well-known landmarks as islands and mountains, to establish location; and the positions of the sun and the Pole star, to give an approximate idea of course.

The first large ships were probably built by the Egyptians, on the Nile, and by the earlier higher cultures in Mesopotamia, on the Tigris and Euphrates. These early ships would have been without keels, and would not have been capable of venturing on to the high seas. In time, however, the interests of trade and the need to carry greater loads for longer distances would encourage the development of sturdier craft.

THE EARLY CIVILIZATIONS

2700–2200BC: The Egyptians of the 'Old Kingdom' begin to develop sea trade with the Syrian coast and the east African land of Punt (probably the area of modern Somali Republic).

2300–2100: During the Bronze Age, the inhabitants of the Cyclades Islands exercise command of the Aegean and the eastern Mediterranean, with many-oared ships. These are the vehicles of an exchange of culture between Asia Minor and south-eastern Europe.

2000–1400: Crete, during the middle and late Minoan period, is the first naval power of significance. With robust ships featuring keels and ribs, she trades with Egypt, Syria, Sicily and the islands of the Aegean.

1990–1790: The Egyptian 'Middle Kingdom' takes up trading relations with Crete.

1850: There begin the first migrations of Indo-European tribes (Ionians and Achaeans) into present-day Greece.

1501–1480: Queen Hatshepsut of the Egyptian 'New Kingdom' undertakes a great trading expedition to Punt, and hardwoods, incense, ivory, metals, cattle and slaves are brought back to Thebes.

From 1400: In the late Mycenaean period, the mainland Greeks become the leading naval powers in the Aegean and central Mediterranean, while the Phoenicians begin to succeed the Cretans as the leading maritime traders. From their settlements along the Syrian coast (Byblos, later Tyre and Sidon), their fleets penetrate to the farthest shores of the Mediterranean, exporting cedars from Lebanon, slaves and purple dye. From Tartessus (or Tarshish), the old trading centre at the mouth of the Guadalquivir in Spain, they

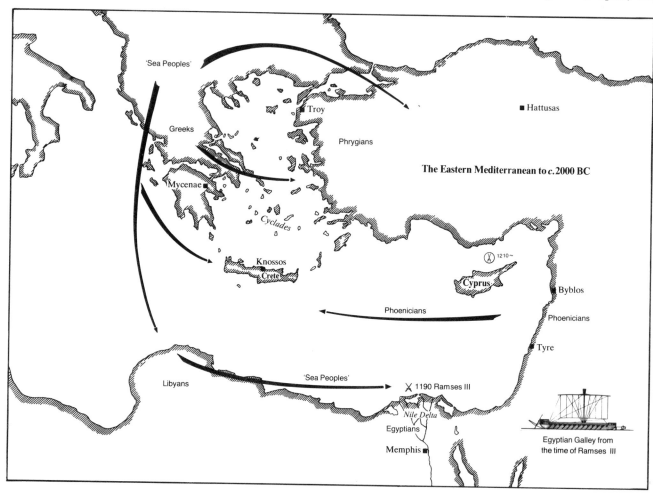

The Eastern Mediterranean to c. 2000 BC

Egyptian Galley from the time of Ramses III

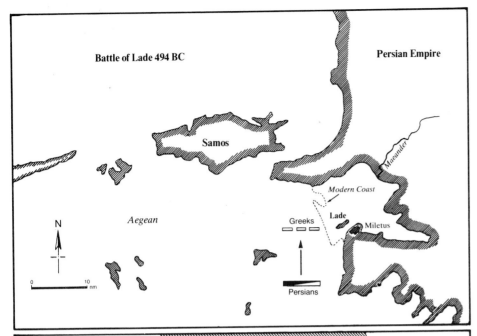

Battle of Lade 494 BC

Samos

Persian Empire

Maeander

Aegean

Modern Coast

Greeks

Lade

Miletus

N

0   10
nm

Persians

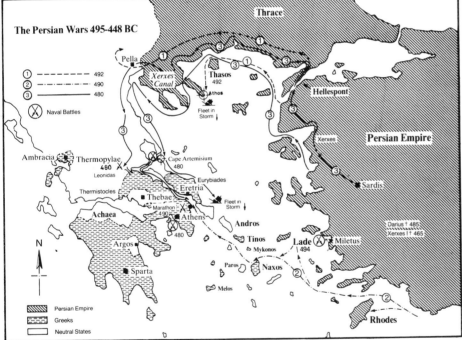

The Persian Wars 495-448 BC

Thrace

① — — — — —   492
② — · — · — ·   490
③ ——————   480

Ⓧ Naval Battles

Pella

Xerxes Canal   Thasos 492

Athos

Fleet in Storm

Hellespont

Xerxes

Persian Empire

Ambracia

Thermopylae 480 X
Leonidas

Cape Artemisium 480

Eurybiades

Thermistocles

Thebae

Eretria

Fleet in Storm

Achaea

Marathon 490 X

Athens

Andros

Sardis

Darius † 485
Xerxes †† 465

Argos

Tinos

Mykonos

Lade Ⓧ 494   Miletus

Sparta

Paros

Naxos

Melos

Rhodes

Persian Empire
Greeks
Neutral States

N

---

upheavals in the eastern Mediterranean: together with the Libyans, they attack Egypt.

1210: Battle off Cyprus. Suppiluliumas II, king of the Hittites, defeats the Cypriot fleet, which is allied to the Sea Peoples, and their ships are burnt at sea. This is the first recorded sea battle (on clay tablets) that can be dated.

About 1190: In a naval battle in the Nile delta, Ramses III repulses an invasion of the 'Sea Peoples', some of whom settle in Palestine (where they become known as Philistines).

1100-900: The Dorian migrations; Greek colonization of the Mediterranean and the Black Sea begins. Many towns are founded, including Ischia (770) and Cumae (750) in southern Italy; Syracuse (734) in Sicily; Naucratis (610) in Egypt; Massilia, modern Marseilles (600); and Malaca (600) in Spain. Greek maritime trade expands rapidly, mainly due to the Ionians, but the extension of trade into the western Mediterranean is obstructed by the Carthaginians in the 6th century. In Greece, a single consolidated state is not formed, since the nature of the country favours separation, so there spring up a plethora of city-states, all sharing a common language and religion. Doric Sparta and Ionian Athens manage, however, to establish a certain hegemony.

From the 8th century: The Assyrians encroach upon Phoenicia.

7th century: Psamatik I maintains a fleet of Greek mercenaries, and brings Greek trade to Egypt.

6th century: For a short time (until its conquest by the Persians in 525) Egypt is a naval power in the eastern Mediterranean. In Greece, the geographer Skylax produces the first noteworthy coastline description (The Periplus) as a navigational aid. The description of the Mediterranean coasts that is usually attributed to him, however, is certainly some 200 years later.

664: A battle at sea is fought between Corinth and her 'daughter city', Corcyra (Corfu), the first naval battle in Greek history for which a written record exists.

560-546: King Croesus of Lydia brings the Greek towns of Asia Minor under his influence. Ephesus is captured, and a treaty concluded with Miletus.

c. 546: Lydia itself falls to King Cyrus the Great of Persia, and the Greeks of Asia Minor thus pass into Persian rule. The Persian attack on Greece proper signals the beginning of organized naval warfare.

The struggles between the Persians and the Greeks constituted the first great combined land–sea operations. The principal warships were galleys with two (biremes) or three (triremes) rows of oars, one above the other, and equipped with a ram at the bow. Offensive tactics would have been ramming or passing close alongside an enemy ship, in order to break off the opponent's oars and render him incapable of manoeuvre. As well as these 'battleships', there were small penteres, with 25 oars on each side. All warships had flat bottoms, so that they could be beached.

THE WARS OF THE ANCIENT GREEKS

The Persian Wars begin with a rising of the Ionians of Asia Minor, under Aristagoras of Miletus, against their Persian overlords. The Greeks receive support from Athens and Eretria (Euboea).

497: Battle off Cyprus. The Greeks on the island rise up against the Persians. The Phoenician fleet brings Persian troops to Cyprus, and is subsequently defeated by an Ionian squadron. However, the troops they have landed suppress the Greek rebellion.

494: Battle of Lade (Asia Minor). The combined Ionian fleet, under the Phocaean Dionysius, is decisively beaten by the Persians. A coalition fleet, the Ionian side is weakened by the

---

bring silver, lead, iron and tin. Phoenicians found many colonies throughout the Mediterranean, including Malta, Panormus (Palermo), Hippo (Bizerta), Utica (near Tunis), Carthage and Gades (Cadiz). Under Hiram I of Tyre (969-936); and, in co-operation with Solomon of Israel (966-926), communal trade is developed in the Red Sea. According to legend, Phoenicians succeed in the first circumnavigation of the African continent. Their warships are the first to have two banks of rowers per side (one above the other), and they also build the first warships with rams.

1220 onwards: The migrations of the 'Sea Peoples' cause great

divergent interests of its contingents, and part of the Greek fleet does not earnestly enter into the battle. The Persians themselves are not sailors: they rely upon the fleets of their vassals, including Phoenicians and Lycians.

The assistance given by Athens and Eretria to Miletus (now destroyed by the Persians) becomes the excuse for a campaign of revenge by the Persians against Greece. One man in Greece recognizes the danger, and knows how to combat it:

493/492: Themistocles of Athens begins construction of a fortified naval base at Piraeus.

492: The First Persian Campaign

The army of King Darius of Persia, commanded by his general Mardonios, crosses the Hellespont and advances into Thrace to secure his flank for the assault on Attica. But the Thracians offer stiff resistance, and the fleet accompanying the Persian army is wrecked in a storm off Mount Athos. Mardonios then abandons the campaign. Sparta and Athens refuse to subject themselves to Persia as demanded.

490: The Second Persian Campaign

This time, Darius' army, under Datis and Artaphernes, is transported direct to Attica and, on the way there, they subdue Rhodes and Naxos, and capture and destroy Eretria on Euboea. To carry their cavalry, the Persians use special horse-transport ships, making this the first large-scale amphibious operation in recorded history. The landing takes place near Marathon, but the road to Athens is blocked by the Greek army under Miltiades. The Persians begin to re-embark their force, but at this point the Greeks attack and, as the Persian cavalry is already on board the ships, the Persian army is defeated. A rapid countermarch by the Greek army prevents another landing near Athens. The Persians withdraw.

On the advice of Themistocles, Athens now builds a strong fleet to guard against future Persian attacks. This construction is financed with the profits of the state-owned silver mines of Laurion near Cape Sounion.

487: The new Athenian fleet, reinforced by 20 ships from Corinth, fights two successful engagements against the hitherto unbeaten Aegina.

486: Death of Darius, the Persian king. His son, Xerxes I (486–65) continues the struggle in 480.

480: The Third Persian Campaign

As in the first campaign, the army advances on land via the Hellespont, and a great war fleet with a large train follows their progress. Xerxes assumes personal command of the operation. Confronted with this great show of force, most of the Greek states submit to the Persians, but a few support Athens and Sparta in their decisive struggle, and Sparta assumes command of the combined armies. The Persians build two bridges of boats over the Hellespont, and dig a canal through the isthmus of Athos to speed the advance of fleet and army, but, at the defile of Thermopylae, the Greeks under Leonidas halt their progress.

480: Battle of Artemisium. In order to cover the army at Thermopylae, the Greek fleet under the Spartan Eurybiades takes up position in a narrow channel off Cape Artemisium. Themistocles commands Athens' strong contingent. Facing the more numerous Persian fleet, the Greek left flank is covered by the mainland, and their right by the island of Euboea. A Persian attempt to sail around Euboea and attack the Greeks from both sides fails when the outflanking force is destroyed in a storm. A Persian frontal attack breaks the first Greek line, but is then taken in the flank by the second line. With the destruction of some of their ships, the Persians withdraw, and have to ride out a storm for a whole night in the unprotected roads. Two days later, they attack again, but the Greeks, reinforced in the meantime, retain control of the battle area until news of the fall of Thermopylae precipitates their withdrawal.

On Themistocles' advice, Athens is evacuated: the population is moved to safety on the island of Salamis, and the fleet takes up a protective position between Salamis and the mainland.

480: Battle of Salamis. In this position, the Persians once again have no chance to bring their numerical superiority to bear. Themistocles places the Greek fleet so that its right wing is pushed forward against Salamis, and its left wing is refused towards the mainland. A small island (Psyttaleia) in the channel by which the Persians must advance further complicates their assault. In spite of these difficulties, and misled by a secret message from Themistocles, Xerxes orders an attack. The Persian order of battle is disrupted by the island and, as soon as the opposing fleets are close enough, Themistocles attacks the disordered Persian left wing with his right. The Persian left wing is surrounded and thrown back on to its own right wing, which itself is being attacked by the Spartan division of the Greek fleet. The ram, with which the Greek triremes are equipped, proves to be the decisive weapon. In the ensuing mêlée, the more numerous Persian fleet cannot deploy, suffers heavy losses, but is not destroyed. The Greeks lose about 40 ships to a Persian loss of approximately 200. Although his remaining fleet is still stronger than that of the Greeks, Xerxes orders a withdrawal to Piraeus. For the first time, naval warfare has affected world history: the Persian threat to Greece is removed, and Athens' command of the sea (initially the Aegean) is established. From now on, Greece is almost immune to Persian attack.

479: After fighting on in Attica for another year, the Persian army under Mardonios is defeated at Plataea. In the same year, the Greek fleet takes the offensive against the Persians at Samos. The Persians withdraw to Asia Minor and lay up their fleet at Mycale.

479: Battle of Mycale. The Greeks, under Leotychides the Spartan and Xanthippos the Athenian, beat the Persians and burn their beached fleet. The Ionian city-states in Asia Minor are liberated.

478: The Greek fleet, under Pausanias, liberates the Greeks on Cyprus and captures Byzantium on the Bosporus, thus reopening the sea lane to the Black Sea. Until this point, Sparta has held supreme command of the Greek fleet in this campaign; but now, after the recall of Pausanias, this is transferred to Athens at the wish of the Ionian towns.

477: Founding of the First Attican Maritime Alliance (the Delian League) by Aristeides; under the command of Athens, this is to liberate and protect the Aegean from the Persians.

470: As a result of political manoeuvring in Athens, Themistocles is ostracized (banished).

466: Twin Battles of Eurymedon. The Greek fleet under Cimon, son of Miltiades, seeks out and defeats a Persian army and fleet.

The growing strength of Athens now begins to bring her into conflict with Sparta, thus far the leading military power in Greece, and (459–49) Sparta repeatedly interferes in Athens' struggles with recalcitrant allies. Aegina and Corinth join this opposition to Athenian hegemony in Greece.

458: Battle off Aegina. The fleet of the League, under Leodorates, defeats the combined forces of Aegina and Corinth.

459–54: The Greek expedition to Egypt. The League supports an Egyptian revolt against Persia. Initial successes take their fleet to Memphis, but, when the Persian king Artaxerxes sends a force to recapture Egypt, the entire Greek expeditionary fleet is destroyed, together with a supporting squadron. This causes the League to move its treasure from the now exposed Delos to Athens.

449: Twin Battles of Salamis (Cyprus). Cimon's Greek expeditionary force beats a Persian fleet composed of Phoenicians and Cicilians.

448: Peace of Callias. In return for a Persian guarantee of the autonomy of the Greek towns in Asia Minor, the Greeks agree not to support any futher revolts against Persian rule in the subcontinent. The aim of the Delian League has thus been achieved, and Pericles converts it into an Athenian Empire.

433–432: The Corinthian War against Corcyra (Corfu)

433: Battle of Sybota. Although the Corinthian fleet defeats that of Corcyra, the presence of an Athenian squadron prevents exploitation of the victory. Corinth subsequently urges jealous Sparta to declare war on Athens.

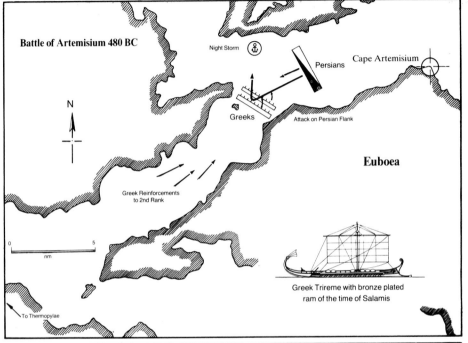

Battle of Artemisium 480 BC

Night Storm

Persians

Cape Artemisium

Greeks

Attack on Persian Flank

N

Euboea

Greek Reinforcements to 2nd Rank

Greek Trireme with bronze plated ram of the time of Salamis

0   5
nm

To Thermopylae

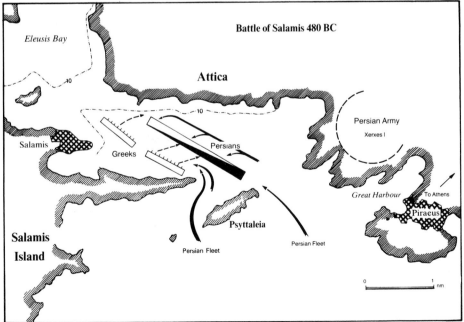

Battle of Salamis 480 BC

Eleusis Bay

Attica

Salamis

Greeks

Persians

Persian Army
Xerxes I

Salamis Island

Psyttaleia

Great Harbour

To Athens

Piraeus

Persian Fleet

Persian Fleet

0   1
nm

431–404: The Peloponnesian War

The opponents are Athens' Attic League and Sparta's Peloponnesian League—sea power versus land power. Corinth provides the fleet of the Peloponnesian League. According to Pericles' plan of campaign, Attica is to be abandoned to the superior land forces of Sparta, and the populace evacuated to the safety of the walls of Athens and Piraeus. The fleet is to conduct offensive operations at sea.

431–421: The Archidamian War. King Archidamos of Sparta opens the land war, seizes the initiative and devastates Attica. Athens is at first only concerned with keeping open her sea lanes, which are vital to her existence, and the fleet is squandered in minor engagements.

429: Pericles dies of the plague, which devastates the population of Athens. A squadron of about 20 Athenian triremes under Phormio is meanwhile maintained in the Gulf of Corinth. Sparta sends 45 triremes against them.

429: Battle of Rhium (Chalcis, off the Gulf of Patras). The Athenians defeat a Spartan squadron, which has taken up an unsuitable 'hedgehog' formation: some ships are sunk, the rest put to flight.

429: Battle of Naupactus (medieval Lepanto). Sparta sends Brasidas, with the concentrated fleets of her confederates, into the Gulf of Corinth. Outnumbered 77 to 20, Phormio initially withdraws, but turns suddenly on the foremost of his adversaries and puts them to flight. Sparta loses 7 ships to Athens' 1, and is forced to give up the offensive in the west.

425: Fight for Pylos. After a battle in the harbour of Pylos, the Athenians win control of the sea and, after a 72-day blockade of the island of Sphacteria, force the Spartan garrison there to surrender.

421: Peace of Nicias between Athens and Sparta ('the rotten peace'), but the old conflicts remain.

415–413: Athens' Sicilian Expedition. The city of Segesta (Sicily) calls on Athens for help against Syracuse, an ally of Corinth. 134 triremes with 25,000 crewmen and a 6,400 landing force under Nicias set off for Sicily. The Athenians are victorious in Syracuse harbour, and firmly establish themselves there in the next year. In the meantime, Sparta sends Gylippus to help Syracuse: he defeats the Athenian landing force, and blockades their camp on the south shore of the harbour from the land side. During three battles in Syracuse harbour, the Athenians suffer considerable losses.

413: Fourth Battle of Syracuse. Gylippus closes the harbour mouth with a blockade of ships and beams, and prepares his fleet in the northern part of the harbour to prevent a break-out attempt by the Athenians. When Nicias makes the attempt, his fleet is heavily defeated; Athens loses 50 ships against 20 from Syracuse. Then, in an attempted break-out by land, all the Athenians are killed. This catastrophe is the beginning of the decline of Athens' sea power; one after the other, her allies desert her.

413–404: The Decelian War. After urging by Alcibiades, Sparta renews the war. She ensures herself the support of Tissaphernes (Persian satrap of Lydia), in return for mastery of the Greeks in Asia Minor. After constitutional changes in Athens, Alcibiades returns there.

411: Battle of Cynossema. Off the coast of Asia Minor, 76 Athenian ships clash with a slightly stronger squadron from Sparta. The Athenians are victorious in this, their first victory since the catastrophe of Syracuse.

410: Battle of Cyzicus. Alcibiades wipes out the main Spartan fleet. By feigned flight, he lures them out of the harbour, and destroys them completely in a surprise attack. Mindarus, commander of the Spartan fleet is killed.

407: Battle of Notium. The Spartan fleet, under Lysander,

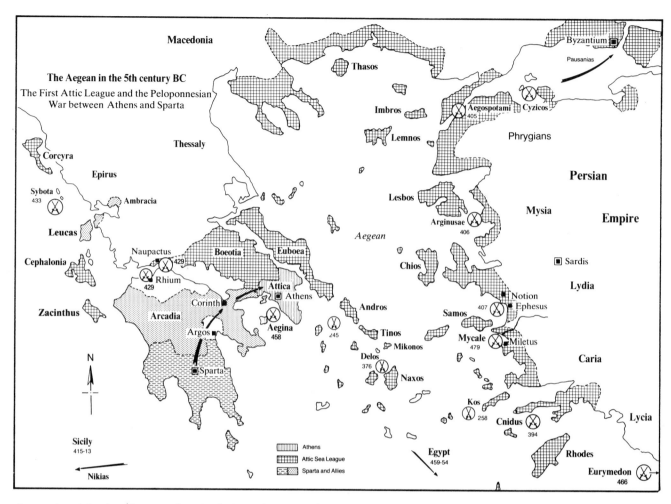

The Aegean in the 5th century BC

The First Attic League and the Peloponnesian War between Athens and Sparta

▥	Athens
▦	Attic Sea League
▨	Sparta and Allies

beats the Athenian fleet, under Antiochus. As a result, Alcibiades' role as a strategist is ended. Athens builds a new fleet of 150 triremes.

406: Battle of the Arginusae. Athens wins another great victory. The passage for supplies from the Black Sea is safe again. The Athenian fleet commanders, however, are condemned to death for not rescuing shipwrecked sailors in a storm following the battle, and for not burying their bodies. (Socrates enters an unsuccessful plea on their behalf.)

405: Battle of Aegospotami. Lysander and the Spartan fleet destroy Conon's Athenian fleet, which is drawn up on the beach. Athens is now besieged by land by a Spartan army and closely blockaded from the sea by the fleet under Lysander.

404: Surrender of Athens. The city is forced to yeild to the first effective blockade in the history of sea warfare. Athens has to deliver her fleet, the city walls are slighted and the confederation of the sea is disbanded. But the real victors in these struggles are the Persians, who regain all of Asia Minor.

395-387: The Corinthian War

The Greeks in Asia Minor rebel against the Persians; they call to Sparta for help, and her intervention is successful. Tissaphernes manages to organize an alliance against Sparta in Greece, under the leadership of Thebes, and Athens also puts a small contingent into the field against her old rival. Initially Sparta is victorious on land.

394: Battle of Cnidus. The fleet of the allied Greeks under Conon decisively beats that of Sparta north of Rhodes; this is a blow from which Sparta never recovers.

376: Battle of Naxos. A Spartan fleet of 60 ships blockades the Saronian Gulf. The Athenians attack with 80 triremes, and inflict a crushing defeat on the Spartans.

After his victory over the Persian army at Issus (333) Alexander of Macedonia turns south in order to take from the Persians their naval bases.

332: At the siege and capture of Tyre, Alexander successfully uses his new fleet for the first time.

323-280: Conflict at sea during the Diadochian Wars

322: After the death of Alexander (323), Athens rises up against the Macedonians; but in two naval battles, at Abydos and Amorgos, the Macedonians destroy the Athenian fleet, and Athens' brief command of the Aegean collapses.

318: Battle of the Bosporus. Antigonus' Syrian fleet under Nicanor meets the Greek-Macedonian fleet under Cleitus. At the first clash, the Syrians lose almost half of their fleet. Shortly afterwards, Nicanor surprises his opponents, whose fleet is drawn up on the beaches. In an attack by land and by sea, the Macedonians are beaten and their fleet is destroyed.

306: Battle of Salamis (Cyprus). Demetrius Poliorcetes, with over 100 large ships beats a somewhat stronger Egyptian

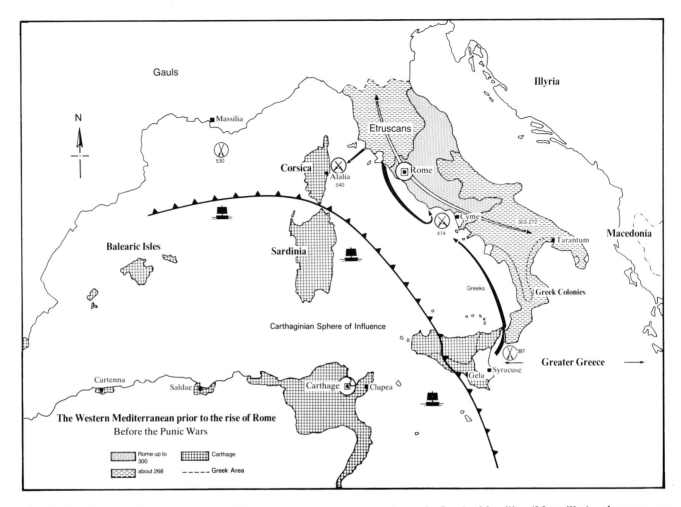

The Western Mediterranean prior to the rise of Rome
Before the Punic Wars

Rome up to 300		Carthage
about 268		Greek Area

fleet under Ptolemy. He captures 40 warships, 100 transports and 8,000 men.

305/304: The island of Rhodes successfully repels an attempted invasion by Demetrius ('the Besieger'). Blockade runners are able to circumvent the attackers and supply the island.

258: Battle of Kos. The Macedonian fleet, under King Antigonus Gonatas II, defeats the superior Egyptian fleet in a large sea battle.

246/245: Battle of Andros. Antigonus II defeats the Egyptians for a second time, and ends their 35-year long domination of the Aegean.

THE NAVAL WARS OF ROME

Events in the Western Mediterranean prior to the rise of Rome

From 1200: Phoenicians found trading colonies in the western Mediterranean.

c.814: Carthage (near Tunis) is founded by a force from Tyre. Following the conquest of Phoenicia by the Assyrians, Carthage assumes the role of protector of all Phoenician colonies.

c.540: **Battle of Alalia** (Corsica). Together with the united Etruscans, the Carthaginians defeat the Phoceans; Greek penetration of the western Mediterranean is thus halted. The Etruscans limit themselves to coastal trade and, with the exception of Greek Massilia (Marseilles), the western Mediterranean becomes a Carthaginian trading area.

c.530: Off the coast of Gaul, the Greeks defeat a Carthaginian squadron, thus securing the survival of their colony at Massilia.

c.510: Carthage destroys Tartessus (or Tarshish) in southern Spain. Punic trade now extends westward via Gades (Cadiz), and reaches to the North Sea and West Africa.

c.480: The Carthaginian Hanno sails around West Africa and reaches the Cameroons.

474: Battle of Cyme (Cumae). Syracuse in Sicily, by now the most powerful city in the Greek sphere, defeats the Etruscan fleet and halts their expansion to the south.

398-396: War between Carthage and Syracuse. Dionysius I of Syracuse attacks Carthaginian possessions on western Sicily.

398: The town of Motya is captured with the help of heavy siege equipment, and an attempted relief by the Carthaginian fleet is beaten off.

397: Battle of Catania. The Carthaginian fleet defeats that of Syracuse. Half of the defeated fleet's ships are destroyed, and Syracuse is then placed under siege. But, after Dionysius I mounts a night raid on the besiegers, by land and sea, the Carthaginians, already weakened by plague, conclude peace.

356: Civil War in Syracuse. The Democrats win control of the sea in a battle outside the city's harbour, and thereby win the civil war.

312-306: War between Carthage and Syracuse. Carthage, holding western Sicily, makes repeated attempts on the Greek half of the island, until the tyrant Agathocles of Syracuse lands with an army at Aspis (Clupea) in Africa, and attacks Carthage in her own heartland. This forces Carthage to sue for peace.

275: Pyrrhus of Epirus fights in Sicily against the Punic allies of Rome. As he crosses from the island to southern Italy, his fleet loses 70 ships as a result of Punic attacks and storms.

272: A Punic fleet supports Rome in her struggle against Greek Tarentum (Taranto). The blockade of this city speeds its capture by Rome, and helps to spread Rome's power over southern Italy. Rome intervenes in the war in Sicily, and thus comes into conflict with Carthage.

The Romans were not a sea-going nation; their power was based on their political and military organization on land. Initially, Rome had not indulged in wars of conquest, entering wars only at the request of allies, but these martial adventures had founded her power base. Lacking the urge to act offensively overseas, navigation was practised on a modest scale and, in 509, 348 and 306, Rome had signed treaties with Carthage acknowledging the supremacy of that sea power in the western Mediterranean. However, a Roman naval victory in 338 (during the Latin War) is known to us: for the prows of captured ships were set up in the Forum as speakers' pulpits (rostra).

264-241: The First Punic War

The war begins as a struggle on land for Sicily. Since victory there cannot be achieved without a fleet, Rome builds a fleet of penteres (quinqueremes), using as its model a stranded Punic vessel. And, to compensate for their inferior seamanship, the Romans invent a boarding ramp (corvus = raven, or crow), transforming ships into battlegrounds. They are thus able to use their legionaries effectively, applying the tactics of land warfare to naval engagements.

260: Battle of Mylae. This is the first clash between the new Roman fleet and that of the Carthaginians. Each fleet is of about 130 ships, the Roman under Consul Caius Duilius, the Carthaginian under Hannibal. Hannibal underestimates the novices, attacks carelessly, and the boarding ramps decide the battle in favour of the Romans. Hannibal loses 50 ships and control of the sea; the Romans now occupy Corsica (259) and Malta (257). But these operations bring no final victory and, to invade Africa, an expeditionary force is assembled on the south coast of Sicily; a reinforced fleet of warships is to escort the transport fleet on the voyage.

256: Battle of Ecnomus. The Roman fleet, led by consuls M. Atilius Regulus and L. Manlius Vulso, numbers about 330 ships; and the awaiting Carthaginian fleet, under Hanno and Hamilcar Barca, is of similar strength. Each fleet is divided into four squadrons. The Romans advance with two squadrons in a v shape in the van, the third squadron towing the troop transports, the fourth bringing up the rear. The Carthaginians adopt a broad formation, all squadrons abreast. As soon as the opposing fleets meet, the two central Carthaginian squadrons feign flight, drawing the two leading Roman squadrons after them. The other two Carthaginian squadrons fall on the transports, and force them and their escorts on to the coast. Atilius Regulus, with one of the two leading Roman squadrons, immediately breaks off the fight and hurries to help his transports; the other Roman squadron follows suit. One of the Punic squadrons that had been attacking the transports manages to escape this envelopment, but the other is caught and practically annihilated. The Carthaginians lose about 90 ships (60 captured, 30 sunk), the Romans 24, all sunk by ramming. In spite of their superior naval tactics, the Carthaginians lose the battle because they have no answer to the Roman boarding ramps in close combat. The sea lanes to Africa are now open to the Romans. Their army lands at Clupea, and advances to the walls of Carthage. The Carthaginians sue for peace, but the terms demanded by Rome—the surrender of Sicily, Sardinia, Corsica and the Carthaginian fleet—are too harsh.

255: With the aid of Greek mercenaries under the Spartan Xanthippos, the Carthaginians defeat the Roman army at Tunis.

255: Battle of Cape Bon. A Roman relief fleet defeats a Punic squadron, capturing or driving 114 ships on to the

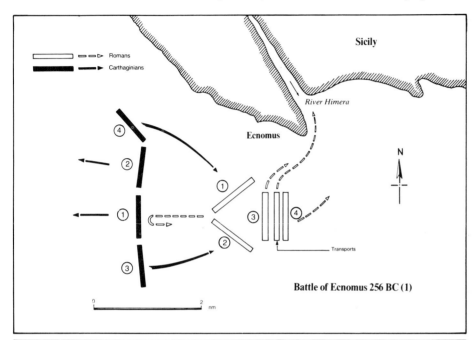

Battle of Ecnomus 256 BC (1)

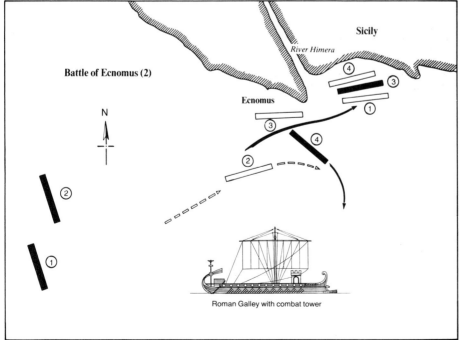

Roman Galley with combat tower

beach. The Roman fleet now seeks to evacuate the remnants of the army to Sicily, but almost the entire fleet is shipwrecked on the south coast of the island in a storm: 280 ships and 100,000 men perish, the greatest known loss by shipwreck in the history of seafaring.

254: A new Roman fleet supports a land army in the capture of Panormus (Palermo).

253: This new fleet is also lost in a storm whilst attempting to carry the war to Africa. The disasters of 255 and 253 are attributable to inadequate Roman seamanship; temporarily, Rome gives up the struggle for naval supremacy. Sicily,

meanwhile, is in Roman hands, with the exception of Lilybaeum (Marsala), Drepanum (Trapani) and Eryx (Erice); small squadrons are used to blockade these harbours.

250: Roman naval victory at Panormus.

249: Battle of Drepanum (or Trapani). The blockading Roman squadron, under consul Publius Claudius Pulcher, attempts to attack the harbour of Drepanum, but the Punic fleet there, under Adherbal (and, like their Roman adversaries, over 100 vessels strong), manages to escape to the open sea. Adherbal succeeds in manoeuvring the Roman fleet, which is advancing along the coast in a long line, between his ships and the shore, and destroys his relatively inexperienced foes almost entirely: Pulcher escapes with only 30 ships.

In the same year, the Romans send a fleet (numbering possibly as many as 800 ships) around the southern tip of Sicily to supply their troops in the west of the island. This fleet is also destroyed in a storm on the south coast, and Rome breaks off the war at sea completely. Punic raiders now harass the entire Italian coast. The Punic fleet can bring reinforcements to Sicily undisturbed, and Hamilcar Barca there gives the Romans stiff resistance, expecially in the struggles for Panormus and Lilybaeum. Finally, rich Roman merchants, citizens and shipowners build and crew a fleet of 200 warships at their own cost. When it is learned in Carthage that the new Roman fleet has set out for Sicily, the Carthaginian fleet is also despatched to support Hamilcar Barca.

241: Battle of the Aegates Islands. The Roman consul C. Lutatius Catulus is met by the Carthaginians off the western point of Sicily, and defeats them heavily: 50 Punic ships are sunk, about 70 are captured, and 100 or so escape to Africa. At one blow, Lutatius Catulus has achieved mastery of the sea. And, without support, Hamilcar Barca cannot maintain himself on Sicily. With the permission of his government, he negotiates peace with L. Catulus, whereby Carthage gives up Sicily and pays an indemnity of 32,000 talents.

238: Sardinian mercenaries rebel against Carthage and call on Rome for help; Rome declares war again, and Carthage is soon forced to yield Sardinia and Corsica too.

229-228: Rome suppresses the Illyrian pirates in the Adriatic, and brings the whole of that coastline under her control.

237-227: The Carthaginian, Hasdrubal, conquers Spain as far north as the Ebro.

226: The Ebro Treaty, between Rome and Carthage, pledges the latter to forgo further conquests in Spain. When, however, she attacks and captures Saguntum (south of the Ebro, and an ally of Rome), Rome declares war yet again. But, before she can deal with Carthage, she must put down a revolt of the Celts in upper Italy and deal with resurgent pirates in the Adriatic.

218-201: The Second Punic War

After the death of Hasdrubal (221), Hannibal assumes command in Spain. Crossing both Pyrenees and Alps, he carries the war into Italy, winning a succession of victories: Ticinus and the Trebbia (218), Lake Trasimenus (217) and Cannae (216). After this, the Roman army avoids battle with Hannibal; their fleet, meanwhile, controls the sea.

217: Action at the mouth of the Ebro. A Roman fleet under Gn. Cornelius Scipio decisively beats the Punic squadron in Spain. There follow combats with varying fortunes in Spain, Sicily and Greece, but command of the sea permits Rome to redeploy her forces rapidly.

215: Successfully wooing the Greeks in southern Italy away from Rome, Hannibal concludes an alliance with Philip V of Macedonia; but, as the Roman fleet controls the Adriatic, the Macedonians are unable to intervene in Italy (First Macedonian War, to 205).

212: The Roman consul Marcellus captures Syracuse (an ally

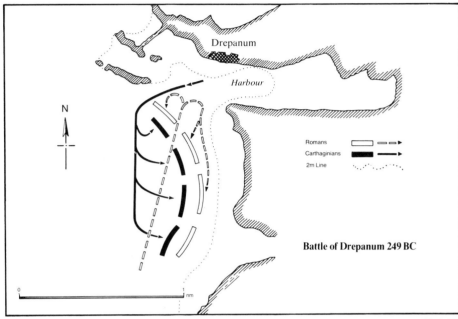

Romans	
Carthaginians	
2m Line	

Battle of Drepanum 249 BC

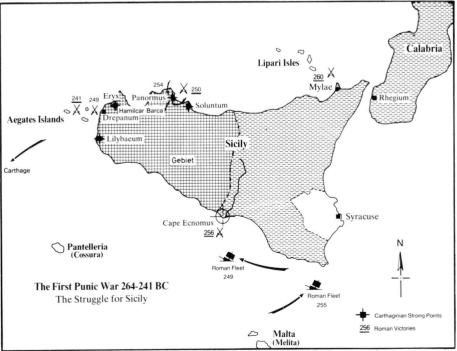

The First Punic War 264-241 BC
The Struggle for Sicily

Carthaginian Strong Points

256 Roman Victories

of Carthage) with fleet and army, despite the ingenious defences of Archimedes (who dies in the fighting). Meanwhile, Hannibal captures Tarentum (Taranto) and wins a battle at Capua (211).

207: Hasdrubal crosses the Alps with reinforcements, but loses a battle on the Metaurus river (near Sena Gallica) and is killed.

206: P. Cornelius Scipio completes the conquest of Carthaginian Spain, while Hannibal's youngest brother, Mago, manages to land at Genoa with the remnants of the Spanish army. Here, he attempts vainly to lead the Ligurians and Gauls against Rome once more. This evacuation is the only large-scale Carthaginian sea operation during the Second Punic War.

204: Consul P. Cornelius Scipio lands in Africa and wins a battle at Tunis (203). Hannibal must now evacuate southern Italy in an improvized transport fleet.

202: P. Cornelius Scipio defeats Hannibal at Zama, and Carthage is finally forced to conclude peace: she loses Spain to Rome, and Numidia becomes independent. Carthage must pay reparations, hand over all but 10 of her warships, and may not declare war without Roman permission.

Carthage, one-time mistress of the sea, made no attempt in this war to regain her lost position: without a fight, the Roman fleet had achieved control of almost the entire Mediterranean.

204–197: The Second Macedonian War

Philip V of Macedonia and Antiochus III of Syria combine to share Ptolemaic possessions in the Aegean and Palestine. Philip's successes in Asia Minor cause the minor states in this area to fear for their independence, and Rhodes, Pergamum and Byzantium together declare war on Philip.

201: The Macedonian fleet captures Samos and destroys the Egyptian fleet there, thus ending Ptolemaic naval activity in the Aegean.

201: Battle of Chios. The allied fleets of Rhodes and Pergamum defeat the Macedonian fleet. Philip loses 27 large and 65 small ships, the Allies 7. At the request of the Allies, Rome enters the war against Macedonia.

200: The Roman fleet captures the strongpoint of Chalcis on Euboea and attains control of the Aegean. After his defeat at Cynoscephalae in Thessaly (197), Philip is forced to negotiate peace and to hand over his fleet to Rome, retaining only 6 ships.

192–188: The War between Rome and Antiochus III of Syria

After Philip's defeat at the hands of Rome, King Antiochus absorbs his conquests in Asia Minor, and begins to extend his rule to Thessaly and Greece. Defeated by the Romans at Thermopylae in 191, it is only his fleet which prevents them and their allies, the Rhodians, from invading Asia Minor.

Sept 191: Battle of Corycus (Cissus). Polyxenidas, Antio-

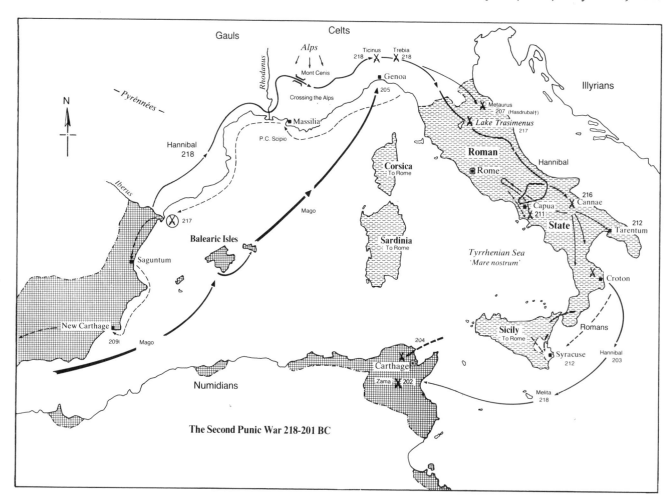

The Second Punic War 218-201 BC

chus' admiral, fails in an attempt to prevent the junction of the fleets of Rome and Pergamum: his 70 large ships are thus opposed by 80 Roman vessels under C. Salinator Livius and 25 ships from Pergamum under King Eumenes. In the ensuing battle the Syrians lose 25 ships, the Allies 1. Polyxenidas is pursued to his naval base at Ephesus.

April 190: The Syrian fleet under Polyxenidas defeats a Rhodian squadron at Panormus, south of Ephesus.

June 190: The reinforced Rhodian squadron under Eudamas defeats a reinforcing Syrian squadron at Side.

Oct 190: Battle of Myonnesus. As no further reinforcements from Syria can be expected, Polyxenidas attempts to regain mastery of the Aegean with the main fleet lying in Ephesus. He commands 89 ships and 24,000 men. These are opposed by 58 Roman 'battleships' under Aemilius, plus 22 lighter ships from Rhodes under Eudamas, with 20,000 men. While the faster Rhodian ships cover the wings, the large Roman vessels break through the enemy centre. The Syrians lose the battle, with 29 ships captured and 13 sunk; the Allies lose 2 Roman ships and 1 from Rhodes. Now secure in their command of the Aegean, the Romans carry the war into Asia Minor, and win a decisive victory at Magnesia (190). As part of Rome's peace terms, Antiochus hands over to Rome all but 10 of his ships.

88-84: After winning the first of three wars with Mithridates VI of Pontus, Rome demands the surrender of his fleet as well; she thus holds a position of unchallenged naval supremacy throughout the Mediterranean.

73: Battle of Lemnos. In the third war against Mithridates, the Romans pursue one of his squadrons from the Dardanelles to the island of Lemnos, and there destroy the ships on the beach.

78-67: Rome's War against the Pirates

From 88 onwards, Rome neglects to police the seas, and piracy assumes great proportions, especially during the Civil Wars. From their lairs in Cilicia, along the coast of of Asia Minor, and on Crete, pirates disrupt supplies to Rome and even stop the flow of grain from Africa. Rome is driven to conduct a formal war against them. Proconsul Servilius and Marcus Antonius the elder campaign for years with varying success, until finally the pirates become downright impudent.

67: In Ostia, Rome's harbour, the pirates attack a squadron being prepared for service against them. Pompey is then given extraordinary executive powers, and placed in command of 500 ships and an army of 120,000 men. In a brilliant 3-month campaign, he secures the western Mediterranean and then defeats the pirates in their eastern lairs: we are told that 10,000 pirates were killed and 20,000 captured. But delegating special powers to Pompey proves to be the first step to dictatorship. In 60, he forms the First Triumvirate, with Caesar and Crassus.

56: In Quiberon Bay, Caesar's fleet of galleys defeats the

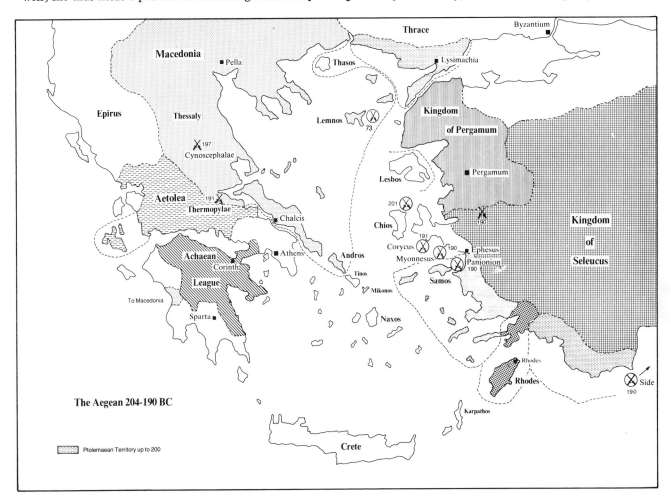

The Aegean 204-190 BC

Ptolemaean Territory up to 200

great sailing ships of the Gallic Venetes, assisted by a lack of wind which becalms their opponents.

48–36: The Roman Civil Wars

After the death of Crassus, Caesar and Pompey clash; and, at Pharsalus (48), Caesar defeats his rival, and becomes dictator for life. After Caesar's murder (44), there follows the Second Triumvirate (Antony, Lepidus and Octavian).

40: Division of the Empire: Antony takes the east, Octavian the west, and Lepidus, Africa. Sextus Pompey, younger son of Caesar's old rival, commands the Roman fleet. By the Treaty of Misenum (39) he secures for himself Sicily, Sardinia, Corsica and Achoria, and guarantees grain deliveries to Rome. Like his father, he is one of the first Romans to recognize the significance of sea power: with his domains and the fleet, he holds the fate of Rome in his hands. To wrest command of the sea from Sextus Pompey, Octavian begins to build his own fleet. The 'battleships' of this era are bigger than those of the Punic Wars. Larger catapults are built into them, and the ships are equipped with towers so that the enemy can be overlooked. By surprise attacks, Octavian captures Sardinia and Corsica.

37: Battle of Cumae. Octavian's fleet is defeated by that of Sextus Pompey, and its remnants destroyed in a storm. Octavian now entrusts the construction of a new fleet to his boyhood friend Marcus Agrippa and, by the Treaty of Tarentum (Taranto) in 37, Antony gives command of his fleet to Octavian for the struggle against Sextus Pompey. Agrippa has his ships strengthened with beams around the waterline, as protection against damage by ramming; this is the first known use of 'belted armour'. A naval base is founded at Portus Julius, near Cumae, closer to the intended theatre of operations, and the ships' crews are given special training for the coming campaign. Then Agrippa seizes one of the southern Lipari Islands, to observe the fleet of Sextus Pompey, lying at Mylae on the northern Sicilian coast and commanded by Demochares, a freed slave. After careful reconnaissance, Agrippa attacks.

36: Battle of Mylae. Demochares accepts the challenge and the battle immediately develops into a series of ship-to-ship combats. Agrippa's ships are the larger and stronger, those of Sextus Pompey the faster and more manoeuvrable. For some time the combat is indecisive, but, as the extra armour on Agrippa's ships makes them immune to enemy ramming attempts, he gradually wins the upper hand, and finally succeeds in sinking Demochares' flagship. Demochares escapes to another ship, but breaks off the fight: Agrippa has won his first sea battle, and has lost only 5 ships compared to 30 of his foe.

At the same time, Octavian lands 3 legions at Messina, on Sicily, but the transport fleet is almost completely destroyed by Sextus Pompey on the return journey. Octavian himself only just escapes. Meanwhile, Agrippa captures Mylae and other points on the northern Sicilian coast, and covers the

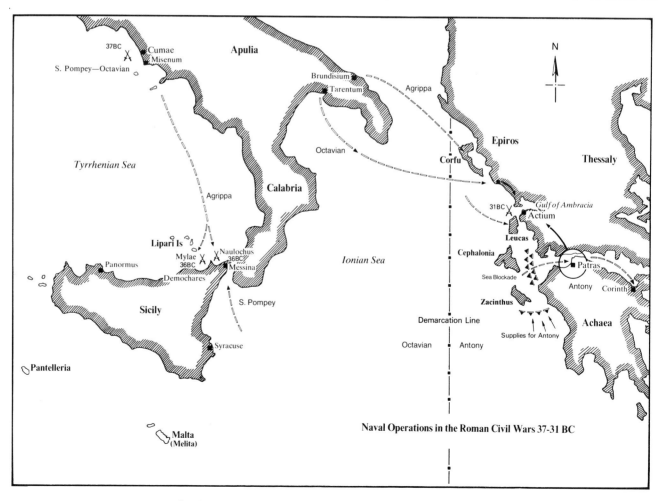

Naval Operations in the Roman Civil Wars 37-31 BC

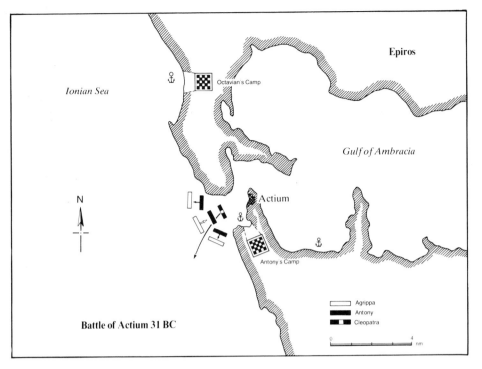

Ionian Sea

Epiros

Octavian's Camp

Gulf of Ambracia

N

Actium

Antony's Camp

Agrippa
Antony
Cleopatra

Battle of Actium 31 BC

0   4
         nm

landing of a strong army. Sextus Pompey now stakes his whole fleet in a gamble to regain command of the sea, north of Sicily.

36: Battle of Naulochus. Almost 300 ships, commanded by Demochares and Apollophanes (also a freed slave), advance through the Straits of Messina. Agrippa moves eastward along the coast to oppose them, also with about 300 ships, but bigger and stronger units than those of his adversary. In this battle, Agrippa uses fire-arrows and a grapple projectile (the harpax, or harpago), a beam equipped with grappling-irons fired at the enemy ship on the end of a line, to drag the two ships together. The fleets meet at almost exactly the same spot as a few months previously; they close up to each other in line abreast, their southern flanks near the Sicilian coast. The fleet of Sextus Pompey is in close formation which allows him to be outflanked on the sea side by the enemy, and does not permit the greater speed and man-oeuvrability of the smaller ships to come into play: instead, they are pushed on to the coast by Agrippa's fleet. The battle ends in a complete defeat for Sextus Pompey. Only 17 ships escape to Messina, 28 are sunk or burnt, while the rest are captured or driven on to the coast; Agrippa, mean-while, loses but 3 ships, by ramming. Demochares takes his own life, Apollophanes surrenders, and Sextus Pompey, watching the battle from the shore, abandons his army and flees to Asia, where he will die a captive of Antony in Miletus. The army of Lepidus, already landed in Sicily, goes over to Octavian, who is now unlimited ruler of the western half of the Roman empire. After the separation of Antony from Octavia (his wife, and sister of Octavian) and his marriage to Cleopatra VII, the relationship between the two Roman rulers becomes strained. Antony builds an oriental empire, makes Caesarion (son of Cleopatra and Caesar) co-Regent, and gives Cleopatra Roman lands.

33: Octavian's publication of Antony's will (deposited with the Vestal Virgins) before his death, provokes War between East and West.

32–30: War between Octavian and Antony

Antony, accompanied by Cleopatra and her war chest, goes to Greece with his forces to conduct the war from there. His fleet of 170 warships contains the mightiest 'battleships' of the era, similar to those used by Agrippa at Naulochus. Although Octavian has consciously precipitated the War with Antony, he is unprepared for it; but, to his good fortune, Antony wastes half a year idling in Greece, holding court in oriental splendour with Cleopatra. This habit drives many Romans from his camp.

31: In spring, Octavian has completed his preparations and takes the offensive, concentrating his army at Brundisium and Tarentum. The fleet which was victorious at Naulochus is missing, however, and its whereabouts unknown. Such great ships are difficult to build and very expensive, so Agrippa assembles a fleet of about 260 liburnians, light, agile one- and two-deckers as used by the Illyrians who gave them their name. Since Antony and his army in Patras are dependent on supplies brought in by sea, Agrippa starts his campaign with a naval blockade. His fast ships catch most of the enemy transports, and Antony's army begins to suffer shortages. Agrippa also takes Corcyra (Corfu), thus securing the Adriatic crossing for Octavian's army to the north of Actium, where Antony has concentrated his fleet and army. Octavian now begins to shut Antony in from the land side without presenting the opportunity for a battle, while Agrippa and the fleet complete the encirclement by capturing Corinth, Patras and Leucas. In Actium, the forces of Antony are now so weakened by shortage of food, sickness and desertion that he no longer dares to chance a confron-tation on land. And, to guard the entrance of the Gulf of Ambracia (on which Actium lies), Agrippa has set a squadron of ships under Arruntius. This force repels attempted blockade-running. Antony's last hope is to break out with the fleet, and to renew the struggle from Egypt. This plan is supported by Cleopatra, 60 of whose ships are with the fleet. Antony embarks 20,000 legionaries and burns the ships for which he now has no crews. Agrippa's fleet embarks 30,000 men of Octavian's army. The preparations for one of the decisive battles in history are complete.

2 Sept 31: Battle of Actium. Antony's fleet is divided into three squadrons: the right wing under Gellius is in the north next to the coast; Justijus commands the centre; and Coelius leads the left wing next to the coast in the south. In the oppos-ing fleet, Agrippa commands the centre, Lurius the southern (right) wing and Arruntius the northern (left) wing. Agrippa holds back his centre, for the larger enemy ships are in close formation and, with their flanks protected by the coasts, cannot be outflanked.

Midday: a north-easterly wind rises, and Antony uses this for a break-out attempt. His wing squadrons advance more quickly than the centre, and Agrippa falls back slowly, knowing that, the more into the open sea the fleets progress, the more he can bring his superior numbers into play. In threes and fours, the liburnians surround the 'battleships' of Antony; many are set on fire with fire-arrows, but the battle is yet undecided.

1pm: Cleopatra makes use of a gap in the fighting line to break out, and Antony manages to follow her with a few last galleys. At this, the resistance of the remainder of his fleet begins to wane, but it is still some hours before they are overpowered. Only a few escape to the army in Actium; the majority are burned or taken. A week later, the encircled and deserted army surrenders. West has beaten East, and Rome remains the centre of the Roman empire. After Octavian's landing in Egypt, Antony and Cleopatra take their own lives.

Agrippa's command at sea had been the deciding factor in this campaign—which featured raids, blockades and, an eminently suitable weapon, the fire-arrow. As in the sea war against Sextus Pompey, the careful training of the crews paid handsome dividends. The Civil Wars and the Republic were thus ended, and the Imperial Age began. For the next five hundred years, Rome would command the whole of the Mediterranean, and the fleet's main tasks would be those of police force and transport medium for numerous armies.

The Age of Imperial Rome

Augustus forms two main fleets: from 22BC, the western fleet is based in Misenum, near Naples. This force intervenes repeatedly in Roman politics, and achieves a political position not unlike that of the Praetorian Guard. From AD29, the eastern fleet is based in Ravenna, and employed in the Adriatic and eastern Mediterranean. For the protection of the provinces, there are various smaller fleet detachments. In AD155, Roman ships operate in the Indian Ocean. Neglect of the fleets in the 3rd century AD, however, allows piracy to increase again, and the consequences of this are supply difficulties and inflation in Italy. The next major conflict at sea concerns the struggle for total power between the emperors Constantine and Licinius.

AD323: **Battle of the Hellespont.** Licinius' fleet, under Amandus, blocks the entrance to the Hellespont; Constantine's fleet, under his son Crispus, is given the task of opening the passage to Byzantium. Amandus assembles his ships in close formation, while Crispus arranges his fleet in two ranks and attacks in a loose formation. The first rank crashes into the enemy fleet and breaks open their line; this is exploited by the second rank. The ships of Amandus are hindered by their own close battle order. After several hours, Amandus withdraws into a harbour on the Asiatic shore, intending to renew the fight on the following day. However, a storm destroys nearly half his ships.

324: Constantine defeats Licinius at Adrianople and Chrysopolis, and becomes sole ruler of the Empire. Byzantium, renamed Constantinople, becomes the second capital.

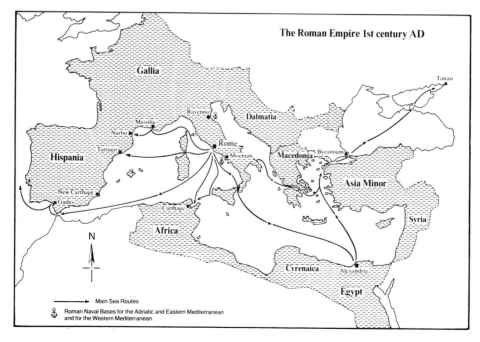

The Roman Empire 1st century AD

→ Main Sea Routes

⚓ Roman Naval Bases for the Adriatic and Eastern Mediterranean and for the Western Mediterranean

The Barbarian Migrations

From 375: For many years the Roman Empire has been fighting with barbarians on her borders, but in the 4th century her resistance begins to wane. With the incursion of the Huns and their victory over the Ostrogoths, the Barbarian Migrations begin. All northern imperial borders are overrun; the Goths push westwards through the Balkans, setting up states in Gaul and then in Spain and Italy.

429: The Vandals move through Gaul and Spain to northern Africa, and there set up an independent German state under Gaiseric. In Carthage harbour, they capture the Roman grain fleet: with this, they achieve command of the western Mediterranean, and go on to capture Sicily, Sardinia and Corsica (440) and plunder Rome (455).

456: Action off Corsica. The commander of the Roman army, Flavius Ricimer, defeats a Vandal fleet. Soon afterwards, the Western Roman Emperor, Majorian (457-61), repels a Vandal fleet from the mouth of the Tiber estuary. He then moves to Spain and begins to build a fleet in Cartagena, only to see this destroyed by Gaiseric just before completion. Odoacer (or Odovacar, King of Italy) leases Sicily from the Vandals.

468: Battle of Cape Bon (Promunturium Mercurii). The Vandal fleet defeats a combined fleet of Eastern and Western Roman warships, thereby securing command of the sea in the western Mediterranean for a further 50 years.

527-65: Emperor Justinian sets out to conquer the decadent western half of the old Roman Empire for Eastern Rome.

Sept 533: The Eastern Roman commander, Belisarius, lands on the African coast with an army of 15,000 men and 800 ships; within a few months he conquers the Vandal kingdom, and Justinian is in sole command of the Mediterranean.

535-52: Eastern Rome's Gothic War

535: Belisarius lands on Sicily and, by 540, has conquered most of Italy.

549: The new Ostrogoth king, Totila, advances southwards; his newly constructed fleet plunders Corfu and many Greek coastal towns.

551: Battle of Sena Gallica. The Eastern Roman Fleet, led by Artabanes and clearly superior to its foe, decisively defeats the Ostrogoths; one year later, they are defeated by the Eastern Roman general Narses.

552-554: Justinian's fleet enables Constantinople to conquer southern Spain, but Eastern Rome's supremacy in the western Mediterranean is short-lived. In the east, there is continual conflict with Persia, and the Slavs bear down from the north.

568: The Langobards (Lombards) overrun almost all Italy. Within a few years Spain too is lost. The Slavs push into the vacuum left by the Germans in the Balkans.

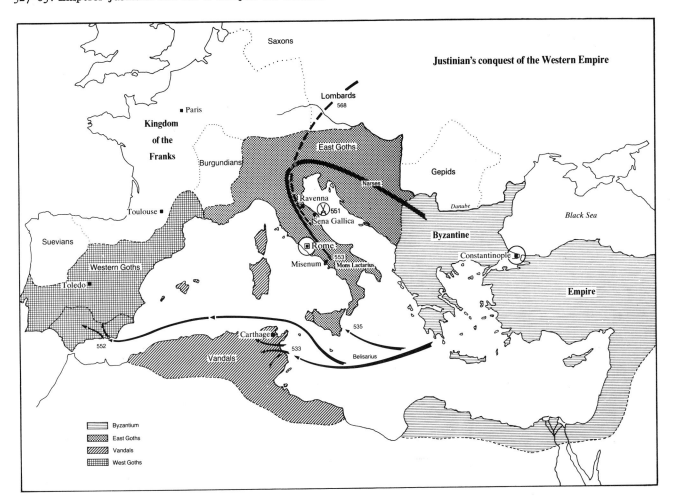

During the 7th century, a new and vital influence began spreading throughout the southern and eastern shores of the Mediterranean—Islam. At the death of Mohammed in 632, the whole of the Arabian peninsula had succumbed, and his successors began a 'Holy War' aimed at establishing an Islamic world order. Damascus (635) and Jerusalem (638) soon fell, and the Sassanid Persian Empire, heavily defeated by Byzantium* in 628, fell an easy prey to the Arabs in the years 636 to 642. Egypt fell in 640, and Alexandria was evacuated by the Byzantines in 642. The stage was now set for some 900 years of conflict between the followers of Allah and Christendom's eastern bastion, Byzantium.

These wars in the medieval Mediterranean would be fought in warships little different from those of ancient times. Construction and propulsion was much the same; secondary propulsion was by lateen sail. Main battle unit was the dromon, a heavily covered galley with two rows of oars and a crew of 200–300 men.

THE ARABS IN THE MEDITERRANEAN

649: Cyprus and Rhodes are captured by the Arabs.

652: First raid of the Arab fleet on Sicily. In Tripoli, Muawiya concentrates a powerful fleet for the conquest of the Aegean; when this fleet is burned by Christian galley slaves, Muawiya has to build a replacement fleet.

* It is at about this point in time that the Eastern Roman Empire becomes known to history as the Byzantine Empire.

655: 'Battle of the Masts' (Dhat al-Sawari). In spring, an Arab fleet of 200 ships under Abdallah ibn Sa'd sets sail for Constantinople. Off the coast of Asia Minor, near Phoenix, their path is blocked by the Byzantine fleet, 500 ships strong under the personal command of Emperor Constans II. After initial indecision, the Arabs attack their more numerous foe, but are soon in difficulties, due to the superior tactics and manoeuvrability of the Greeks. In the nick of time, a Byzantine dromon is prevented from towing off the Arab flagship with its grappling tackle. The Arabs then chain their ships together to form a floating fortress, and begin to destroy the enemy ship by ship with boarding parties. Emperor Constans II escapes with difficulty, and the Arabs have won their first great naval victory: the way to Constantinople seems open.

659: The assassination of Caliph Othman (656) and the struggle for the succession, between Ali ibn-abi-Talib and Muawiya, force the latter to conclude peace with Byzantium.

661: Muawiya gains the caliphate and founds the Umayyad dynasty in Damascus.

663: Muawiya resumes the offensive against Byzantium; his armies push through Asia Minor to the Sea of Marmara.

670: The Arabian fleet forces the Dardanelles and enters the Sea of Marmara, occupying a strongpoint on the Cyzicus peninsula for use in the coming attack on Constantinople. To secure their rearward communications they also occupy the islands of Rhodes, Chios and Kos in the Aegean and, to

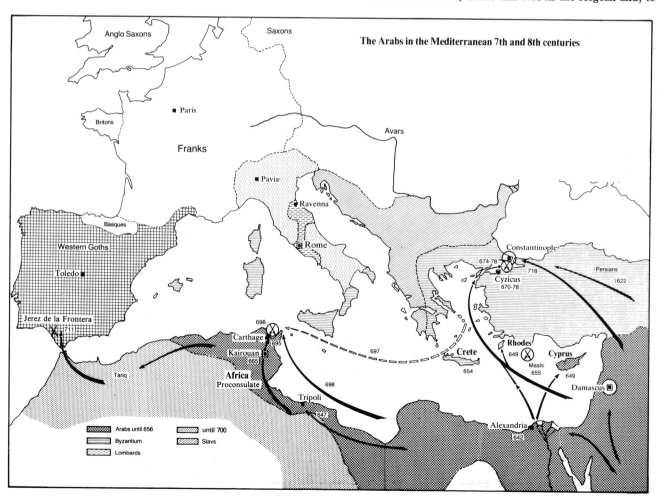

The Arabs in the Mediterranean 7th and 8th centuries

Arabs until 656		until 700	
Byzantium		Slavs	
Lombards			

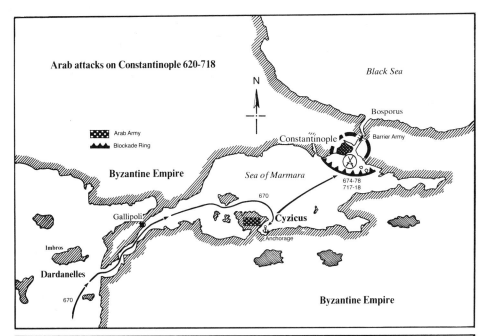

Arab attacks on Constantinople 620-718

Black Sea

N

Bosporus

Constantinople

Barrier Army

Arab Army
Blockade Ring

Byzantine Empire

Sea of Marmara

674-78
717-18

670

Gallipoli

Cyzicus

Anchorage

Imbros

Dardanelles

670

Byzantine Empire

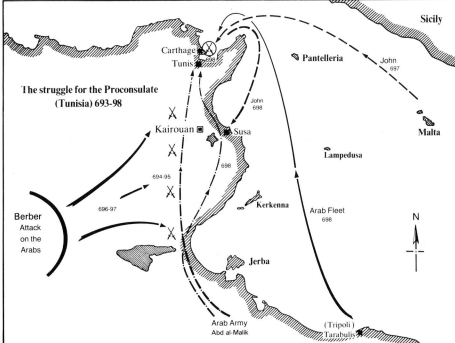

Sicily

Carthage
698

Tunis

The struggle for the Proconsulate (Tunisia) 693-98

Pantelleria

John
697

John
698

Kairouan

Susa

Malta

John
698

Lampedusa

694-95

698

Berber
Attack
on the
Arabs

696-97

Kerkenna

Arab Fleet
698

N

Jerba

Arab Army
Abd al-Malik

(Tripoli)
Tarabulis

conceal their real aim, they make attacks on the Proconsulate (Tunisia) and raid Sicily.

674-78: First Attack on Constantinople. In the summer of 674, the Arabs under Yazid, son of the Caliph, begin a carefully planned, large-scale attack on the capital of the Byzantine Empire. Throughout the summer, they blockade the city by land and sea; for the winter, they withdraw to Cyzicus. This programme is repeated each year until 678, but still the Arabs cannot breach the immensely strong city walls. The city is finally saved by the Greek fleet with the aid of a new weapon: Kallinikos, a Syrian in Byzantine service, invents a primitive

flame-thrower. (A mixture of saltpetre, pitch, sulphur and oil is ignited, and projected on to an enemy ship by 'siphon'; this mixture, once aflame, cannot be quenched with water, and the victim ship is doomed to burn out.) Later known as 'Greek Fire', this weapon so decimates the Arab fleet that Yazid breaks off the siege in the summer of 678. On the way home, the remnants of the Arab fleet are lost in a storm. The first Islamic assault on Constantinople has been repulsed.

693-98: Struggle for the Proconsulate (Tunisia). An Arab army begins the conquest of the last Byzantine province in Africa and, with the fall of Carthage in 695, the Arabs control the entire state. Emperor Leontius counterattacks with a strong fleet under the Patrician John, who defeats the fleet sent against him, forces entry into Carthage harbour and recaptures the city. He then regains control of the other Tunisian towns. In the hinterland, the Arabs are decisively beaten by the Berbers under their prophetess the 'Kahena'. So, the next year, Caliph Abd al-Malik sends a new army to the west, this time escorted by a strong fleet.

698: Battle of Carthage. John positions the Greek fleet outside the city harbour; the Arabs break his line, enter the harbour and seize the city from within. John escapes with part of the fleet. North Africa, with the Arab capital at Kairouan, is now firmly in Islamic hands.

8th century: Basra is the starting point for Arabian trading voyages to India, China and the Sunda Isles (the East Indies). Initially, they have to fight their way through the pirates of the Persian Gulf to gain the open seas.

704: Arabs begin privateering in the western Mediterranean with their new African-based fleet.

711: Arab general Tariq lands in Spain, and destroys the army of the Visigoths under Roderic. In a short time almost all of Spain is captured.

717-18: Second Arab Attack on Constantinople. In spring 717, the brother of the Caliph, Maslama, opens the offensive by land and sea against the city.

15 Aug 717: The army crosses the Dardanelles, and blockades the city from the land side.

1 Sept 717: A great Arab fleet under Suleiman appears before the city, but the Byzantine fleet is lying in the Golden Horn, which is closed by a chain.

3 Sept 717: The Byzantine fleet, under the personal command of Emperor Leo III ('the Isaurian') makes a sortie, and 15 Arab 'battleships' are destroyed by 'Greek Fire'. The Arabs maintain the siege throughout the winter, suffering extreme losses from the weather.

Spring 718: An Arab supply fleet from Egypt arrives at Constantinople, and a number of Christian sailors with this fleet escape to the Byzantines, using the smaller boats of the supply fleet. On their advice, Leo III undertakes another sortie with his 'battle dromons' and, in the ensuing battle, the Arabs suffer a serious defeat. A large part of their fleet is burnt, leaving the sea front of Constantinople and the supply routes from the Black Sea open again.

15 Aug 718: Maslama lifts the siege, and the Arab army withdraws through Asia Minor. The remnants of the Arab fleet are practically all destroyed in storms in the Sea of Marmara and in the Aegean.

Similar in its significance to the boarding ramp in the First Punic War, 'Greek Fire' was the decisive weapon in this war. By its use, the fleet of Byzantium had regained command of the Aegean.

From the beginning of the 8th century, the Arabs of Tunisia undertake repeated raids in the central Mediterranean, but whole fleets succumb to autumnal storms; the Arabs, like the Romans in the First Punic War, pay dearly for their lack of experience in seamanship.

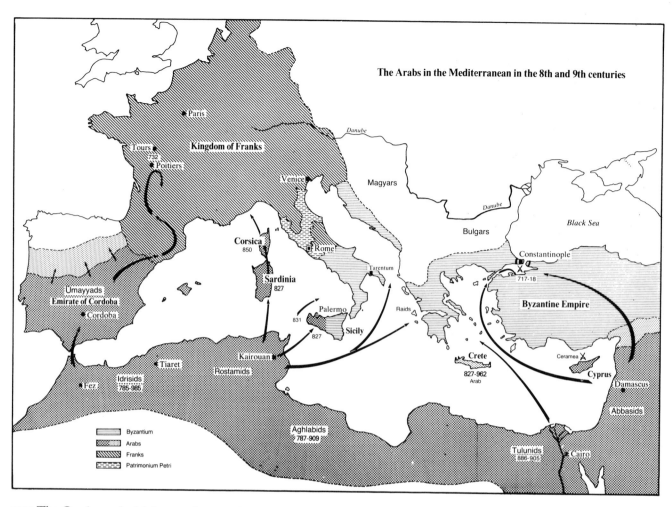

The Arabs in the Mediterranean in the 8th and 9th centuries

727: The Greek provincial Aegean fleet revolts against Byzantium, and is destroyed in a battle with the central fleet.

732: Charles Martel defeats the Arab invasion of France at the battles of Tours and Poitiers.

747: Battle of Ceramea (Cyprus). The Byzantine fleet completely destroys an Arab fleet of 100 ships. With this victory, Byzantium wins back control of the Mediterranean for over 50 years.

821: Civil War breaks out in the Byzantine Empire. The provincial fleets are defeated in a series of conflicts with the central fleet off Constantinople, and the naval defences of Byzantium are thus weakened.

827: Arabs land on Sicily, and begin a struggle for this island that lasts until 964.

828: Rebellious Arabs from Spain land on Crete, and soon capture the island. Repeated Byzantine attempts to recapture it fail.

831: Arabs capture Palermo, and make it their Sicilian capital.

841: A Venetian squadron is defeated by the Arabs off Taranto; Venice now begins to equip a fleet with which to attain command of the Adriatic.

846: An Arab fleet from Palermo appears off Rome; the Arabs do not attempt to storm the city, but plunder the area of St. Peter's.

853: A Byzantine squadron of 100 ships seizes the Nile delta town of Damietta and, almost without loss, returns home with rich booty. This expedition is repeated successfully in 854 and 859.

867: Arabs plunder the Illyrian and Greek coasts.

868: Byzantine admiral Niketas Oryphas leads 100 ships against the Arabian pirates; 20 Arab ships are destroyed off the coast of Thrace. Oryphas then has his ships dragged over the isthmus of Corinth, and, launching a surprise attack on Arabs busy plundering the Gulf of Corinth utterly destroys them.

878: Arabs capture Syracuse on Sicily.

880: Night Battle of Cephalonia (Peloponnese). An Arab fleet is destroyed by the Byzantines under Nasaris, who then takes his fleet through the Straits of Messina to the north coast of Sicily.

880: First Battle of Milazzo. Nasaris destroys an Arab fleet from Palermo, temporarily strengthening Byzantium's position in southern Italy.

888: Second Battle of Milazzo. The Arabs from Palermo defeat a fleet from Byzantium; 5,000 Greeks drown.

904: The town of Thessalonica is captured by an Arab fleet: to get over the walls, battle gondolas are hoisted over them on long yardarms from the ships. After plundering, the Saracens withdraw.

908: Battle in the Aegean Sea. The Byzantine fleet under Admiral Himerios defeats the Arabs; Himerios then temporarily occupies Cyprus and, from there, mounts raids on the Syrian coast.

912: Battle of Chios. The Syrian–Cilician fleet defeats a

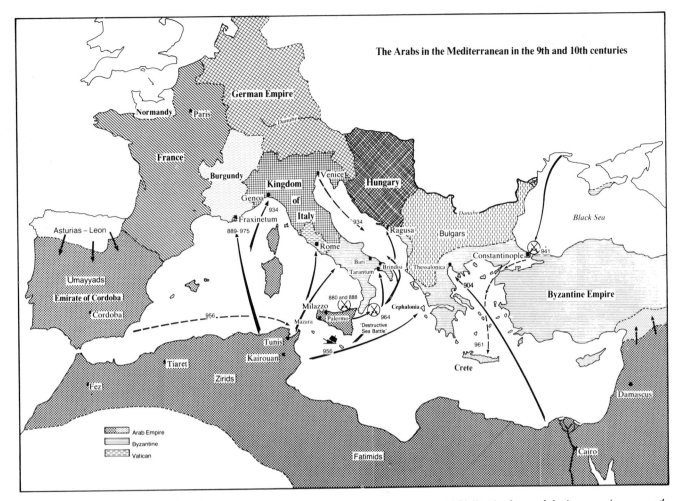

The Arabs in the Mediterranean in the 9th and 10th centuries

Byzantine squadron under Himerios.

At the beginning of the 10th century, Venice is engaged in a bitter war with Dalmatian pirates.

934: Genoa is plundered by Arabs.

941: The Kievan fleet of Igor is destroyed off the Bosporus by a Byzantine fleet.

956–64: The Tripartite Naval War

Byzantium and the Spanish Umayyads are allied against the Arabs on Sicily and in North Africa.

956: An Arab fleet from Tunis, bound for Sicily, is decimated by a storm.

956: A new fleet from Tunis is destroyed by the Allies off Mazara. In the same year, an Umayyad fleet raids the coast of North Africa.

958: In the Straits of Messina, Allied and Tunisian fleets fight an indecisive battle; the Tunisian fleet is subsequently destroyed in a storm off Palermo.

960–61: Byzantium captures Crete, the key to command of the eastern Mediterranean. The Arabs capture Taormina (962) and the fortress of Rametta (964), and thus secure the whole of Sicily.

964: 'The Destructive Sea Battle'. A fleet under the Patriarch Niketas evacuates the last Byzantines from Sicily, but an Arab fleet blocks their escape off the Calabrian coast, and completely destroys them. Combat swimmers set fire to many Greek dromons.

After the conquest of Sicily, the force of Arab expansion seemed, temporarily at least, to have been spent; at the beginning of the 11th century, Arab naval offensives against Greece were repulsed with heavy loss, and there began a Christian counterattack that would reach its climax in the Crusades.

From northern Europe, meanwhile, new forces were beginning to exert their influence on the civilized world. From the 2nd century onwards, the inhabitants of southern Scandinavia had been migrating into eastern and central Europe, while, by the end of the 4th century, the Barbarian Migrations (see page 23) had effected great changes on the map of the continent. Tribes of Germans had set up states in the territory of the dying Roman Empire; and, when the Romans abandoned the British Isles, their place was taken by Angles, Saxons and Jutes, who pushed the natives back into Wales, Scotland, Cornwall and Brittany.

In the 8th century there began a new wave of emigration from Scandinavia: the 'Norsemen' (or Vikings, 'Varangians' in Russia, 'Normans' in France) began to embark on pirate expeditions, prompted by overpopulation and a lust for adventure. Spending the summers privateering, and wintering at home, they travelled in boats that had reinforced hulls for masts and keels (as demonstrated in examples discovered at Gokstad and Oseberg). Their raids eventually extended over the entire North Sea and Channel coasts (prompting Charlemagne to attempt a coast guard system against their depredations).

THE VOYAGES OF THE 'NORSEMEN'

838: Norsemen capture Dublin.

From **840:** Large groups begin to settle for long periods on the coasts and in the river estuaries.

844: Norsemen reach Spain and Portugal.

859–62: Raiding parties pass through the Straits of Gibraltar to the coasts of Provence and Tuscany; the town of Luna is destroyed.

At the end of the 9th century, stronger groups of Norsemen begin to occupy territory on a permanent basis.

860: Norse raiders plunder Provence and Liguria, and a Varangian fleet from Kiev attacks Constantinople, but is repulsed.

866: Danes settle in England (East Anglia and Northumberland, or 'Danelag').

871–99: Anglo-Saxon King Alfred the Great (of Wessex) builds the first English fleet and uses it to beat off the Danes. His ships are larger than the Danes' dragon-headed long-ships.

874: Norwegian Vikings settle in Iceland.

896: Rollo begins raiding in northern France. These raids culminate in the Treaty of St. Clair-sur-Epte (911) by which Rollo becomes a vassal of the King of the Franks, and thus first Duke of Normandy.

984: Norwegians discover Greenland, and settle there for 500 years.

c. 1000: From Greenland, Leif Eriksson discovers America; but the attempt to found a permanent settlement fails.

Meanwhile, the successors of Alfred the Great neglect the English fleet, and the Danes renew their penetration into England.

1016: Knut (Canute) the Great of Denmark becomes King of England, temporarily uniting the two countries.

1062: Battle of Nissa. Harald Hardrada of Norway, with 150 ships, defeats a stronger Danish fleet in the Kattegat.

1066: King Harold of England defeats a Norwegian army at Stamford Bridge; at the same time, Duke William of Normandy lands on the south coast of England with a strong army. William beats Harold at the Battle of Hastings (or Senlac), and becomes King of England. This is the last invasion of England.

Jan 1156: A fleet of 58 Celtic ships defeats a Viking squadron off the west coast of Scotland.

Scandinavian expansion and colonization in the 8th and 9th centuries

Greenland 984
Vinland about 1000

A 'Drakkar.' Typical Viking Warship

Iceland
874

Faeroes
800

Shetland
700

Lindisfarne
793
866-71

Varangians

Kingdom of Kiev

German
Empire

Elbe Oder Vistula

Hastings
1066

Normandy
896-911

Brittany

France

Noirmoutier

Biscay

Kingdom of
Italy
Luna
859-62
Rome

Hungary

Danube

886-909-941

Bulgaria

Black Sea
941
Sinope

Asturias-Leon

Emirate of
Cordoba
Caliphate From
929

844

Arabs

Constantinople

Byzantine Empire

Arabs

Viking Homelands
Conquered Areas
Viking Journeys
Target Areas

In the meantime, internal dynastic strife had led to the Arabs gradually relinquishing control of the Mediterranean, while the penetration of nomads into their northern African territories and Egypt had seen the decay of these hitherto blooming provinces. At the same time, Normans began to settle in southern Italy and Sicily and, in the 11th century, took a large area of southern Italy from the Byzantines, and all Sicily from the Arabs. By the Synod of Melfi in 1059, Robert Guiscard, the Norman leader, recognized the feudal authority of the Pope in return for the title of duke.

Through the consolidation of many European states during the later Middle Ages, world trade enjoyed a considerable increase, with the main trading routes leading from the Middle East and Constantinople to the northern Italian ports. Here, Genoa, Pisa and Venice had achieved almost complete independence and had become great trading states. Each built her own navy to protect her trade, and fought continuously against the others for supremacy; but, since no one of them was strong enough to dominate the seas, the contest for trade advantages and strongpoints dragged on without decision.

In the eastern Mediterranean, the Byzantine Empire was now in decline, a fact ominously signalled by her defeat by the Turks at Manzikert in 1071. The growing Islamic threat in the eastern Mediterranean was recognized by Pope Urban II, who, at the Synod of Clermont in 1095, called for a Crusade to recapture Jerusalem for Christianity.

NAVAL WARS IN THE MEDITERRANEAN FROM THE 11th TO THE 14th CENTURY

1004: A Venetian fleet, under Doge Pietro Orseolo II, defeats the Arabs off Bari.

1005: A fleet from Pisa defeats the Arabs at Messina.

1016: A combined fleet from Genoa and Pisa captures Sardinia and Corsica from the Arabs.

1043: A Russian squadron is defeated in the Bosporus by a Byzantine force.

1052: An Arabian fleet from Tunis, bound for Sicily, is wrecked in a storm off Pantelleria.

1071: Robert Guiscard captures Bari and then Palermo (1072) and begins the Norman conquest of Sicily.

1080-85: The Normans attack Byzantium: Robert Guiscard lands with an army in Albania.

1081: **Battle of Durazzo.** A Venetian–Byzantine squadron of 60 ships defeats the Norman fleet, and supplies the beleaguered town.

1082: For her naval assistance to Albania, Venice receives trade and legal privileges from the Byzantine empire. (Byzantium's naval supremacy in the eastern Mediterranean is by now at an end.)

1084: The Venetian fleet is defeated by the Norman fleet in a series of engagements off the Albanian coast.

1087: A fleet from Genoa and Pisa, with several ships from Amalfi, captures Tunis, and does not leave until a treaty is

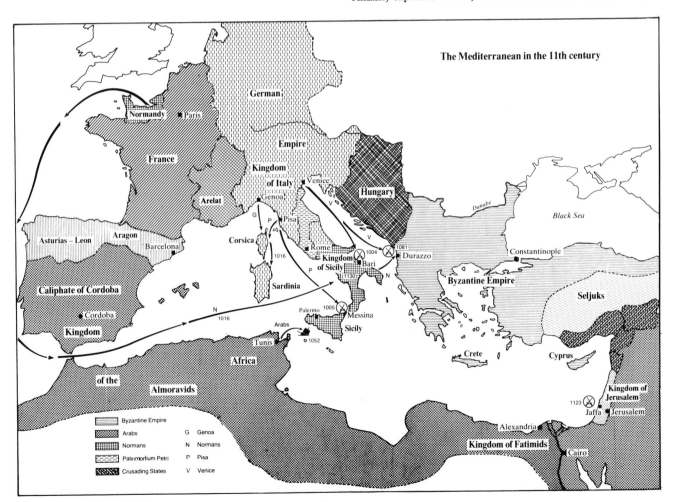

The Mediterranean in the 11th century

made in the following year.

1096–99: The First Crusade. Genoa and Venice produce a supply fleet for the Crusaders.

1104: Genoa provides a further 70 ships for the Crusade and, in return, receives strongpoints in the Holy Land.

1119–33: Genoa defeats Pisa in a struggle for supremacy in the western Mediterranean.

1123: The Venetian fleet defeats an Arab fleet off Jaffa.

1130: The Norman possessions in Sicily and southern Italy are united by Roger II to form a kingdom.

1137: The Venetian fleet defeats the Normans off the Apulian coast at Trani.

1135–48: Roger II establishes himself temporarily in Tunisia.

1147–58: The Byzantine–Sicilian War
King Roger utilizes the weakness of Byzantium to attack Greece during The Second Crusade.

1147: Corfu and the Ionian islands are occupied, and the coast of the Peloponnese is devastated by the Norman fleet.

1148: A thrust by the Normans through the Dardanelles and towards Constantinople is unsuccessful.

1149: Battle of Cape Malea. The united Venetian and Byzantine fleets defeat the Normans. Byzantium renews and extends the privileges of 1082 for this Venetian aid. In the same year, Byzantium recaptures Corfu.

1155: Byzantium assumes the offensive, and attacks Italian soil in Apulia: Ancona, Bari and Trani are taken. At this,

Venice, concerned for her control of the Adriatic, concludes peace with the Normans.

1158: Without Venetian naval assistance, Byzantium cannot maintain her forces in Apulia, and so comes to terms with the Normans.

1177: In the roads of Pirano, the Venetians (in league with the Pope) defeat a squadron from Genoa and Pisa, who are allied with the German emperor.

1185: In renewed hostilities between the Normans and Byzantium, Alexius Branas wins a decisive victory over the Normans off the coast of Greece at Demetrists.

1187: Sultan Salah ed-Din (Saladin) defeats the Crusaders at Hattin, and reconquers Jerusalem.

1188: A Norman fleet saves Tripoli (Palestine) from the Arabs.

1190–92: The Third Crusade. The German knights under Frederick Barbarossa advance overland; Kings Richard I ('the Lionheart') of England and Philip II Augustus of France arrive in the Holy Land by sea. For the first time, large fleets from Atlantic states appear in the Mediterranean.

1202–4: The Fourth Crusade. Venice assumes responsibility for the logistics of the Crusade, and places her fleet at its disposal. In return, she demands the capture of Zara (Zadar), in Dalmatia.

1203: The Crusaders capture Constantinople.

1204: Constantinople is taken a second time by the Crusaders, and the city is plundered. The Venetian fleet, under Doge

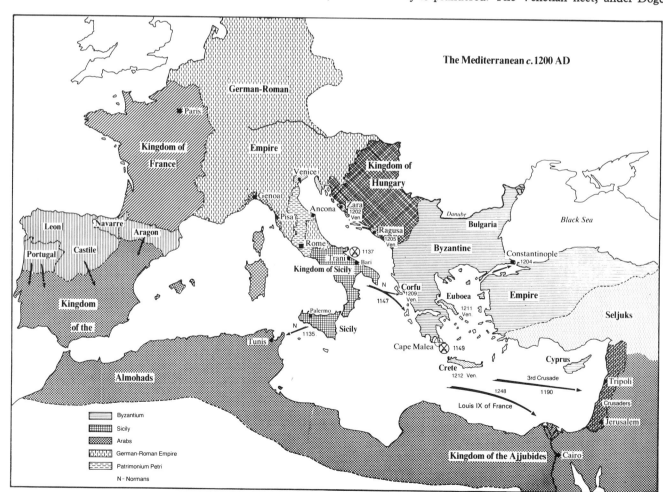

The Mediterranean c.1200 AD

Byzantium
Sicily
Arabs
German-Roman Empire
Patrimonium Petri
N – Normans

Enrico Dandolo, is actively engaged in the capture. A Latin Empire is set up in Constantinople (which lasts until 1261), and Venice secures vital strongpoints for herself in the Aegean.

1241: In the struggle of Emperor Frederick II against the Pope, the fleet of Pisa (an imperial ally) under Admiral Ansald de Mari defeats the Genoese fleet. A number of cardinals and bishops en route to the council in Rome are captured.

1248: King Louis IX of France undertakes a Crusade to Egypt; Genoa helps equip the French fleet.

1261: Genoa aids the Byzantine emperor in the recapture of Constantinople, and thus displaces Venice from her sphere of influence in the Empire.

1253-84: The First Venetian-Genoese War

1263: Gilberto Dandolo's Venetian fleet beats the Genoese in the Bay of Nauplia, at Settepozzi.

1264: Off Saseno, by Valona (Albania), the Genoese fleet under Simone Grillo captures the heavily laden Venetian Levantine fleet, with the exception of the great galley *Roccaforte*, which escapes to Ragusa.

1266: Battle of Trapani. Dandolo, with 25 galleys, encounters a Genoese fleet under Borborino off the north-west coast of Sicily. The latter declines action, and the Geonese link their galleys together in defence. After three attempts, however, the Venetians break through, and destroy most of Borborino's ships.

1284: Battle of Meloria (near the mouth of the Arno), the decisive battle in the War between Pisa and Genoa (1282–84). A Genoese fleet under Oberto Doria beats a Pisan fleet under Morosini; Elba falls to Genoa. (The harbour of Pisa is now visibly silting up, and the city is eventually forced to recognize the supremacy of Genoa.)

1282-87: The War for Sicily

Charles of Anjou is endowed with the kingdom of Sicily after the death of Emperor Frederick II, and conquers the island in 1266. After the War of the Sicilian Vespers (1282), Pedro III of Aragon (related to the Staufen family) occupies the island with the aid of his fleet. Charles, in alliance with France, tries to recapture Sicily from Naples.

1283: The fleet of Aragon, under Roger di Loria, beats the French fleet off Malta.

1284: Roger defeats the Neapolitan fleet.

1285: Roger is victorious in a night battle, which frustrates a French invasion of Catalonia.

1287: For a second time, Roger di Loria beats the Neapolitan fleet, and captures 42 ships. Through his naval victories, Sicily is now firmly under the control of Aragon.

1293-99: The Second Venetian-Genoese War

1294: The Genoese defeat the Venetians off the coast of Kilikian, the latter losing 25 ships out of 68.

1298: Battle of Curzola Island (Dalmatia). A Venetian fleet

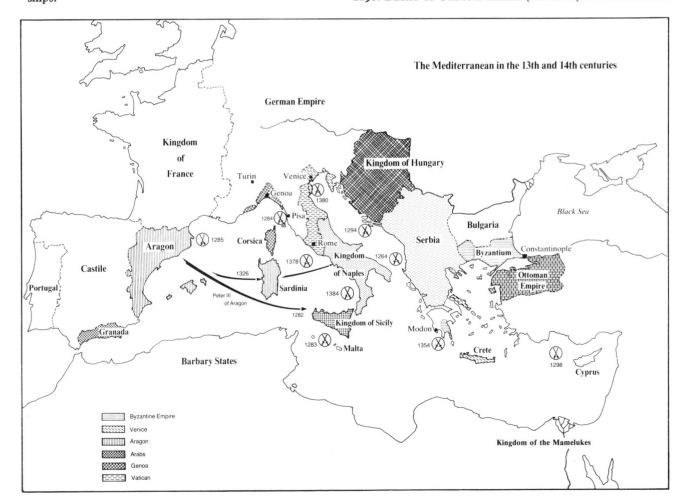

The Mediterranean in the 13th and 14th centuries

German Empire

Kingdom of France

Kingdom of Hungary

Turin

Venice

Genoa

Pisa

1380

1284

1294

Black Sea

Corsica

Bulgaria

Serbia

Aragon

1285

Rome

Byzantium

Constantinople

Castile

Kingdom

1264

Ottoman Empire

Portugal

1378

of Naples

1326

1384

Peter III of Aragon

Sardinia

Modon

1282

Kingdom of Sicily

1354

Granada

1283

Malta

Crete

1298

Cyprus

Barbary States

Byzantine Empire
Venice
Aragon
Arabs
Genoa
Vatican

Kingdom of the Mamelukes

of 98 ships, under Andrea Dandolo, meets a Genoese fleet of about 78 ships. The Venetians are heavily defeated. (Among the prisoners is the world traveller, Marco Polo.)

1350–55: The Third Venetian–Genoese War
1352: Battle of the Bosporus. An indecisive battle is fought between a Genoese squadron and an allied squadron that includes ships from Venice, Aragon and Byzantium.

Aug 1353: The united fleets of Venice and Aragon, under Nicolo Pisani, defeat the Genoese fleet off Sardinia.

1354: Battle of Modon. In the Ionian Sea, Paganino Doria's Genoese fleet inflicts a crushing defeat on the Venetians under Nicolo Pisani.

1378–81: The Fourth Venetian–Genoese War (The Chioggia War)
1378: The Venetian fleet under Vittore Pisani defeats the Genoese fleet off Cape Anzio, in the Tyrrhenian Sea.

7 May 1379: Battle of Pola. The Genoese under Luciano Doria beat the Venetians under Vittore Pisani, off Pola. Later that year, the Genoese establish themselves in the harbour town of Chioggia, only a few miles south of Venice.

1380: Battle of Chioggia. After a 6-month campaign on land and sea, the Venetian fleet under Doge Andrea Contarini decisively defeats the Genoese. At the Peace of Turin (1381), Venice secures her position of supremacy in the eastern Mediterranean.

Farther north, the possessions of the English kings in France constituted continual grounds for conflict between the two monarchs, resulting in many wars, and culminating in The Hundred Years War (1337–1453). With no regular navies, warlike operations were generally undertaken with the use of armed merchantmen. France sometimes employed Genoese fleets (and, during the 14th century, Genoa became politically semi-dependent on France). Genoese contingents consisted mostly of galleys, while the other fleets included vessels of the Norse type.

WARFARE IN THE ENGLISH CHANNEL FROM THE 13th TO THE 15th CENTURY

May 1213: Battle of Damme (Bruges). France collects a fleet in the harbour of Bruges in order to act against the Count of Flanders, whom England sends a fleet to help. The French ships are only weakly crewed, as France is pre-occupied with the siege of Ghent, and the English capture some of the enemy ships and destroy a large part of the fleet on the beach—in all, some 400 ships. Two years later, the French invade southern England.

Aug 1217: Battle of Dover (or 'the Fight off Sandwich'). A French fleet of 80 ships under Eustace the Monk is bringing reinforcements to the Thames. The Governor of the Cinque Ports (Dover, Romney, Hythe, Hastings and Sandwich), Hubert de Burgh, is loyal to the English crown, and attacks

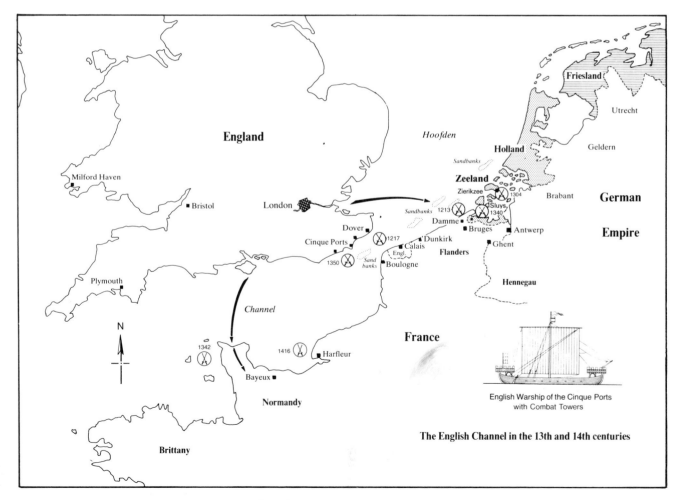

English Warship of the Cinque Ports with Combat Towers

The English Channel in the 13th and 14th centuries

the French in the Channel with about 40 ships. He encounters the enemy as they sail northeast and, passing them, turns and attacks them from the rear, one by one. The English bowmen keep the French crews down and their ships are captured, only 15 ships escaping. This is the first recorded instance of a battle conducted by sailing ship tactics.

1294-97: Edward I seeks to win back his ancestral possessions in France, and raises three fleets, one in Yarmouth, to operate in the Hoofden and the North Sea, one in Portsmouth, for the Channel, and one for the Irish Sea. However, even with control of the sea, his operations on the Continent are unsuccessful.

18 Aug 1304: Battle of Zierikzee. The Count of Flanders is besieging Zierikzee, in the Scheldt estuary, by both land and sea. France sends a relief fleet under Admiral Raignier de Grimaldi of Genoa (this is the first use of the title 'admiral' in the North). The fleet consists of ships from Normandy and Spain, and galleys from Genoa. In a 2-day battle, the Flemish fleet is defeated and a number of their ships taken, including the Count's flagship. He himself is captured. In the narrow waterways, galleys are still superior to sailing ships; this is also the first recorded occasion of the use of fire-ships in the North.

1337-1453: The Hundred Years War

Edward II raises his claim to the French throne; Philip VI of France, meanwhile, rents a fleet of Genoese galleys to clear the Channel of English ships (1338); the big vessels *Christopher* and *Edward* are captured.

1339: French ships burn Hastings, Plymouth and Bristol, whilst the English fleet is employed against Flanders and Scotland.

1339: Ships from the Cinque Ports, under Sir Robert Morley, defeat a French squadron off Dover, pursue the enemy to Boulogne and destroy the ships lying there.

24 June 1340: Battle of Sluys. Edward III prepares a landing in France, covered by a strong fleet. The French fleet takes up a strong position in the western Scheldt, in the neighbourhood of Sluys. It is divided into three squadrons, two of sail under Admiral Quiéret and Treasurer Balmuchet, and one of galleys under the Genoese Barbenoire. The French sailing ships drop anchor in an arm of the Scheldt, the ships, of the individual ranks being chained together. This is a defensive position, sacrificing mobility. The galleys are behind them in reserve. The English fleet of over 200 ships, led by the King and Morley, attack and, due to the greater mobility of the English ships, the French first rank is defeated ship by ship. The remaining French sailing ships are abandoned by their crews and Barbenoire's galleys can only escape with difficulty. As a result of this victory, the battles of the Hundred Years War are fought on French soil: even without a regular navy, England has sufficient resources to maintain control of the Channel.

1342: Battle of Guernsey. A French squadron of 33 ships (mainly Genoese) mounts a surprise attack on English ships transporting reinforcements to Brittany, and capture 4 or 5 ships. The remaining English ships land their troops as intended.

1347: Capture of Calais. The effective blockade of the town by the English fleet leads, after a siege of almost a year, to the fall of Calais.

During this period, there were no regular navies available to protect trade routes from the depredations of pirates; merchantmen were therefore armed, and tended to travel in large convoys.

29 Aug 1350: 'Les Espagnols sur mer'. Between Dungeness and Hastings, a convoy of 40 armed merchantmen under Don Carlos de la Cerda is attacked by Edward III's English fleet. After a sharp fight, the English capture about 20 Spanish ships for a loss of two of their own, including their flagship *Thomas*.

22-23 June 1372: Battle of La Rochelle. The English send a fleet under Lord Pembroke to the Bay of Biscay to relieve the besieged La Rochelle. During an attempted forcing of the harbour entrance, they are subject to a surprise attack by a Franco-Castillan fleet under Ambrosio Bocanegra. On the first day the contest is indecisive, but, on the second day, Pembroke is captured and the English fleet almost completely destroyed.

1377-79: During the reign of Richard II, the French fleet repeatedly devastates the southern coasts of England.

1403-1407: French squadrons again ravage the English southern coast. As a result, the Cinque Ports and Plymouth again equip squadrons, which destroy a French squadron in Milford Haven (there to aid the rebellious Welsh), capture two great merchant fleets, and devastate towns on the coast of Brittany.

August 1416: The harbour of Harfleur (captured by the English in 1415) is blockaded by the French on land and at sea. An English squadron defeats the French blockading ships, and ends the operation.

1417: Action in the Channel. The English fleet defeats that of the French, to permit the landing of Henry V's army in France. Henry is successful: but holding France is beyond the power of the English and, during the reign of the French Charles VII, the English are driven (with the initial inspiration of Joan of Arc) from all but Calais.

A co-operative compact of German export merchants had existed since the beginning of the 11th century. Simultaneous with the German colonization of the east, the northern German towns gradually brought the Baltic trade under their control, their trading capital being Wisby. By the end of the 12th century, Lübeck had become the leading Hanseatic trade centre, and remained so until the decline of the Hanseatic League. In addition to their 'Hanse-kogge' (ships of about 100 tons), which were superior to the Norse ships and distinguished by their great carrying capacity, Lübeck and Hamburg maintained a fleet of their own war 'Koggen'.

THE HANSEATIC LEAGUE FROM THE 12th TO THE 16th CENTURY

1358: The Hanseatic League. This is a loose union of merchants (without any formal constitution or executive) from up to 200 towns in north Germany. It maintains trading accounts in foreign countries, with special privileges: Novgorod (Peterhof), Bergen (German Bridge) and others; later also, London (Steelyard) in 1474.

1361–63 and 1368–70: The Danish–Hanseatic Wars
The Danish seizure of the League's base, Wisby, leads the League to retaliate by taking and sacking Copenhagen.
1362: Off Helsingborg, the League's fleet, under Wittenberg, is defeated by the Danes. The League sues for peace.
1368: The Hanseatic fleet captures Copenhagen and Helsingor, and forces the Danish king, Waldemar IV to leave the country.
1370: Peace of Stralsund. The Hanseatic League wins trade privileges and the right to veto the succession to the Danish throne unless their monopoly is renewed.

About 1400: Struggle of the Hanseatic League against the Nordic pirates, the Likendeeler or 'Equal Sharers' (Vitalien-bruder) who severely affect Hanseatic trade.
1402: Capture and execution of the leader of the Likendeeler, Klaus Stortebecker.
1420–35: Danish–Hanseatic War.
It achieves the liberation of the Wendish towns from the Sundzoll (Sound Tax).
1474: A Hanseatic fleet devastates the east coast of England, and forces King Edward IV to reinstate their suspended privileges.

From the beginning of the 16th century, the trade of the lower Rhine towns becomes increasingly west-orientated, and they withdraw from the Hanseatic League.
1523: Gustav Vasa of Sweden flees, from Christian II of Denmark, to Lübeck. The Hanseatic fleet forces the Danes in Stockholm to surrender, and sets Gustav Vasa on the Swedish throne as Gustav I.
1524: The Hanseatic fleet captures Zealand and Copenhagen, deposes King Christian II, and gives Denmark to Frederick I of Holstein.
1535: The Danish fleet under Peder Skram defeats the Hanseatic fleet in the Little Belt; the Hanseatic League lose most of their trade privileges (1537).

1563–70: The Northern Seven Years War
Lübeck and Denmark are at war with Sweden; but the other Hanseatic towns remain neutral, and the League falls apart.
1564: The Danish fleet, under Herlof Trolle, defeats the Swedes, under Jakob Bagge, in a 2-day sea battle between Oeland and Gotland.
4 June 1565: Trolle, with 28 Danish and Lübeck ships, encounters the Swedish fleet off Bukow, on the coast of Mecklenburg. The fighting is indecisive, but Trolle is mortally wounded.

7 July 1565: A Swedish fleet of 46 ships, under Klas Horn, beats an Allied fleet of 36 ships between Rügen and Bornholm. Both sides suffer heavy losses.
1566: 11 Danish ships and 6 Lübeckers run aground at Wisby after an inconclusive action with the Swedish fleet. By the end of the war, Lübeck's role as a seapower has ceased.

1598: Steelyard in London, the last Hanseatic counting house in a foreign country, is closed.

The decline of the Hanseatic League reflected changing conditions in northern Europe: the rising power of the Scandinavian states, the absence of herring shoals—a vital source of income—in the North Sea, and the transfer of the main trading routes to the northern Atlantic. The scene was now set for the rise of the Netherlands and England.

In the Mediterranean, meanwhile, a new power had arisen in Asia Minor: the Ottoman Turks. During the 14th century, they began to penetrate into the Balkans, their main goal Constantinople. Initially, however, their attempts on this last relic of the Byzantine Empire were repulsed.

WARS IN THE MEDITERRANEAN FROM THE 15th TO THE 17th CENTURY

1416: The first Turkish fleet in the Mediterranean is decisively beaten by the Venetians, under Pietro Loredano, off Gallipoli.
1453: The Turks capture Constantinople.
12–14 Aug 1499: In two engagements off Zonchio and Lepanto, Borrait Rais' Turkish fleet inflicts crippling defeats on the Venetians, under Grimani, a major point in the decline of Venice as a naval power. On 25 Aug, the Venetians (in company with the French) suffer their final defeat near Sapienze Island.
At the beginning of the 16th century, the remaining Islamic states in North Africa make the western Mediterranean unsafe with their piracy. The Turkish Sultan, Suleiman, entrusts command of his fleet to the Algerian Corsair, Khair al-Din (Barbarossa).
1522: The Turks capture Rhodes, driving the Knights of St. John from the island.

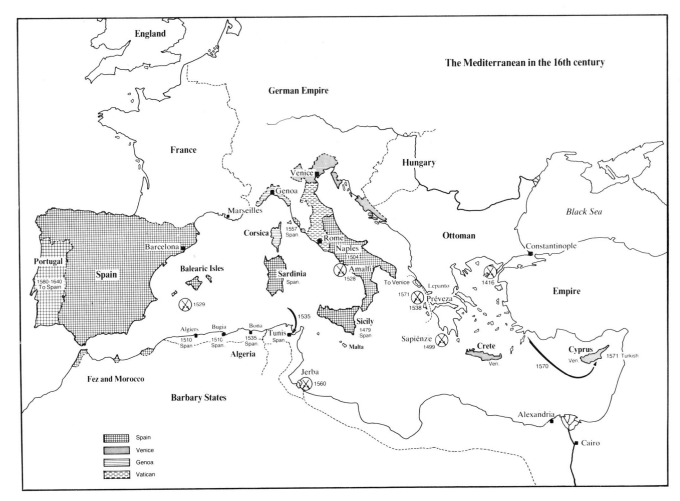

The Mediterranean in the 16th century

Spain
Venice
Genoa
Vatican

1521–29: The War between Emperor Charles V and Francis I of France

1521: Marseilles, besieged by Imperial forces from the land side, is able to hold out until relief arrives, thanks to the support of the French fleet.

1528: Naples is blockaded from the land side by the French army, and from the sea by the Genoese fleet under Andrea Doria; off Amalfi, Doria beats a relieving Spanish fleet. Shortly afterwards, however, he changes sides, and Naples is saved. France then calls on the Turkish fleet for help.

1529: Barbarossa defeats a Spanish fleet off the Balearic Isles. Despite this, however, Francis I is forced to renounce his claims on Italy at the peace treaty of Cambrai.

1532: Andrea Doria captures Koron and installs a Spanish garrison there.

1533: Barbarossa ravages the Sicilian and Italian coasts.

1534: Now admiral of the Ottoman Empire, Barbarossa captures Tunis and retakes Koron. Tunis is taken from Mulai-Hassan, who flees to Europe to seek aid from Charles V of Spain.

June–July 1535: Charles V's army, with the assistance of Doria's fleet, wrests Tunis from the Turks, and reinstates Mulai-Hassan. Doria destroys Barbarossa's fleet.

1536: Barbarossa devastates Minorca with his new fleet.

1537: Suleiman declares war on Venice, and sends Barbarossa to attack Venetian shipping.

18 Aug to 6 Sept 1537: Turkish land and naval forces lay siege to Corfu, assisted by the French, but withdraw on the approach of Doria's fleet.

1538: Barbarossa's activities in the Adriatic and Aegean intensify, and he captures many Venetian islands and mainland outposts. Then in a 3-day battle off Prevéza, Doria's fleet suffers a resounding defeat, which leaves the Turks in complete command of the Ionian Sea.

1541: Charles V's invasion of Algiers is thwarted when his fleet is wrecked in a storm.

1542–44: Barbarossa continues to terrorize the western Mediterranean.

1560: Battle of Jerba (Djerbeh). While attempting to capture Tripoli, the Spanish-Genoese fleet under Gian Andrea Doria is defeated by Piali Pasha's Turkish fleet.

May–Sept 1565: The Knights of the Order of St John (later the Knights of the Maltese Order) successfully defend Malta against a Turkish army under Mustapha and Piali. Christian losses are 7,000 men, Turkish losses 25,000.

1570–71: The Turks capture Cyprus, after landing a strong army with Piali Pasha's fleet.

1571: An alliance against the Turks is formed by Philip II of Spain, Pope Paul V and Venice.

7 Oct 1571: Battle of Lepanto. The Allies assemble a fleet of over 200 ships under Don John of Austria, half brother of the Spanish king. The fleet consists mainly of galleys; each has a crew of 200–400 men (about 100 of these being marines)

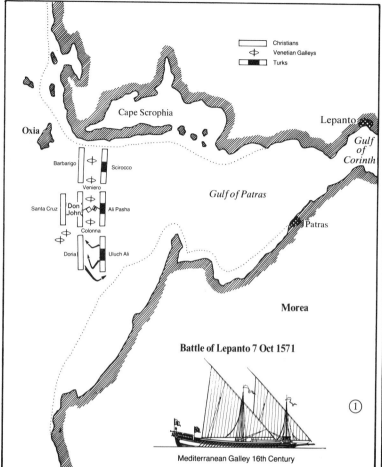

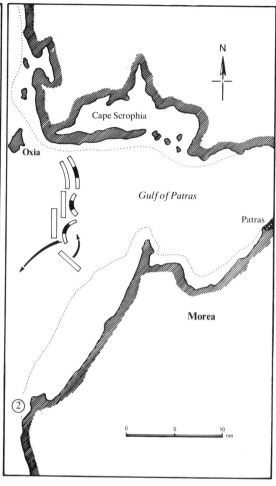

Christians
Venetian Galleys
Turks

Battle of Lepanto 7 Oct 1571

Mediterranean Galley 16th Century

① ②

and a platform in the bows, mounting 5-8 guns. Venice provides 6 galliots (large galleys with 4 masts, lateen sails and 50 guns). The Turkish fleet, under 'Kapudan Pasha' (Commander of the Fleet) Ali Pasha, is about 220 ships strong, and consists mainly of galleys armed with only a few guns. The crews of the Allied fleet total almost 80,000 men; half of them being rowers; the Turkish fleet has about the same number, the rowers being mainly Christian slaves. Don John forms the Christian fleet into three squadrons: the centre (Spanish and Venetian ships) under his personal command: the left wing (Venetians) under Barbarigo; and the right wing (Venetian and Spanish ships) under the Genoese Gian Andrea Doria. Behind the centre is a mixed squadron under the Spaniard Santa Cruz. The Commander of the Venetian contingent, Veniero, has his flagship in the centre near Don John. Two galliots are placed ahead of each squadron. The Turks also form three squadrons: the centre (90 ships) commanded personally by Ali Pasha; the left wing (about 90 ships), composed mainly of Algerians, under the renegade Uluch Ali; and the right wing (60 ships) under Scirocco.

Dawn: The opponents sight each other at the entrance to the Gulf of Patras, and approach each other in slightly crescent-shaped formations, the wings slightly ahead of the centres. The northern wings are close to the coast. The battle is opened by the Venetian galliots with their artillery, and a number of Turkish galleys are hit and some even sunk.

Midday: The fleets are in close combat range; in the centre and the north, ships begin fighting alongside their enemies. Doria swings out to the south, allowing a gap to develop between his wing and the centre: Uluch Ali moves into this gap, and soon has the Christian centre in dire straits. Only the intervention of Santa Cruz's reserve saves it from destruction. On the northern wing, the Turks succeed in outflanking the Christians, and the situation here is also critical; the squadron commanders on both sides, Barbarigo and Scirocco, are killed. In the centre, however, Don John succeeds in gaining the upper hand. His galleys close up on the Turkish flagship and capture it; Ali Pasha is killed, and the Turks lose heart. The centre and right wing of the Turkish fleet are crushed; only Uluch Ali with his Algerians manages to escape with most of his ships, fighting a successful rearguard action. The Turks lose over 150 ships, 30 of which are beached, and 110 captured by the Christians. Turkish losses are about 25,000 dead and 5,000 captured; 12,000 Christian galley slaves are freed. On the Christian side, there are about 8,000 dead and over 20,000 wounded; 12-15 Christian ships are lost, mostly on the right wing during Uluch Ali's attack.

Lepanto was one of the great naval battles of history, and especially significant in having been the last major clash involving galleys. It was also the last decisive battle in the Mediterranean for a long time, although its long-term strategic effects were squandered by the break-up of the Christian coalition shortly afterwards.

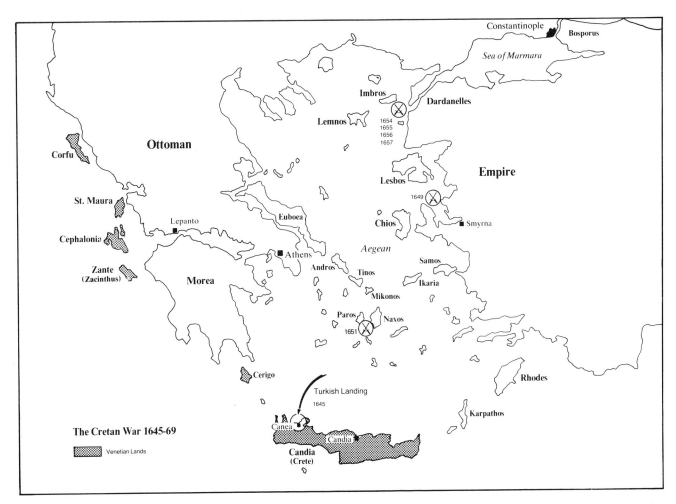

The Cretan War 1645-69

Venetian Lands

1573: Venice concludes peace with the Porte.

1575: Uluch Ali, with a fleet of 230 ships, lands a strong army in Tunis and captures the city.

1609: For the first time, a Spanish squadron composed wholly of warships of sail operates in the Mediterranean against the Barbary states.

1645-69: The Cretan War

Provoked by the piracy of the Knights of Malta in the Levant, Turkey launches a naval offensive.

1645: The Turkish fleet lands an army on Crete, starting a 25-year logistic struggle to supply the opposing armies on the island. The fleets involved are almost always a mixture of sail (galleons) and galleys.

1647: First clash between two squadrons off Negropont (Euboea).

12 May 1649: Battle of Focchies (near Smyrna). 19 Venetian galleons under Giacomo Riva defeat a Turkish fleet of 93 ships; the Turks lose 17 ships to the Venetians' 3.

July 1651: Battle of Paros Island. The Venetian fleet, 58 ships strong under Alvise Mocenigo, clashes with a 100-ship Turkish fleet. In a 3-day pursuit battle, the Turks lose about 15 ships. The Venetians finally try to suppress the Turkish supply route by blockading the Dardanelles.

16 May 1654: First action off the Dardanelles. The Turkish fleet of 76 ships fights its way out of the Narrows against a Venetian blockading force of 26 ships.

21 June 1655: Second action off the Dardanelles. 36 Venetian ships, under Lazaro Mocenigo, oppose a Turkish fleet of 100 ships in the Narrows. This time the break-out costs the Turks 16 ships.

26 June 1656: First Battle of the Dardanelles. The Venetian fleet, 29 sail and 38 galleys under Lorenzo Marcello, blockades the Narrows. In attempting a break-out, the Turkish fleet (28 sail and 70 galleys) is decisively defeated; only 14 galleys escape. The Venetians lose only 3 ships.

17 July 1657: Second Battle of the Dardanelles. In a 3-day battle, the Venetians under Lazaro Mocenigo, cannot prevent a Turkish break-out.

1669: As the Venetians cannot suppress the Turkish logistic effort, Candia, their last strongpoint on Crete, falls. And, in the same year, Venice concludes peace with the Porte.

During the 17th century, Ottoman expansion to the west was largely curtailed by internal unrest within the Turkish Empire. Coincidentally, the age of the galley came to an end; although they were still to be used both in the Mediterranean and in the Baltic throughout the 18th century, they would no longer play a significant role in decisive naval actions.

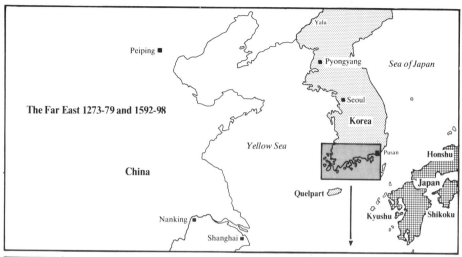

The Far East 1273-79 and 1592-98

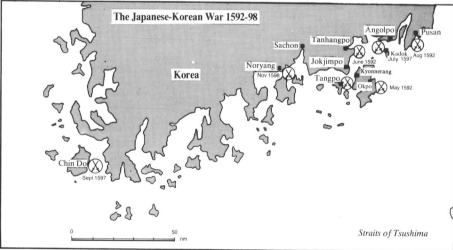

The Japanese-Korean War 1592-98

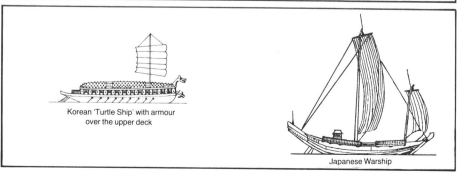

Korean 'Turtle Ship' with armour
over the upper deck

Japanese Warship

From earliest times to the end of the 19th century, the coast of Asia had been plagued by pirates. In particular, the island status of Japan had led to the early development of seafaring skills among her people and, during the Middle Ages, Japanese pirates maintained an almost total blockade of the Chinese coast. When, in 1273 and 1279, Kublai Khan attempted to invade Japan, typhoons came to Japan's aid, badly damaging the invasion fleets.

In the 15th century, however, the Ming dynasty in China achieved naval supremacy; their considerable fleet controlled the China seas and undertook numerous voyages into the Indian Ocean. By the time the Portuguese reached the area in the 16th century, this fleet had already fallen into disuse and decay. Starting in the 11th century, meanwhile, Korea had maintained her own fleet.

THE FAR EAST IN THE 16th CENTURY

1592-98: The Japanese-Korean War

Japan, united under the Shogun Hideyoshi, attempts to make conquests on the Asian mainland. An army of about 140,000 men is assembled, and 800 ships make ready for the invasion of Korea. Korea's fleet consists of only 80 galleys, but they include the first warships with iron plating; on these, an iron-plated turtleback deck provides protection against missiles, and iron spikes deter boarders. The stem is strengthened for ramming, and the sides are pierced by archery ports.

Most ships already carry light cannon and catapults for fire-arrows. In the shoal-ridden waters of south Korea, these galleys are very much superior to the Japanese sailing ships. At the beginning of 1592, the Japanese carry out an almost unopposed landing at Fusan (or Pusan), and penetrate inland.

May 1592: Battle of Okpo. Korea's fleet, under Yi Sun-sin, intercepts a Japanese supply squadron, and destroys 26 ships. Next day, 13 more Japanese ships are destroyed at Jokjimpo.

June 1592: At two further battles, Sachon and Tangpo, Yi Sun-sin sinks 12 and 21 Japanese ships, respectively, without loss to his own fleet.

June 1592: Battle of Tanhangpo. Yi Sun-sin destroys 30 ships of a Japanese squadron.

July 1592: Near Kyonnerang, Yi Sun-sin destroys a large Japanese logistic convoy; and, at Angolpo, another convoy loses 42 ships. The sea supply routes of the Japanese army (now at Pyongyang) are cut.

Aug 1592: Battle of Pusan. Yi Sun-sin attacks the 500-strong Japanese supply fleet lying in Pusan harbour, and destroys over 130 of them. Lack of supplies now forces the Japanese army to evacuate north and central Korea.

July 1597: The Korean fleet, under Won Kyun, is defeated by the Japanese off Kadok.

Sept 1597: Action off Chin Do Island. Yi Sun-sin, with only 12 ships, beats a 133-ship strong Japanese squadron.

Nov 1598: Battle of Noryang. Yi Sun-sin attacks two Japanese squadrons in sequence: the first loses 50 ships; the second is almost completely destroyed with a type of flame-thrower (fire-arrows?). Yi Sun-sin is killed shortly before the end of the battle.

At the end of 1598, the Japanese evacuate Korea.

The Age of Sail

Illustration by Geoff Hunt

During the later Middle Ages, the sailing ship had gradually developed into a truly ocean-going vessel. The upsurge of trade during the 13th century had produced broad-beamed ships with rigging, evolved from the longboats of the Norsemen and from the various sail-powered vessels of the Mediterranean. The fore- and after-castles became part of the main hull, resulting in the northern 'cog' and the Mediterranean 'caravel' and 'nef'. The average displacement rose from 100 to 300 tons, and the larger sailing ships were fitted with up to four masts, generally carrying square sails, an arrangement that much improved their sailing properties.

During the course of the 14th century, the fixed rudder controlled with a tiller replaced the old steering system of an oar fixed to the starboard side, and improved instruments, such as the compass (attributed to the Italian Flavio Gioja) and the astrolabe, enabled long-distance oceanic voyages to be undertaken, and charts to be drawn up.

Ship's armament became immensely more powerful in the 15th century, with the introduction of a weapon of much greater range and destructive potential than catapults and slings—the cannon. Initially mounted in the 'castles', they were later carried amidships; the invention of gun ports (attributed to the Frenchman Décharges) in 1501 enabled the heavy guns to be carried lower in the ship, with a consequent improvement in stability. Warships, too, had by now increased considerably in size: the English Great Harry (or Henry Grâce de Dieu), one of the largest ships of the early 16th century, had a displacement of 1,500 tons.

VOYAGES OF THE DISCOVERERS

The rise of the Ottoman Empire across the European trade routes to Asia resulted in the imposition of heavy taxes on oriental trade. Prompted by this situation, and now equipped with ships better suited to crossing the oceans, the seafarers of the West now sought afresh new routes to the East. The Portuguese Prince Henry the Navigator gathered the leading geographers and navigators of his time to Portugal to instruct his sea captains and, at the beginning of the 15th century, the voyages of discovery southward along the west coast of Africa began. Following the rediscovery of the fact that the world is round, attempts were also made to sail to India in a westerly direction, but the circumference of the globe proved to have been hopelessly underestimated.

1488: After some 50 years of cautious exploration by various Portuguese captains, Bartolomew Dias is the first to go round the horn of Africa.

1492: Christopher Columbus, on a westerly voyage in the caravels *Santa Maria, Nina and Pinta*, discovers America for the Spanish crown. Following this, Columbus undertakes three more similar journeys before 1504.

1494: Treaty of Tordesillas. After Papal mediation, Spain and Portugal divide between them the newly discovered lands and those yet to be discovered. The dividing line is to be the

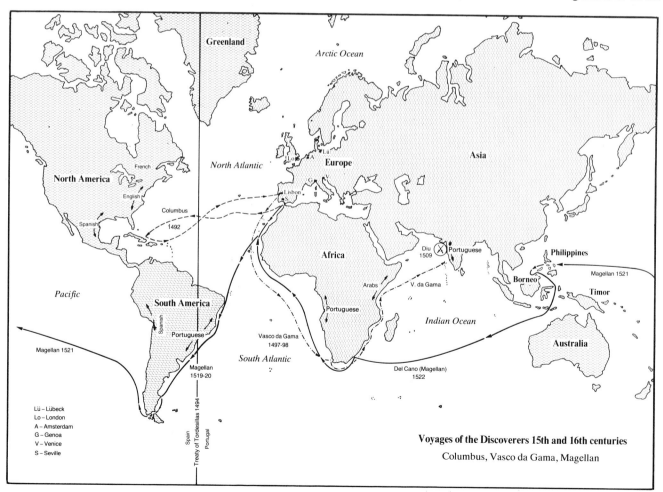

Lü – Lübeck
Lo – London
A – Amsterdam
G – Genoa
V – Venice
S – Seville

Voyages of the Discoverers 15th and 16th centuries
Columbus, Vasco da Gama, Magellan

Western Europe in the 16th century

Shetland Is.

Kingdom of Norway

Oslo

Hebrides

Kingdom of Scotland

Storm

Copenhagen

Kingdom of Denmark

Lübeck

Kingdom

of England

London

Southampton

1545

6.8 – 8.8

Calais
Span.

Antwerp

Netherlands

Union of Utrecht

Amsterdam

German

Storm

31.7

Paris

Luxembourg

Empire

Kingdom

of

France

Burgundy

Confederation

Tyrol

The Spanish Armada
1588

La Rochelle

Savoy

Milan

Venice

Parma
Modena Papal
States

22.7

22.9

Genoese
Rep.

Tuscany

Corunna

Santander

Vigo

Corsica
Gen.

Elba

Rome

Barcelona

Portugal

Kingdom of Spain

Sardinia
Span.

1580-1640
To Spain

Madrid

Lisbon

14.5

Balearic Isles

Seville

Cadiz

Drake 1587

Algiers

Tunis

Barbary States

squadron at Dabul (Chaul). After 3 days of bitter fighting, 2 Portuguese ships escape.

February 1509: The Portugeuse viceroy, with the aid of reinforcements, destroys the Gujerati-Egyptian fleet at Diu, thereby establishing Portuguese supremacy in the Indian Ocean.

1519-21: First circumnavigation of the globe by Ferdinand Magellan and Sebastian del Cano. But, of the 5 ships that set out, only 1 comes back.

1577-80: Second circumnavigation of the globe, by Francis Drake.

During the 16th century, the trading centre of gravity began to shift from the Baltic, North Sea and Mediterranean in favour of the Atlantic, resulting in the rise of Lisbon, Seville, Amsterdam (and later, London), while trade in Lübeck, Venice and Genoa tended to stagnate. The voyages of discovery and the growth of colonies in America and India brought a dramatic increase in sea traffic: great fleets of sailing vessels were now bringing the riches of the New World to the Iberian Peninsula and the Spanish Netherlands. Each year, the Spanish silver fleet crossed the Atlantic from the West Indies to Cadiz, laden with treasure; but it was a treasure from which the other European nations were excluded.

And, while the Iberians imported bullion, the people of the Spanish Netherlands prospered on the spin-off of intermediate trade; during the 16th century, the Dutch carried practically all the Spanish trade with the Baltic, while their fishing fleets in the North Sea earned them a handsome living too. The Reformation, however, divided Europe into two religious blocs; and, when it became clear that Philip II of Spain would grant no political or religious freedom to his subjects in the Low Countries, those provinces revolted. Precipitated by the execution of Egmont and Hoorn by the Spanish, the Netherlands rose against Spain, under William of Orange.

At the same time, Catholic Spain's relations with Protestant England deteriorated, and Elizabeth I began openly to assist the Netherlanders. In the West Indies, the declaration of war had been anticipated, and there Drake, Hawkins, Frobisher and others caused considerable damage to Spanish trade.

SPAIN AND THE THIRTY YEARS WAR

1545: The French attempt to invade England. A mixed French fleet of galleons and galleys, under d'Annebaut, attempts a landing. The weaker English fleet, under Lord Lisle, repels the enemy after a short artillery duel off Spithead. The English *Mary Rose* heels over when her helm is put about, and she sinks with heavy loss of life.

1582: Battle of Punta Delgada (Azores). The Azores (with French aid) rise in opposition to the succession of Philip II to the Portuguese throne. The Azores are vital for the security of the sea routes to America, however, and a squadron of Spanish sail under the Marquis of Santa Cruz defeats a French squadron under Philip Strozzi, and occupies the Azores. This is the first battle to be fought in mid-Atlantic, and it leads Spain to place special emphasis on the building of sailing ships.

1568-1648: The Dutch War of Independence (The Eighty Years War)

1572: Calvinist rebels, fleeing from Spanish oppression in their native Netherlands, become privateers (the 'Sea Beggars') and sieze Brill.

Oct 1573: Action at Enkhuizen. A Spanish squadron of 30 ships tries to wrest control of the Zuider Zee from the 'Sea Beggars', but is defeated, losing 6 ships.

Jan 1574: Battle of Romerswael. A Spanish squadron attempting to break the Dutch siege of Middelburg suffers a

degree of longitude running about 370 miles west of the Azores, 46° 37' w.

1498: Vasco da Gama completes the discovery of the sea route to India around the southern tip of Africa.

At the beginning of the 16th century, the Portuguese establish naval bases along the African coast, on the route to their new colonies in India. To oppose Portuguese expansion in the east, Mahmud Begara of Gujerat allies with the Sultan of Egypt and, early in 1507, an Egyptian fleet is despatched to India.

March 1508: Gujerati-Egyptian forces surprise a Portuguese

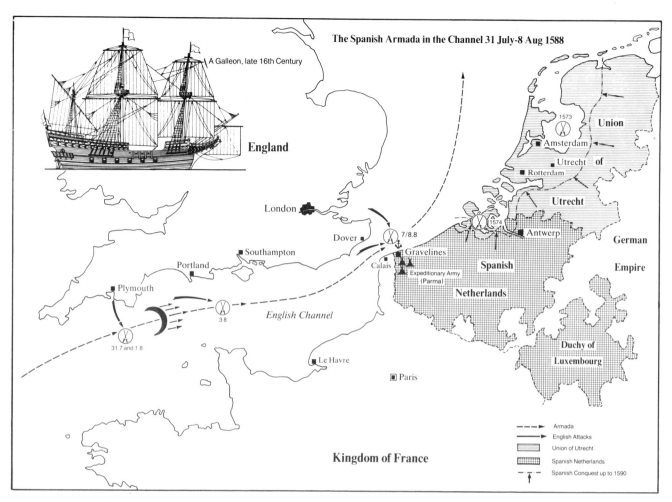

The Spanish Armada in the Channel 31 July-8 Aug 1588

A Galleon, late 16th Century

England

London

Dover

7/8.8

Southampton

Portland

Plymouth

31.7 and 1.8

3.8

English Channel

Gravelines

Calais

Expeditionary Army
(Parma)

Spanish

Netherlands

Union

Amsterdam

Utrecht

of

Rotterdam

1574

Utrecht

Antwerp

German

Empire

1573

Duchy of
Luxembourg

Le Havre

Paris

Kingdom of France

- - - - ▶ Armada
———▶ English Attacks
Union of Utrecht
Spanish Netherlands
Spanish Conquest up to 1590

heavy defeat, and loses 15 ships. Middelburg surrenders.

1581: Declaration of independence by the Seven Provinces. Maurice of Orange leads the struggle from 1585 to 1625.

1585: Spain captures Antwerp: the southern half of the Low Countries remains in Spanish hands. But, meanwhile, the Dutch drive Spanish–Portuguese trade from South Africa and the Far East, and firmly establish themselves there.

1587: The execution of Mary Queen of Scots precipitates open war between England and Spain.

1587: Raid on Cadiz. With 6 warships and 17 armed merchantmen, Francis Drake attacks the Spanish fleet under preparation in Cadiz. He drives off the protecting galleys and, in 3 days, destroys most of the Spanish ships, including 6 of over 1,000 tons. Drake then sails off to the Azores on a privateering raid, and returns to England after 3 months, almost without loss. The planned Spanish attack on England has to be postponed by a year, so that a new fleet can be built.

1588: The Spanish Armada. After numerous delays, Spain's fleet enters the English Channel. Commanded by the Duke of Medina Sidonia, it includes 6 squadrons of sail, 1 of galleys (including 4 large galliots) and a supply squadron; the 130 ships have on board 30,000 men, two-thirds of them soldiers. The artillery consists of a great number of small calibre cannon set on the high castles of the galleons, but the Spaniards rely, as at Lepanto, on their strength in boarding: the artillery is regarded as a secondary weapon. Elizabeth entrusts the English fleet to the Lord High Admiral, Lord

Howard; he is supported by Drake, Hawkins and Frobisher. The English fleet has almost 200 ships, mainly small armed merchantmen: crews total 15,000 men, a third of them soldiers. All are sailing ships, and carry heavy-calibre broadside guns. The sizes of the ships of sail in the fleets are as follows:

	SPAIN	ENGLAND
Over 1,000 tons	7	2
500–1,000 tons	50	11
100–500 tons	20	150
Below 100 tons	25	30

31 July: As soon as the Armada is sighted, the English fleet sets out from Plymouth. The Spaniards approach in crescent formation, while the English, taking advantage of the superior sailing properties of their ships, sail around the enemy causing the rearmost ships heavy losses with their artillery, while avoiding close combat.

1 Aug: The English capture two damaged stragglers, *Nuestra Senora de Rosaria* and *Nuestra Senora de Rosa*, two of the biggest Spanish ships.

2 Aug: The English replenish their ammunition.

3 Aug: Howard, in his flagship *Ark Royal* is in combat against several Spanish ships.

4 Aug: The Spanish ship *Santa Anna* runs aground at Le Havre.

6 Aug: The Spanish fleet anchors off Calais. Howard calls Seymour's Thames-based squadron lying in the Downs to his assistance.

7/8 Aug: The English undertake a night attack with fire-ships. Eight old sailing ships, loaded with inflammable materials, are set aflame and sent into the enemy anchorage. The Spanish cut their anchor cables and try to escape by sailing along the shallow coastal waters; there, several of them go aground.

8 Aug: The Spanish fleet is now scattered about Gravelines. Drake launches an energetic attack, and the Spanish are driven onto the Flanders coast, suffering heavy losses from grounding and artillery fire. The combats in the Channel have cost them a total of 20 ships and about 5,000 men. When the wind turns from the south, the badly mauled Spaniards escape into the North Sea, but, as the Channel is controlled by the English and the Dutch harbours are in hostile hands, Medina Sidonia decides to return to Spain by sailing around the British Isles. Storms cost him about half his remaining ships, and he reaches Spain at the end of September with but 65 ships and 10,000 men.

This was the first sea battle to be decided by artillery alone, for the superior handling characteristics of their ships had enabled the English to avoid close combat with their larger adversaries. Spain's naval hegemony was now at an end.

1589: An Anglo-Dutch fleet under Drake and Norris sails for Spain; the harbours of Vigo and Corunna are destroyed and a large number of merchant ships captured.

June–July 1596: Capture of Cadiz. An Anglo-Dutch fleet, under the joint command of Lord Howard and Lord Essex, captures Cadiz. After destroying the Spanish ships, harbour installations and supply depots, the town is evacuated again.

1598: A Dutch fleet plunders Spanish bases in the Canaries.

1601: The Spanish land troops in Ireland, but, unsupported, these are soon forced to surrender.

1602: English galleons destroy a Spanish squadron of 9 galleys in the Channel; only one escapes. This is the last conflict between sail and galley in the waters around the British Isles.

1604: Elizabeth's successor, James I, makes peace with Spain; the Netherlands continue the war alone against a weakened Spain.

1607: The Dutch, under Jacob van Heemskerck, defeat a Spanish squadron in Gibraltar Roads.

1609-21: Armistice (The Twelve Years Truce) between Spain and the Netherlands. Dutch trade increases greatly in this period of peace.

1628: A Dutch squadron under Piet Hein captures the Spanish silver fleet off Cuba.

1631: At Antwerp, the Spanish equip a fleet to attack the Netherlands, but the Dutch annihilate this in a night attack.

Sept 1639: A Spanish fleet, under Admiral Oquendo (flagship *Santiago*), appears in the Channel. It is about 70 ships strong, over a dozen of which displace more than 1,000 tons (e.g., *Santa Theresa*, 2,400 tons); the crews total 24,000 men, including a number of marines aboard transports.

16-17 Sept 1639: With 20 much smaller ships, the Dutch admiral Martin Van Tromp (flagship *Amelia*) attacks the Spaniards and, in a pure artillery duel, he forces the Spanish fleet towards the English coast. Oquendo anchors in the Downs to replenish supplies and to repair damage. An English squadron under Pennington also anchors in the Downs, in order to protect English neutrality, while Tromp observes and blockades the Spaniards, and is constantly reinforced with ships from Holland.

21 Oct 1639: Battle of the Downs. The 70 Spanish ships are finally confronted by about 100 Dutch vessels (all of them much smaller than their enemy). Tromp divides his fleet into six squadrons, one of them, under de With, to observe the English squadron (which takes no part in the ensuing action). Eleven fire-ships are prepared and, on the morning of the 21st, a favourable wind enables Tromp to attack. The Spaniards, not reckoning to be attacked under the eyes of the English, can scarcely cut their cables in time, and their fleet is thrown into complete confusion. The Dutch fire-ships find a number of victims, and a great number of Spanish ships run aground, there to be finished off by the Dutch. Oquendo is only able to escape with a dozen or so ships; the Dutch take 14 prizes; the rest of the Spanish fleet is destroyed or stranded; Spanish losses include 7,000 dead and wounded and 1,800 captured. Tromp's losses are but 1 ship lost and 500 men dead. The Battle of the Downs confirms Spain's naval eclipse.

By the beginning of the 17th century, the Dutch had become the world's leading trading nation. Into the Baltic, Mediterranean and Far Eastern seas sailed great convoys of merchantmen—travelling together as security from the pirates of the Barbary states, and from those of Dunkirk operating specifically against the Dutch and English. For service to the East Indies, the Dutch built especially big, strong ships; in time of war, these were to form a large part of the combat fleets—naval powers still maintained very few regular warships. Although the first 100-gun three-decker, the 1,520-ton Sovereign of the Seas, was built in 1637, the standard principal unit of sea power remained the two-decker, mounting 50–80 guns.

Frigates, however, were now beginning to be built: of about 400 tons displacement and with 30–40 guns, they were slim, fast, yet powerful vessels. Ideal for anti-pirate activities, they would prove excellent for cruising and reconnaissance roles in war.

In France, Richelieu was now building up that nation's first regular navy, with its main base at Brest; for flagship, it could already boast the 1,800-ton Couronne. And, like Spain, France continued to maintain a strong fleet of galleys in the Mediterranean.

Nov–Dec 1640: The Dutch fleet supports Portugal in its struggle for independence from Spain.

1648: Peace of Westphalia. Spain finally acknowledges the independence of the Netherlands.

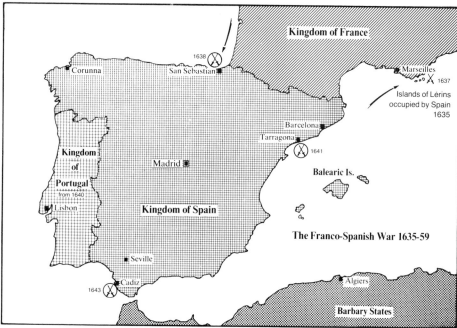

The Franco-Spanish War 1635-59

1635–59: The Franco-Spanish War
France, under Richelieu, intervenes in the Thirty Years War on the Protestant side.

1635: A Spanish mixed fleet captures the islands of Lérins (off the coast of Provence); these are subsequently developed into a strong Spanish naval base.

March–May 1637: A strong French fleet of sail, galleys and fire-ships, under command of Marquis de Sourdis and Comte d'Harcourt, lands an army on the islands and ejects the Spanish.

22 Aug 1638: Action near San Sebastian. In the roads of Guetaria lies a Spanish squadron of 28 ships; they are attacked by the French under de Sourdis, with 18 large galleons and 7 fire-ships. Almost all the fire-ships reach their targets, and most of the Spanish ships are destroyed.

20 Aug 1641: Action off Tarragona. A Spanish galley squadron is destroyed by a few French sailing ships.

1642: Death of Richelieu. The young French fleet begins to decline again.

4 Sept 1643: Action off Cadiz. The French admiral de Brezé defeats a Spanish squadron by cleverly manoeuvring them between two fires.

1659: Treaty of the Pyrénées brings the war to a close. Spain is finally dislodged from her position of European hegemony.

To the north, meanwhile, Denmark and Sweden were fighting for control of the Baltic; each side maintained a standing fleet of sail no less effective than those of the western sea powers.

1643–45: The War between Sweden and Denmark
May 1644: A Swedish squadron (fitted out in Holland) is beaten by the Danish fleet under King Christian IV.

11 July 1644: Action off Femern. (Colberger Heide). The Swedish fleet of about 40 ships, under Klas Fleming, meets an approximately equal Danish fleet under Jorgen Wind, with the Danish King Christian IV aboard Trefoldighed. The fight lasts for 10 hours and ends indecisively, neither side losing a ship. King Christian, however, loses the sight of an eye in the battle.

23 Oct 1644: Action off Laaland. The Swedish fleet under Count Wrangel, with 42 ships, meets a Danish squadron of 17 ships, under Pros Mund, off the southern Danish island. In a 6-hour fight, the Danish squadron is destroyed, Mund is killed, and only 3 ships escape.

1645: The Peace of Brömsebro. Sweden receives Gotland and Osel, and is exempted from the Sound Tax.

1648: The Peace of Westphalia brings the Thirty Years War to a close. Sweden acquires possessions in northern Germany.

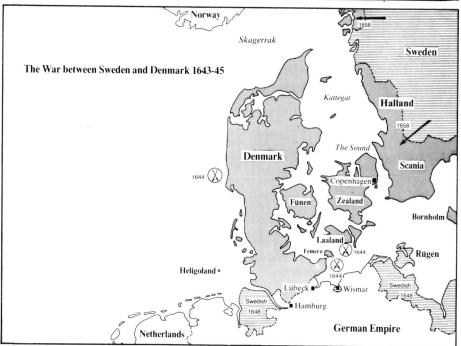

The War between Sweden and Denmark 1643-45

In 1652 began the first of three great wars for the world's trade. After the English Civil Wars (1642–46, 1648, 1650–51) and the execution of the vanquished King Charles I in 1649, England became temporarily a republic. At sea, royalist resistance lingered on for a few years, as Prince Rupert led a small fleet in a war of piracy. Cromwell, taking the helm in England, now proceeded to embark upon an expansive foreign policy, aimed principally at reducing the Dutch share of world trade. The words of Ralegh were to become deeds: 'Whosoever commands the sea commands the trade; whosoever commands the trade of the world commands the riches of the world, and consequently the world itself.' Whilst Blake chased Prince Rupert out of the Channel and around the Iberian peninsula, gradually destroying his ships, Popham and Deane cleared the Channel of privateers, and Ayscue sailed to North America to force the English colonies to abandon the Royalist cause.

1652–54: THE FIRST ANGLO-DUTCH WAR

The Anglo-Dutch War in the 'Narrow Seas'

1651: The Navigation Act. Goods travelling to or from England may do so only on English ships or on ships of the exporting country. This is a blow aimed against Dutch shipping. England demands that all ships, including whole fleets, must accord English warships 'the honours of the flag' when in English waters. Also, Dutch ships may be searched for Royalist pirates. To lend effect to his laws, Cromwell begins

to strengthen the English fleet in 1649: by 1654, 86 ships of the line (mostly two-deckers of up to 1,000 tons, with 60–80 cannon) have been built. Command is given to 'General-at-Sea' Robert Blake. At the outbreak of war, the Dutch fleet consists of about 60 ships of the line, generally smaller than the English ships and carrying only 40–50 guns. Both fleets augment their strength with large armed merchantmen. To maintain their vital trade, the Dutch assemble large convoys; it is these that often become the centre of the conflict.

29 May 1652: Battle of Dover. Dutch admiral Tromp meets an English squadron under Blake in the Channel. The English, with 25 ships, are numerically inferior to the 40 Dutch, but despite this Blake demands that the Dutch dip their ensigns first, and reinforces his demand with a few cannon shot. Tromp answers with a broadside from his flagship, and there follows a battle of some hours' duration, in which the Dutch lose two ships. Both countries prepare for war, the official declaration of which follows in two months. The Dutch gather all their merchantmen approaching from the west into a convoy, and only convoys will henceforward be sent in the opposite direction.

26 Aug 1652: Action off Plymouth. Dutch admiral Michiel de Ruyter is escorting a Dutch west-bound convoy. At midday, an English squadron of 40 ships and 5 fire-ships under Ayscue attempts to stop the convoy, but, with his 30 warships and 6 fire-ships, de Ruyter successfully fights off the English and forces them back to Plymouth. The convoy sails safely

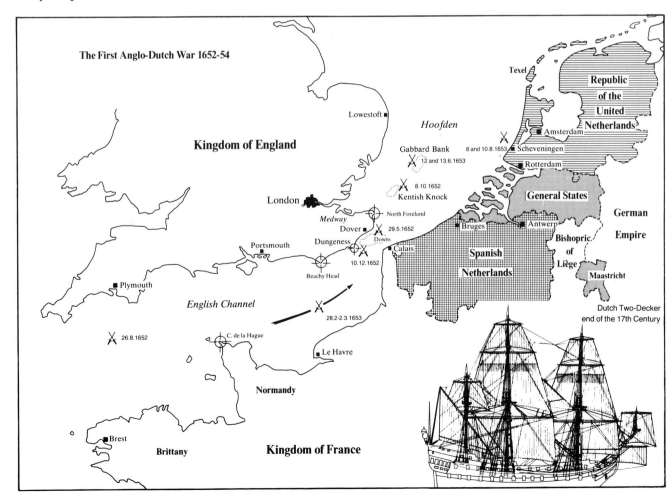

The First Anglo-Dutch War 1652-54

Kingdom of England

Republic of the United Netherlands

Texel

Lowestoft

Hoofden

Amsterdam

Gabbard Bank
8 and 10.8.1653 Scheveningen
12 and 13.6.1653

Rotterdam

8.10.1652
Kentish Knock

General States

London

Medway
North Foreland

Dover 29.5.1652

Bruges Antwerp

German Empire

Dungeness Downs

Calais

Bishopric of Liège

Portsmouth

Beachy Head

10.12.1652

Spanish Netherlands

Maastricht

Plymouth

English Channel

28.2-2.3.1653

Dutch Two-Decker end of the 17th Century

26.8.1652

C. de la Hague

Le Havre

Normandy

Brest

Brittany

Kingdom of France

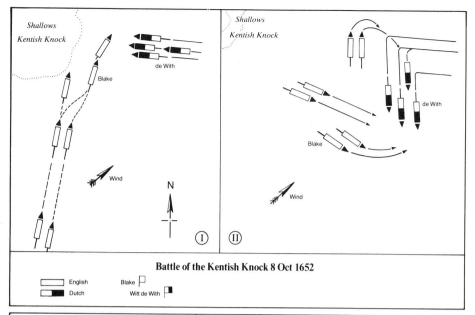

Battle of the Kentish Knock 8 Oct 1652

☐ English   Blake ☐
▬ Dutch   Witt de With ▭

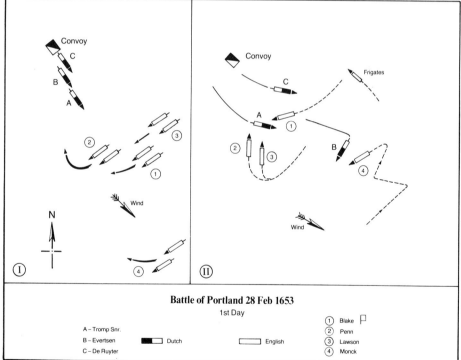

Battle of Portland 28 Feb 1653
1st Day

A – Tromp Snr.
B – Evertsen   ▬ Dutch   ☐ English
C – De Ruyter

① Blake ☐
② Penn
③ Lawson
④ Monck

badly damaged. Cromwell now believes the Dutch fleet destroyed, and sends parts of his own fleet out into the North Sea and Western Approaches on convoy escort duty and privateering. Only 45 ships remain with Blake in the Downs.

10 Dec 1652: Battle of Dungeness. Tromp, with the reinforced Dutch fleet, is to escort a great convoy to La Rochelle and return to Holland with another convoy. In order to clear his path, Tromp attacks Blake, who is outnumbered by 70 ships to 42. Blake opens the battle with his flagship *Triumph*. Two English ships lay alongside Tromp's flagship *Brederode* and attempt to board, but a second Dutchman comes to Tromp's aid, and both English ships are captured. Blake loses 3 other ships and has to accept defeat. Tromp takes his convoy safely to La Rochelle, and starts back with another convoy of 150 ships.

28 Feb to 2 March 1653: Battle of Portland (The Three Days Battle in the Channel). The English have now had time to concentrate their fleet and reinforce it with new ships. Blake thus commands 70 ships. The van is commanded by Penn, and the rear by Monck.

28 Feb: The fleets sight each other off Cape la Hague. Tromp orders the convoy to turn away, and attacks the English with his 70 ships. He commands the van himself, Evertsen the centre, de Ruyter the rear. The battle rages indecisively all afternoon and, during the night, Tromp orders the convoy to proceed towards Holland alone, and places his fleet between it and the English ships.

1 March: In the pursuit, the English try repeatedly (and in vain) to get at the convoy; but they only manage to take a few stragglers. Some Dutchmen already begin to run out of ammunition.

2 March: In the morning, the Dutch are off Beachy Head. At 9am, Blake again attacks Tromp, who now has only 30 ships capable of fighting. The English at last succeed in reaching the convoy with their fast frigates, and capture a number of merchantmen. Tromp can only maintain his position with difficulty, one ship after another running out of ammunition; but, as darkness falls, Blake breaks off the battle. In spite of this, the English victory is great: the Dutch lose 11 warships, 30 merchantmen and almost 2,000 dead; the English only 1 ship, but almost 1,000 men. Blake himself is wounded, and Monck assumes command. Tromp has, however, achieved his aim by bringing in the majority of the convoy. Both countries now work furiously at their armaments, and look ahead to the struggle for command of the sea. In April, Cromwell dissolves the 'Long Parliament' and begins his solitary rule. In spring, the Dutch fleet is back up to fighting strength, and Tromp runs into the Kattegat and escorts 200 merchantmen home. After bombarding Dover and destroying some English merchantmen in the Downs, he meets the battle-ready English fleet once again.

through the Channel.

8 Oct 1652: Battle of the Kentish Knock. The Dutch fleet, under Witte de With, enters the Channel to attack Blake's fleet lying in the Downs. Each side is about 65 ships strong, and they meet at the Kentish Knock, a shallow in the Thames estuary. Some English ships go aground and the battle moves off southwards, developing into a series of irregular combats between individual ships and groups of ships. The larger English ships finally win the day owing to the suddenness of Blake's attack and the reluctance of the Dutch crews to engage: the Dutch lose 3 ships, and many of the others are

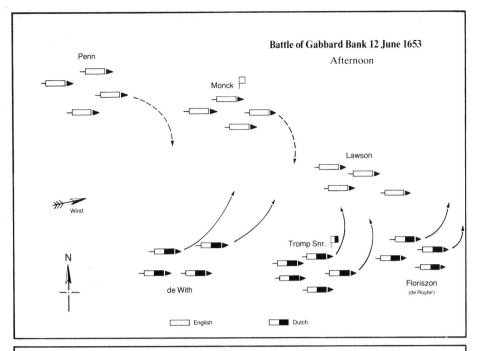

Battle of Gabbard Bank 12 June 1653

Afternoon

Penn

Monck

Lawson

Wind

N

Tromp Snr.

de With

Floriszon
(de Ruyter)

☐ English   ■ Dutch

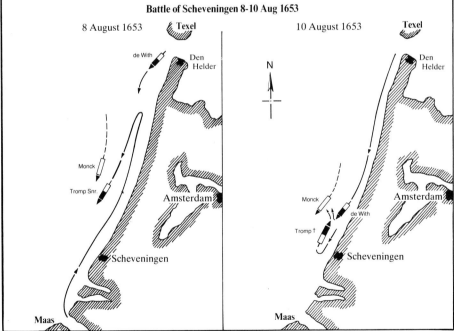

Battle of Scheveningen 8-10 Aug 1653

8 August 1653   Texel

de With   Den
Helder

Monck

Tromp Snr.

Amsterdam

Scheveningen

Maas

10 August 1653   Texel

N

Den
Helder

Monck

de With

Tromp †

Amsterdam

Scheveningen

Maas

12–13 June 1653: Battle of Gabbard Bank (North Foreland). Monck and Deane command the English fleet of 115 ships, including 5 fire-ships and 30 armed merchantmen, with a total of 3,840 guns and 16,300 men. Tromp's Dutch fleet has 104 ships, 6 of these being fire-ships.

12 June: Monck keeps his fleet concentrated, and tries to hold the enemy at a distance with his stronger artillery. Tromp succeeds in trapping the English rear (Lawson) between his own main body and his rear (de Ruyter), but Monck manages to extricate Lawson and a general mêlée develops. The Dutch manage to hold their own against the stronger English until evening; then Blake arrives with 18 reinforcements.

13 June: Next morning, the English superior numbers begin to tell. In the afternoon, the Dutch withdraw into the Flanders shallows, where the larger English ships cannot follow. The Dutch lose 20 ships (including 11 captured) and 1,400 men; English losses are 1 ship and 400 men. The Dutch coast is now blockaded by the English fleet and all their sea trade stopped. The re-equipping of the Dutch fleet proceeds in the Maas under Tromp and in the Texel under de With.

8–10 Aug 1653: Battle of Scheveningen (Ter Heide). Tromp leaves the Maas to join up with de With; he has 82 ships including 5 fire-ships.

8 Aug: Off Scheveningen, he falls in with Monck, who has over 100 ships; when Tromp tries to shake off his adversary by sailing south, de With hears the combat and, that night, leaves the Texel with 24 ships to support him.

9 Aug: Heavy storms prevent action, but by evening, Tromp and de With unite in sight of the English fleet.

10 Aug: Overnight, the weather improves: the battle begins on the next day in a light south-westerly wind. The fleets pass each other several times in badly ordered line ahead, until the Dutch penetrate the English line from the windward side, and a general fight develops. Tromp is killed by a musket ball. Several English ships are caught by fire-ships, and one frigate explodes, but Dutch losses are greater, and several of their ships are sunk. The flagships of de Ruyter and Evertsen are no longer capable of combat. In the afternoon, 20 Dutch ships take flight, and de With covers their withdrawal to Texel with the rest of his fleet; but English losses are so heavy that no energetic pursuit is mounted. In these three days, the Dutch lose 15 ships, but the English are forced to lift their blockade in order to refit their fleet, and the Dutch start their convoys again. Their trade, however, suffers heavily from English privateering.

The Anglo-Dutch War in the Mediterranean

For some time, the English and the Dutch have maintained small squadrons in the Mediterranean, in order to protect their merchantmen from Algerian pirates. The Dutch squadron consists of 14 warships with 26-30 guns each, and is reinforced by 22 armed merchantmen. The English have 15 warships of 30-54 guns, and their squadron is divided into two, one half in the western Mediterranean, the other in the Levant. At the outbreak of war, these two halves seek to unite in the Tyrrhenian Sea.

6 Sept 1652: The Dutch commander, van Galen, defeats the English Levant squadron south of Elba and then blockades the English in Elba and Leghorn (Livorno) for 6 months.

13 March 1653: He finally manages to lure the other English squadron out of Leghorn, and destroys it completely. This causes the second English half-squadron to leave the Mediterranean. English trade there is now paralysed by the Dutch. These events (and mutinies in the English fleet) cause England to open peace negotiations with an equally war-weary Holland.

15 April 1654: Treaty of Westminster (1). Holland achieves only slight concessions to the Navigation Act, and the honouring of the flag clause remains. England is permitted to trade with the Far East, and Holland cedes St. Helena.

The First Anglo-Dutch War marked the true beginning of England's rise as a maritime power, and it brought in some 1,700 prizes for a loss of only 440. English colonies in North America now began to grow, sowing the seeds of the future transatlantic empire. In the middle years of the 17th century, naval science made several significant steps forward. Although England's Instructions for the better ordering of the Fleet in Fighting, issued in 1653, advocated line ahead formation and attack from the weather gage, the many armed merchantmen operating with the fleets hindered such tactical innovations. The short range of the artillery tended also to lead to mêlées—uncontrolled group combat aimed at boarding the enemy.

At the outbreak of the First Dutch War, the English warships had become classified or 'rated' approximately as follows:

1st rate 90 guns and more	*4th rate 38–50 guns*
2nd rate 80–90 guns	*5th rate 18–38 guns*
3rd rate 50–80 guns	*6th rate 18 guns and less*

Subsequently, other nations began to follow this example. Only the ships of the first three ratings were really suitable for fighting in the line of battle, and they were therefore referred to as 'ships of the line'; 4th rates equated to frigates, while the last two ratings were generally corvettes and sloops.

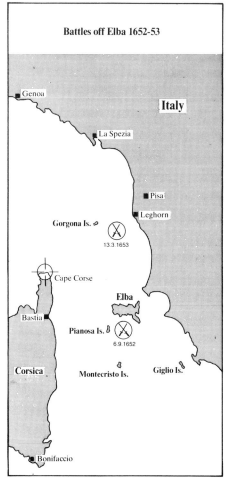

Battles off Elba 1652-53

The Anglo-Dutch War in the Mediterranean

1655: Blake undertakes a Mediterranean cruise with a squadron of 25 ships, in order to show the flag.

9 April 1655: Attack on Porto Farina (north of Tunis). With 15 ships, Blake forces the harbour entrance to this corsair base, silences the land batteries, and destroys the 9 ships belonging to the Bey of Tunis lying there.

1654-59: THE ANGLO-SPANISH WAR

In order to break the Spanish monopoly on West Indian trade, England declares war on Spain.

1655: Penn takes a squadron of 38 ships to the West Indies, fails to take Santo Domingo, but captures Jamaica for England.

1655-56: From July to April, Blake blockades Cadiz harbour with his squadron, and intercepts a silver fleet from America, destroying part of it and capturing the rest.

20 April 1657: Raid on Santa Cruz (Tenerife). Blake learns that a silver fleet has entered the harbour of Santa Cruz; he immediately lifts the blockade of Cadiz, and attacks the strongly defended harbour. The Spaniards have arranged the 22 galleons within the harbour so that their guns bear on the entrance; batteries of artillery have been set up on the beach, and a strong fort guards the entrance. Blake's squadron approaches in two groups: one attacks the fort and the beach batteries, the other attacks the silver fleet. The fight begins at 8am and, after 6 hours, the Spanish ships are destroyed: two galleons are sunk, the rest burned out, and the beach batteries are silenced; only the fort keeps up a defence to the end. However, the Spaniards have managed to unload the silver before the onslaught. By 7pm, Blake has reached the open sea again, in spite of an unfavourable wind. Of his squadron, only some frigates are badly damaged. On the homeward voyage, Blake dies. The attacks on Santa Cruz and Porto Farina, two years previously, are two of the rare cases in which sailing ships successfully engage land fortifications.

1658: Death of Oliver Cromwell.

1659: Peace between England and Spain.

1657-60: THE SWEDISH-DANISH WAR

Denmark, with Dutch support, declares war on Sweden to frustrate Charles X's ambitious plans in the Baltic.

22/23 Sept 1657: Action off Falsterbö. An indecisive action between the equally sized Swedish and Danish navies.

1658: The Peace of Roskilde stills the fighting for only 5 months; even before the various points of that treaty have been agreed, Charles X renews the fighting. The Swedes land on Zealand, and blockade Copenhagen by land and by sea with a fleet under Count Wrangel. Holland sends a relief fleet, under Jacob van Wassenaer van Obdam, to the Sound.

8 Nov 1658: Battle in the Sound. The Swedish fleet, under Wrangel, has 35 ships of the line and 8 frigates, with 1,900 guns and 7,500 men. The Dutch fleet also has 35 ships of the line, and is escorting 30 transports with 2,000 soldiers. The Dutch sail into the Sound in the early morning, with a northerly wind. The Swedish fleet awaits them at Helsingör and, at 8am, a bitter ship-to-ship combat develops in the narrow waters. Both flagships, *Victoria* (Wrangel) and *Eendracht* (Wassenaer), are soon out of action, and both fleets suffer heavily. Apart from the *Brederode* (Tromp's old flagship), the Dutch lose several smaller ships; 2 admirals and 1,700 men are killed. The Swedes lose 3 ships and slightly fewer men than the Dutch, but Copenhagen is relieved and the Dutch fleet controls the Sound.

In Feb 1659, the Swedes try to take Copenhagen by storm, but are repelled with heavy losses. Numerous combats between the Swedes and the Dutch-Danish flotillas develop in the waters around the Danish islands, and 1 Swedish ship of the line is captured. Swedish troops remain on Zealand until hostilities are ended.

At the beginning of 1659, an English squadron appears off the Sound to 'observe'. An auxiliary fleet under de Ruyter lands troops on Fyen and helps to capture the fortress of Nyborg.

1660: Treaty of Copenhagen, Denmark retains her territories, but the barrier of the Sound is finally lifted.

1665-67: THE SECOND ANGLO-DUTCH WAR

Two years after Cromwell's death, the monarchy is reinstated in England, and Charles II ascends the throne. In the Netherlands, meanwhile, the house of Orange is excluded from the Dutch government, which is in the control of Jan de Witt. Mercantile jealousy creates more tension and, on all the world's seas, the English and Dutch emerge as competitors. Both countries reinforce their navies; particularly fast reconnaissance and despatch boats ('avisos') are built. The decision in this war will be reached in the 'Narrow Seas' on either side of the English Channel.

1664: The English open hostilities by taking over Dutch possessions in West Africa and North America. De Ruyter recaptures the West African bases with his Mediterranean squadron, but is thus not available in home waters when war breaks out.

29 Dec 1664: In the Straits of Gibraltar, an English squadron falls on a rich Dutch convoy out of Smyrna. Only 3 ships are captured, but the Dutch take reprisals.

14 March 1665: Charles II declares war on the Dutch republic.

13 June 1665: Battle of Lowestoft. The Duke of York, brother of the English king, is Commander-in-Chief of the English fleet as 'Lord High Admiral'. The fleet totals 109 ships, including 35 ships of the line, 53 other warships (4th-6th rates), 21 armed merchantmen and 21 fire-ships and 7 small craft. In total, this makes 4,200 guns and 22,000 crewmen. The fleet is divided into three: the centre, under personal command of the Duke of York in *Royal Charles* (with Sir William Penn as captain of the fleet), the van under Prince Rupert, and the rear under the Earl of Sandwich. The Dutch fleet, commanded by Jacob van Wassenaer van Obdam on *Eendracht,* is slightly weaker, with 103 warships, 11 fire-ships and 7 avisos. It contains a greater proportion of armed merchantmen, the ships of the line are smaller than their English counterparts, and their 4,900 guns are generally of smaller calibre. Their crews total 21,000 men, and the fleet is divided into 7 squadrons. Although it is not yet fully equipped, Wassenaer van Obdam receives a directive from de Witt to attack at once.

3am-10am: The fleets meet; after passing and cannonading each other twice, the English fleet turns into the Dutch line in squadrons, and a general artillery duel develops with both fleets sailing south.

3pm: Some Dutch ships of the centre turn to flee, causing gaps in their line which the English penetrate. *Eendracht,* fired upon from both sides, explodes, and Wassenaer van Obdam is killed. More Dutch ships flee, while Evertsen (the elder) and Tromp (the younger) cover the withdrawal. The Dutch lose 17 ships by artillery fire, boarding and fire-ships, with 3 admirals and 4,000 men. English losses are 2 ships, 2 flag officers and 800 men. De Witt orders the immediate reconstruction of the fleet.

In Bergen is a Dutch convoy of 70 merchantmen; the English try to capture these ships in harbour, but they defend themselves strongly and beat off the attack.

Aug 1665: As soon as he reaches home, de Ruyter sails for Norway with the Dutch fleet, and brings the Bergen convoy safely into the Ems estuary. A storm partially scatters his fleet, and the English fleet, always lurking in wait, capture about 10 stragglers.

In the second half of 1665, the English fleet is unusually reticent, and this allows de Ruyter to protect Dutch sea trade effectively, by cruising between Harwich and the Downs off the Thames estuary, until heavy crew losses due to sickness force him to return to base.

Autumn 1665: Great Plague breaks out in England.

Jan 1666: King Louis XIV of France declares war on England, but, in the event, the French fleet takes no active part in hostilities. De Ruyter hopes for French assistance and moves to the Flanders coast to meet them. To counter the French, Prince Rupert takes 20 ships to the west end of the Channel, leaving Monck (now Duke of Albemarle) with a significantly weakened fleet to watch for the Dutch.

11-14 June 1666: The Four Days Fight in the Channel. On the morning of 11 June, de Ruyter anchors off Dunkirk with the Dutch fleet. To the south is the rear, under Tromp (junior); in the centre is de Ruyter, and in the north the van, under Evertsen (senior). The fleet has 84 ships with 4,600

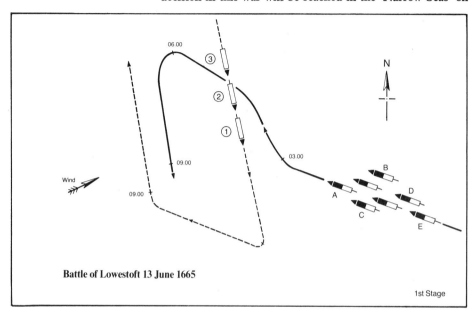

Battle of Lowestoft 13 June 1665

1st Stage

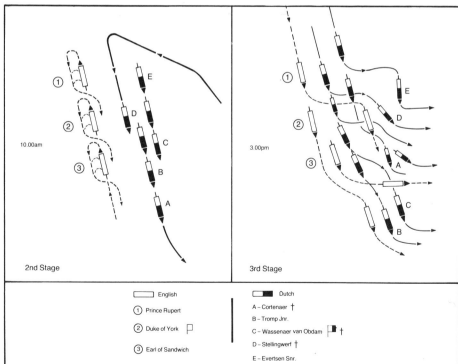

2nd Stage

3rd Stage

	English
①	Prince Rupert
②	Duke of York
③	Earl of Sandwich

	Dutch
A –	Cortenaer †
B –	Tromp Jnr.
C –	Wassenaer van Obdam †
D –	Stellingwerf †
E –	Evertsen Snr.

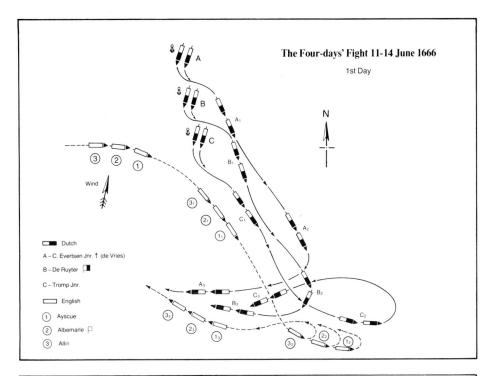

The Four-days' Fight 11-14 June 1666
1st Day

Wind

Dutch
A – C. Evertsen Jnr. † (de Vries)
B – De Ruyter
C – Tromp Jnr.
English
① Ayscue
② Albemarle
③ Allin

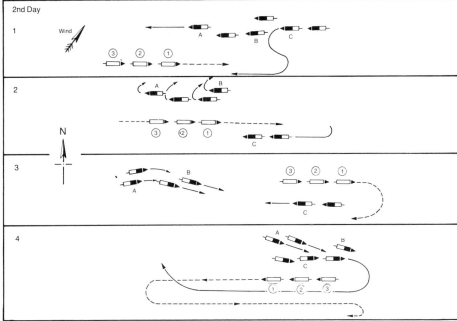

2nd Day

1 Wind

N

2

3

4

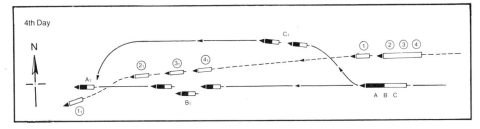

4th Day

N

A₁
B₁
A B C

guns and 22,000 crewmen. The English fleet is under the joint command of Albemarle and Prince Rupert, with 78 ships, 4,500 guns and 21,000 crewmen; but, for some days, Prince Rupert and his 20 ships have been detached to intercept a French force mistakenly believed to be coming to the aid of the Dutch. Commander of the English van is Sir George Ayscue; Sir Thomas Allin commands the rear. As soon as Albemarle learns of the presence of the Dutch fleet he orders an attack despite his numerical inferiority.

Midday 11 June: In a very close line ahead formation, Albemarle attacks the southern Dutch squadron (Tromp), which scarcely has time to cut its anchor cables and take up the fight, moving south. For some hours, Tromp has great difficulty against the English.

4pm: Finally, Albemarle has to change on to a westerly course, because of the nearness of the Flanders coast. De Ruyter and Evertsen now join in the fight, and the superior Dutch numbers begin to tell. The English *Swiftsure* is taken, and her flag officer, Sir William Berkeley, is killed. Sir John Harman, aboard *Henry*, fights a heroic battle, repelling attacks by several Dutch ships of the line and fire-ships: he manages to quench the fires in his rigging, kills Evertsen with the last salvo of his decimated artillery, and brings his battered ship to safety. By evening, both sides have lost several ships. During the night, damage is repaired and ships no longer capable of fighting are sent to the rear. Vice Admiral de Vries takes command of the Dutch van.

12 June: Albemarle attacks the Dutch, who are sailing parallel to his fleet again. The odds are now 47 English ships to 77 Dutch. Tromp tries to take his rear to the windward side of the English fleet, and finds himself in a very critical situation: de Ruyter has to bring ships to his aid, and the Dutch fleet loses all semblance of order. Albemarle, however, is unable to capitalize on the enemy's misfortunes, due to his numerical inferiority and after both sides have lost several ships, he breaks off the fight, hoping that Prince Rupert will soon return.

13 June: Now with only 30 ships fit for action, Albemarle pulls back westward. De Ruyter cannot catch him with his damaged ships, and only a few shots are exchanged. *Royal Prince*, Ayscue's flagship, and one of the strongest English ships, runs aground: surrounded by the Dutch fleet, Ayscue has to strike, and his ship is burned by the Dutch. That evening, Albemarle is at last joined by Prince Rupert's 20 ships.

14 June: Next morning, both fleets seek a final decision. They both sail to the west, the Dutch on the windward side. At the start of the combat, the English van sails faster than the main body, and a gap appears in the English line. Dutch Rear Admiral van Nes enters this gap with part of his van and, at the same time, Tromp and his rear come around the lee side of the English rear. The centre and rear of the English fleet are thus under fire from both sides. Now De Ruyter breaks through the centre of the English line; both parties

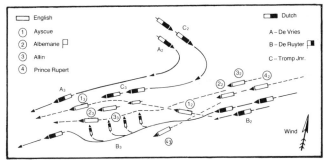

English
① Ayscue
② Albemarle
③ Allin
④ Prince Rupert

Dutch
A – De Vries
B – De Ruyter
C – Tromp Jnr.

Wind

suffer heavy loss in the ensuing struggle, and the English finally break off the fight. The Dutch have almost exhausted their ammunition and also turn for home. By the evening, one of the most prolonged and hard-fought sea battles of all time has ended. English losses are 17 ships, 5,000 men killed and 3,000 taken; the Dutch lose 6 ships and 2,000 men killed. De Ruyter has won a victory, but the English fleet is by no means destroyed. He blockades the Thames for some time, but the refurbished English fleet takes to the sea again on 2 August.

4–5 Aug 1666: St. James's Day Fight (Battle of the North

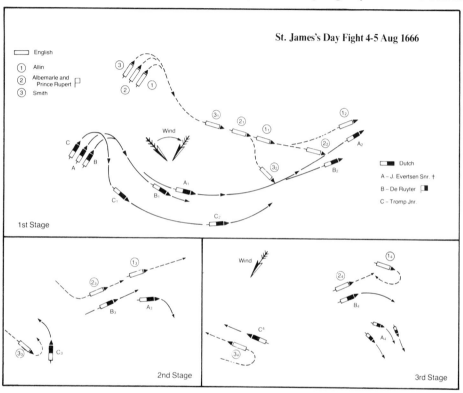

St. James's Day Fight 4–5 Aug 1666

English
① Allin
② Albemarle and Prince Rupert
③ Smith

Wind

Dutch
A – J. Evertsen Snr. †
B – De Ruyter
C – Tromp Jnr.

1st Stage

Wind

2nd Stage

3rd Stage

Foreland). Both Fleets are about 90 warships and 20 fire-ships strong. Albemarle and Prince Rupert are in joint command of the English fleet; on the Dutch side, de Ruyter has the centre, Cornelius Tromp the rear and Evertsen the van.

Morning: A running fight develops in an easterly direction, the English on the windward side. Within a short time, all admirals in the Dutch van are killed and their ships take flight. Tromp is pursuing some fleeing English ships with his rear, leaving de Ruyter's centre to face a superior number of English ships. In a masterful manner, de Ruyter covers the withdrawal of the Dutch fleet, with 20 ships.

5 Aug, early: Tromp is completely out of sight; now with only 8 ships, de Ruyter covers the arrival of stragglers behind the shallow sandbanks along the Dutch coast. Tromp is in danger of being cut off, but arrives back safely next day. Dutch losses are 2 ships and 1,000 men, those of the English 1 ship and 300 men. De Ruyter's masterful conduct has saved the Dutch fleet from destruction, but the English have attained control of the sea.

8 Aug 1666: A small English squadron, under Sir Robert Holmes, destroys 150 Dutch merchantmen in the Texel ('Holmes's bonfire').

10 Sept 1666: Great Fire of London. This event, plus the effects of the plague (which has been raging for a year) and the great costs of King Charles II's court demand economies. The ships of the line are laid up at the wharfs, and the trade war is carried on with the smaller vessels. Peace negotiations are opened; but in contrast, Holland makes full use of the command of the seas presented to her without a fight.

May 1667: A Franco-Dutch squadron of 17 ships attacks English possessions in the West Indies. Off Nevis Island, they are confronted by 12 English ships; in the following battle the English lose 3 ships, but frustrate the attempted landing.

19–23 June 1667: The Dutch fleet enters the mouth of the Thames with 24 ships of the line, 20 smaller vessels and 15 fire-ships.

19 June: An attack on Gravesend fails, due to unfavourable wind.

20 June: Sheerness is captured, facilitating entry into the Medway, where some of the English ships are laid-up.

22–23 June: De Ruyter sails up the Medway, his ships silencing the shore batteries. Landing parties and fire-ships remove or destroy the river barriers at Upnor, and nine of the laid-up ships are either captured or burnt. *Royal Charles*, Albemarle's flagship in the last battles, is taken as a prize to Holland. De Ruyter then blockades the Thames estuary.

6 July 1667: To speed up the peace negotiations, de Ruyter returns to Gravesend; panic breaks out in London.

21 July: Treaty of Breda. Holland gives up the New Netherlands (her colony in North America), and achieves some relaxation of the Navigation Act.

1668: Treaty of Aix-la-Chapelle. The Triple Alliance of Holland, England and Sweden prevents Louis XIV from completing the French annexation of Brabant. Louis now embarks upon a policy of encircling Holland, and gathers England, Sweden, Cologne and Munster into a coalition.

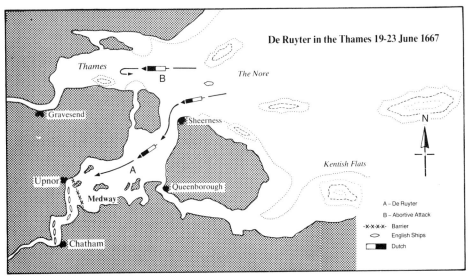

De Ruyter in the Thames 19-23 June 1667

Thames

The Nore

B

Gravesend

Sheerness

Kentish Flats

N

Upnor

A

Queenborough

Medway

A – De Ruyter
B – Abortive Attack

-x-x-x- Barrier
⬭ English Ships
▭ Dutch

Chatham

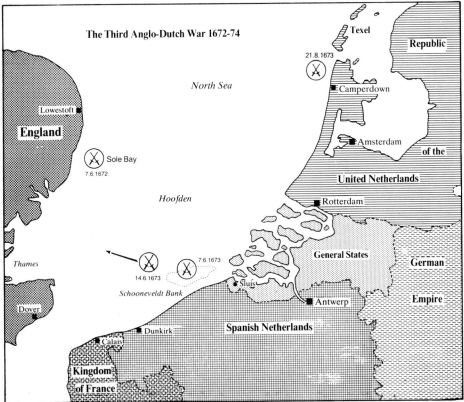

The Third Anglo-Dutch War 1672-74

Texel

Republic

21.8.1673

North Sea

Camperdown

Lowestoft

England

Amsterdam

of the

Sole Bay

7.6.1672

United Netherlands

Hoofden

Rotterdam

14.6.1673

7.6.1673

General States

German

Thames

Schooneveldt Bank

Sluis

Dover

Antwerp

Empire

Dunkirk

Spanish Netherlands

Calais

Kingdom of France

1672–74: THE THIRD ANGLO-DUTCH WAR
1672–80: THE FRANCO-DUTCH WAR

The War in the 'Narrow Seas'

March 1672: Raid on the Channel Convoy. Before the declaration of war, an English squadron of 18 warships (12 of them ships of the line) attacks a Dutch convoy consisting of 72 merchantmen (24 of these armed) and 5 warships, under den Haen. He conducts so successful a defence that the English can only take 3 merchantmen; one Dutch ship sinks, but the rest reach safety.

April 1672: After Louis' coalition declares war, Jan de Witt is murdered by the mob in Holland. Admiral de Ruyter re-assumes command of the Dutch fleet. As Holland in this war is also menaced from the landwards, he must conduct his sea operations with great care. He thus keeps his fleet mainly in the shallows along the coast, but takes every opportunity for offensive action if chances of success seem good. To make his task the more difficult, the English fleet opposing him is now joined by the new French fleet. Brought to a high standard of readiness by Colbert, the French navy needs but battle experience to complete its schooling.

7 June 1672: Battle of Sole Bay (or Southwold Bay). The Allied fleet lies at anchor in Sole Bay, replenishing its stores. The Duke of York (flagship *Royal Prince* with 120 guns) commands the centre; the Earl of Sandwich in *Royal James* (100 guns), commands the rear, and d'Estrées, aboard *St. Philippe* (78 guns), has the van, which is comprised of the French contingent. In all, there are 45 English and 26 French ships of the line; including the smaller warships, fire-ships and transports, the Allied fleet totals almost 150 ships, with 5,100 guns and 33,000 men.

The Dutch fleet, under de Ruyter (flagship *Zeven Provincien* with 82 guns), has about 130 ships (including 61 ships of the line) with a total of 4,500 guns and 21,000 men. Vice Admiral Banckert commands the van, Vice Admiral van Ghent the rear. De Ruyter attacks the Allies in a wide formation and it is only with difficulty that the Anglo-French fleet can manoeuvre away from the coast in the prevailing easterly wind. D'Estrées takes his squadron south, and is intercepted by Banckert with part of the Dutch van; the French content themselves with a long-range artillery duel with these ships, and do not earnestly enter the battle. The main body of the Dutch fleet falls on the English fleet, which, with difficulty, forms line ahead going north. Sandwich and van Ghent are both killed early in the battle. About midday, the nearness of the coast forces both fleets to turn south-east, and the bitter fighting continues until dark. That evening, Banckert rejoins de Ruyter. English losses are 4 ships and 2,500 men; the Dutch lose 2 ships and 2,000 men. With this attack, de Ruyter has frustrated a planned invasion of Holland; together with Prussia's intervention on land, it saves the country, which is already partly overrun by Allied troops. The battle is thus a tactical and a strategic success for de Ruyter, who again retires with his fleet into the coastal shallows. From here, he may choose when to accept battle with his shallow-draught ships, a successful application of the use of the strategy of internal lines of communication.

July 1672: An Allied fleet with a large landing force arrives off the Texel, but, with the intact Dutch fleet on their flank, no landing is attempted.

Aug 1672: Beset by land and sea ('Holland in peril'), the Dutch turn to the young William III of Orange, who takes over the duties of head of state.

Spring 1673: Prussia and France conclude peace, but Austria and Spain enter the war on Holland's side against France.

7 June 1673: First Battle of Schooneveldt. The Allies plan a new landing in Holland, and their fleet arrives off the Dutch coast; de Ruyter accepts battle. The relative strengths of the opposing fleets are as follows.

	NETHERLANDS	ALLIES
Ships of the line	52	81 (27 of these French)
Frigates	12	11
Fire-ships	25	35

De Ruyter's subordinate commanders are admirals Tromp (junior) and Banckert. The Allied fleet is commanded by Prince Rupert, who has the van under his personal command; d'Estrées commands the centre, and Sir Edward Spragge

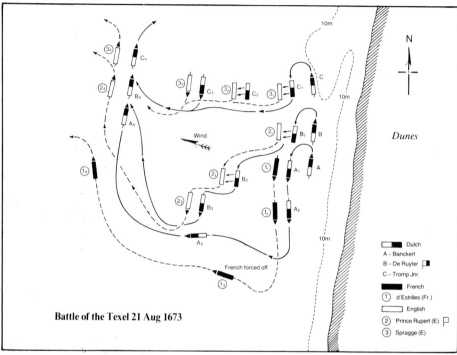

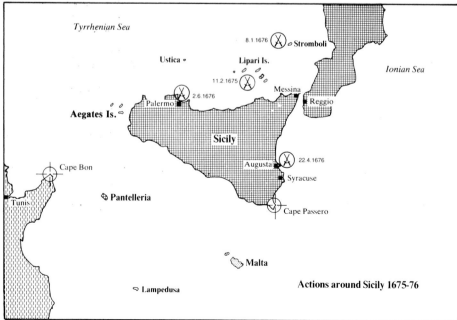

N

Dunes

Wind

□ Dutch
A – Banckert
B – De Ruyter
C – Tromp Jnr.

■ French
① d'Estrées (Fr.)
□ English
② Prince Rupert (E)
③ Spragge (E)

A₃

French forced off

Battle of the Texel 21 Aug 1673

Tyrrhenian Sea

Stromboli 8.1.1676

Ustica

Lipari Is.

Ionian Sea

11.2.1675

Messina

2.6.1676

Palermo Reggio

Aegates Is.

Sicily

Cape Bon

Augusta 22.4.1676

Syracuse

Pantelleria

Tunis

Cape Passero

Malta

Lampedusa

Actions around Sicily 1675–76

the rear. The Allied fleet approaches on a westerly wind in a broad line abreast formation. De Ruyter moves north, and a running battle develops. Although de Ruyter breaks the French centre, he then has to fall back to aid the hard-pressed Banckert; and meanwhile, Tromp has allowed himself to be cut off by the superior English van and is also in difficulties: he has to change flagships three times. De Ruyter thus abandons his duel with the English rear and moves with Banckert to Tromp's aid.

The fleets disengage in the evening; de Ruyter anchors off the coast, Prince Rupert to the west of him, and the fleets make good their damage in full view of each other. Losses on both sides are restricted to just a few small ships.

14 June 1673: Second Battle of Schooneveldt. The wind suddenly turns to the east, placing the Dutch in the windward position: de Ruyter attacks at once. The Allies are unready, seek to escape, and the battle runs onto the English coast. Only Tromp and Spragge enter into serious fighting, however. After 6 hours, de Ruyter breaks off the battle. With only slight losses, he has again frustrated an attempted invasion, and Holland can again bring in precious convoys.

July 1673: De Ruyter cruises off the Thames for ten days. The land situation turns against Holland in the summer and the allies aim to mount a combined land–sea attack. Invasion forces of 20,000 men are assembled in England, and the first wave (almost 10,000) is taken aboard the fleet.

21 Aug 1673: Battle of the Texel (Camperdown). The Allied fleet, under Prince Rupert, proceeds to Texel to cover the landing. The relative naval strengths are as follows.

	NETHERLANDS	ALLIES
Ships of the line and frigates	75	90
Fire-ships	30	30

Prince Rupert commands the centre, d'Estrées the French van, and Spragge the rear. On the Dutch side, de Ruyter has the centre, Banckert the van, and Tromp the rear. During the night, with an easterly wind, de Ruyter succeeds in putting himself between the coast and the enemy fleet. At dawn, and having the weather gage, de Ruyter attacks. Moving on a southerly course, the parallel fleets are matched as follows: Banckert v. d'Estrées, de Ruyter v. Prince Rupert, and Tromp v. Spragge. D'Estrées tries to surround the Dutch van, but Banckert breaks the French line and throws it into complete confusion. Leaving a few ships to watch the French, he returns with the rest of his squadron to aid the centre. (D'Estrées does not re-enter the combat.) Prince Rupert gradually moves his centre westwards, in order to keep de Ruyter at a distance. The rearward squadrons clash at once, and remain locked in combat. Spragge is killed. Both main bodies eventually turn to help join the battle astern of them, and Banckert also re-enters the battle. This continues until nightfall, when d'Estrées eventually returns. The English fleet sails home, and the landing is abandoned. No ships have been sunk, but a great number on both sides have been heavily damaged. The Allies lose about 2,000 men, the Dutch about half this number. Holland is free of the threat from the sea, and a large East India convoy can be brought in safely. England is outraged at the conduct of the French fleet and makes peace with Holland.

Feb 1674: Treaty of Westminster (2). With the removal of her major opponent at sea, Holland can concentrate on the struggle against France. When war breaks out between Spain and France in 1675, part of the Dutch fleet supports the Spanish in the Mediterranean.

1674: The majority of the French fleet moves into the Mediterranean, whereupon Cornelius Tromp blockades the French Atlantic coast.

The War in the Mediterranean

11 Feb 1675: Action off the Lipari Islands. The French Mediterranean fleet, consisting of 20 ships (including 9 of the line) under Count Vivonne, defeats the Spanish fleet, under Admiral de la Cueva. The Spaniards have 30 ships, half of them galleys, and are no match for the French.

Dec 1675: De Ruyter takes 15 ships of the line and frigates into the Mediterranean, to aid Spain in defending Sicily against France.

8 Jan 1676: Battle of Alicudi (or Stromboli). This is the first clash between de Ruyter and Admiral Duquesne, the new commander of the French Mediterranean fleet. Duquesne has 20 ships of the line, with a total of 1,500 guns; de Ruyter has 19 ships of the line (one of these Spanish) and frigates, with about 1,200 guns. Duquesne attacks boldly from windward; de Ruyter keeps his ships in very close formation, and receives the enemy with such an effective broadside that they are unable to break the Dutch line. The fight ends indecisively at nightfall. The French lose 3 fire-ships and, next day, a badly damaged Dutch ship of the line sinks. De Ruyter has shown how a fleet to leeward of a stronger enemy can successfully defend itself. The leeward position is much favoured in the following wars, particularly by the French; but decisive victories can scarcely be achieved from this position.

22 April 1676: Battle of Augusta (Sicily). Duquesne has 29 ships of the line, with 2,200 guns and 10,700 men; the Allied fleet has 17 ships of the line (4 of these Spanish), 9 frigates (5 of these Spanish), with 1,330 guns. The Allied commander is the Spanish admiral, Don Francisco de la Cerda; de Ruyter commands the van, den Haan the rear. The Allies attack from windward: de Ruyter closes up to the enemy and batters some of his ships out of action, but, as the Spanish centre remains at long range, Duquesne can outflank de Ruyter and bring him under fire from two sides. Only an energetic attack by den Haan with the Allied rear saves the van. The battle ends indecisively, but de Ruyter is badly wounded and dies a few days later on his flagship *Eendracht*, a severe blow to the Dutch.

2 June 1676: Battle of Palermo. The Allied fleet of 27 ships is anchored in the harbour awaiting the French attack. The French, under Comte de Vivonne, have 60 ships, including galleys; under the covering fire of 9 ships of the line, they send 6 fire-ships into the Allied fleet. These and the artillery fire cause their opponents heavy losses: 6 ships of the line, 2 galleys and several other vessels; 6 admirals, including den Haan and de la Cerda, are killed and 2,000 men are dead or wounded. This victory costs the French practically nothing. At one blow, they have achieved control of the Mediterranean.

The War in the West Indies

May 1676: Admiral Binkes with a small Dutch squadron captures Tobago, in the West Indies.

3 March 1677: Action off Tobago. Vice Admiral d'Estrées tries to take Tobago from the Dutch. In a heavy battle with Binkes' squadron, d'Estrées loses 5 out of his 10 warships, the Dutch 3 out of 6. Later, with a reinforced squadron, d'Estrées captures the island.

5 Feb 1679: Peace of Nijmegen. Holland retains her territories. But, during these wars, the English have succeeded in replacing Holland as the world's leading trading nation.

So ended the epic Anglo-Dutch struggle for maritime supremacy. While the first war had been essentially centred on Dutch convoys, the second war saw a shift of emphasis, with battle fleets contending for command of the sea. The third war introduced combined land and sea operations, as the Allies attempted in vain to mount invasions of the Low Countries. By the end of the struggle, naval tactics had reached a high level of sophistication, helped considerably by the removal of armed merchantmen from the warring fleets and the increasing standardization of ships. Fire-ships were now of but limited use: effective against stragglers or ships at anchor (as amply demonstrated at Palermo), they did not work against a close line ahead formation.

During these wars, French and Dutch privateers were waging their own campaigns in the waters around France; the activities of the Dunkirk pirates were especially successful.

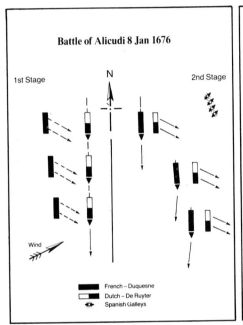

Battle of Alicudi 8 Jan 1676

1st Stage   N   2nd Stage

Wind

- ■ French – Duquesne
- □ Dutch – De Ruyter
- ✦ Spanish Galleys

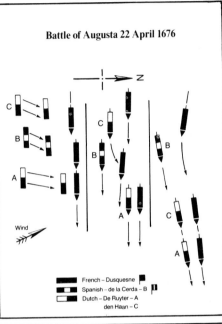

Battle of Augusta 22 April 1676

Z

Wind

- ■ French – Dusquesne
- ■ Spanish – de la Cerda – B
- □ Dutch – De Ruyter – A
-     den Haan – C

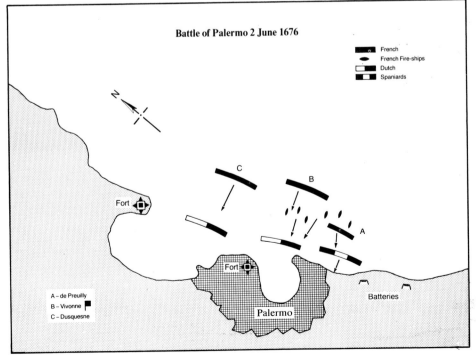

Battle of Palermo 2 June 1676

- ◨ French
- ⬭ French Fire-ships
- □ Dutch
- ■ Spaniards

N

Fort

Fort

Palermo

Batteries

- A – de Preuilly
- B – Vivonne
- C – Dusquesne

1675–79: THE SCANIAN WAR

Sweden (Charles XI), as an ally of France, wages war in the Baltic against Denmark (Christian V) and Brandenburg (the Great Elector). In a combined land and sea campaign, the Danish fleet (19 small ships of the line) is supported by the Dutch against the superior Swedes.

3–4 June 1676: Action off Jasmund. First action between the Dutch–Danish fleet under Admiral Niels Juel and the Swedish fleet under Baron Creutz. The battle begins in the evening and lasts until midday on the 4th, both fleets attempting to manoeuvre into favourable positions. Casualties are slight, and there is no decisive outcome. Two days later, Cornelius Tromp assumes command of the Allied fleet.

11 June 1676: Battle of Oeland. The Allied fleet, of 25 ships of the line (10 of these Dutch) and 10 frigates, is slightly stronger than the Swedish fleet. Tromp overtakes the Swedes, who are sailing north-east along the coast of Oeland, and comes up on their weather side to attack in line ahead. Admiral Creutz tries to double back with his van, so as to have the Allies between two fires, but his flagship, *Krona* (124), the largest warship of her time, capsizes in the strong wind. This throws the Swedish ships into confusion, and Tromp is quick to take advantage of the fact. The flagship of the Swedish second in command is dismasted and taking severe punishment. She strikes her colours, but is destroyed by a fire-ship. In all, the Swedes lose 4 ships of the line (1 of these having been boarded), 2,000 dead and wounded and 600 prisoners. The Allies incur only slight losses.

11 June 1677: Action off Moen. Admiral Niels Juel, with a Danish squadron of 9 ships of the line and 2 frigates, destroys a Swedish squadron under Admiral Sjöblad. The Danes capture 5 of 7 Swedish ships by boarding.

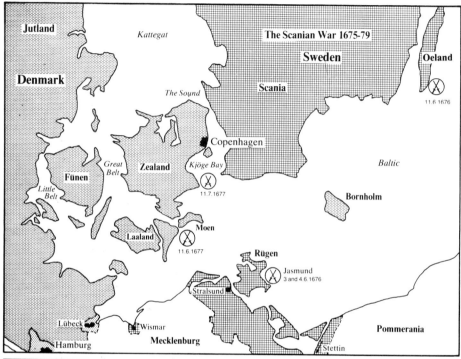

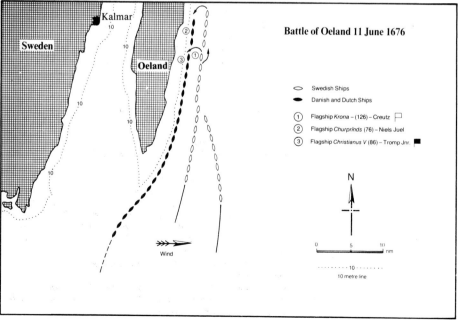

11 July 1677: Battle of Kjöge Bay. The Swedish fleet seeks a decision before the expected arrival of another Dutch squadron can reinforce the Danes. Relative fleet strengths are as follows:

	SWEDEN	DENMARK
Ships of the line	25	19
Frigates	11	6
Fire-ships	6	3
Total no. guns	1,800	1,270
Total crews	9,000	6,500

Admiral Niels Juel in *Christianus Quintus* leads the Danes; Field Marshal Henrik Horn in *Viktoria* the Swedes.

6am: On a north-westerly course, the fleets approach the coast of Zealand, with the wind changing from southerly to westerly.

7am: A Swedish ship of the line goes aground; Horn leaves 6 other ships of the line to protect it, and sails south-east with the rest of the fleet, to regain the open sea. Niels Juel sends 6 ships of the line to attack the Swedes around their stranded vessel (*Drake*), which, with 2 other Swedish ships, has to surrender. The 6 Danish ships sail towards their own main body, and this leads to a running fight with the Swedes, whose line gradually becomes disordered. Niels Juel pushes his fleet into a gap between the Swedish centre and rear, separating them. The 6 detached Danish ships then arrive, and attack the Swedish rear from the opposite side. The Swedes take flight. In a series of ship-to-ship combats, they are pursued by the Danes until nightfall. On the following two days, the 4 Swedish ships which originally escaped from the stranded *Drake* are either taken or sunk. In all, the Swedes lose 10 ships of the line (7 of these captured) and 3 fire-ships, 2 admirals and 3,000 men captured and about 1,500 dead and wounded. The Danes have only 4 ships seriously damaged and lose 350 men. As a result, the Danish fleet controls the western Baltic to the end of the war. Niels Juel's tactical mastery reminds one of de Ruyter.

1679: Peace of Nijmegen. The Scandinavian states also make peace, each nation maintaining its territories, for the success of the Danish fleet has been balanced by the defeat of its army in Scania.

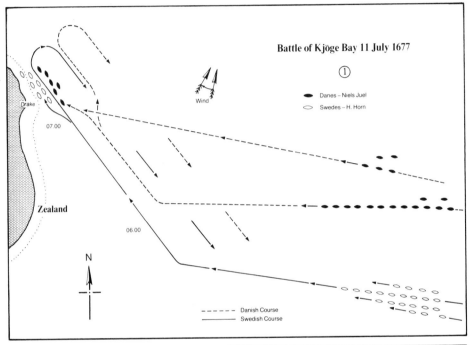

Battle of Kjöge Bay 11 July 1677

①

● Danes – Niels Juel
○ Swedes – H. Horn

- - - - Danish Course
——— Swedish Course

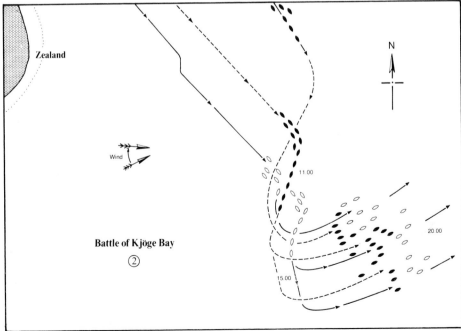

Battle of Kjöge Bay

②

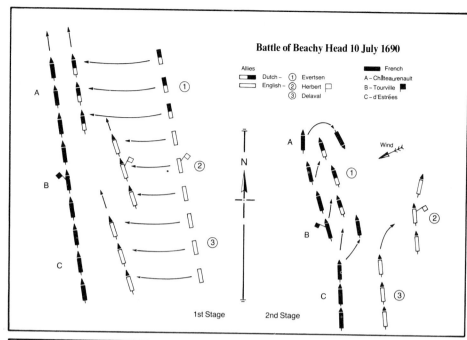

Battle of Beachy Head 10 July 1690

Allies			French
Dutch –	① Evertsen		A – Châteaurenault
English –	② Herbert		B – Tourville
	③ Delaval		C – d'Estrées

Wind

1st Stage   2nd Stage

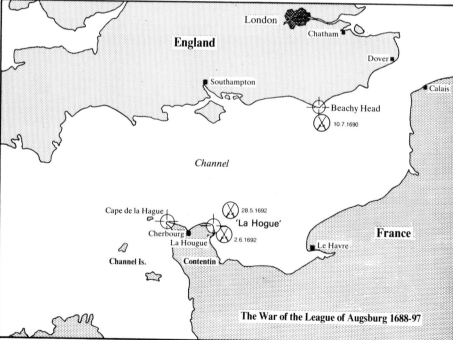

London
Chatham
England
Dover
Southampton
Calais
Beachy Head
10.7.1690

Channel

28.5.1692
Cape de la Hague
'La Hogue'
Cherbourg
La Hougue   2.6.1692
Channel Is.
Contentin
Le Havre
France

The War of the League of Augsburg 1688-97

1688–97: THE WAR OF THE LEAGUE OF AUGSBURG*

1688: The 'Glorious Revolution' in England. For religious reasons the English parliament calls on William III of Orange to accept the English throne. William lands unopposed in England and is crowned in 1689, to rule jointly with his consort Mary (daughter of James II).

After the French move into southern Germany, William of Orange forms a coalition aimed at countering the power of Louis XIV on the Continent. By virtue of the 'personal union' between England and Holland, the fleets of both countries are combined against France. Thanks to Colbert, France has the best fleet in the world at this time, if not numerically then certainly in terms of quality of equipment. At the outbreak of war, the French fleet has 80 ships of the line, the strongest of the period. The English fleet has about 100, and the Dutch 50 ships of the line.

March 1689: A French squadron lands the deposed James II and 8,000 men in Ireland.

11 May 1689: Action off Bantry Bay. An English squadron of 18 ships of the line, under Admiral Herbert, attempts to attack a further French landing force, but is driven off by the French covering squadron of 24 ships of the line, under Vice Admiral Châteaurenault. Each side loses a ship. Although James II is initially successful in Ireland, the English squadron controlling the Irish Sea helps to prevent the capture of the important city of Londonderry, and then lands William III near Belfast. In little over a month, he recaptures all Ireland.

10 July 1690: Battle of Beachy Head (or Bévéziers). The French concentrate their Atlantic and Mediterranean squadrons at Brest, in order to seize control of the Channel. Commander of their fleet is Vice Admiral Count Anne Hilarion de Tourville, who attacks the Allies off the southern coast of England. At the express order of the British government, Admiral Herbert (now Lord Torrington) accepts battle with his numerically weaker fleet.

	FRANCE	ALLIES	
Ships of the line	70	57	(21 Dutch)
Total no. guns	4,600	3,850	
Total crews	28,000	23,000	

Each fleet is divided into three squadrons.

	VAN	CENTRE	REAR
French	Châteaurenault	Tourville	d'Estrées (jr.)
Allied	C. Evertsen (NL)	Torrington (E)	Delaval (E)

Tourville waits south of Beachy Head, as the Allies approach from the east. Torrington manoeuvres onto the windward side of the French, and closes up squadron for squadron on parallel course. The Dutch van opens the fight at close range, and the English rear does the same, but the main body stands off. By bringing up his main body, Tourville is thus able to attack the Dutch van from both sides. Torrington does not go to the Dutchmen's aid, and Evertsen saves his squadron only with great difficulty; terribly shot up, soon only 3 ships are capable of further action. The Allied fleet withdraws and the French follow slowly. Several of the badly damaged Dutch ships have to be scuttled or beached. Total Dutch losses are 10 ships of the line: if Tourville had pursued energetically, the whole squadron could have been lost. The French do not exploit their command of the Channel.

* Otherwise known as 'The War of the Grand Alliance', 'King William's War' and 'The Nine Years War'.

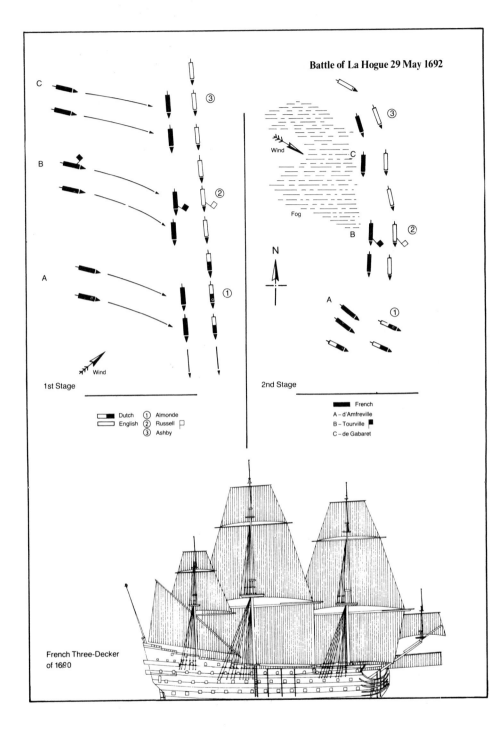

Battle of La Hogue 29 May 1692

C

B

A

Wind

1st Stage

N

Wind

Fog

2nd Stage

Dutch	① Almonde
English	② Russell
	③ Ashby

French
A – d'Amfreville
B – Tourville
C – de Gabaret

French Three-Decker
of 1690

1691: Tourville has instructions to avoid battle, and to concentrate on the trade war and protection of the French coast. This he does by undertaking a week-long cruise on the high seas ('campagne du large'), the Allied fleet under Admiral Russell pursuing him without being able to bring him to battle. Tourville fails, however, to intercept an awaited large convoy from Smyrna. Meanwhile, French privateers attack Allied shipping with renewed vigour.

1692: Louis XIV concentrates an army of 30,000 men in the Cotentin Peninsula, ready to land in England and restore James II to the English throne; 500 transports have been assembled to carry the troops. Tourville is charged with gaining control of the Channel, but the Mediterranean squadron, intended to reinforce the Atlantic fleet, is delayed, and Tourville has to venture out with the Brest squadron alone. In mid-May, the Anglo-Dutch squadrons gather off Hastings.

28 May–2 June 1692: Battle of La Hogue (or Barfleur). Fleet strengths are as follows.

	ALLIES		FRANCE
Ships of the line	88	(26 Dutch)	45
Frigates and fire-ships	37		13
Total no. guns	6,750		3,240
Total crews	39,000		21,000

The commanders are as follows.

	VAN	CENTRE	REAR
Allied	Almonde (NL)	Russell (E)	Ashby (E)
French	d'Amfreville	Tourville	de Gabaret

29 May, 10am: The fleets meet off the Cotentin Peninsula, under a weak south-westerly wind. Obeying his orders, Tourville at once attacks his doubly strong enemy from the windward side and closes up squadron for squadron; in order to guard against being outflanked, the French line is as long as that of the Allies, but much thinner. The French fight splendidly, and initially the Allies can gain no advantage: d'Amfreville holds the Dutch van in check, and Tourville lays his *Soleil Royal* (110) against Russell's *Britannia*, showering her with shot.

2pm: *Britannia*'s neighbours come to her aid, and Tourville fights all three enemy ships. The battle lines of the opposing centres and rears gradually dissolve into a series of ship-to-ship combats.

3pm: *Soleil Royal* wards off 5 fire-ships. Gradually, a thick fog rises which almost silences the guns.

8pm: As soon as the fog lifts, a rising wind permits Tourville to disengage. Up to this point, the French fleet has fought magnificently: only *Soleil Royal* is badly damaged and almost uncontrollable.

30 May, 7am: Tourville gathers 35 ships; the rest are scattered, and reach Brest independently.

8am: Russell sights the French and orders a chase. In the almost calm conditions, it is a slow affair. Tourville is forced to change flagships.

From 11pm: During the night, 20 French ships save themselves by running through the dangerous Race of Alderney.

31 May, early: *Soleil Royal* and 2 other ships of the line go aground off Cherbourg and Tourville transfers his flag to *Ambiteux*. With the other 12 ships, Tourville goes to La Hougue, where the vessels are hauled close inshore.

2 June: The 3 ships at Cherbourg are destroyed by English fire-ships.

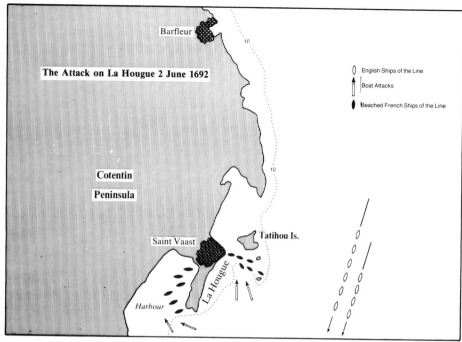

The Attack on La Hougue 2 June 1692

Barfleur

Cotentin
Peninsula

Saint Vaast

Tatihou Is.

La Hougue

Harbour

○ English Ships of the Line

▐ Boat Attacks

⬗ Beached French Ships of the Line

The War for the Morea 1684-1698

Ottoman

Corfu

Leucas 1684

Cephalonia

Zante 1686

Morea 1699-1718 Ven.

Patras

Corinth

Athens

Nauplia

Kalamata

1685

Cerigo

Negroponte

Skyros

Imbros

Lemnos 20.9.1698

Mytilene 15.9.1695

Lesbos

Chios 9.2.1695

22.8.1696 Andros

1 and 20.9.1697

Tinos

Mikonos

Melos

Naxos

Samos

Ikaria

Cos

Rhodes

Karpathos

Crete

Izmir

Empire

Venetian Territory

6pm: Vice Admiral Rooke (E) mounts a night attack with small boats on the French ships at La Hougue and, under the eyes of James II with the army on the Cotentin Peninsula, captures and burns them all. In all, the battle costs the French 15 ships of the line. The morale of the French fleet is dealt a severe blow by the destruction of its ships in full view of the French army.

June 1693: Tourville, with the French fleet, attacks a great Smyrna convoy of 140 merchantmen off St. Vincent, and captures 80 of them.

Feb and June 1694: Jean Bart escorts a large grain convoy from the Baltic to Dunkirk, and thus saves France from near starvation. In a clash with a Dutch squadron, he captures 3 ships. Privateering from French harbours, particularly Dunkirk, blooms throughout the war (especially after 1693). Despite the French taking 4,000 prizes, the world trade of the sea powers is profitable enough to finance the war. Meanwhile, the blockade of the French coast completely ruins that country's trade, and Louis XIV can no longer afford to wage war.

Sept 1697: Peace of Ryswick. France has to relinquish all her recent conquests except Strasbourg. After this war, the Dutch fleet begins to decline; now only the great powers can afford to maintain fleets of the size needed to fight for world trade.

1697: Paul Hoste, ship's chaplain of *Soleil Royal* writes what is now the earliest surviving book on naval tactics. In it, he favours the retention of attack in close line ahead formation, if possible from the windward side, and gives exact rules for the attack, combat, withdrawal and pursuit. He rejects attacking the enemy from both sides, and penetration of the enemy line. His book is an important influence on naval tactics in the following century.

1684-98: THE MOREAN WAR

After the defeat of the Turks at Vienna (1683), Venice joins the 'Holy League' (Vatican, Austria and Poland) against them, her principal aim being to capture the Morea. In contrast to the last Turkish war (for Crete), the backbone of navies (even in the Levant) is now the sailing ship: the squadrons of galleys still maintained are consigned to subsidiary roles. At Venice's side from time to time are also ships from Spain, Portugal, Malta, Tuscany and the Vatican. The numerous sea battles are often long, sometimes bloody, but rarely decisive.

1685: The Venetians land in the Gulf of Messenia, and capture Koron and Kalamata.

1686: The Venetians land in Navarino Bay.

9 Feb 1695: Battle of Chios. 21 Venetian sail and 26 galleys are opposed by 20 Turkish sail and 24 galleys in a mêlée fought without any battle order. The two fleets clash again, inconclusively, 10 days later and, on 21st, the Venetians abandon Chios.

15 Sept 1695: Action off Mytilene. After a 3-hour artillery fight, the two fleets part with light casualties.

22 Aug 1696: Action off Andros. Another indecisive engagement.

1 and 20 Sept 1697: Two actions off Negroponte. Both combats are indecisive; Contarini commands the Venetian fleet.

20 Sept 1698: Battle of the Dardanelles. After a hard but indecisive struggle, both fleets part.

1698: The Peace of Carlowitz. Venice retains her conquest, the Morea.

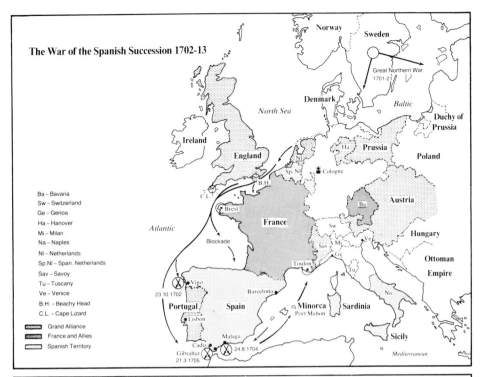

The War of the Spanish Succession 1702-13

Ba – Bavaria
Sw – Switzerland
Ge – Genoa
Ha – Hanover
Mi – Milan
Na – Naples
Nl – Netherlands
Sp.Nl – Span. Netherlands
Sav – Savoy
Tu – Tuscany
Ve – Venice
B.H. – Beachy Head
C.L. – Cape Lizard

Grand Alliance
France and Allies
Spanish Territory

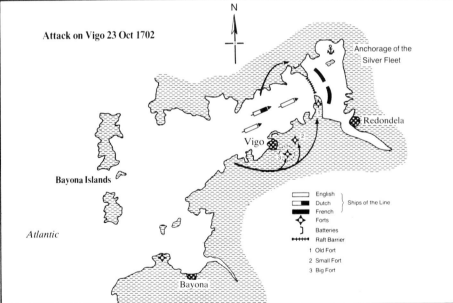

Attack on Vigo 23 Oct 1702

English
Dutch
French
Ships of the Line
Forts
Batteries
Raft Barrier

1 Old Fort
2 Small Fort
3 Big Fort

Anchorage of the Silver Fleet

Redondela
Vigo
Bayona Islands
Atlantic
Bayona

1702-13: THE WAR OF THE SPANISH SUCCESSION

The last Habsburg king of Spain, Charles II, is succeeded by Philip of Anjou (a grandson of Louis XIV). This concentration of power is opposed by the 'Grand Alliance' of Austria, England, Holland, Prussia, Hanover and, later, Portugal, the Holy Roman Empire of German states (1702) and Savoy (1703). Allied with France are the House of Wittelsbach (Bavaria and the Electorate of Cologne). The land campaigns are fought in the Netherlands, Germany, Italy and Spain. England's reason for fighting, apart from protecting her interests overseas, is because Louis XIV has recognized James II's claim to the English throne. Simultaneously, but independently of this war, Scandinavia and Eastern Europe are torn asunder by the Great Northern War. At the outbreak of war, the English fleet has 110 ships of the line, including a number of three-deckers with over 90 guns; the Dutch fleet has 50 ships of the line, almost all dating from the last war; and the French fleet has about 100 ships of the line, most of these also being old; the Spanish fleet is very run down and can scarcely be counted as an instrument of war. The first clash takes place in the West Indies.

29 Aug–3 Sept 1702: Action off Cartagena (Santa Marta). A small French squadron of 4 ships of the line and a frigate, under du Casse, escorts a troop transport. An English squadron of 7 ships of the line, under Admiral Benbow, attacks them; but, as 5 English commanders abandon their admiral, Benbow is beaten off, and is himself mortally wounded. After the action, 4 English commanders are tried for cowardice, and 2 are sentenced to death.

Aug/Sept 1702: An Allied fleet under Admiral Rooke lands troops at Cadiz to capture the city, but the attack is half-hearted, mismanaged and repulsed.

23 Oct 1702: Attack on Vigo. At the urging of Admiral van Almonde (NL), Rooke (returning from the Cadiz failure) undertakes an attack on a Spanish treasure fleet, which has just entered Vigo harbour. The narrow harbour entrance is blocked by a floating barrier, behind which is the French escorting squadron of 13 ships of the line under Admiral Châteaurenault. The Allies first land troops to capture the forts at the harbour entrance; then a squadron of 25 ships forces the barrier and suppresses the French escort. Six ships of the line and 5 silver-carrying galleons are captured, together with the greater part of the silver; all other ships are burnt. Allied losses are slight. After this victory, Portugal joins the side of the sea powers.

7 Dec 1703: In a severe storm, the English lose 13 ships, and more than 1,500 men perish.

4 Aug 1704: Raid on Gibraltar. On the initiative of Prince George of Hesse-Darmstadt, Admiral Rooke attacks Gibraltar and, after a short fight, the 500-man garrison surrender. The commander of the French fleet, the Comte de Toulouse (a natural son of Louis XIV), is given the task of recapturing the Rock; this leads to the only fleet-to-fleet clash in this war.

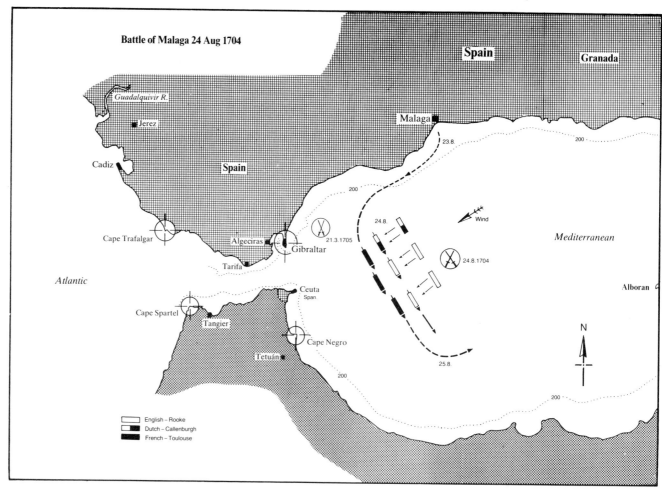

Battle of Malaga 24 Aug 1704

English – Rooke
Dutch – Callenburgh
French – Toulouse

24 Aug 1704: Battle of Malaga (or Velez Malaga). Both fleets are about equal in strength, with 51 ships of the line and some 3,600 guns. Commanders of the individual squadrons are as follows.

	VAN	CENTRE	REAR
Allied	Shovell (E)	Rooke (E)	Callenburgh (NL)
French	d'Infreville de Saint-Aubin	Toulouse	Marquis de Langeron

Rooke, on the windward side, steers a parallel course to the enemy in combat range. A running ship-to-ship battle begins, and the heavy artillery duel lasts until evening with no tactical manoeuvring. Toulouse breaks off the fight at nightfall, without knowing that some of his adversaries' ships are out of ammunition (for much of it has been used in the capture of Gibraltar). Both sides suffer heavy casualties (2–3,000 men), but no ships are lost. Although the tactical outcome of the battle is undecided, the retention of Gibraltar in Allied hands is a strategic victory.

7 Nov 1704: Vice Admiral Leake (E) relieves Gibraltar, which is under heavy Spanish attack.

21 March 1705: Action off Gibraltar. With a squadron of 13 ships of the line, Leake attacks the French fleet blockading the fortress. The French try to escape, but the English capture 3 ships of the line, and burn 2 more that are beached (including the French flagship). Simultaneously, the English

land provisions and reinforcements in Gibraltar: possession of the fortress is now secure.

Aug–Oct 1705: The English fleet under Admiral Shovell brings an army of 10,000 men under the Habsburg pretender, Charles III, to Barcelona, which is captured in a combined operation. Catalonia falls to the Habsburgs.

April 1706: The fleet relieves Barcelona, which has been under French attack.

11 May 1707: Action off Beachy Head. Forbin (F), with 8 warships, attacks a British* convoy of 56 merchantmen and 4 warships. In a sharp fight, he captures 2 warships and 22 merchantmen.

End of June 1707: Prince Eugène arrives before Toulon with an Allied army; the advance on the coast is covered by the Allied fleet under Shovell. As the Allies arrive at the town, the French sink their ships in the harbour: 15–20 ships are total losses, but the rest are later raised and refitted.

21 Oct 1707: Convoy skirmish off the Lizard. The French DuGuay-Trouin and Forbin, with 12 warships, meet a British supply convoy bound for Lisbon, consisting of about 130 transports and 5 ships of the line. French capture 4 of the warships and 15 transports.

7 June 1708: The British destroy a Spanish silver fleet off Cartagena in the West Indies.

* In Jan 1707, a treaty between England and Scotland brings union between the two countries, to form Great Britain.

1708: With the aid of the British Mediterranean fleet, Charles III captures Sardinia (Aug) and Minorca (Sept); on the latter island, Port Mahon becomes a British naval base for decades.

1711: Death of Emperor Joseph I. The Habsburg pretender to the Spanish throne becomes Emperor Charles VI of the Holy Roman Empire. In Britain, Marlborough falls from favour and Britain leaves the Grand Alliance.

Sept 1712: Raid on Rio de Janeiro. DuGuay-Trouin takes a squadron of 15 men of war (including 7 ships of the line) and 2,000 troops to Brazil in an undertaking financed by a private trading company. In a bold attack, the harbour entrance is forced and the town captured; a high ransom is extracted, and rich booty taken.

1713: Peace of Utrecht, between the sea powers and France. Spain is divided: Philip V retains the mainland and the colonies, while the other provinces fall to Austria, Sicily and Savoy. Britain keeps Gibraltar, Minorca, Newfoundland and Nova Scotia.

1714: Peace of Rastatt and Baden. The Holy Roman Empire recognizes the conditions of the Peace of Utrecht.

The War of the Spanish Succession had been decided by trade warfare, rather than by fleet actions. Each side lost about 1,500 merchantmen, but, while French trade was ruined and the country *financially broken, Britain could more than absorb her losses— indeed, the war brought England vast profits.*

This war was also noteworthy as the first occasion in modern times when fleets were not laid up during the winter months, and Britain began permanently to maintain a Mediterranean fleet. About this time, too, the steering of sailing ships was further improved by the replacement of the old tiller by a much more practical device, the wheel.

1700-21: THE GREAT NORTHERN WAR

Peter I (the Great) of Russia organizes an alliance with Frederick IV of Denmark and Augustus II of Saxony (and exiled King of Poland) to counter Charles XII of Sweden's expansionist policy. At the start of the war, 42 Swedish ships of the line are matched against 33 Danish.

1700: Denmark is forced to agree to peace by the landing on Zealand of a Swedish army under Charles XII. Charles now turns on Russia, defeats Peter at Narva (1700), and subsequently forces Augustus II to give up his claim to Poland (1704).

1702: Peter I advances to the Gulf of Finland again, and there founds St. Petersburg. His immediate construction of a Russian fleet is not disturbed by the Swedes.

1709: Following the destruction of the Swedish army at Poltava, Denmark re-enters the war.

4 Oct 1710: Battle of Kjöge Bay. The Danish fleet under

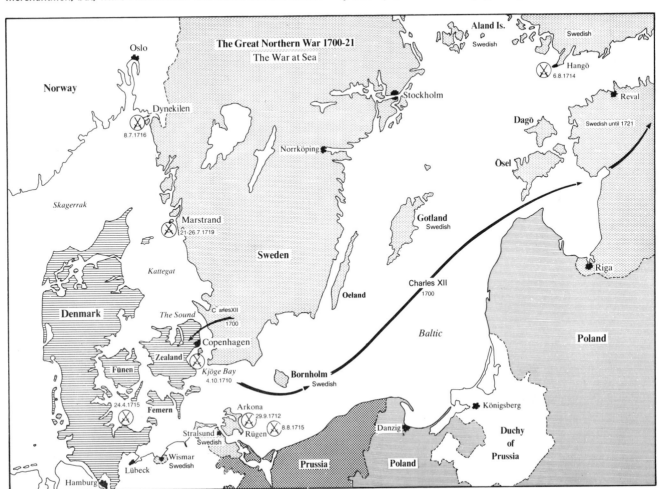

Admiral Gyldenlove lies in Kjöge Bay, with 26 ships of the line; the flagship is *Elephant* (90). The Swedish fleet under Admiral Hans Wachtmeister, 21 ships of the line, flagship *Götha Lejon* (96), mounts a surprise attack in the morning. In a brief fight, the Danish *Dannebrog* (82) blows up, and 2 Swedish ships of the line run aground and have to be burned.

28 Sept 1712: Action off Arkona. A Swedish transport fleet of 95 ships land troops and equipment on Rügen; nearby is a Swedish fleet of 29 ships under Wachtmeister. The Danish fleet under Gyldenlove manages to get between the two Swedish fleets, and 40 transports are burned, 15 captured.

The Swedish fleet is not in a position to counterattack and sails off.

6 Aug 1714: Action off Gangut (or Hangö Head). A fleet of 100 Russian galleys meets a Swedish flotilla under Rear Admiral Ehrenskjold, who fights heroically with his 7 ships, and is defeated, but only after hours of fighting. Only 60 of the victor's ships remain intact at the end of the engagement.

24 April 1715: Action off Femern. A Danish squadron of 9 ships of the line and frigates, under Rear Admiral Gabel, puts 6 Swedish ships of the line and frigates to flight. Next day, the Swedes run aground in Kiel Bay and are forced to surrender by the Danes.

8 Aug 1715: Battle of Rügen. The Swedish and Danish fleets clash again; each has 21 ships of the line, the Danes under Admiral Raben, the Swedes under Admiral Sparre. At 1pm, the battle opens with the fleets in line ahead, running eastwards before the wind. From time to time, ships leave the lines in order to repair damage: on the Danish side, their place is always taken by a frigate. Until 8pm, this heavy artillery duel is fought out in strict formation, with no tactical manoeuvring. Each side loses about 600 dead and wounded, but no ships are sunk and, next day, the Danes anchor off Rügen and thus cut the Swedish supply lines to Stralsund.

15 Nov 1715: The Danes and the Prussians (who have now joined the Allies) land an army of 12,500 infantry, 5,000 cavalry, 5,200 horses and a train from 330 coastal ships on the island of Rügen within a few hours, in a perfect amphibious operation. Stralsund is completely cut off, and surrenders after a month.

8 July 1716: Action off Dynekilen. Tordenskjold (DK) destroys a fleet of Swedish galleys, under Rear Admiral Sjöblad, in a fjord in the Kattegat. Charles XII's intended invasion of Norway is thereby frustrated.

July 1717: The Russian fleet (galleys and gunboats) plunders the settlements in the Swedish waters from Stockholm to Norrköping.

1718: Death of Charles XII of Sweden.

21–26 July 1719: Attack on Marstrand. In this harbour is the Swedish Kattegat squadron of 5 ships of the line, 1 frigate, and 10 other ships. Rear Admiral Tordenskjold attacks with a Danish squadron of 7 ships of the line, 2 frigates and a dozen galleys and gun 'punts'. He lands marines, sets up an artillery battery, and shoots the harbour into a condition ripe for storming. Of the Swedish ships in the harbour, he captures 1 ship of the line and 4 other ships; the others are scuttled by their crews.

7 Aug 1720: Action off Åland Island. The Russian coastal fleet lures a Swedish squadron of 4 ships of the line, 6 frigates and some smaller ships into the shallower waters and, after a stiff fight, captures 4 frigates. But 43 Russian galleys are damaged beyond repair, and 2 are sunk.

1719–21: In the peace negotiations, Sweden loses her German possessions to Prussia and Hanover, and her Baltic provinces to Russia, who now replaces Sweden as the major sea power in the Baltic.

*In **this** war, the fleets did not engage directly in a struggle for command of the sea; rather, their clashes developed out of convoy escort duties. The Swedish fleet had failed to disrupt the construction of the Russian fleet. And, in the close, shallow waters, ships propelled with oars proved themselves still worth while.*

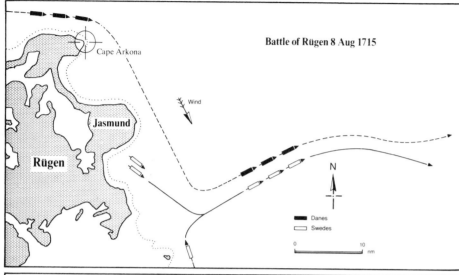

Battle of Rügen 8 Aug 1715

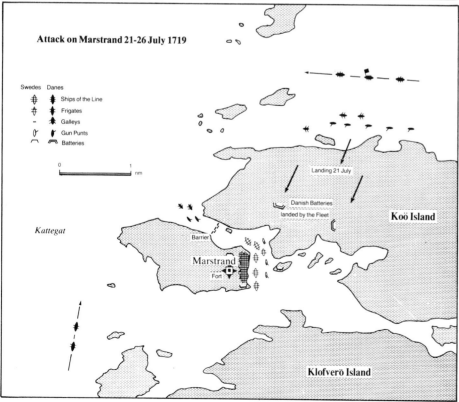

Attack on Marstrand 21–26 July 1719

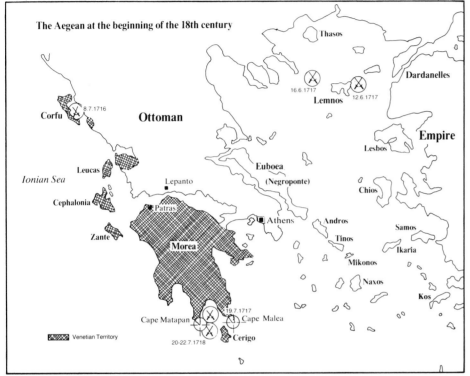

The Aegean at the beginning of the 18th century

Thasos

Dardanelles

16.6.1717 ⊗

⊗ 12.6.1717

Lemnos

Corfu ⊗ 8.7.1716 **Ottoman**

Lesbos

Empire

Leucas

Ionian Sea

Euboea

(Negroponte)

Chios

Lepanto

Cephalonia

★ Patras

Zante

⊙ Athens

Andros

Samos

Tinos

Ikaria

Morea

Míkonos

Naxos

Kos

Cape Matapan ⊗ 19.7.1717

⊗ ⊙ Cape Malea

⊠ Venetian Territory

⊗ 20-22.7.1718 Cerigo

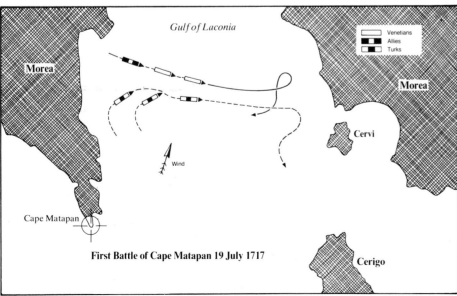

Gulf of Laconia

Morea

Morea

☐ Venetians
■ Allies
☐■ Turks

Cervi

Wind

Cape Matapan

First Battle of Cape Matapan 19 July 1717

Cerigo

WARS IN THE MEDITERRANEAN, 1714–20

1714–18: The Venetian-Turkish War
After the Peace of Adrianople with Russia (1713), the Turks have a free hand in the Mediterranean. Now they aim to recapture the Morea from Venice. While the Turkish fleet is considerably reinforced with ships from the north African states, the weaker Venetian fleet receives practically no support initially from the West. It is only after the fall of the Morea (in the first year of the war) that Venice gets military support from Austria and, from 1717 on, naval support from Portugal.

8 July 1716: Battle of Corfu. The Venetian fleet (27 ships of the line under Andrea Corner) meets the Turkish fleet, which is twice as strong. After 5 hours, the battle ends indecisively: the Venetians lose 360 men.

12 and 16 July 1717: The Two Battles of Lemnos. 26 Venetian and 37 Turkish ships of the line are opposed; the battles rage for two days without result. Venetian losses are 1,400 men.

19 July 1717: First Battle of Cape Matapan. The Venetian fleet under M. Diedo (flagship *Trionfo*, 70 guns) consists of 33 ships of the line, and awaits a Turkish attack by 44 ships of the line. After 9 hours bitter fighting, the Turks are repelled. Many ships on both sides are badly damaged, and Venetian casualties amount to 600 men.

20–22 July 1718: Second Battle of Cape Matapan. 26 Venetian ships of the line (with 1,800 guns) under Diedo clash with 36 Turkish men-of-war (with 2,000 guns). For 3 days, Diedo tries vainly to gain the windward side of the Turks, and only on the 22nd does battle commence. The Turks are repelled with loss; Venetian losses are 1,800 men and their flagship *Trionfo* is dismasted.

July 1718: Peace of Passarowitz. Austria gains Belgrade, but Venice loses the Morea.

1718–20: The War for Sicily
Spain attempts to regain some of the territories she lost in the War of 1702–13. Her fleet covers troop landings on Sicily, which is rapidly occupied with the exception of Messina. The Quadruple Alliance (Great Britain, Austria, Holland and France) turns on Spain, and England sends her Mediterranean squadron to Sicily.

11 Aug 1718: Battle of Cape Passaro (Messina). The Spanish fleet, of 20 ships of the line and some other vessels under Vice Admiral Castañeta, is south of Messina when it sights an equally strong British fleet under Admiral George Byng. The Spanish immediately take flight to Malta and, in the ensuing chase, they lose 11 ships of the line, 7 of which are captured by the British. As the British now control the seas, Austrian troops recapture the island in the following year. Byng destroys the last Spanish ships in Sicily.

Autumn 1719: The British fleet devastates the Spanish coast from Vigo to San Sebastian.

1720: Treaty of The Hague. Austria exchanges Sardinia for Sicily, with Savoy.

1727: Spain's attempt to recapture Gibraltar fails.

South-west Europe in the middle of the 18th century

War of the Austrian Succession 1741-48

The Seven Years' War 1756-63

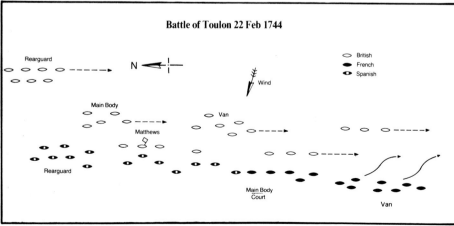

Battle of Toulon 22 Feb 1744

○ British
● French
◉ Spanish

1740-48: THE WAR OF THE AUSTRIAN SUCCESSION

War breaks out over the succession of Maria Theresa to the Habsburg possessions, and it involves the great sea powers. Spain, France, Prussia and Bavaria are on the one side; Austria, Great Britain and Holland on the other. At the outbreak of war, Britain has 80 ships of the line, France over 45 and Spain over 25, although the two latter fleets are in poor condition.

22 Feb 1744: Battle of Toulon. The British Mediterranean fleet, under Admiral Matthews, meets the Allied fleet under the French Admiral La Bruyère de Court and Don José Navarro. The 28 British ships, opposed by 15 French and 12 Spanish, attack from the windward side in extended line ahead, so that their van opposes the Allied centre, and the English centre, their rear; the British rear is not engaged. An attempt by the French van to surround the British van is frustrated by the leading British ships. However, few of the British ships manage to close the enemy, and the battle ends indecisively with minor losses. The Allied fleet returns unmolested to Barcelona, and Admiral Matthews is cashiered for not having pressed the battle.

July 1746: Action off Negapatam (or Fort St. David). The commander of the French Indian Ocean squadron, Admiral de la Bourdonnais, defeats a British squadron under Peyton; Madras falls to the French.

3 May 1747: Action off Cape Finisterre. Admiral Anson (GB), with 17 ships of the line, meets a large French convoy escorted by 5 French ships of the line, under de la Jonquière. With his superior numbers, Anson orders 'general pursuit' and, in the ensuing fight, all the French warships and 6 merchantmen are captured, while the rest of the convoy escapes.

14 Oct 1747: Action North of Cape Finisterre. Rear Admiral Hawke (GB), with 14 ships of the line, meets a French convoy escorted by 9 ships of the line, under Commodore de l'Etenduère, who leaves one warship with the convoy and offers battle with the rest. Hawke also declares the hunting season open, but enemy resistance is so stiff that the fight goes on until nightfall. The British capture 6 ships of the line, while the other 2 escape in the dark, badly damaged. The convoy has been saved, but the French have lost their last battleworthy escort squadron.

France and Britain now carry their struggle into the colonies: in the West Indies, Britain captures several places, while the French are successful in the East Indies.

1 Oct 1748: Action off Havana. A British squadron of 6 ships of the line meets an equal number of Spanish ships. 1 Spanish ship strikes its flag, while another is burned by its crew in order to avoid capture.

1748: Treaty of Aix-la-Chapelle. Prussia retains her conquest, Silesia; the other captured territories are handed back.

During this war, French successes on land were more than outweighed by her lack of power at sea. The trade war had resulted in a loss of over 3,300 ships on each side: France's trade was now in ruins, and even Britain had suffered more than usual. Peace lasted but a short time, for there persisted in the colonies considerable tension between France and Britain. In 1754, fighting gradually spread in these disputed areas and, by 1755, Hawke was conducting what amounted to a trade war in the Bay of Biscay. Then, in 1756, Frederick the Great invaded Saxony, and Europe once again erupted into war.

Sea power (Britain, soon to be led by William Pitt the elder) combined with land power (Frederick the Great's Prussia) against France (Louis XV), Austria (Maria Theresa) and Russia (Catherine the Great). At sea, 120 British ships of the line were set to oppose 70 French. At the heart of the fleets, ships of the line were now up to

2,000 tons displacement, while the new, fast, 700-ton frigates were soon to prove their worth in all the theatres of a world-wide war.

1756–63: THE SEVEN YEARS WAR

The War in European Waters

April 1756: Landing on Minorca. A French transport fleet of 150 ships lands troops on the island and besieges the British naval base at Port Mahon. A French squadron of 12 ships of the line, under Admiral de la Galissonière, covers the operation.

20 May 1756: Battle of Minorca. Admiral John Byng, with 11 ships, attacks the French squadron off Port Mahon; de la Galissonière meets him with 10 ships in a very close leeward position. Only the British van closes the enemy, and is received with effective broadsides; the other British ships fight from a distance. The French fail to surround the British van and the battle ends without tactical result. Worse, Byng retires to Gibraltar, leaving the French free to compel the British garrison at Port Mahon to surrender. The public outcry in Britain causes the embarrassed government to recall Byng. He is court martialled, found guilty, and shot, a fate that arouses widespread comment and prompts Voltaire's famous remark: 'Dans ce pays-ci, il est bon de tuer de temps en temps un admiral pour encourager les autres.'

France prepares an invasion of England, and concentrates an army of 30,000 men north of the Loire estuary. The French fleet is due to concentrate off the Morbihan inlet of Quiberon Bay, and the Toulon fleet makes for the Atlantic.

Aug/Sept 1758: A British attempt to land troops at St. Malo fails, and they suffer heavy losses while re-embarking.

18–19 Aug 1759: Battle of Lagos Bay (Cape Santa Maria). The French are sighted as they pass Gibraltar, and the British Mediterranean squadron (which happens to be in harbour there) catches up with them after a short chase. The 15 British ships of the line under Boscawen are opposed by 7 French under de la Clue, whose other 5 ships have fled to Cadiz during the night. The rearmost French ship, *Centaure*, holds up the British long enough before sinking for 2 other French ships to escape into the Atlantic; the other 4 ships are run aground in Lagos Bay, Portugal. In spite of Portuguese neutrality, Boscawen attacks next day, capturing 2 ships and burning the other two. The French Mediterranean squadron has thus ceased to exist.

The French, meanwhile, stick to their invasion plans: in favourable weather, their Atlantic squadron under Marshal Conflans runs out of Brest and sets course for the mouth of the Loire. Admiral Hawke gives immediate chase with his blockading squadron.

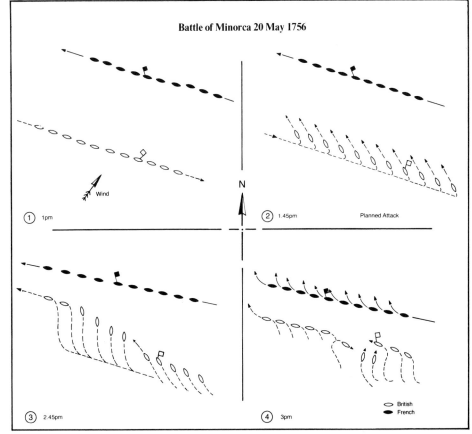

Battle of Minorca 20 May 1756

① 1pm   Wind   N

② 1.45pm   Planned Attack

③ 2.45pm

④ 3pm

○ British
● French

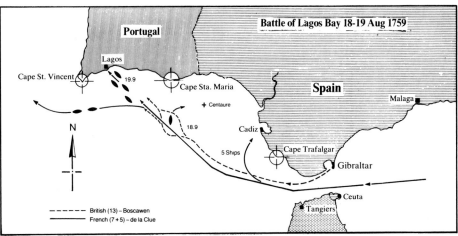

Battle of Lagos Bay 18-19 Aug 1759

Portugal

Lagos

Cape St. Vincent   19.9

Cape Sta. Maria

Spain

✛ Centaure

Malaga

18.9

Cadiz

N

5 Ships

Cape Trafalgar

Gibraltar

Ceuta

Tangiers

– – – – British (13) – Boscawen
——— French (7 + 5) – de la Clue

20 Nov 1759: Battle of Quiberon Bay. In a rising westerly storm, the French are overtaken by the British blockade squadron in Quiberon Bay. Hawke (flagship *Royal George*) commands 27 ships of the line; Conflans (flagship *Soleil Royal*) 21 of the line plus 2 frigates. Conflans decides to run into the bay, where the waters are treacherous, with many small islands, and can only be negotiated with the aid of pilots with local knowledge (who are aboard the French ships). Despite the rising WNW wind, which makes the entrance to the bay particularly dangerous, Hawke orders a general pursuit.

2pm: Even as the French leading ships enter the bay, the British van is upon them, and the fight begins.

3.30pm: In bitter fighting, the French rearguard is beaten: *Formidable* is captured, *Superbe* capsizes. As the other British ships join the fight, the badly damaged *Héros* strikes her flag and runs aground; and *Thesée* in combat with *Torbay*, founders with over 700 men aboard. Practically no survivors can be saved from the sunken ships. Darkness causes the British to break off the fight and anchor overnight. Two of their ships run aground and have to be destroyed, while some of the French vessels also run aground, including *Soleil Royal*, which is then burnt by her crew. Some French ships escape over the bar into the mouth of the River Vilaine, after jettisoning their cannon to reduce their draught; only a year later can they leave this haven. Only 8 French ships manage to escape to Rochefort; their losses are 7 ships of the line compared with 2 of the British (those that had run aground). The stormy battle of Quiberon Bay is one of the most famous victories in the Royal Navy's history. The French battle fleet is now non-effective, the threat of a French invasion is removed, and the English can now turn their attention to the naval war in the far seas, whilst closely blockading the French coast to cut communications with her colonies.

8 June 1761: The British capture the island of Belle Isle off Quiberon Bay, and retain it until the end of the war.

The War in the Indian Ocean

Jan 1757: The British Indian squadron captures Calcutta and Chandernagore from the French.

29 April 1758: Action off Cuddalore. The first indecisive fight between the British and French squadrons in the Indian Ocean matches 7 British ships of the line, under Admiral Pocock, to 8 French under Count d'Aché.

3 Aug 1758: Action off Negapatam. The second indecisive combat.

10 Sept 1759: Action off Porto Novo (or Pondicherry). The third indecisive clash, as Pocock's 9 ships face 11 French. Due to lack of bases, Count d'Aché has no opportunity of repairing damages and replenishing his equipment, so he finally has to surrender command of the sea to the British. The land forces under Clive rapidly drive the French out of India.

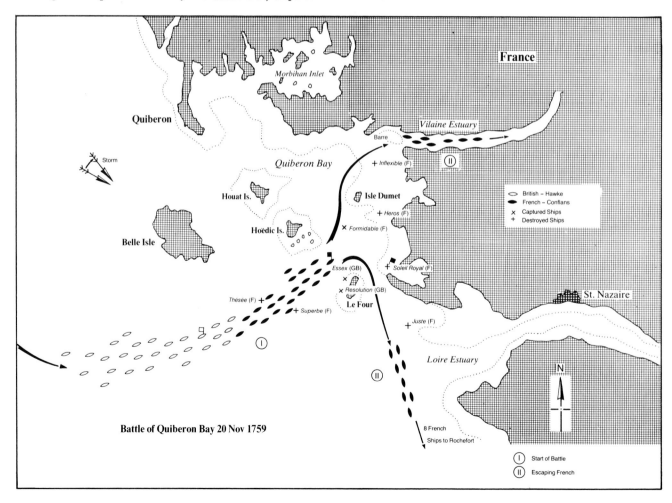

Battle of Quiberon Bay 20 Nov 1759

The War in the Americas

1758: Admiral Boscawen captures Louisburg, the French naval base, near the mouth of the St. Lawrence. Six French ships of the line in the harbour are also captured.

1759: Quebec falls to a British army led by General Wolfe and a fleet under Vice Admiral Saunders.

1759: A British squadron under Commodore Moore captures Guadeloupe.

1760: The British capture Montreal. Cut off from France, all the French colonies in Canada are eventually lost.

1761: Dominica is taken by a British squadron under Commodore Douglas.

1761: A British expedition captures Manila and the majority of the Philippines from Spain.

1762: Spain enters the war on the side of France, but, as the Spanish fleet is totally ineffective, Britain can continue her rampaging in the colonies.

1762: A British squadron under Rear Admiral Rodney captures Martinique.

June–Aug 1762: Attack on Havana. A British squadron of 22 ships of the line, 30 other ships and 100 transports, under Admiral Pocock, lands troops on the Spanish island of Cuba.

13 Aug: After two months, Havana is captured. Of the 12 ships of the line of the Spanish West Indies squadron in the harbour, 9 are captured and 3 sunk.

1763: Peace of Paris and Hubertusburg. Great Britain gains Canada, Louisiana, Florida and Senegambia: North America becomes Anglo-Saxon. Prussia remains intact.

During the course of this war, it had again been demonstrated that trade was a very considerable factor in the conduct of military operations. Following the Battle of Quiberon Bay, the British had instituted a blockade that succeeded in practically driving the French flag from the sea lanes of the world. France's foreign trade was ruined, and the finances of the land exhausted. Even in neutral vessels, Britain had taken rigorous measures to seek out contraband. Despite Pitt's resignation in 1761, and the resultant slackening in the British war effort, Britain emerged from the Seven Years War in firm command of the seas, and could now (in Ralegh's words) bid fair to control the riches of the world.

The victor of Quiberon Bay, Hawke, was the forerunner of a generation of naval officers who would be ready to deviate from the rigidity of formal tactics, and who would seek victory through boldness and attack (virtues which would be tested to the utmost in the next war, when Britain would be in danger of being overwhelmed at sea for the first time in two hundred years).

Battle, however, was not the greatest reaper of lives at this period: heavier casualties were incurred, on long cruises and gruelling blockade duties, through disease. With a monotonous diet and impossible sanitary conditions aboard ship, scurvy and intestinal disorders were rife. During the Seven Years War, the Royal Navy had lost 1,500 men in action; disease accounted for another 100,000.

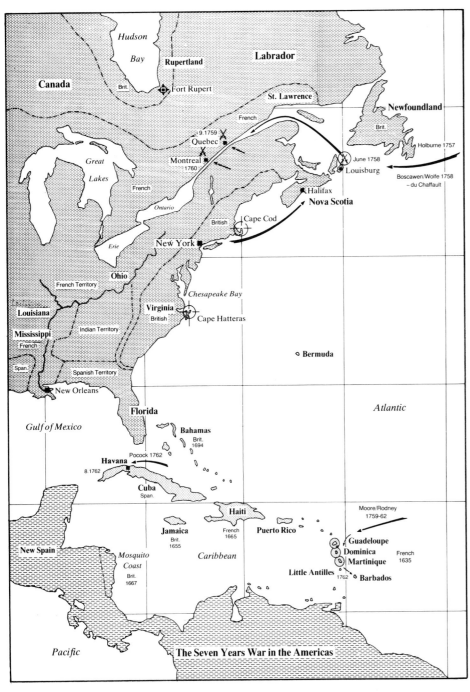

The Seven Years War in the Americas

1768-74: THE FIRST RUSSO-TURKISH WAR

Empress Catherine II (the Great) sends a Russian squadron into the Mediterranean for the first time; this is in order to support the Greeks in their struggle against Turkish rule. (The Russians at this time have no Black Sea fleet.)

1770: The Russian squadron, under Count Orlov, concentrates in Navarino Bay, while the Turkish fleet lies in the roads of Chios.

5 July 1770: Battle of Chios. The Turkish fleet (20 ships of the line plus frigates) opposes Orlov's 9 ships of the line and 3 frigates. With a following wind, the Russians attack the anchored Turkish fleet in line ahead. The Russian van, under Vice Admiral Spiridov, bears the brunt of the fight: his flagship, *St. Eustachius*, is dismasted and, running up against a Turkish ship, catches fire and explodes. By evening, the Turks are badly mauled, and they cut their cables in the night and flee into the bay of Chesme.

6-7 July 1770: Battle of Chesme (or Tchesme). A Turkish fleet of 20 ships of the line and 3 frigates lies unprotected in the narrow bay. Orlov decides on a night fire-ship attack, and Commodore Greig (a Scotsman in Russian service) escorts the fire-ships up to the enemy with 4 ships of the line. The leading ship is heavily bombarded by the Turks, but the fire-ships reach their target. The Russians capture 1 ship of the line and 10 other vessels; all other Turkish ships are burned or explode, and the Turks lose about 9,000 men. With their ships' boats the Russians tow their vessels out of the bay.

Oct-Nov 1771: Orlov twice attempts to force the Dardanelles by bombardment, but is driven off with loss.

1774: Peace of Kutchuck-Kainardji.

The voyages of exploration that began in the 15th century had, by the middle of the 18th century, resulted in a considerable opening-up of the world's oceans to European influence. Charting of the Pacific was now proceeding apace. In 1568, the Spaniard Mendana had sailed from South America to the Solomons and back and, in the early 17th century, the first Dutch voyagers on their way to Indonesia had discovered the western coast of Australia. Abel Tasman, sent to explore the extent of this southern continent by the governor of Batavia (headquarters of the Dutch East Indies Company), had circumnavigated Australia in 1642–43, touching en route Van Diemens Land (Tasmania), New Zealand, Fiji and New Guinea.

Following in the footsteps of Magellan and Drake, Anson, Byron, Wallis, Carteret and Bougainville now traversed the Pacific from east to west. In order to improve the accuracy of longitudinal and latitudinal measurements by astronomical observation, James Cook undertook his voyages of research in the South Seas during the late 1760s and 1770s.

THE CHARTING OF THE PACIFIC

1768-71: Cook journeys from Cape Horn, and visits Tahiti, New Zealand and Australia before returning westwards.

1772-75: On his second journey, Cook enters the Pacific from the Indian Ocean, crosses the Pacific in a series of circles, and establishes the extent of the island groups.

1776-79: On his third journey, Cook explores the northern Pacific, discovers the Sandwich Islands (Hawaii), sails through the Bering Straits, and vainly attempts to find the 'north-west passage' to Europe. On returning to Hawaii, he is killed by the natives.

Battle of Chios 5 July 1770

N

St. Eustachius

Chios Channel

Wind

Battle of Chesme 7 July 1770

Fire-ship Attack

Batteries

Batteries

Chesme

Chios
Chesme
Izmir
Samos

Russians
Turks

1775-83: THE AMERICAN REVOLUTION (THE WAR OF AMERICAN INDEPENDENCE)

The white settlers in Britain's American colonies rise against the mother country, mainly because of restrictions on settling, limitations on trade and the tax laws. The first clash between British troops and American militia occurs at Lexington on 19 April 1775. George Washington takes command of the army of liberation and, on 4 July 1776, the Declaration of Independence of the 13 United States is signed. After the American victory at Saratoga (1777), Benjamin Franklin succeeds in gaining France as an ally for the revolting colonies.

1778: France declares war on Britain; one year later, Spain, too, declares war.

1780: Formation of the League of Armed Neutrality. At the urging of the Empress Catherine II of Russia, a number of neutral states band together to resist British 'high-handed' methods at sea. When Holland joins the League, Britain declares war on her. With the entry of France and Spain into hostilities, the war hinges on command of the sea: the decision will be reached in the Atlantic. The British fleet at the outbreak of war is 130 ships of the line strong, all in good condition, but spread over a very wide area. Since the last war, France has much improved her fleet: she now has 80 ships of the line, almost all less than 20 years of age and in good condition. The Spanish fleet is also numerically strong, but the standards of personnel training and supply organization are very poor. As this war takes place mainly in the colonies, the possession of good harbours and bases is vital; part of the struggle is concerned with their possession.

The War in European waters

Although the British fleet is mainly deployed far from home, the French fail to blockade the English coast.

27 July 1778: Battle of Ushant. The British Channel fleet and the French Brest squadron meet. Thirty British ships of the line under Admiral Keppel (flagship *Victory*, 100 guns) oppose 27 French under Count d'Orvilliers (flagship *Bretagne*, 110 guns). In a westerly wind, the French are on the weather side and the fleets meet on opposing courses. The British fleet gets into disorder, but the French fail to grasp the opportunity. The battle ends indecisively after 3 hours; the British lose 500 men, the French 700, and some British ships are badly damaged.

1779: After the entry of Spain into the war, the Allied fleet in the Channel has about 60 ships of the line, and is thus twice as strong as the British. However, the Allies fail to exploit this advantage: Spain's aim in the war is the recapture of Gibraltar and Minorca, while France is taking the offensive in the West Indies.

16 Jan 1780: Battle of Cape St. Vincent (the 'Moonlight Battle'). Admiral Rodney, with 22 ships of the line and 9 frigates, meets the 11 ships of the Spanish squadron, under Admiral Langara, which are blockading Gibraltar. A running fight develops. Although there is a strong westerly wind and the coast is dangerous, Rodney presses the chase, breaking it off only at nightfall and almost on the coast. Six ships are taken from the Spanish (but 2 of these are lost by running aground), and some of the British ships only narrowly escape being shipwrecked. Rodney resupplies Gibraltar.

1780: The Allied fleet captures a British convoy of 60 ships laden with booty returning from the West Indies.

Spring 1781: Another British West Indies convoy is captured.

April 1781: The British Channel fleet takes a supply convoy into Gibraltar.

5 Aug 1781: Action at the Dogger Bank. A British and a Dutch convoy, both from the Baltic, meet in the North Sea.

Each is covered by 7 ships of the line, the British under Vice Admiral Hyde Parker, the Dutch under Rear Admiral Zoutman. Both enter into a furious combat at close range in line ahead, and it develops into one of the bloodiest clashes of the war. Both convoys proceed on their respective ways.

Dec 1781: Rear Admiral Kempenfelt, with 12 ships of the line, completely destroys a large French convoy off Ushant; 15 prizes are taken. The French Brest squadron, under Rear Admiral de Guichen, is in the neighbourhood, but is downwind of the convoy and can thus do nothing.

Feb 1782: The Spanish capture Port Mahon on Minorca.

Sept 1782: Attack on Gibraltar. The Allies concentrate their Atlantic fleet to storm the fortress from land and sea.

9-13 Sept: A 4-day bombardment begins. Ten floating batteries, made almost unsinkable by cork bolstering, are anchored in the bay of Algeciras; together with a number of mortars, they begin to pound the fortress. The defenders counter the floating batteries with heated shot and 2 of them are burnt out. The remainder are then destroyed in a bold night attack, mounted in small boats.

Oct 1782: Admiral Howe arrives in Gibraltar with the Channel fleet and a supply convoy of 140 ships. He succeeds in luring the Allied fleet into the Mediterranean, while, in two days, the convoy unloads its cargo and escapes into the Atlantic again. Howe then slips away from a developing battle with his stronger foes.

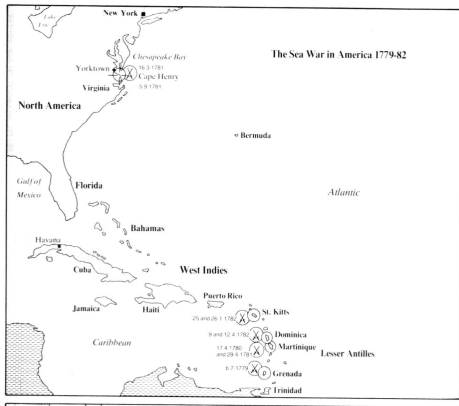

The Sea War in America 1779-82

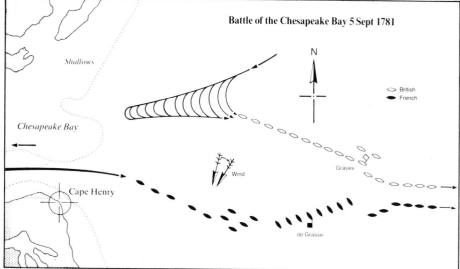

Battle of the Chesapeake Bay 5 Sept 1781

○ British
● French

The War in North America and the West Indies

1776: The American David Bushnell builds a primitive 1-man submarine, and tries to attack the British fleet in New York harbour. The first clashes between opposing squadrons of ships, however, result from the struggle for the West Indies.

15 Dec 1778: Action off Santa Lucia. At the outbreak of war, the French take advantage of the British naval weakness in the West Indies and attack their possessions there. Off Santa Lucia, the British successfully ward off an attempted raid by a stronger French squadron.

6 July 1779: Battle of Grenada. Having landed troops on the island, Admiral d'Estaing's transports and escorts (25 ships of the line) lie in the harbour at Georgetown. The British (21 ships of the line under Vice Admiral Byron) attack, but Byron underestimates the enemy strength and orders an open hunt. The leading British ships are badly battered by the still-forming French line, so Byron reverts to line of battle. The fight ends at midday without a decision, and d'Estaing misses the opportunity of destroying the damaged British ships. Losses on both sides are about 1,000 men.

17 April 1780: Battle of Martinique. Admiral Rodney (flagship *Sandwich*, 90 guns), with 20 ships of the line, meets 24 French ships of the line under Rear Admiral de Guichen. The entire forenoon is taken up with manoeuvring for position until, finally, Rodney is on the windward side. He orders an attack on the enemy rear, but a misunderstanding leads the British ships to close up against the whole enemy fleet. The two lines batter each other with their artillery from 1pm to 7pm. The damaged *Sandwich* drifts through the French line and is followed by other British ships: de Guichen takes this to be an intentional tactical breakthrough, and breaks off the engagement. Both sides have lost about 500 men.

1781: Land combat in America enters the decisive phase: British troops under General Cornwallis are surrounded by the Americans at Yorktown. Control of the sea, and in particular of Chesapeake Bay, is vital to them.

16 March 1781: Action off Chesapeake Bay. Indecisive combat between 8 ships of the line and 4 frigates, under Vice Admiral Arbuthnot, and 7 French ships of the line and 2 frigates, under Commodore des Touches (F).

29 April 1781: Action off Martinique: The British West Indian squadron of 18 ships of the line, under Rear Admiral Hood, meets 24 French ships under Vice Admiral de Grasse, who contents himself with repelling the British attack. Three British ships are badly damaged, and both sides lose about 300 men.

Sept 1781: De Grasse brings troop reinforcements for Washington from the West Indies. He anchors his fleet in the entrance of Chesapeake Bay, thus cutting Cornwallis' sea supply route. Rear Admiral Graves must drive de Grasse away.

5 Sept 1781: Battle of Chesapeake Bay (Virginia Capes, or Cape Henry). Graves (flagship *London*) arrives off Chesapeake Bay with 19 ships in the morning of 5th; his second in command is Rear Admiral Hood in *Barfleur*. As soon as de Grasse (flagship *Ville de Paris*) sights the British fleet, he raises anchor and sails his 24 ships of the line into battle line on an easterly course. Instead of attacking the enemy while he was engaged in formation of line, Graves also forms line ahead, and then comes down on the French from the north.

4pm: Only the British van comes within combat range of the enemy; the British main body and rear, becalmed as the wind drops, remain out of artillery range. The British van is badly shattered by French fire.

6pm: *Terrible* is so badly damaged that she has to be abandoned 5 days later. The French van also suffers, but Graves breaks off the fight. Next day he does not renew the attack, and de Grasse re-anchors off Cape Henry. Cornwallis' sea route remains cut, and this sea battle thus has the most far-reaching strategic effects.

19 Oct 1781: Capitulation of the British army at Yorktown. The war for American independence has been won.

The centre of gravity of the war at sea now returns to the West Indies. French troops land on St. Kitts and surround the British garrison on a hill. De Grasse covers the landing

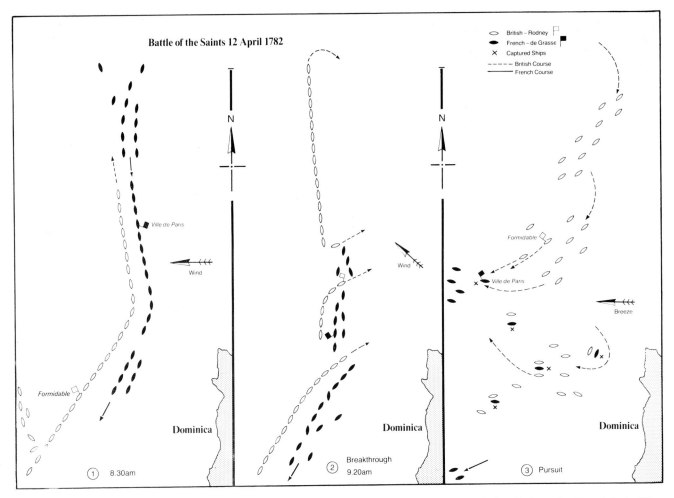

Battle of the Saints 12 April 1782

○ British – Rodney ⚐
● French – de Grasse ⬛
✕ Captured Ships
---- British Course
—— French Course

N

Ville de Paris

Wind

Formidable

Dominica

① 8.30am

N

Wind

Breakthrough
② 9.20am

Formidable

Ville de Paris

Breeze

Dominica

③ Pursuit

with 26 ships of the line.

25–26 Jan 1782: Battle of St. Kitts. Rear Admiral Hood manages to slip into the harbour, with his 22 ships of the line, past the 24 French ships of the line.

25 Jan: Even as his ships drop anchor, de Grasse attacks; but under enemy fire, Hood anchors his squadron so that the French ships are received with full broadsides. De Grasse breaks off the fight.

26 Jan: Next day the French attack again, sailing past the British ships in line ahead. The leading French ships, however, receive broadsides from all the British ships, and are badly damaged. After a second attempt, de Grasse breaks off the action. But, as the British troops on the island have surrendered, Hood slips away unnoticed to join Admiral Rodney, who has meanwhile returned to the West Indies. This makes over 30 ships of the line on the British side, so that they can now operate more offensively against the French. Rodney plans to intercept the French fleet, which is to escort a large convoy from Martinique to Cuba.

9 April 1782: The opposing fleets meet off Dominica, each about 30 ships strong. In the lee of the island, they are becalmed, and only some of the French and the British van can catch a light breeze. A combat develops between 8 British and 15 French ships, but, after a few hours, the British main body approaches. The French break off the fight, and return to guard the convoy. Three days later the fleets meet again.

12 April 1782: Battle of the Saints (or Dominica). The British fleet under Rodney (flagship *Formidable*) has 36 ships; Hood is second in command in *Barfleur*. De Grasse (flagship *Ville de Paris*) has 31 ships, and his fleet is off The Saints, a small group of islands south of Guadeloupe. The British approach from the south in the forenoon.

7am: The French form line ahead on a southerly course, and pass the leading British ships on the weather side.

9am: As the fight opens, the French line develops some gaps. The wind suddenly turns south-easterly, and Rodney immediately turns his flagship into the wind, breaking through the French line. A ship of his van, and the rear under Hood follow this manoeuvre.

11am: The French fleet is in complete confusion; some ships are already badly damaged.

2pm: De Grasse fails to re-order his fleet, and the French begin to withdraw.

6pm: The British manage to capture some stragglers and eventually *Ville de Paris*—which alone has 400 dead aboard— is also forced to strike her flag. De Grasse is captured and, if Rodney's pursuit had been more energetic, his victory would have been greater still. French losses are 5 ships and over 2,000 men dead and wounded as well as a large number captured. British losses are just over 1,000 men. As the first victory by penetration, after many indecisive combats, this battle introduces a new phase in naval warfare. The struggle in the West Indies is decided in Britain's favour.

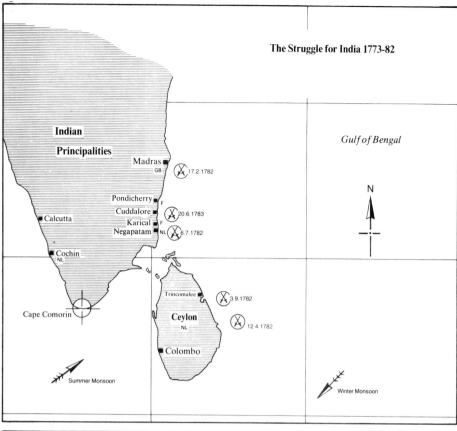

The Struggle for India 1773-82

Indian

Principalities

Madras
GB — ⊗ 17.2.1782

Gulf of Bengal

Pondicherry F
Cuddalore F — ⊗ 20.6.1783
Karical F
Negapatam NL — ⊗ 6.7.1782

Calcutta

Cochin
NL

N

Trincomalee — ⊗ 3.9.1782

Cape Comorin

Ceylon
NL

⊗ 12.4.1782

Colombo

Summer Monsoon

Winter Monsoon

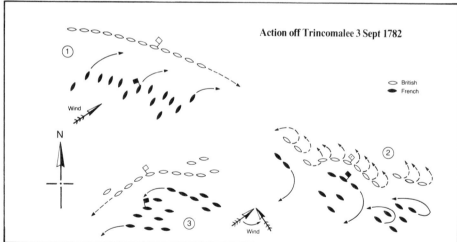

Action off Trincomalee 3 Sept 1782

①

Wind

N

②

③

Wind

○ British
● French

The War in the East Indies

1781: Britain and France send reinforcements to their naval
forces in the Indian Ocean. The British squadron has a task
en route: to capture the Dutch Cape Colony. The French
send troop reinforcements there.

16 April 1781: Action in Porto Praya Bay (Cape Verde). On
the way there, the French squadron of 5 ships of the line
under Commodore Suffren, meets the British in the harbour
of Porto Praya. Suffren attacks at once, but, as only 2 ships
follow him, the British avoid destruction. Suffren breaks off
the fight and moves on to land his reinforcements in the

colony, which is thus secure. He then sails into the Indian
Ocean (where he has no bases), to carry the fight to the
British.

17 Feb 1782: Action off Madras. Suffren meets his adversary,
Hughes, for the first time. Twelve French ships oppose 9
British. Suffren attacks the British rear from the windward
side, but changing winds bring the British van into the fight
too, and the combat ends indecisively at nightfall.

12 April 1782: Battle of Providien (off Ceylon). Second
meeting of the opponents, 11 British ships versus 12 French.
Although more serious, this fight is also indecisive. Each
side loses about 500 men.

6 July 1782: Action off Negapatam. This time 11 ships are
on each side; 2 French ships are cut off from the main body
and badly shot up. Suffren only extracts himself with
difficulty, and French losses are heavier this time, even
though no decision is reached; however, Suffren fails in his
objective, the recapture of Negapatam.

3 Sept 1782: Action off Trincomalee. Suffren attacks im-
petuously with his 14 ships; Hughes with 12 ships awaits the
French assault in good order. Some French ships are again
badly damaged, and Suffren's flagship *Héros* becomes
unmanageable. But Hughes fails to press his advantage. Both
sides lose about 300 men, and Suffren has to withdraw to
Sumatra to repair.

20 June 1783: Action off Cuddalore. Hughes is blockading
this harbour with 16 ships of the line; Suffren attacks with 15.
The running fight leads to no decision, but Hughes has to
lift the blockade. Both sides lose about 500 men. Shortly
after this, news of peace arrives from Europe. Suffren has
conducted a naval campaign for almost two years without
proper bases and almost without support.

1782: Recognition of the United States of America by Britain.

1783: Peace of Versailles. The territorial picture is basically
as before; conquests on both sides are exchanged, but Spain
retains Minorca and Florida.

*In the Royal Navy, several technical improvements had by now
proved their worth: copper plating on ship's hulls afforded greater
speeds; cannon now had flintlock firing mechanisms to replace the
dangerous match; and a new type of gun, the carronade, provided a
short-range weapon of devastating effect. Signalling had meanwhile been improved by the introduction of a new book of signals by
Howe and Kempenfelt.*

*In the 1780s and 1790s, the Scot, John Clerk of Eldin, wrote his
Essay on Naval Tactics, which criticized the rigid line ahead
formation and the pure ship-to-ship artillery duel. Rather, he
favoured a more flexible control of the fleet, and a concentration of
force against one part of the enemy fleet, which was to be crushed
by superior numbers. He was also a proponent of piercing the
enemy line and of attack from both sides.*

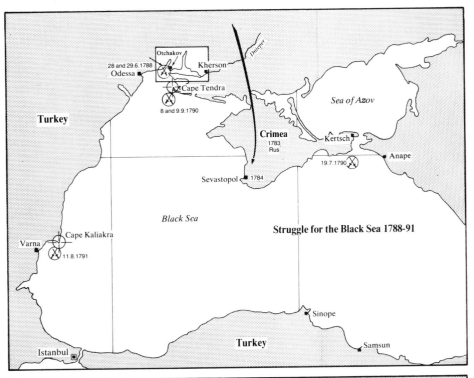

Struggle for the Black Sea 1788-91

Map labels: Otchakov, 28 and 29.6.1788, Odessa, Kherson, Dnieper, Cape Tendra, 8 and 9.9.1790, Turkey, Sea of Azov, Crimea 1783 Rus, Kertsch, Anape, 19.7.1790, Sevastopol 1784, Black Sea, Cape Kaliakra, Varna, 11.8.1791, Sinope, Turkey, Samsun, Istanbul

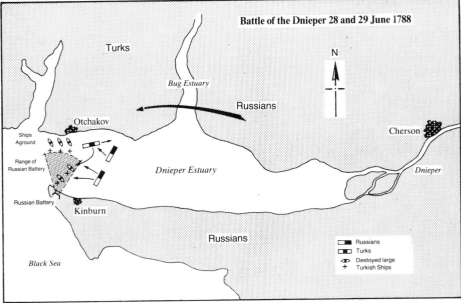

Battle of the Dnieper 28 and 29 June 1788

Map labels: Turks, Bug Estuary, Russians, N, Otchakov, Ships Aground, Cherson, Range of Russian Battery, Dnieper Estuary, Dnieper, Russian Battery, Kinburn, Russians, Black Sea

Legend:
- Russians
- Turks
- Destoyed large
- Turkish Ships

RUSSIA'S WARS WITH TURKEY AND SWEDEN, 1787-91

1787-91: The Second Russo-Turkish War

Russia annexes the autonomous Crimea, and founds the naval base of Sevastopol; Turkey senses a threat to her control of the Black Sea, and declares war. Relative strengths of the fleets at outbreak of hostilities are as follows.

	TURKEY	RUSSIA (Black Sea fleet)
Ships of the line	22	5
Frigates	8	20
Total no. guns	1,700	1,100

Apart from this, both fleets have strong river flotillas of galleys, gunboats and artillery punts.

1788: In the second year of the war, the Russians begin an attack on the fortress of Otchakov, at the mouth of the Dnieper.

28-29 June 1788: Battle of the Dnieper. The combined Turkish fleet of about 100 vessels, including some small ships of the line, under Hassan el Ghazi, lies off Otchakov. The Russians gather a flotilla of 70 gunboats, under Prince Nassau-Siegen (a Franco-German mercenary), and a light sail squadron of 13 ships under the the American Paul Jones. A battery is set up at Kinburn, opposite Otchakov, to control entry to the river. On the first day of the combat, the Turkish fleet is repulsed with loss and in an attempt to pass the Russian battery and gain the open sea, the squadron of Turkish sail runs aground and all the ships are captured or destroyed by the Russians. Turkish losses are 10 ships and 1,600 prisoners; Russian losses are one frigate and 100 men.

June 1790: Rear Admiral Ushakov attacks the harbours of Sinope, Samsun and Anape with a light squadron, and destroys or captures over 20 Turkish ships.

19 July 1790: Action off Kertsch. Ushakov, with 16 ships of the line and frigates, meets a Turkish fleet 2 vessels stronger. After a 2-hour combat, the Turks withdraw.

8-9 Sept 1790: Battle of Tendra. West of the Crimea, Ushakov again falls in with the Turkish fleet.

	RUSSIA	TURKEY
Ships of the line	10	14
Frigates	6	8
Guns	830	1,200

The battle begins at 3pm, both fleets in line ahead; towards evening the Turks gradually take flight. Next morning, the Russians catch up with 2 damaged Turkish ships of the line: one surrenders at once, while the other, Vice Admiral Said Bey's flagship, puts up bitter resistance and surrenders only when it has been overwhelmed by 3 opponents. But then, after striking her colours, the ship explodes, killing almost the entire crew. Russian losses are 50 men.

11 Aug 1791: Action off Cape Kaliakra. Ushakov engages the Turkish fleet for the last time. After a 3-hour battle, the Turks withdraw and, on this day, an armistice is agreed.

1792: Peace of Jassy (Iassi). Russia retains all conquered territory east of the River Dniesta, including the port of Otchakov. She now has firm control of part of the northern Black Sea coast.

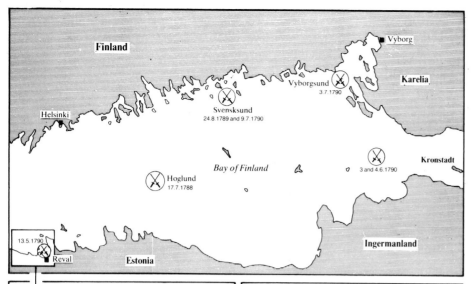

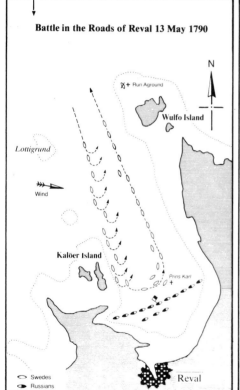

Battle in the Roads of Reval 13 May 1790

Run Aground

Wulfo Island

Lottigrund

Wind

Kalöer Island

Prins Karl

○ Swedes
● Russians

Reval

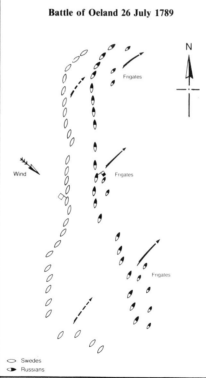

Battle of Oeland 26 July 1789

N

Frigates

Wind

Frigates

Frigates

○ Swedes
● Russians

1788–90: The Russo-Swedish War

To strengthen his own internally weak position, Gustav III of Sweden prepares for war on Russia, which is already at war with Turkey. Fleet strengths are as follows.

	SWEDEN	RUSSIA (Baltic Fleet)
Ships of the line	15	17
Frigates	11	8

Both countries also have considerable fleets of galleys for use in the shallow coastal waters.

17 July 1788: Battle of Hoglund. Initial contact between the fleets occurs in the Bay of Finland: Admiral Greig (flagship *Rostislav*, 100 guns) has 17 Russian ships of the line with 1,220 guns; Duke Carl, a brother of the Swedish king (flagship *Gustav III*, 70 guns) has 15 ships of the line and 5 large frigates, a total of 1,180 guns. An indecisive artillery duel lasts from afternoon until nightfall, each side losing one ship of the line by boarding. The Swedes sustain 1,200 casualties, the Russians 1,800: but the Swedish advance has been stopped.

1789: Icing-up of the Baltic stops hostilities during the winter. In spring, the Swedes put 21 ships of the line and 13 frigates into action, and try to prevent the junction of the main Russian fleet from Kronstadt with their squadron in the Sound.

26 July 1789: Battle of Oeland. The Swedish fleet of 21 ships of the line and 8 frigates, under Duke Carl, meets the main Russian fleet of 21 ships and 10 frigates, under Admiral Chichagov. The latter evades serious combat, and the action soon ends indecisively with minor losses. The Swedes proceed to Karlskrona, where they are blockaded by the now-united Russian fleet.

24 Aug 1789: First Battle in Svensksund. The Russians attack the Swedish inshore fleet in Finnish waters. Nassau-Siegen commands 86 vessels (frigates, galleys, gunboats, etc.) with 1,283 guns: Admiral Ehrensvärd has 30 Swedish vessels, with 680 guns, in a strong defensive position. The Russians attack in two groups. The southern one under Major General Ballé is repulsed, but the eastern group penetrates the Swedish defences, and the Swedes are pursued until late in the night. They lose 8 fighting ships, 16 other vessels, 14 transports burnt to avoid capture, and 2 hospital ships captured; the Russians lose 1 galley, 1 gunboat and a number of smaller vessels badly damaged.

13 May 1790: Battle in the Roads of Reval (Tallin). Here lies a Russian squadron of 10 ships of the line, 5 frigates and 2 bomb vessels, under Admiral Chichagov in *Rostislav*. The Swedish fleet of 22 ships of the line and 12 frigates attacks, but, as they sail past the Russians, the wind freshens and they become disorganized. Duke Carl breaks off the fight. The Swedes lose the now-uncontrollable *Prins Karl*, as well as 130 dead and wounded and 600 prisoners. Russian losses are negligible.

3–4 June 1790: Battle of the Bay of Kronstadt (Cape Styrsudden, or Krasnala Gorka). At the end of May, the main Russian fleet, under Admiral Kruse, makes for the open sea. It includes 17 ships of the line and 19 frigates, with 1,600 guns. In order to prevent the union of this force with the Russian Reval squadron, the Swedes attack with a fleet of equal strength on 3 June. The whole day is taken up with a long-range artillery duel, the Russians always to the east, in the direction of Kronstadt.

4 June: The fight is renewed at 2pm and, at 9pm, Chichagov's Reval squadron arrives. The Swedes break off the fight before the Russians unite, and run into the Bay of Vyborg, where the Swedish galley fleet is waiting. The Swedes are at once blockaded by the Russians.

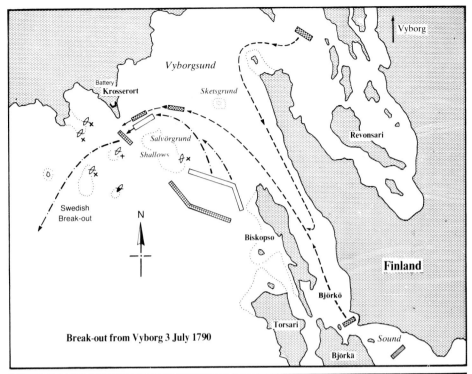

Break-out from Vyborg 3 July 1790

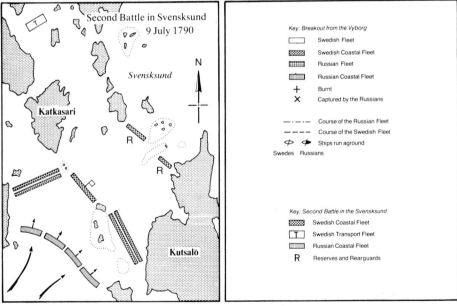

Second Battle in Svensksund
9 July 1790

Key: Breakout from the Vyborg

▢	Swedish Fleet
▨	Swedish Coastal Fleet
▥	Russian Fleet
▦	Russian Coastal Fleet
+	Burnt
×	Captured by the Russians
—·—·—	Course of the Russian Fleet
— — —	Course of the Swedish Fleet
⊅ ⊅	Ships run aground
Swedes Russians	

Key: Second Battle in the Svensksund

▨	Swedish Coastal Fleet
T	Swedish Transport Fleet
▦	Russian Coastal Fleet
R	Reserves and Rearguards

3 July 1790: Break-out of the Swedish Fleet from Vyborg. After a long delay, the Swedish king (with the galley fleet) orders a break-out attempt. Chichagov is anchored across the entrance of the bay, with 31 ships of the line, 24 frigates and a large number of smaller vessels; the Swedes have 21 ships of the line, 15 frigates and 240 smaller units—in all, 3,000 guns, 24,000 men, plus 120 transports carrying 12,000 soldiers. In the morning, the Swedes mount a surprise attack on the western flank of the Russian fleet, the galleys and transports moving under the covering fire of the bigger ships. The Russian ships are badly battered by the passing Swedish ships, and almost all of the latter manage to escape. Four ships of the line run aground, one of which is ignited by a Swedish fire-ship, and explodes. The Russians manage to capture 2 more Swedish stragglers in the ensuing chase, while the galley fleet keeps to shallow waters and escapes to Svensksund. The Swedes lose 7 ships of the line, 3 frigates, 30 smaller warships, 30 transports and 6,000 men; 11 Russian ships of the line are out of action and they lose 7,000 men. The well executed Swedish break-out has not only succeeded, but heavier losses have been inflicted than sustained in the operation.

9–10 July 1790: Second Battle in Svensksund (or Rochensalm). The Russian inshore fleet attacks the Swedes. The strengths are as follows.

	SWEDEN	RUSSIA
Ships	195	140
Total no. guns	1,200	1,500
Total crews	14,000	18,500

The Swedish inshore fleet is anchored in a strong L-shaped formation in Svensksund. The Russians attack from the south, and are badly mauled by the Swedish fire. Next day, the Swedes counterattack, and the Russians flee, in disorder, towards Aspo. Russian losses are 64 vessels, 6,000 men captured and 3,000 dead and wounded: Swedish losses are very light. Catherine of Russia is now ready to make peace.

14 Aug 1790: Peace of Verela (Wereloe). The status quo is restored.

This was the last war in which large numbers of oar-propelled vessels were to be used; however, in the course of the fighting, both gun punts and gunboats had proved their worth.

The climax of the long series of wars between Britain and France was now at hand. The French Revolution in 1789 acted as the trigger to over twenty years of warfare, both in Europe and in the colonies.

The British navy started the war at some advantage, with an officer corps second to none, well-trained and experienced crews, and adequate dockyards and equipment. The backbone of the fleet would still be the two-decker with 74 guns, but there were also some 100-gun three-deckers (with a displacement of 2,300 tons and a crew of 850). The 'workhorse' of the fleet was the frigate, which by now could be as large as 1,000 tons.

The French navy was not so well off, for about 80% of the officers of the pre-Revolution navy had disappeared; their replacements lacked training and experience. Dockyards and arsenals were also in a poor state, and the British blockade soon made it difficult to get materials to equip the ships. On average, the French warships were bigger and heavier than the British; the three-deckers carried 116 guns, displaced about 3,000 tons and had crews of 1,300 men.

The Spanish ships were generally in good condition, but they lacked trained manpower. Holland's fleet was in good condition too, and there were adequate well-trained crews; but the smaller ships of the line, designed for action in shallow coastal waters were much inferior as fighting units to their larger adversaries. The relative strength of the four navies, in ships of the line started as follows: Britain, 115; France, 80; Spain, 60; Netherlands, 50.

1793-1802: THE FRENCH REVOLUTIONARY WARS

1792: France is proclaimed a republic and declares war on Austria. In the War of the First Coalition (1792–97), almost all France's neighbours oppose her.

Feb 1793: England enters the war, after France has executed Louis XVI and occupied the Austrian Netherlands (Modern Belgium).

Aug 1793: French Royalists surrender Toulon to the British Mediterranean fleet under Admiral Samuel Hood. The British and Spanish occupy the town, and the 31 ships of the line (plus 27 frigates and corvettes) of the French Mediterranean fleet thus fall into Allied hands. Toulon is now beseiged by the forces of the French Convention.

17 Dec 1793: The Allies evacuate Toulon; but nothing has been prepared for the removal of the French ships, so only 3 of them are taken away and 9 others are burned. The rest are later repaired by the French and put back into service.

28 May to 1 June 1794: The Glorious First of June (Battle of Ushant). Shortage of food in France leads to large quantities of grain being bought in America and transported across the Atlantic in a large convoy of merchantmen. The French Brest squadron is sent out to escort the convoy in. Four hundred nautical miles west of Ushant, they meet the British blockade squadron under Admiral Howe (flagship *Queen Charlotte*, 100 guns), with 26 ships of the line. The equally strong French squadron is commanded by Rear

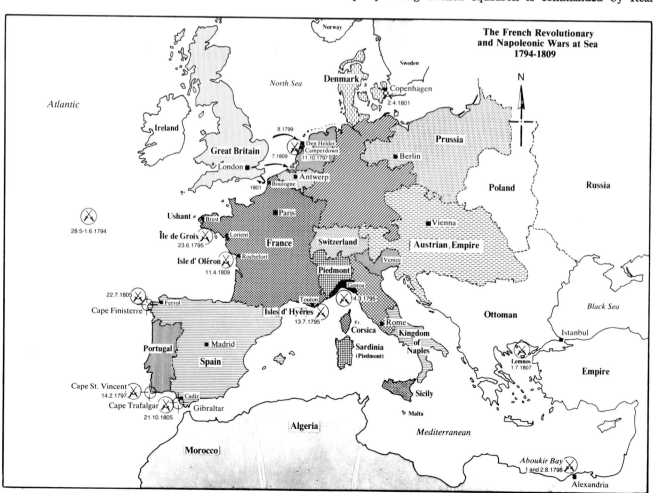

The French Revolutionary and Napoleonic Wars at Sea 1794-1809

Admiral Villaret-Joyeuse in the 120-gun *Montagne*.

28 May: On the first day, the only fighting is between some British 74s and the French 3-decker *Révolutionnaire* (110), after which the French ship and the British *Audacious* have to retire badly damaged.

29 May: Next morning, the opposing fleets form line ahead, the British on the lee side. Howe orders his ships to pass through the French line in order to obtain the weather gage, but only a few ships obey. Some French warships are badly damaged and, after an 8-hour fight, the French fleet withdraws. *Tyrannicide* and *Indomptable* are towed home by other ships.

30 May: Villaret, his losses replaced by warships of the convoy escort, draws the British after him, and the convoy crosses the battle area of the last few days unimpaired.

30–31 May: Bad visibility prevents combat.

1 June: The fleets, both on a westerly course, meet: this time the British are on the windward side, and they attack energetically. Some of them break through the French line, and both fleets suffer heavy losses in the close combat. After a duel between the flagships lasting several hours, *Montagne* breaks away from her opponent. Villaret finally succeeds in re-forming his battle line on an easterly course. Eight of the badly damaged French ships are cut off and forced to strike their colours; one of these is subsequently recaptured by the French. *Vengeur du Peuple* is so battered by *Brunswick* that she sinks. Early in the afternoon, Villaret breaks off the

fight and returns to Brest, towing a number of dismasted vessels. The British fleet is so badly battered that Howe does not pursue. French losses are 7 ships of the line (of these 1 sinks); others badly damaged and 7,000 men dead, wounded and captured. Howe has 8 ships badly damaged and 1,150 casualties; he needs several days to secure the captured ships. In spite of this tactical defeat, the French succeed in their strategic aim of bringing the grain convoy in to Brest, repulsing Montagu's attack on the 9th.

1794: Holland is occupied by French troops and, as the Batavian Republic, becomes a French satellite. An amphibious force, under Samuel Hood and Nelson, captures Corsica. (Nelson loses the sight of an eye in the fighting.)

Jan 1795: The Brest fleet loses 5 ships of the line in a storm.

1795: Peace of Basle. Prussia leaves the Coalition.

14 March 1795: Action off Genoa. The British Mediterranean fleet (13 ships of the line under Vice Admiral Hotham) meets a French squadron of 15 ships of the line under Rear Admiral Martin, on an expedition to recapture Corsica. As a result of the action the French lose 2 ships and their expedition to Corsica is frustrated; a damaged British ship later sinks off La Spezia.

17 June 1795: Action off Belle Isle. In the north of the Bay of Biscay, Vice Admiral Cornwallis (GB), with 5 ships of the line, encounters 12 French ships of the line under Admiral Villaret-Joyeuse. In a skilful withdrawal, Cornwallis avoids loss, and Villaret breaks off the chase fearing the intervention

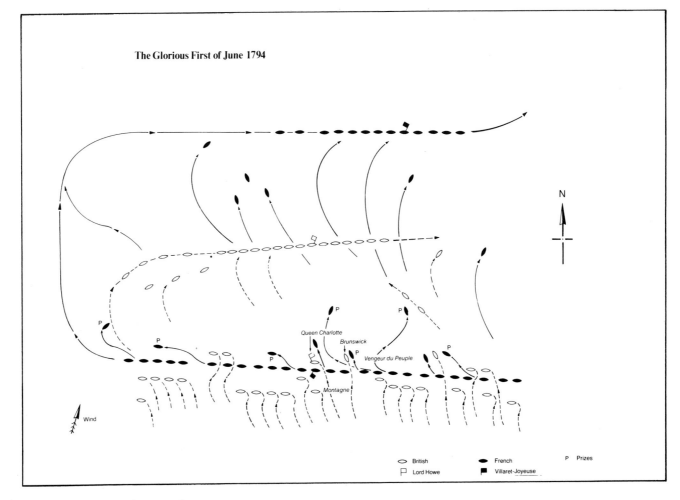

The Glorious First of June 1794

N

Wind

○ British   ● French   P Prizes
⌂ Lord Howe   ◼ Villaret-Joyeuse

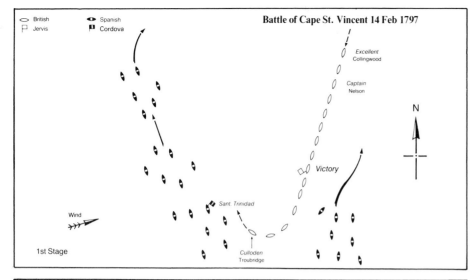

Battle of Cape St. Vincent 14 Feb 1797

1st Stage

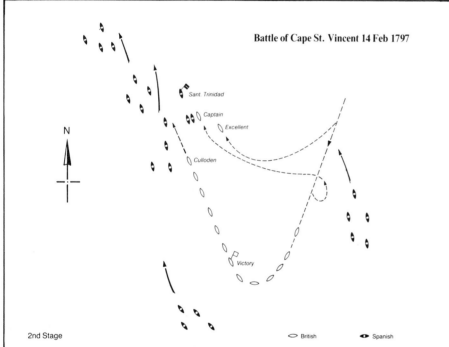

Battle of Cape St. Vincent 14 Feb 1797

2nd Stage

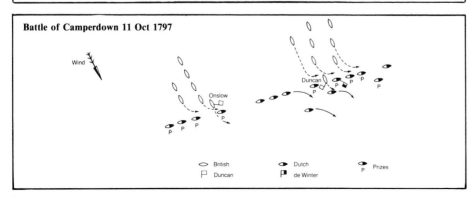

Battle of Camperdown 11 Oct 1797

of the British main fleet.

23 June 1795: Action off the Île de Groix. Admiral Alexander Hood's blockade squadron of 14 ships of the line, off Brest, meets 12 French ships of the line under Villaret-Joyeuse. In a pursuit battle, the French lose 3 ships; the rest escape to Lorient.

13 July 1795: Action off the Hyères Islands (near Toulon). The British Mediterranean fleet, 23 ships of the line under Vice Admiral Hotham, meets 17 French ships of the line under Rear Admiral Martin. After a short skirmish, the French lose 1 ship which catches fire and blows up.

1796: Treaty of Ildefonso. Spain allies with France against Britain. This (as well as French victories ashore) poses a serious threat to British naval forces in the Mediterranean: Corsica and Elba are evacuated, and, in December, Jervis removes his fleet to Gibraltar, in order to concentrate on activities off the Atlantic coasts of Spain and Portugal.

End of 1796: French Expedition to Ireland. An army under General Hoche is taken aboard the French Brest fleet under Vice Admiral Morard de Galles. They successfully avoid the British blockading force, but a storm allows only 35 ships under Rear Admiral Bouvet to reach the Irish coast and, since he cannot decide on independent action, he returns to Brest in January 1797.

Jan 1797: Success of the French army under General Napoleon Bonaparte in Italy.

14 Feb 1797: Battle of Cape St. Vincent. The Spanish Mediterranean fleet, under Don José de Cordova, is en route to Brest to unite with the French Atlantic squadron. After passing through the Straits of Gibraltar, they come upon Admiral Sir John Jervis's Mediterranean Fleet off Cadiz. The Spanish have 27 ships of the line; flagship is the huge *Santissima Trinidad*, a 4-decker with 130 guns. The British squadron has 15 ships of the line, and the flagship is *Victory*, with 100 guns. The Spanish sail in two irregular groups, 8 ships some miles east of the main body, while Jervis, in line ahead, comes from the north, splitting the two Spanish groups. The British ships then turn north, and attack the main Spanish group from astern. In order to prevent a junction of the two parts of the Spanish fleet to the north of the British, the third-from-last British ship, *Captain* (under Commodore Nelson), leaves the battle line independently and attacks the leading Spanish ship. The rearmost British ship, *Excellent* (Captain Collingwood), follows Nelson and, for some time, these 2 ships fight the Spanish alone, until the leading British ships, *Culloden* in the van, join them. Nelson personally boards the Spanish *San Nicolas* and *San José*, and two other Spanish ships are captured. Jervis then breaks off the fight and secures his prizes, while Cordova runs into Cadiz. Apart from the 4 ships lost, the Spaniards have 10 ships badly damaged and 5,000 men dead, wounded or captured; 5 British ships have been badly damaged, and 300 men lost. Jervis seizes the opportunity to blockade the Spanish fleet in Cadiz.

24/25 July 1797: An attack on the harbour of Santa Cruz de Teneriffa by a British squadron under Nelson (now a rear admiral) fails; the silver convoy is not in the harbour, as had been expected. In spite of this, Nelson attempts a landing, which is repulsed with heavy loss. Nelson loses his right arm in the fighting.

17 Oct 1797: France forces Austria to the Peace of Campo Formio. In exchange for Milan and Belgium, Austria receives Venice, bringing to an end the independence of the 1,000-year-old republic. France takes from Venice the Ionian islands and her fleet, thus securing her position in the Mediterranean. Britain is now France's only opponent.

11 Oct 1797: Battle of Camperdown. The Dutch fleet, under Admiral de Winter, is to cover a landing of French troops in Ireland. Soon after leaving the Texel, the Dutch meet a British squadron under Admiral Duncan (which has been blockading them since summer). Both sides have 16 ships of the line, but the Dutch are considerably smaller. The British attack from the weather side in two columns: both leading ships pierce the enemy line, and the following ships come alongside the enemy on the weather side. (A style of attack similar to that used eight years later by Nelson at Trafalgar.) In a bloody fight, in which the Dutch put up bitter resistance, the British take 9 ships. The rest escape, and the British squadron is in no condition to pursue. Each side loses about 1,000 men, and the planned expedition to Ireland is delayed.

April–Aug 1797: Mutinies in the Royal Navy. Arduous blockade duty, arrears of pay, lack of leave, bad treatment and bad food lead to mutinies of the Channel Fleet at the Nore and Spithead. Howe and Jervis can only restore discipline with draconian measures.

May 1798: Napoleon Bonaparte leaves Toulon, with a transport fleet of 400 ships carrying an army of 36,000 men and 2,000 cannon. The Mediterranean fleet under Vice Admiral Brueys provides the escort. A reconnaissance squadron of frigates is formed.

10–12 June 1798: The French capture Malta.

May 1798: Britain sends a squadron under Rear Admiral Nelson to the Mediterranean to find the French fleet. Bonaparte meanwhile lands in Alexandria to conquer Egypt, and the fleet anchors in Aboukir Bay, at the mouth of the River Nile.

1–2 Aug 1798: Battle of the Nile (Aboukir Bay). Brueys has 13 ships of the line and 4 frigates; flagship is the 3-decker *L'Orient* (120 guns). The French ships total 1,200 guns, but not even the guns of one broadside can be manned as most of the crews are on shore getting water. The ships lie north-west to south-east, the van just south of Aboukir Island.

1 Aug, 2pm: Nelson appears with his 14 ships (1,000 guns); two of the ships are still off Alexandria harbour and do not arrive until nightfall, and *Culloden* runs aground off Aboukir Island and is also not available for the battle.

4.30pm: Nelson opens the battle with his available 11 ships. The first 5 ships pass inside the French van, while Nelson (in his flagship *Vanguard*) and the other ships attack from the seaward side. In a light north-westerly wind, the French ships lie at bow anchors; the English ships are anchored at the stern.

8pm: The French van is thus attacked from both sides by superior forces. *Bellerophon*, however, anchors opposite *L'Orient*, and, after an hour, has been shot to a wreck; *Majestic* is also badly damaged and lets herself drift.

Nightfall: The 5 leading French ships are by now battered into silence by the superior British fire. The British ships thus released from that fight, together with the newly arrived *Alexander* and *Swiftsure*, now attack the French centre.

10pm: *L'Orient* catches fire and explodes. In the next hour, *Tonnant* and *Franklin* both strike their flags after bitter resistance. Two other ships run aground.

2 Aug, 3am: After a short pause, the British attack the French rear (which is under the command of Rear Admiral Villeneuve); until now, it has taken no part in the battle. *Timoléon* is beached and set on fire by her crew and Villeneuve, distinguished by his extraordinary day-long inactivity, escapes with 2 ships of the line, *Guillaume Tell* and *Généreux*, plus a frigate. All the other ships are overpowered by the British. French losses are 11 ships of the line and 2 frigates, 1,700 men dead, 1,500 wounded and 3,000 captured. Some British ships are badly damaged and they lose just 1,000 dead and wounded, but they take 6 of the captured enemy ships of the line home as prizes. The Battle of the Nile as well as being a brilliant tactical tour de force, also has extensive strategic and political consequences: the French army in Egypt is cut off from France, Britain again controls the Mediterranean and is able to re-form a coalition against France.

12 Oct 1798: Action off Lough Swilly. The French try to land 3,000 men in Ireland with 1 ship of the line and 8 frigates. In a clash with 3 British ships of the line and 5 frigates, they lose their ship of the line and 3 frigates. A few days later, the French lose 3 more frigates.

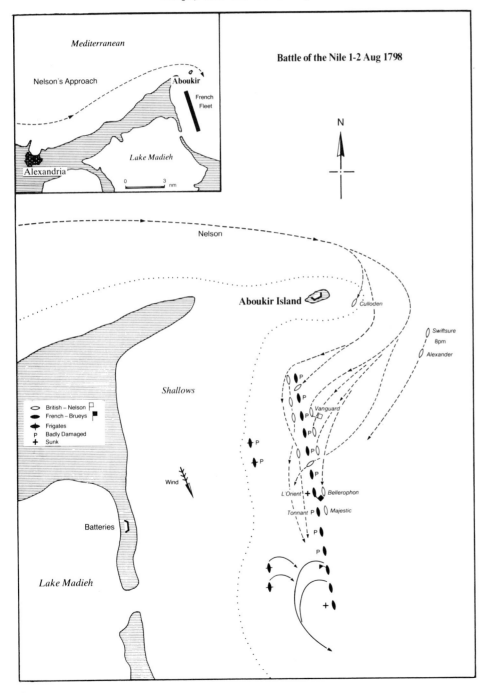

Battle of the Nile 1-2 Aug 1798

Mediterranean

Nelson's Approach

Aboukir

French Fleet

Alexandria

Lake Madieh

0   3   nm

N

Nelson

Aboukir Island

Culloden

Swiftsure
8pm

Alexander

Shallows

British – Nelson
French – Brueys
Frigates
P Badly Damaged
+ Sunk

Vanguard

Wind

L'Orient   Bellerophon

Tonnant P   Majestic

Batteries

Lake Madieh

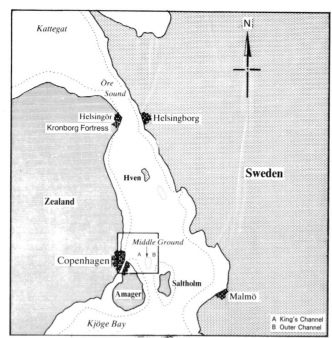

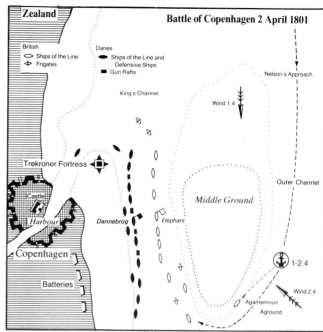

1799: The Second Coalition. Turkey, Russia, Austria, Naples and Portugal join Britain against France.

March 1799: Russo-Turkish forces capture the Ionian Islands.

Aug 1799: Landing in Holland. The British fleet with 250 transports, under Admiral Duncan, lands an army of 30,000 men (including 2,000 Russians) at Den Helder, and also captures some Dutch Republican ships of the line. But two months later the French force the expeditionary army to re-embark.

Oct 1799: Napoleon Bonaparte returns to France from Egypt. Following his coup d'état he becomes effectively the dictator of France. Russia, meanwhile, leaves the Coalition.

Sept 1800: The French garrison on Malta surrenders to the British blockading fleet.

Feb 1801: Treaty of Lunéville. After her defeats at Marengo and Hohenlinden, Austria is forced to adhere to the provisions of the Peace of Campo Formio. Britain is again France's only opponent.

Spring 1801: Renewal of the 'Armed Neutrality of the North' by Scandinavian states and Russia.

8 March 1801: In face of French opposition, the British land troops in Aboukir Bay: within a few months, almost all French forces in Egypt are forced to surrender.

2 April 1801: Battle of Copenhagen. Britain sends a squadron under Admiral Sir Hyde Parker to Denmark; second in command is Vice Admiral Nelson. Parker's task is to persuade Denmark to revoke its armed neutrality, and he brings 20 ships of the line, 5 frigates and 28 other warships to the Sound. His flagship is *London* (98); Nelson's is *Elephant* (74). The Danes expect an attack and are prepared, but entry into the Copenhagen roads is also complicated by shallows and islands in the Sound. The Middle Ground sandbank divides the channel into two arms, the King's Channel and the Outer Channel. In the northern entrance to the King's Channel, the strong Trekroner fort covers the entry to Copenhagen harbour and, south of this, are the floating defences, consisting of 2 ships of the line, 1 frigate, 8 defence ships and 7 gun rafts or floating batteries. The defence ships are old, stripped-down ships of the line and

frigates, and are commanded by Commodore Fischer in *Dannebrog*. Parker leaves Nelson to attack the Danish fleet, and Nelson decides to attack from the south in order to avoid Trekroner. He commands 12 ships of the line, 5 frigates and 19 other vessels. On the night of 1st, Nelson takes his squadron through the Outer Channel and the Sound, and awaits a southerly wind. The rest of the British fleet anchors off the Middle Ground.

2 April, 9am: The wind turns and Nelson attacks; one ship of the line goes aground on the sandbanks, but the other ships anchor about 500 metres from the Dutch vessels. The British have over 600 cannon, 60 carronades and 9,000 men; the Danes have 370 guns and 6,000 men.

10am: A bitter battle begins in which the Danes resist stoutly.

1pm: Three British ships of the line are already badly damaged and run aground near Trekroner. At this, Hyde Parker gives the signal to break off the battle, but Nelson ignores it, considering that to take the already damaged ships past Trekroner would be disastrous.

3pm: After a further 2 hours combat, 11 Danish ships have struck their colours and Nelson offers them an armistice (which he hopes will also allow him to escape from his precarious position). The Danes accept, and Nelson is able to sail his battered squadron to safety past Trekroner. The Danish defensive line loses 15 ships, even though the British are only able to take one as a prize. Danish casualties are over 1,000 dead and wounded and 2,000 prisoners, to 1,200 British dead and wounded. Shortly after this battle, Denmark agrees to the British demands, a decision influenced by the murder of Tsar Paul I, the main driving force behind the armed neutrality.

6 July 1801: Action off Algeciras (Straits of Gibraltar). Three French ships of the line, under Admiral Linois, repel an attack by Admiral Saumarez's 6 English ships, and capture one of them which has gone aground.

12 July 1801: Night action off Cadiz. A Franco-Spanish squadron of 9 ships of the line under Linois encounters a British squadron under Admiral Saumarez. Linois loses 3 ships to the British 1.

15 Aug 1801: An attempt by a British flotilla of gunboats, under Vice Admiral Nelson, to destroy French landing craft at Boulogne fails with heavy loss.

1801: Robert Fulton builds a primitive submarine and offers it to the French for use against the British blockading fleet, but his offer is rejected.

March 1802: Peace of Amiens. Pitt's government falls, and the Anglo-French struggle pauses. Britain gives up her colonial conquests, except for Ceylon and Trinidad; France completes her evacuation of Egypt.

During the French Revolutionary Wars, naval tactics revived after a long lapse: Howe, Jervis, Duncan and, above all, Nelson had shown the value of concentration of force and the advantage to be gained by breaking the enemy line. In the overall strategy of the war, colonies were of but secondary importance, although in the early years of the conflict, the British had succeeded in taking some West Indian islands from the French and, when Holland became a French satellite, had begun to capture Dutch colonies too. Cape Colony, Malacca, Ceylon and all the Dutch possessions in the West Indies fell into British hands. And, when Spain joined in, her colonies became fair game as well: in capturing Trinidad, 4 Spanish ships of the line had also been taken. With the passage of time, however, the struggle at sea became increasingly a blockade war. The important French, Spanish and Dutch harbours, such as Brest, Toulon, Cadiz, Rochefort and Den Helder, were each blockaded by a British squadron that watched for every move the enemy should make, and left its station only in the severest storms. French, Spanish and Dutch trade was now crippled; even neutral vessels (which had increased rapidly in numbers) were being stopped and searched for contraband by the Royal Navy.

1803–15: THE NAPOLEONIC WARS

Following his seizure of power in 1799, Napoleon Bonaparte rules France; and in 1804, after a plebiscite, he crowns himself 'Emperor of the French'. In Britain, Pitt the younger takes over leadership of the government again. A squabble over the return of Malta, ostensible French invasion preparations in the Channel, and their occupation of Hanover cause Britain to declare war again. Pitt forms the Third Coalition with Russia (Alexander I), Austria (Francis II), Sweden and Naples; Spain is again a French ally. The French fleet is in as bad a condition as it was at the outbreak of the Revolutionary Wars, and England at once imposes a blockade of enemy harbours. Relative naval strengths (combat-ready ships of the line) are: Britain 120; France 40; Spain 30; Holland 20.

1803–5: At Boulogne, Napoleon prepares for an invasion of England. An army of 130,000 men is concentrated and 2,000 transport vessels prepared. As the Channel crossing must be covered by a battle fleet, the French squadrons begin to make break-out attempts from their various harbours. Relative strengths, in ships of the line, at the end of March are:

AREA	FRANCE/SPAIN		BRITAIN	
Texel	9		11	
Brest	21	(Gantaume)	17	(Cornwallis)
Lorient	3		–	
Ferrol	12		8	(Calder)
Cadiz	7	(Gravina)	6	
Cartagena	6		–	
Toulon	11	(Villeneuve)	11	(Nelson)

March 1805: Villeneuve slips out of Toulon; he is joined in Cadiz by Gravina, with 6 ships of the line. The Allied fleet now sets sail for the West Indies. Nelson at first assumes that they have gone to the eastern Mediterranean.

May 1805: Only a month later does he follow Villeneuve to the West Indies, where the Allied fleet has captured a British convoy of 14 ships. Villeneuve learns of Nelson's arrival in the West Indies, and sets sail back to Europe.

June 1805: The British Admiralty, informed by Nelson of fleet movements, reinforces the squadron off Ferrol, and warns Cornwallis at Brest. Nelson leaves the West Indies 3 days after Villeneuve, and heads for Cadiz.

July 1805: As soon as Nelson, at the Straits of Gibraltar, learns that he has missed Villeneuve again, he sails his squadron to meet Cornwallis at Brest, and goes himself to Portsmouth. Meanwhile, the dispositions arranged by the First Lord of the Admiralty, Admiral Lord Barham, begin to bear fruit; upon his return to Europe, Villeneuve meets the reinforced blockade squadron at Ferrol.

22 July 1805: Battle of Cape Finisterre. Villeneuve, with 20 ships of the line and 7 frigates, is opposed by Vice-Admiral Calder, with 15 ships of the line and 2 frigates. At noon, and in spite of the misty weather, Calder attacks, trying to cut off the enemy rear. But bad visibility renders the fleets uncontrollable for a fleet action. The British do succeed in forcing 2 Spanish ships to strike their colours, but the battle is indecisive. Casualties are 200 British and 500 of the Allies. Calder contents himself with bringing in his prizes, while Villeneuve runs into Ferrol. (Calder's failure to bring the enemy to a decisive action earns him a court martial and severe reprimand.)

Aug 1805: Villeneuve leaves Ferrol with 29 ships of the line, to unite with the Rochefort squadron and then enter the Channel. The rendezvous fails and Villeneuve returns to Cadiz. Napoleon now abandons his invasion plans for England, and turns on his mainland enemies.

1805: The War of the Third Coalition. While Napoleon advances through south Germany against Austria, Collingwood blockades Cadiz, until Vice Admiral Nelson assumes command of the blockade fleet. A threatened removal from command forces Villeneuve to break out of Cadiz in October, in order to go into the Mediterranean. Alerted by his patrol frigates, Nelson takes up the chase and in the afternoon of 20 October, Villeneuve is sighted by the English fleet. He turns north, intending to give battle next day.

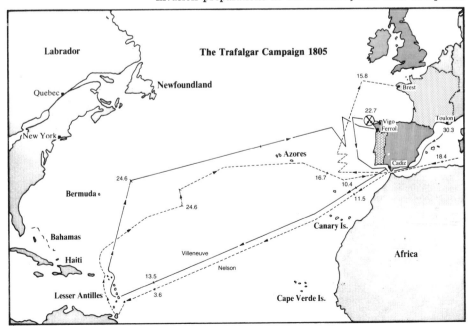

The Trafalgar Campaign 1805

Labrador · Quebec · Newfoundland · New York · Bermuda · Bahamas · Haiti · Lesser Antilles · Azores · Canary Is. · Cape Verde Is. · Africa · Brest · Vigo · Ferrol · Toulon · Cadiz · Villeneuve · Nelson

15.8 · 22.7 · 30.3 · 18.4 · 24.6 · 16.7 · 10.4 · 11.5 · 24.6 · 13.5 · 3.6

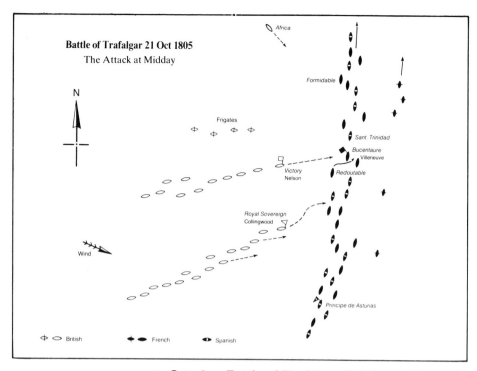

Battle of Trafalgar 21 Oct 1805
The Attack at Midday

N

Africa

Formidable

Frigates

Sant. Trinidad

Bucentaure
Villeneuve

Victory
Nelson

Redoutable

Royal Sovereign
Collingwood

Wind

Principe de Asturias

⊄ ○ British   ◆—● French   ◖ Spanish

21 Oct 1805: Battle of Trafalgar. Relative naval strengths this day are as follows.

	BRITAIN	ALLIES	
Ships of the line	27	33	(15 Spanish)
Frigates	4	5	
Total no. guns	2,500	3,000	
Total crews	20,000	30,000	

Nelson's flagship is *Victory*; second in command is Collingwood in *Royal Sovereign*. Commander-in-Chief on the Allied side is Villeneuve in *Bucentaure*; commander of the Spanish squadron (and commander of the rear) is Admiral Gravina. The Allied van is commanded by Rear Admiral Dumanoir (F) in *Formidable*.

11am: The Allied fleet sails north in a rather disorderly formation; Spanish and French ships are mixed throughout the fleet. As soon as he receives sighting reports from his patrolling frigates, Nelson orders an attack based on a plan previously discussed in great detail with his captains: further commands are unnecessary. Nelson attacks from the west in two columns, leading the van (or weather division) of 12 ships himself; Collingwood leads the rear (lee) division. There is only a light wind, but signs of a gathering storm are evident and, with a coast close in their lee, this could be dangerous for the fleets. Nelson's column is to pierce the enemy line at the point of their flagship, hold this ship in close combat, and prevent any interference from the van; the southern column is to attack the Allied rear. This concentration of forces ensures superiority of numbers for the British at the beginning of the battle.

Midday: Collingwood's *Royal Sovereign* is the first ship to break the Allied line, and Nelson's *Victory* leads the other prong through soon after. All British ships follow closely, and at once close up to the enemy.

1.30pm: *Victory* comes up to *Redoutable*, and a marksman in her rigging mortally wounds Nelson. With the aid of *Téméraire*, *Redoutable* is taken and, shortly afterwards, *Téméraire* captures *Fougueux*. The other ships of the northern column attack *Bucentaure* and *Santissima Trinidad* (strongest ship of the fleet and the only four-decker) with superior numbers: both are overwhelmed, and Villeneuve is captured. Meanwhile, Collingwood's ships are in close combat with the Allied rear.

4pm: By this time, 15 ships of the line are already out of action. Nelson hears of his victory just before he dies at 4.30 pm. Now some of the Allied van join the battle, attacking the already badly battered *Victory*, but other British ships come to her aid at once. The Allies lose *Neptuno* and *San Augustino*; Dumanoir, with the van, who has not yet really felt the heat of battle, breaks off the fight, and the mortally wounded Gravina collects the remaining Allied ships of the centre and rear and withdraws to Cadiz.

5.30pm: *Achille*, which has been burning for some time, explodes. The real battle is now over. The Allies have lost 18 ships, 17 of which are in the hands of the victors, 2,600 men are dead or wounded, and 7,000 prisoners are on the prizes in enemy hands. The British lose no ships, but 1,700 men are casualties, and half of the ships are badly damaged. Collingwood now faces a difficult task: to bring his fleet and the prizes to safety in the gathering storm. *Redoutable* sinks the next day, while in tow.

23 Oct 1805: Commodore Cosmao (F), with 5 ships of the line and 5 frigates, recaptures 2 prizes from the British; 9 other prizes run aground or have to be scuttled or burnt by the British, as they cannot be brought to safety. The badly damaged *Berwick* also runs aground. Only 4 of the prizes survive the night at anchor in the storm, and can be taken to Gibraltar; the Allies lose 5 of their surviving ships in the

BRITISH WEATHER DIVISION			BRITISH LEE DIVISION			FRANCE			SPAIN		
Victory	100	(b)	*Royal Sovereign*	100	(b)	*Bucentaure*	80	(c)	*Principe de Asturias*	112	(e)
Téméraire	98	(b)	*Belleisle*	74	(b)	*Redoutable*	74	(cd)	*Montannes*	74	(e)
Neptune	98	(e)	*Mars*	74	(b)	*Indomptable*	80	(e)	*Argonauta*	80	(c)
Conquerer	74	(a)	*Tonnant*	80	(b)	*Neptune*	80	(a)	*Bahama*	74	(c)
Leviathan	74	(a)	*Bellerophon*	74	(b)	*Fougueux*	74	(c)	*San Juan de Nepumuceno*	74	(c)
Britannia	100	(e)	*Colossus*	74	(b)	*Pluton*	74	(e)	*San Ildefonso*	74	(c)
Agamemnon	64	(a)	*Achilles*	74	(e)	*Intrépide*	74	(c)	*San Justo*	74	
Ajax	74	(a)	*Polyphemus*	64	(a)	*Algésiras*	74	(c)	*Santissima Trinidad*	130	(c)
Orion	74	(a)	*Revenge*	74	(c)	*Berwick*	74	(c)	*San Leandro*	64	
Minotaur	74	(a)	*Swiftsure*	74	(e)	*Aigle*	74	(c)	*Santa Ana*	112	(c)
Spartiate	74	(a)	*Defiance*	74	(e)	*Swiftsure*	74	(c)	*Monarca*	74	(c)
Africa	64	(b)	*Thunderer*	74	(e)	*Argonaute*	74	(e)	*Neptuno*	74	(c)
			Defence	74	(a)	*Achille*	74	(d)	*San Augustino*	74	(c)
			Dreadnought	98	(a)	*Scipion*	74	(a)	*Rayo*	100	(e)
			Prince	98		*Formidable*	80	(a)	*San Francisco de Asis*	74	(e)
						Mont Blanc	74	(a)			
						Duguay Trouin	74	(a)			
						Héros	74	(e)			

Key: a, lightly damaged; b, badly damaged; c, prize; d, sunk; e, unspecified damage.

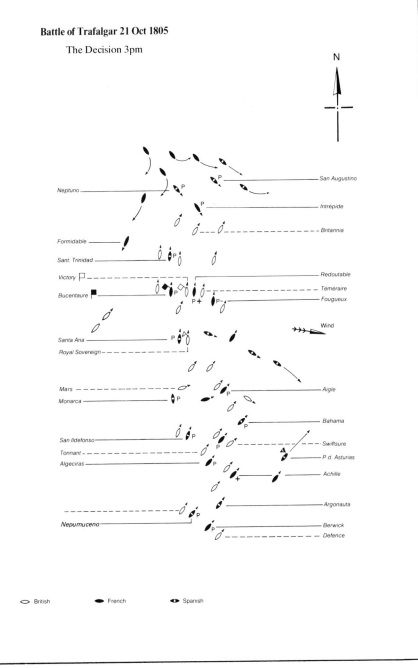

Battle of Trafalgar 21 Oct 1805

The Decision 3pm

N

Neptuno
San Augustino
Intrépide
Britannia
Formidable
Sant. Trinidad
Redoutable
Victory
Téméraire
Bucentaure
Fougueux
Wind
Santa Ana
Royal Sovereign
Mars
Aigle
Monarca
Bahama
San Ildefonso
Swiftsure
Tonnant
P.d. Asturias
Algeciras
Achille
Argonauta
Nepumuceno
Berwick
Defence

○ British   ● French   ◐ Spanish

same storm. The 5 French ships which escaped from the battle are now blockaded in Cadiz (and fall into Spanish hands when that country rises against Napoleon in 1808). Britain is now in unlimited command of the seas.

4 Nov 1805: Action off Cape Ortegal. Dumanoir, with his 4 surviving ships of the line, meets a British squadron of 4 ships of the line and 4 frigates under Captain Sir Richard Strachan. All 4 French ships are dismasted, captured, and eventually added to the Royal Navy.

25 Dec 1805: Peace of Pressburg. After the Battle of Austerlitz (the 'Battle of the Three Emperors'), Austria comes to terms with Napoleon. Britain continues the fight.

Jan 1806: Commodore Popham (GB) captures Cape Town with 4 ships of the line, 4 other vessels and 4,000 troops.

23 Jan 1806: Death of Pitt the younger. A peace offer by Napoleon is rejected by Britain.

6 Feb 1806: Action in the Roads of San Domingo. Five French ships of the line and 2 frigates break out of Brest and make for the West Indies, there to carry on a successful privateering campaign. Vice Admiral Duckworth (GB) surprises them with 7 ships of the line and 2 frigates in the Roads of San Domingo and in individual combats, 3 French ships are captured, 2 driven ashore.

April 1806: An expedition under Popham against Buenos Aires and Montevideo fails.

8 October 1806: First successful use of the Englishman Congreve's rockets. Eighteen 'rocket boats' set the town of Boulogne afire with 200 rockets.

1 Jan 1807: Captain Brisbane (GB), with 4 frigates, captures the strongly defended island of Curaçao in a bold raid.

1806-7: The War of the Fourth Coalition begins, as Britain, Prussia, Russia and Saxony combine against France.

Oct 1806: Napoleon defeats Prussia and Saxony at the twin battles of Jena and Auerstädt.

21 Nov 1806: Napoleon declares his 'Continental System' operational: Britain is to be ruined by exclusion from European trade.

1806: Under French pressure, Turkey closes the Dardanelles to Russian ships. Russia declares war, and sends a squadron to the Mediterranean.

Feb 1807: A British squadron, under Vice Admiral Duckworth, forces the Dardanelles and appears before Constantinople, demanding the delivery of the Turkish fleet. He is driven off, and sustains heavy damage.

1 July 1807: Battle of Lemnos (Athos). The Russian Mediterranean squadron, under Vice Admiral Senjavin (10 ships of the line and 2 frigates), brings the Turkish fleet (10 ships of the line and 5 frigates) to battle off the Dardanelles. After 3 hours, the Turks flee and, in the 4-day pursuit that ensues, they lose 3 ships and 3 frigates.

July 1807: At the agreement of Tilsit, Prussia loses her possessions west of the Elbe and in Poland; Russia and Prussia undertake to join the Continental System.

Aug 1807: Britain attacks Denmark. As Denmark has been forced into the Continental System, Britain sends a strong force (25 ships of the line, 40 frigates, etc., and 380 transports with 29,000 men) under Admiral Lord Gambier and Lieutenant General Lord Cathcart into the Sound and demands the handing over of the Danish fleet. The demand is rejected, so Gambier attacks: troops land on Zealand and blockade Copenhagen from the land side, while the fleet anchors on the seaward side.

2-4 Sept 1807: Bombardment of Copenhagen. The British fleet bombards the city with incendiary projectiles, including the new Congreve rocket. On 5 September, the Danes surrender, and hand over their fleet (16 ships of the lines, 10 frigates and 43 other vessels). Danish military casualties are 200 dead and 350 wounded; civilian losses are 1,600 dead and 1,000 wounded.

1807-14: Denmark subsequently wages a 'small' war against Britain in the Sound and the Kattegatt, the so-called 'gunboat war'.

Sept 1808: The Russian Mediterranean fleet, on its way home, is blockaded in Lisbon by the British. Against a promise of free conduct home for the crews, Vice Admiral Senjavin surrenders his ships.

From 1808: By her command of the seas, Britain is now able to prevent the final subjection of Portugal by Napoleon, and can prepare to enter the war in the Iberian Peninsula.

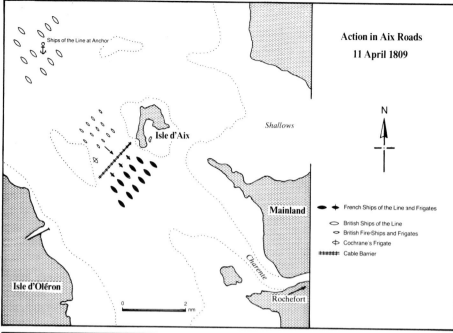

Action in Aix Roads
11 April 1809

Ships of the Line at Anchor

Shallows

Isle d'Aix

N

Mainland

● ┿ French Ships of the Line and Frigates
○ British Ships of the Line
○ British Fire-Ships and Frigates
◇ Cochrane's Frigate
┼┼┼┼┼ Cable Barrier

Charente

Isle d'Oléron

0   2
nm

Rochefort

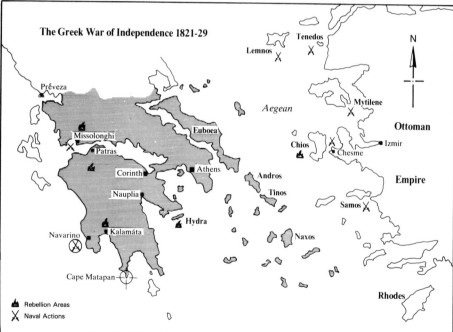

The Greek War of Independence 1821-29

N

Préveza

Tenedos

Lemnos   ✗

✗

Aegean

Mytilene   ✗

Missolonghi

Euboea

Patras   ✗

Ottoman

Chios

Corinth

Athens

Chesme

Izmir

Andros

Nauplia

Tínos

Empire

Samos   ✗

Hydra

Navarino   ⊗

Kalamáta

Naxos

Cape Matapan ⊕

Rhodes

🔥 Rebellion Areas
✗ Naval Actions

1808–9. The Swedish–Russian War

There are numerous clashes between the opposing shallow water fleets, including an action at Sandström (2 Aug 1808), in the Palva Sound (18 Sept 1808) and at Ratan (20 Aug 1809). The main fleets of the two countries are not involved.

10–11 April 1809: Action in Aix Roads (or Oléron Roads). Rear Admiral Willaumez (F) slips out of Brest with 8 ships of the line, and sails to Rochefort, where he anchors in a well-secured position in the Roads of Aix. He is joined by 3 more ships from Rochefort. Admiral Gambier (GB) blockades them with 11 ships of the line, and mounts a night attack with frigates and fire-ships led by Captain Cochrane. However, Gambier fails to support Cochrane at the decisive moment and only 2 of the French ships of the line are scuttled, 2 more and a frigate are burnt, while the remainder escape into the Charente estuary.

Aug 1809: The Walcheren expedition. The British land an army of 40,000 men on the island of Walcheren, with a fleet of 520 transports escorted by 42 ships of the line, 25 frigates and 60 smaller vessels, under Rear Admiral Strachan. Vlissingen is captured, but an assault on Antwerp fails. After considerable losses, the army is re-embarked.

1809: The Fifth Coalition is formed: Austria rises again. Napoleon's first setback at Aspern-Essling (May) is followed by his victory at Wagram (July).

Oct 1809: Peace of Schönbrunn. Austria is further reduced.

26 and 31 Oct 1809: Actions of Cette and Rosas. The British destroy a French squadron, under Rear Admiral Baudin, taking troops to Barcelona.

13 March 1811: Action off Lissa. An English squadron of 4 frigates, under Hoste, defeats a Franco-Venetian squadron of 6 frigates, under Commodore Dubourdieu, who loses 3 frigates, and is killed when his flagship blows up.

June 1812: The United States declares war on Britain, enraged by her handling of neutral shipping (including the impressment of seamen from American ships), and also hoping to acquire Canada.

Nov 1812: Destruction of Napoleon's 'Grande Armée' in Russia.

10 Sept 1813: Action on Lake Erie. A small American squadron under Perry defeats an English squadron under Captain Barclay.

11 Sept 1814: Action on Lake Champlain. An American flotilla under Macdonough defeats a British flotilla, and thus secures the United States northern frontier.

1813: Beginning of the 'Wars of Liberation'. Prussia, Russia, Austria, Britain and Sweden close in upon Napoleon.

Oct 1813: At the 'Battle of the Nations' (Leipzig) Napoleon is defeated in Germany. Forced to abdicate in 1814, his resumption of power in 1815 is ended at the Battle of Waterloo.

1814–15: Congress of Vienna. Britain is the real victor of the war: she acquires Malta, Ceylon, Cape Colony and Heligoland. Russia and Prussia also increase their territories.

During the Napoleonic Wars, aggressive Nelsonian tactics, applied with concentration of force, had brought conflict in the age of sail to peak effectiveness. Decisive victories had been won time and time again, despite all the technical limitations. (The only notable innovation had been the use of Congreve's rockets to bombard Copenhagen, and even these would, in time, be overtaken by improvements in artillery.) And, yet again, the blockade maintained by the British with dogged perseverence, had brought French maritime trade to an almost complete standstill.

1816: Squadrons of ships from Britain, Holland and the

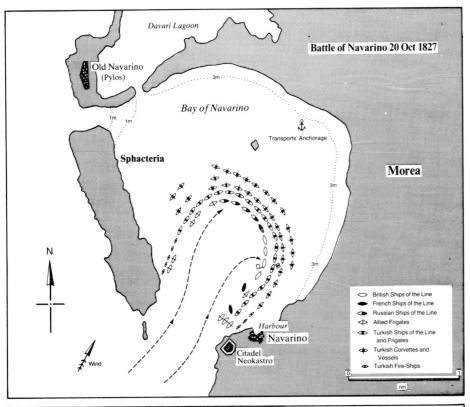

Battle of Navarino 20 Oct 1827

Davari Lagoon

Old Navarino
(Pylos)

Bay of Navarino

3m

1m

1m

Sphacteria

Transports' Anchorage

Morea

3m

3m

N

Harbour

Wind

Navarino

Citadel
Neokastro

⬭	British Ships of the Line
⬬	French Ships of the Line
⬭	Russian Ships of the Line
⬥	Allied Frigates
⬯	Turkish Ships of the Line and Frigates
⬦	Turkish Corvettes and Vessels
⬮	Turkish Fire-Ships

0   1
nm

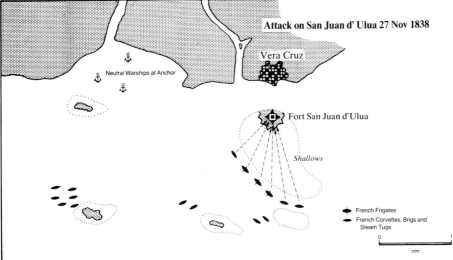

Attack on San Juan d' Ulua 27 Nov 1838

Vera Cruz

Neutral Warships at Anchor

Fort San Juan d'Ulua

Shallows

French Frigates

French Corvettes, Brigs and
Steam Tugs

0   1
nm

United States act against the pirates of the North African coast. An Anglo-Dutch squadron under Lord Exmouth successfully bombards Algiers.

1824: In Burma, the British employ the steam-driven paddle steamer *Diana* against the native craft.

1821–29: The Greek War of Independence

The Greeks fight for their independence against the Turks and, in this struggle, command of the sea plays a role. During the first years, they manage to hold the Turkish fleet in check with an improvised navy.

1821/22: In the Aegean, the Greeks destroy several Turkish ships of the line with fire-ships. (The big Turkish ships abandon the Aegean.) With the support of the Egyptian navy, the Turkish fleet takes the offensive in the Morea.

20 Oct 1827: Battle of Navarino Bay. In the Bay of Navarino lies the Turkish–Egyptian fleet under Admiral Ibrahim Pasha. An Anglo-Franco-Russian fleet, under Vice Admiral Sir Edward Codrington, is to mediate between the Greeks and the Turks. The Turkish ships are anchored in a horse-shoe formation, so that their broadsides cover the harbour entrance. Codrington, ordered to use force only as a last resort, sails into the bay, anchors up against the Turkish ships, and an unintentional battle breaks out. Relative fleet strengths are as follows.

	ALLIES	TURKEY
Ships of the line	11	3
Frigates	9	19
Small vessels	7	35
Total no. guns	1,300	2,000

In the following close combat, the superior training of the European crews is decisive; even the Turkish fire-ships miss their targets and cause damage to their own ships. The Turks resist desperately (only one Turkish ship strikes its flag) but after one hour, the Turkish fleet is destroyed; some of the Turkish ships are destroyed by their own crews. Many of the allied ships are also badly damaged. This is the last great battle of the age of sail, for, with the rapid advance of technology in the 19th century, the days of the 'wooden walls' are over.

1829: Peace of Adrianople. Greece attains political freedom from Turkish rule.

1830: France invades Algeria. Continuing piracy based on north Africa causes France to intervene: a fleet under Admiral Duperré, of 100 men-of-war (including the first French paddle steamer) and 350 transports, lands an army of 38,000 men. (Algeria becomes a French colony in 1847.)

1828–34: The Miguelite Wars (Portugal). The navy is equally divided between the contending parties.

5 July 1833: Action off Cape St. Vincent. Britain's Sir Charles Napier, commanding the 'Liberation squadron', defeats a Miguelite squadron, and then captures Lisbon (24 July).

27 Nov 1838: Attack on San Juan d'Ulua. A French squadron under Rear Admiral Baudin attacks the Mexican harbour of Vera Cruz. With the guns of 3 frigates and 2 corvettes plus other vessels, he silences the strong island fort of San Juan de Ulua. For the first time, the French use the explosive shells developed by the Frenchman Paixhans.

1839–40: The Turko-Egyptian War. The Great Powers intervene.

3/4 Nov 1840: Capture of St. Jean d'Acre. A combined squadron of 8 ships of the line, 5 frigates, 2 brigs and 5 steamers (including 3 Austrian and Turkish warships) under Vice Admiral Stopford forces the strong fortress to surrender, after a bombardment lasting some hours.

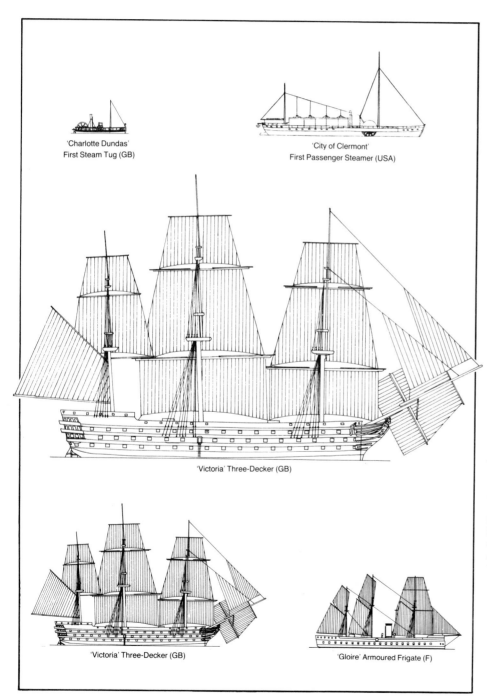

'Charlotte Dundas'
First Steam Tug (GB)

'City of Clermont'
First Passenger Steamer (USA)

'Victoria' Three-Decker (GB)

'Victoria' Three-Decker (GB)

'Gloire' Armoured Frigate (F)

The 'age of sail' was, by now, drawing to a close. In the making was a revolution in warship construction that would usher in the 'age of iron and steel'. Three factors were at work to bring this about: the development of the steam engine; improvements in artillery; and, consequent upon this, the growing necessity to protect ships with armour.

The first experiments with a steam engine for ships had been carried out at the end of the 17th century, by Denis Papin and others; but it was only in 1765, with the construction of James Watt's steam engine, that a power unit suitable for use aboard ship became available. Even so, attempts to apply steam to nautical propulsion during the 18th century brought no success.

In 1802, the first practical paddle steamer, Symington's Charlotte Dundas, was built and, 5 years later, Robert Fulton's City of Clermont became the first steamer to enter regular service, plying between New York and Albany. Fulton also built the first double-hulled steam frigate, Demologus, during the War of 1812, but this was a failure. In 1819, Savannah made the first crossing of the Atlantic by a steam ship (spending 18 of the 26-day voyage under steam power). And then, in 1820, the first iron steam ship, Aaron Manby, was constructed.

These early steam ships, propelled as they were by paddle wheels, had limited application for fighting, since the paddle wheels would have been very vulnerable to artillery fire, and valuable space, which would otherwise have housed guns, was wasted on each side of the ship. So, to begin with, steam was only used for small, fast despatch boats and tugs. However, the invention of a practical ship's screw by the Austrian, Joseph Ressel, in 1829 (improved by Ericsson and Pettit-Smith), was an altogether different matter. Steam engines were now installed as an auxiliary propulsion system in frigates and, following Dupuy de Lômes' Napoleon in 1848, in ships of the line. The merchant marine was rather faster in adopting screw propulsion than the navies: the first iron, screw-driven steamer to enter transatlantic service was Brunel's Great Britain, which made her maiden voyage in 1838.

The artillery revolution, meanwhile, was brought about by the introduction of rifling, which greatly increased accuracy, and the explosive shell, invented by the Frenchman Paixhans, in 1821. The effect of explosive shells on wooden ships' sides was catastrophic: armoured ships were the obvious answer, and the French took an early lead in this field. During the Crimean War, they employed floating batteries that were armoured and, in 1859, they launched the armoured frigate Gloire, the first sea-going armoured ship. Britain and the other naval powers now began to follow the French lead. By the time of the American Civil War, armoured coastal ships were to be employed in large numbers.

The Age of
Iron and Steel

Illustration by Geoff Hunt

1850: The first submarine telegraph cable is laid between France and England.

1850: The Bavarian artillery officer, Wilhelm Bauer, builds *Brandtaucher* ('Fire Diver'), a primitive submarine. An unsuccessful trial dive gives him the initiative to develop techniques for raising sunken vessels.

1853-56: THE CRIMEAN WAR

In the Black Sea, Russia has 16 ships of the line and 19 frigates and corvettes. The Turkish fleet is roughly equal in strength, but badly equipped. Some of the frigates are already steam driven.

30 Nov 1853: Action at Sinope. A Turkish squadron under Vice Admiral Osman Pasha anchors in the Roads of Sinope in November. It includes 7 frigates, 3 corvettes and 3 steam-ships. It is detected and blockaded by a Russian squadron, until reinforcements arrive from Sevastopol. As the Turks lie at anchor on the afternoon of 30 Nov, Pavel Stepanovich Nakhimov attacks, with his squadron of 6 ships of the line, 2 frigates and a brig. Initially, the Russians aim at ship targets with explosive shells and, after 2 hours, a Turkish frigate explodes, while 3 others are already burning; only 1 small steamer escapes. The rest of the Turkish squadron is badly battered, and the Turks lose 2,960 dead to the Russians' 37. The old solid shot is clearly inferior to the new explosive shell. After this clash, Britain and France enter the war on Turkey's side, and declare war on Russia. (In January 1855, Sardinia follows suit.)

16 Aug 1854: French forces capture the Russian fortress of Bomarsund on the Åland Islands in the Baltic. As the fortress cannot be maintained during the winter, it is evacuated again. The main theatre of the war, however, is the Black Sea. Shortly after Sinope, an Anglo-French squadron under Admirals Dundas (GB) and Hamelin (F) enters the Black Sea. With this fleet is the first screw-driven ship of the line, *Napoléon*. An Anglo-Franco-Turkish invasion army is transported to Varna and in the transportation of so many troops over long distances, the steam ships prove their worth.

14 Sept 1854: Landing in the Crimea. The Allied expeditionary army of about 60,000 men is taken from Varna by a fleet of 400 warships and transports, and landed at Eupatoria. The Russian fleet remains in Sevastopol, where some of the ships are sunk to strengthen the harbour defences.

17 Oct 1854: Bombardment of Sevastopol. To support the Allied land forces in their siege of the city, the fleet bombards the Russian defences from the sea. Six screw-driven ships of the line and 21 sail are involved, the latter being towed into position by steamers. The bombardment begins at midday and lasts 6 hours. Damage to the Russian defences is slight, but losses on the Allied side total 340 dead and wounded. Two British ships are so badly damaged that they have to be towed to the arsenal in Constantinople; other ships are also in a bad state. The wooden ships' sides simply cannot stand up to the new shells: the race between shell and armour thus begins, and the construction of armoured warships is started.

9-11 Aug 1855: The Anglo-French fleet successfully bombards the fortress of Sveaborg in the Baltic.

9 Sept 1855: Sevastopol falls to the Allies.

Before capitulating, the Russians scuttle their Black Sea fleet of 14 ships of the line and about 100 other warships.

17 Oct 1855: Bombardment of Kinburn. Fort Kinburn controls the entrance to Nikolaev harbour; to silence this weak fort, the Allies form a bombardment squadron of 10 ships of the line and 80 other vessels, including 3 new French armoured batteries, *Tonnante*, *Lave* and *Dévastation*, the first armoured warships to be used in fleet action. Their fire silences the fort, and the armoured batteries suffer negligible losses.

1856: Peace of Paris. Here is made the Declaration of Paris, in which 'free ships and free merchandise' is the principle: Piracy is outlawed.

The Crimean War provided something of a landmark in naval development: not only did steam power prove its superiority over

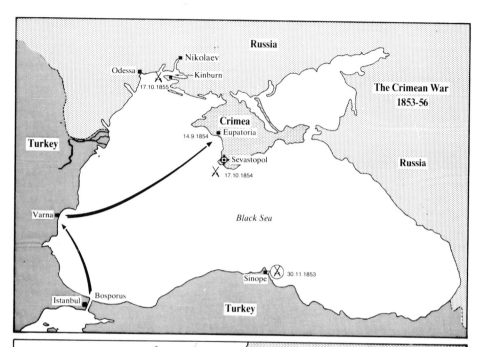

The Crimean War 1853-56

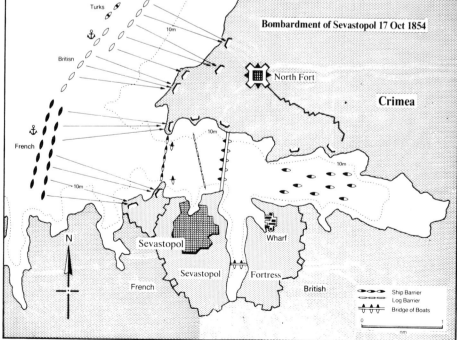

Bombardment of Sevastopol 17 Oct 1854

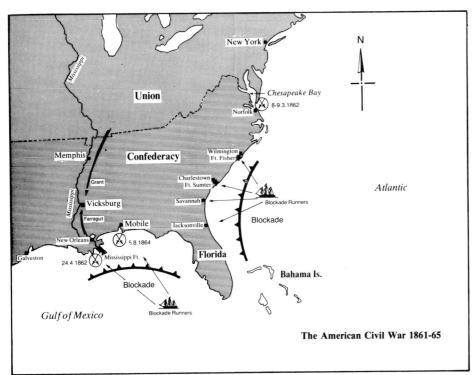

The American Civil War 1861-65

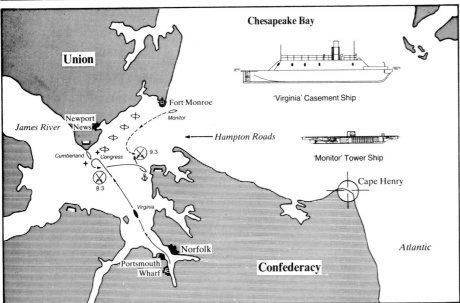

'Virginia' Casement Ship

'Monitor' Tower Ship

1861–65: THE AMERICAN CIVIL WAR

Friction develops between the industrial northern states and the agrarian south, which is dominated by aristocratically governed plantation states, mainly cotton growing, whose economy features the employment of negro slaves. Demands for the abolition of slavery lead to the formation of the .secessionist Confederate States of America.

12 April 1861: Hostilities are opened when the Southerners attack Fort Sumter. (It falls to the Confederates the next day.) The North opens a blockade to strangle the Confederate economy.

3 Aug 1861: Union forces use a captive balloon, from the balloon-ship *Fanny* in Hampton Roads, for artillery observation.

1861: With the capture of Fort Hatteras (Aug) and Port Royal Sound (Nov), a tight blockade of Confederate coasts is started by the Unionists.

8 and 9 March 1862: Action in Chesapeake Bay. The South has converted the steam frigate *Merrimack* to an armoured ship in Norfolk docks, and re-named her *Virginia*. On 8 March, she steams to Hampton Roads to attack the Northern blockade ships there. In a violent action, *Virginia* destroys the frigate *Congress* and the corvette *Cumberland*. *Virginia* is only lightly damaged. That same evening, the Federal states' new armoured ship, *Monitor* arrives at Hampton Roads and, on 9 March, the first battle between armoured ships takes place. But the armour plate defeats the artillery; an attempted ramming by *Virginia* fails and, after 2 hours, the fight ends in a draw.

propulsion by sail, but the new explosive shells demonstrated their great penetrative power. Armour was obviously going to be essential. In the floating batteries at Kinburn, the first steps towards the modern battleship had been taken and, in the Baltic, the Russians had made the first use of the mine as a strategic weapon.

1857/58: The first transatlantic submarine telegraph cable is laid between Ireland and Newfoundland. This cable soon fails, however, and it is only when a second one is laid (completed in 1866) that communications are finally established. A world-wide news system is begun.

24 April 1862: The forcing of the Mississippi forts. The Union gathers 8 steam corvettes, 9 gunboats and a number of mortar vessels, under Commodore Farragut, to attack the river delta at New Orleans. The Confederate Commodore Mitchell has the ram *Manassas,* the armoured ship *Louisiana* and a number of armed steamers. South of New Orleans, the river is guarded by Forts Jackson and St. Philip and, on 18 April, Farragut bombards these forts with his fleet. This goes on for 8 days and, on 24 April, Farragut forces a passage past the forts, losing 1 armed steamer in the process. The Confederates lose the ram *Manassas* and some steamers; the forts are badly damaged. New Orleans and practically the whole Mississippi now fall into Union hands, and only Vicksburg remains to connect the western and eastern halves of the Confederacy.

12 Dec 1862: The Federal gunboat *Cairo* sinks after striking a Confederate mine in a tributary of the Mississippi. She is the first victim of mine warfare.

4 July 1863: At the eighth attempt, the Unionists capture Vicksburg and cut the Confederacy in two.

17 Feb 1864: The Southern submersible *H. L. Hunley* (Lt. George E. Dixon) sinks the blockade ship *Housatonic* in Charleston Harbor. This is the first success by a primitive submarine using 'spear' torpedoes.

5 Aug 1864: Battle of Mobile Bay. After the blockading of her Atlantic harbours, the Confederates are left with only Mobile as a port of any size. Farragut attacks the entrance to the Bay of Mobile, in order to close this avenue as well. The Confederate flotilla includes the armoured ram *Tennessee* and 3 gunboats, under Rear Admiral Buchanan. The entrance to the bay is covered by Fort Morgan, and behind a mine barrier in the entrance to the bay lies Buchanan's little force. Farragut's fleet includes the monitors *Tecumseh, Manhattan, Chickasaw* and *Winnebago,* 9 screw-driven frigates and corvettes, and 10 gunboats. In the morning, Farragut attacks in 2 columns aimed at Fort Morgan, with the 4 monitors closest to the fort, the other ships in the larboard column, each frigate and corvette with a small steamer on its port side. Fort Morgan is held down with heavy fire, and replies only weakly. When the leading monitor, *Tecumseh,* enters the minefield, she strikes a mine and sinks rapidly with heavy loss of life. As the other Federal ships fall into disorder, Farragut orders 'full steam ahead', and takes his flagship, the frigate *Hartford,* through the minefield; the other Federal ships cross the mines without further loss. *Tennessee*'s ramming attempts fail and, bombarded into submission, she surrenders at 10am. Two of her gunboats are also sunk. Some Unionist ships have also suffered badly (Hartford and 2 corvettes are badly damaged), but Mobile can no longer be used by Confederate blockade runners.

Throughout the war, the Confederacy conduct an effective commerce raiding campaign. The most successful of their raiders is *Alabama,* which captures 71 Union ships in 20 months, before being sunk off Cherbourg on 19 June 1864, in a duel with *Kearsarge.*

9 April 1865: The successful blockade, resulting in a lack of war materials and foodstuffs, forces the Confederates to capitulate.

The technological revolution has thus proceeded a step further. Monitors and smaller armoured ships have fought one another, and the armour has, so far, shown itself superior to the artillery. But the mine has had its first success, the torpedo has made its first kill, and experiments with submarines are now under way.

9 May 1864: Action off Heligoland. In the Danish war against Prussia and Austria (for Schleswig-Holstein), 2 Austrian frigates under Commodore Tegetthoff fight an indecisive combat with the stronger Danish blockading squadron.

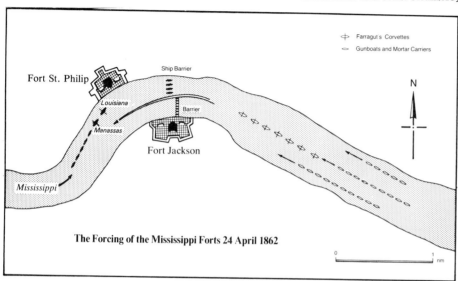

The Forcing of the Mississippi Forts 24 April 1862

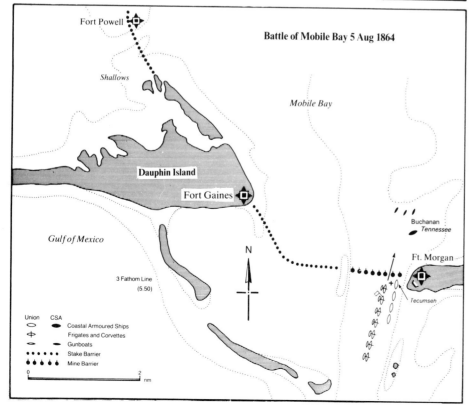

Battle of Mobile Bay 5 Aug 1864

1866: THE AUSTRO-ITALIAN WAR (THE SEVEN WEEKS WAR)

After the defeat of the Italian Army at Custozza, the Italian fleet takes the initiative.

16 July 1866: Admiral Persano, commander of the Italian fleet, takes all available ships from Ancona to attack Lissa, and to cover a landing operation on the island.

18 July 1866: The Italians bombard the coastal defences, but cannot silence the Austrian guns.

19 July 1866: Two armoured ships penetrate the harbour of San Giorgio, but are successfully bombarded by the Austrian batteries. *Formidabile* is damaged and has to withdraw. Hearing of the attack on Lissa, Rear Admiral von Tegetthoff leaves Pola with the Austrian fleet.

20 July 1866: Battle of Lissa. Fleet strengths are as follows.

	ITALY	AUSTRIA
Armoured ships	Re d'Italia	Erzherzog Ferdinand Max
	Re di Portogallo	Habsburg
	Ancona	Kaiser Max
	Maria Pia	Prinz Eugen
	Castelfidardo	Don Juan d'Austria
	San Martino	Drache
	Principe di Carignano	Salamander
	Terribile	
	Palestro	Kaiser (screw driven
	Varese	ship of the line)
	Affondatore	
Steam frigates	3	5
Steam corvettes	4	1

Each fleet is divided into an armoured and an unarmoured division. At 10am Tegetthoff nears the island. Persano breaks off the landing operation and, with his 11 armoured ships, sails against the enemy in irregular line ahead. (*Formidabile* is steaming home.) The unarmoured Italian ships do not enter the battle, but Tegetthoff commits all his ships. He approaches in three arrow-head lines, the 7 armoured ships in the van, and breaks through the Italian line. In the ensuing mêlée, the Austrian flagship *Erzherzog Ferdinand Max* rams *Re d'Italia*, which sinks in a few minutes. Even the Austrian wooden wall *Kaiser* rams an armoured Italian ship, but is itself badly damaged. The Italian armoured ship *Palestro* is set on fire and explodes at 2.30pm. Persano then breaks off the fight.

Lissa was the first naval battle in the open sea since Trafalgar, and it was also the first sea battle between armoured ships. As in the American Civil War, naval artillery was still having little effect on ships' armour, despite scoring many hits at close range. But Lissa was a battle that would influence warship construction for 30 years, and lead to forward-firing guns and ram bows—as in the 'age of galleys', the ship itself would be considered a weapon.

1869: Opening of the Suez Canal.

1870–71: During the Franco-Prussian War, the French fleet starts a blockade of the German coast, but the rapid advance of the German armies soon causes this to be abandoned. The crews of the ships are used in the defence of Paris.

1876–80: The Italian Benedetto Brin builds the battleship *Duillo*, the first heavy turret-ship.

26 Jan 1878: Russian torpedo-boats sink the Turkish gunboat *Intibah* off Batum, in the first successful use of the Whitehead torpedo.

1878: John P. Holland builds his first submarine.

8 Oct 1879: Action off Angamos. In the war between Chile and Peru, the Chilean armoured ships *Almirante Cochrane* and *Blanco Encalada* force the Peruvian turret ram *Huascar* (which has been causing havoc by hit-and-run raids along the coast) to capitulate after a valiant 90-minute conflict.

1882: Thorsten Nordenfelt, a Swedish industrialist and inventor, finances George Garrett's construction of the submarine *Nordenfelt I*, which begins trials in 1885. The first submarine to carry a surface armament, it also carries a Whitehead torpedo in an external bow casing.

11 July 1882: The British Mediterranean Fleet, 8 armoured ships and several smaller vessels, bombards Alexandria, to quell anti-foreign riots.

1880–90: Since steam engines have become strong and

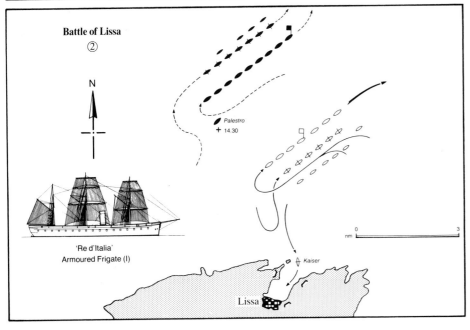

Battle of Lissa 20 July 1866
①

Italians	Austrians	
⬤	◯	Armoured Ships
✦	✧	Wooden Ships
⬤	◯	Gunboats
■	☐	
Persano	Tegetthoff	

11.30
+ Re d'Italia
Erh. Ferdin. Max
Kaiser
Affondatore

Lissa

'Erzherzog Ferdinand Max'
Armoured Frigate (A)

Battle of Lissa
②

N

Palestro
+ 14.30

Kaiser

Lissa

'Re d'Italia'
Armoured Frigate (I)

0   nm   3

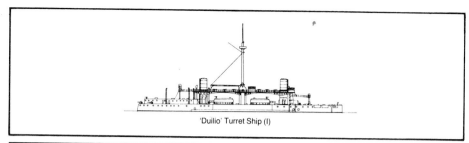

'Duilio' Turret Ship (I)

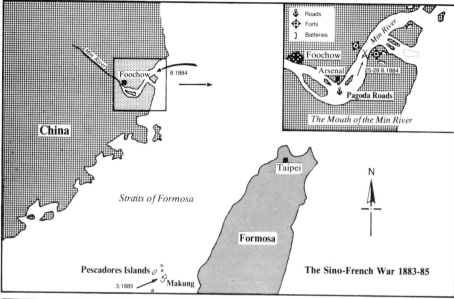

Roads
Forts
Batteries

Foochow
Arsenal
25-29.8.1884
Pagoda Roads

The Mouth of the Min River

China

8.1884
Foochow
Min River

Taipei

N

Straits of Formosa

Formosa

Pescadores Islands

3.1885 → Makung

The Sino-French War 1883-85

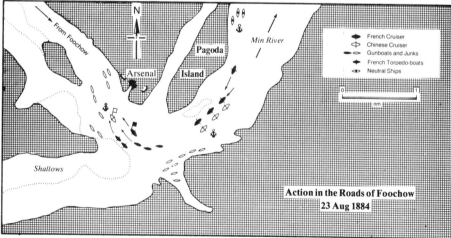

From Foochow

N

Min River

Pagoda

Arsenal   Island

French Cruiser
Chinese Cruiser
Gunboats and Junks
French Torpedo-boats
Neutral Ships

Shallows

0   1
nm

**Action in the Roads of Foochow
23 Aug 1884**

reliable, rigging is now a useless hindrance, so warships are now modified with only combat and signal masts. Apart from training ships, the fleets contain no sail.

1888: The Frenchman Gustav Zédé completes the first electrically-driven submarine, de Lôme's *Gymnote*.

April 1891: In the Chilean Revolutionary War, a torpedo-boat succeeds in sinking *Blanco Encalada*, the first sinking of an armoured warship with a self-propelled torpedo.

April 1894: In the Brazilian Civil War, a torpedo-boat sinks the sea-going turret ship *Aquidaban* (which is later raised).

1897: John P. Holland launches his submarine, *Holland*, for the US Navy.

1899: The Frenchman Laubeuf designs *Narval*, prototype of the modern submarine.

WARS IN THE FAR EAST, 1883-95

1883-85: The Sino-French War

The struggle is for recognition of French sovereignty over Indo-China. In order to force the Chinese to comply with French wishes, the French Far East naval commander, Rear-Admiral Courbet, decides to attack the Chinese fleet lying in the Pagoda Roads at Foochow.

23 Aug 1884: Action in the Roads of Foochow. Courbet has 5 cruisers, 3 gunboats and 2 torpedo-boats; the Chinese fleet, under Admiral Ting, includes 6 cruisers, a number of smaller vessels and 9 armed junks. At 2pm, Courbet opens fire: a torpedo-boat hits the Chinese flagship with a towed torpedo and, after half an hour, the Chinese fleet is destroyed. French losses are very slight. The coastal batteries are now silenced and, next day, the arsenal is bombarded.

25-29 Aug 1884: Leaving Foochow, the French fleet bombards and silences the forts at the mouth of the River Min.

29-31 March 1885: Capture of Mekong by a French squadron under Courbet.

9 June 1885: Peace of Tientsin.

1894-95: The Sino-Japanese War

Japan and China go to war over Korea. After a rebellion in Seoul, the Japanese demand that the Chinese withdraw, but the Chinese respond by reinforcing their troops. Prior to the official declaration of war, 4 Japanese cruisers attack a Chinese troop convoy, sinking a transport and damaging an escorting cruiser. War is declared on 1 Aug. Both countries rely on sea-borne supply routes for their armies in the peninsula. In September, the Chinese fleet escorts a convoy to northern Korea; the Japanese attempt to intercept this, but only find the Chinese fleet on its return journey.

17 Sept 1894: Battle of the Yalu River. The Chinese fleet, under Admiral Ting, consists of the battleships *Ting-Yuen* and *Chen-Yuen*, 8 armoured cruisers and 3 torpedo-boats. The Japanese Admiral Sukenori Ito has 8 armoured cruisers, an old armoured ship, *Fuso*, an old coastal armoured steamer, a gunboat and an armed transport. Ito divides his fleet into a fast squadron (the 4 newest and fastest cruisers) and the main body. The Chinese fleet steams in a broad arrow-head formation, the two battleships in the centre. Ito uses his fast squadron to outflank the starboard wing of the Chinese fleet, and his ships then shoot up the two Chinese ships on this wing. The fast squadron then turns to port, brushes off the Chinese torpedo-boats and turns on the enemy cruisers. The Japanese main body circles the Chinese in a clockwise direction, but this brings the slowest of the Japanese ships close to the Chinese battleships; these ships are badly damaged, and Ito's flagship, *Matsushima*, receives a serious direct hit, forcing Ito to transfer to *Hashidate*. The Chinese suffer even more, however; of their port wing ships, one

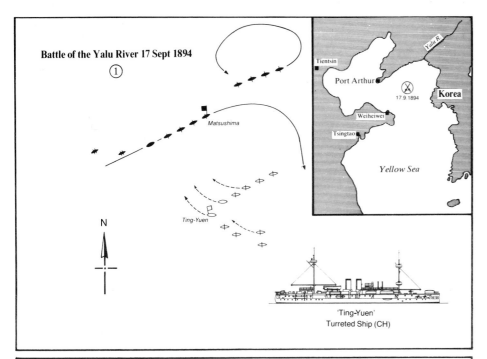

Battle of the Yalu River 17 Sept 1894

①

Matsushima

Ting-Yuen

N

'Ting-Yuen'
Turreted Ship (CH)

Tientsin

Port Arthur

⊗ 17.9.1894

Korea

Weiheiwei

Tsingtao

Yellow Sea

sinks and another catches fire and, in the centre, 2 cruisers are sunk and another catches fire. (The day after the battle, 2 other cruisers which ran aground are also destroyed.) The 2 battleships are hit many times, but their armour is not pierced by the Japanese shells and after 5 hours of combat, both fleets have almost expended their ammunition. The Chinese withdraw to Port Arthur, and the Japanese do not pursue. Total Chinese losses are 5 cruisers sunk and all other ships damaged; on the Japanese side, the flagship, the gunboat, armoured coastal steamer and the transport are all badly damaged.

Oct 1894: Japanese landing near Port Arthur; the Chinese fleet moves to Weiheiwei.

22 Nov 1894: Port Arthur falls to the Japanese. In winter, the land operations in northern Korea are suspended.

19 Jan 1895: A Japanese army lands on the Shantung Peninsula, either side of Weiheiwei.

29 Jan 1895: Opening of the siege. In the harbour are both Chinese battleships, some cruisers and 10 torpedo-boats. The besieging Japanese fleet suffers some losses from the fire of the battleships.

4/5 and 5/6 Feb 1895: Torpedo-boats attack the Chinese fleet. During the first night attack, the Japanese torpedo-boats penetrate the harbour and sink the battleship *Ting-Yuen* for the cost of 2 torpedo-boats, 1 beached, the other sunk by enemy fire. The following night, the Japanese torpedo-boats sink two more ships. On the evening of 7 February, the Chinese torpedo-boats attempt to break out: 2 escape, and 8 are forced to beach themselves by the Japanese cruiser *Joshino* and other ships.

12 Feb 1895: Capitulation of Weiheiwei. Japan has achieved command of the northern Chinese seas. However, under pressure from the Great Powers, she has to return Port Arthur to China.

The Battle of the Yalu River had far-reaching effects, for it showed the advantage of the close line ahead, with its resultant concentration of firepower. Battleships, although invulnerable to the fire of smaller vessels, were demonstrably too slow to catch cruisers, so that fleets now began to be divided into battleships, fast armoured cruisers, and smaller cruisers.

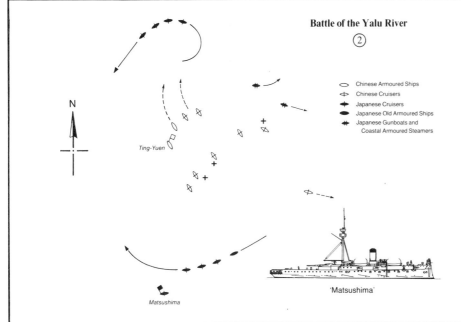

Battle of the Yalu River

②

N

Ting-Yuen

Matsushima

◯ Chinese Armoured Ships
⬭ Chinese Cruisers
➤ Japanese Cruisers
⬬ Japanese Old Armoured Ships
⬭ Japanese Gunboats and
    Coastal Armoured Steamers

'Matsushima'

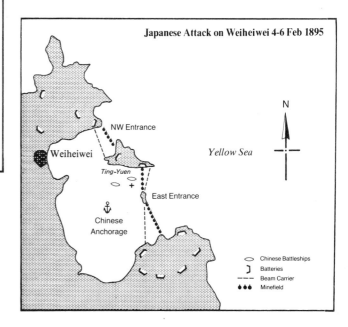

Japanese Attack on Weiheiwei 4-6 Feb 1895

N

Weiheiwei

NW Entrance

Ting-Yuen

Yellow Sea

East Entrance

⚓
Chinese
Anchorage

◯ Chinese Battleships
⌐ Batteries
--- Beam Carrier
●●● Minefield

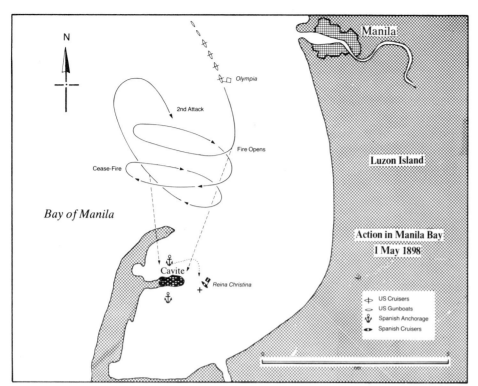

N

Olympia

2nd Attack

Fire Opens

Cease-Fire

Bay of Manila

Cavite

Reina Christina

Manila

Luzon Island

**Action in Manila Bay
1 May 1898**

US Cruisers
US Gunboats
Spanish Anchorage
Spanish Cruisers

1898: THE SPANISH-AMERICAN WAR

In February 1898, the American warship *Maine* explodes in Havana harbour (probably due to the spontaneous detonation of unstable explosives). The United States accuses Spain of sabotage, and declares war in April. At the outbreak of war, the US Navy consists of 5 ships of the line, 2 armoured cruisers, 16 cruisers and a number of monitors, gunboats and torpedo-boats. Spain has 1 ship of the line, 6 armoured cruisers, 11 cruisers, a great number of gunboats and some torpedo-boats. The war centres on Spanish possessions in the Philippines and the West Indies. In the Far East, the Americans have a squadron under Commodore Dewey, including the cruisers *Olympia*, *Baltimore*, *Raleigh* and *Boston*, plus 2 gunboats. Dewey leaves Hong Kong for Manila to destroy the Spanish squadron there. The Spanish commander, Rear Admiral Montojo, has 2 old, weak cruisers and 5 gunboats; his flagship is *Reina Christina*.

1 May 1898: Action in Manila Bay. As his squadron is not combat-ready, Montojo remains under the protection of the Cavite shore batteries. At dawn, Dewey enters the Bay of Manila with his squadron in close line ahead. At 5,000 yards (4,570 metres), the Americans open fire, passing the Spanish on a westerly course until they have to turn because of the near coastline. This process is repeated several times, the range reducing to 2,000 yards (1,830 metres). After 2 hours, all Spanish ships are sunk, burning or aground and after a short pause, the latter are also destroyed. Dewey's ships have only been hit 19 times.

12 May 1898: The bombardment of San Juan de Puerto Rico opens the American offensive in the West Indies. Spain

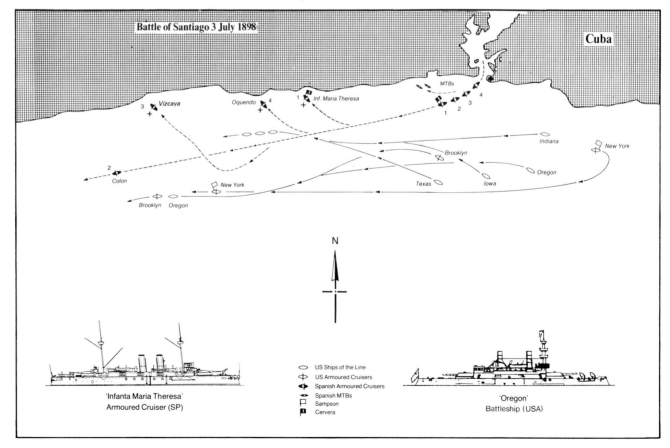

Battle of Santiago 3 July 1898

Cuba

MTBs

Vizcaya

Oquendo

Inf. Maria Theresa

Colon

New York

Brooklyn

Indiana

New York

Oregon

Texas

Iowa

Brooklyn *Oregon*

N

US Ships of the Line
US Armoured Cruisers
Spanish Armoured Cruisers
Spanish MTBs
Sampson
Cervera

'Infanta Maria Theresa'
Armoured Cruiser (SP)

'Oregon'
Battleship (USA)

sends a squadron under Admiral Cervera to protect her colonies in the West Indies.

19 May: Admiral Cervera enters Santiago harbour on Cuba, and is blockaded there by the US fleet under Admiral Sampson.

31 May: An attempt to block the harbour mouth with a blockship fails.

22 June: An American invasion force lands near Santiago, precipitating Cervera's decision to attempt a break-out on 3 July.

3 July 1898: Battle of Santiago. The blockading fleet includes the armoured cruiser *Brooklyn* (flagship of Commodore Schley) and the battleships *Iowa*, *Indiana*, *Oregon* and *Texas*. Sampson in his flagship, the armoured cruiser *New York*, is far to the east and assumes command only at the end of the battle.

9.30am: The Spanish steam out. Cervera's flagship, the armoured cruiser *Infanta Maria Theresa*, is followed by the armoured cruisers *Vizcaya*, *Cristobal Colon* and *Almirante Oquendo*, and 2 torpedo-boats. They move west along the coast.

9.40am: *Brooklyn*, *Texas* and *Iowa* open fire.

10am: The Spanish flagship and *Oquendo* are badly hit and run aground.

12am: *Vizcaya* is now on fire and aground, and the 2 torpedo-boats are sunk.

1.30pm: The fast *Cristobal Colon* is only caught after a 50-mile (80-kilometre) chase by *Brooklyn* and *Oregon* and is now also aground. All Spanish ships are destroyed; 2 American ships are lightly damaged. Combat range during this battle is between 1,650 and 3,300 yards (1,500–3,000 metres).

12 Aug 1898: An armistice is signed. In the following peace treaty, Cuba becomes independent and the United States receives Puerto Rico, Guam and the Philippines.

By the end of the 19th century, the general classification of warship types had become clearer. The backbone of the fleet would be the battleship, with heavy armour and big guns, the 'line of battle' ship. Lighter in armour, and consequently faster than the battleship, would be the cruiser; the light cruiser would provide the main reconnaissance unit, while the torpedo-boat had bred the 'torpedo-boat destroyer' (or, more simply, the 'destroyer'). The general features of these types, during the early years of the new century, can be summarized as follows.

TYPE	TONNAGE	ARMAMENT	SPEED	CREW
Battleship	12–15,000	4 × 12in (30·5cm) guns	18 knots	800
Cruiser	7–14,000	4–6 × 8in (20cm) guns	23 knots	600
Light cruiser	2–4,000	10 × 4in (10·5cm) guns	25 knots	300
Destroyer	300–600	2 × 3in (7·6cm) guns	28 knots	70

1904–5: The Russo-Japanese War

Russia's east Asian expansion brings her increasingly into conflict with the emergent Great Power, Japan, and Russia begins to concentrate large naval forces in the Far East; when Russia rents Port Arthur from China, the clash becomes inevitable. Successful land warfare in Korea and Manchuria is dependent upon control of the Yellow Sea. Relative strengths at the outbreak of war are as follows.

	JAPAN	RUSSIA
Battleships	6	7
Cruisers	6	4
Light cruisers	12	6
Destroyers	19	27

Japan also has 4 old armoured ships, and is awaiting delivery of 2 cruisers which she has bought from Argentina. In the Baltic, Russia has some new battleships fitting out and some older armoured ships and cruisers. At the beginning of February 1904, the majority of the Russian First Pacific Squadron is lying in the roads of Port Arthur.

6 Feb 1904: Japan breaks off diplomatic relations with Russia, and attacks without declaration of war.

8/9 Feb: Attack on Port Arthur. Ten Japanese destroyers mount a surprise night attack on the Russian squadron. Their torpedoes hit the battleships *Tsesarevich*, *Retvizan* and the cruiser *Pallada*: the battleships are out of action for months.

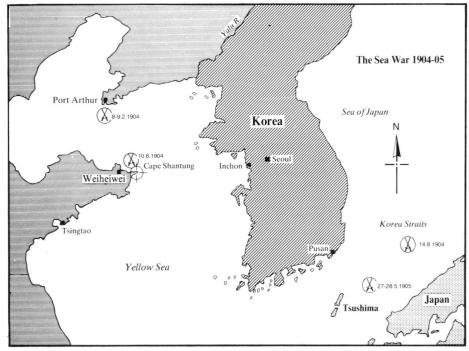

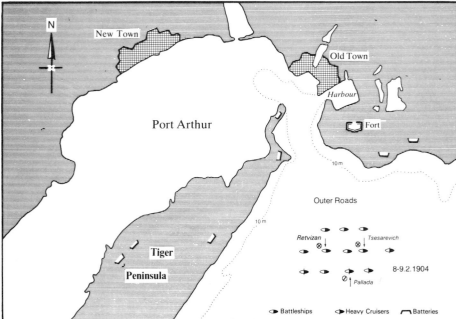

9 Feb: In the morning, Admiral Togo appears with the Japanese fleet, and fights a short action with the Russian ships still lying in the roads. They suffer very little damage. On the same day, a group of Japanese cruisers escorts the first wave of transports to land troops at Inchon, the harbour of Seoul. There, the Russian cruiser *Variag* and a gunboat are badly damaged by the Japanese, and scuttled.

10 Feb: War is declared.

13/14 Feb: A night attempt by the Japanese to block the entrance to Port Arthur with cement-filled steamers fails.

March 1904: The energetic Vice Admiral Makarov takes command of the First Russian Pacific Squadron. Both sides begin a policy of tactical minelaying.

12 April 1904: The battleships *Petropavlovsk* and *Pobieda* run into a minefield; Makarov goes down with his ship.

April: The Japanese set up a naval base on Elliot Island and, from there, cover the landing of an army on the Kwantung Peninsula, to besiege Port Arthur.

3/4 May 1904: Another attempt to block Port Arthur with blockships fails.

15 May: The Japanese battleships *Yashima* and *Hatsuse* sink in a Russian minefield.

23 June 1904: A break-out attempt by the Russian squadron, now under Admiral Vitgeft, fails. By the end of the month, Japanese siege artillery is already putting shells into the harbour, and Vitgeft tries another break-out to Vladivostok.

10 Aug 1904: Battle of the Yellow Sea. In the morning, the Russians sail out of Port Arthur. The relative strengths of the contending fleets are as follows.

	FIRST PACIFIC SQUADRON	JAPANESE FLEET
Battleships	*Tsesarevich*	*Mikasa*
	Retvizan	*Asahi*
	Pobieda	*Fuji*
	Peresviet	*Shikishima*
	Sevastopol	
	Poltava	
Armoured cruisers		*Nishin*
		Kasuga
Cruisers	4	8
Destroyers	14	18
Torpedo-boats	–	30

Midday: The Japanese main body blocks the Russians' path off the Shantung Peninsula.

1pm: The artillery fight opens; in a brief, one-hour fight, the Russians succeed in breaking out. Togo takes up the chase and gradually comes up from the south-west, overtaking the Russian line.

4pm: The fire-fight is re-opened at ranges of 9,000 to 10,000 yards (8,000–9,000 metres).

6pm: Vitgeft is killed by a shell splinter.

6.12pm: A hit on the Russian flagship kills the commander and practically all the bridge personnel; the Russian line becomes disordered, and most ships turn for Port Arthur. In the

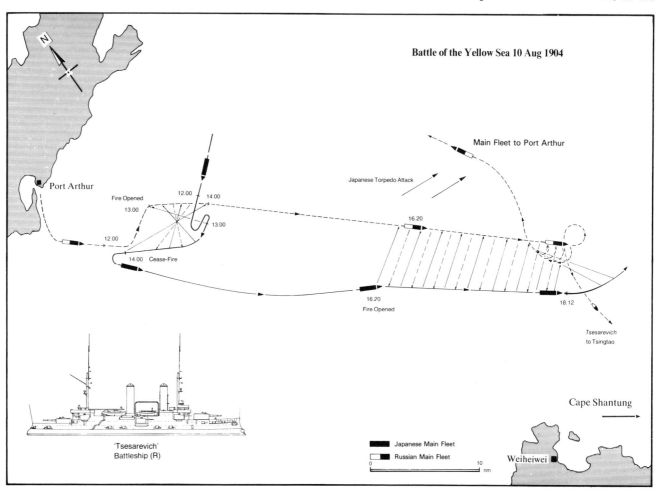

Battle of the Yellow Sea 10 Aug 1904

gathering darkness, Togo breaks off the fight, and gives his destroyers the chance of a night attack. Several such attacks are repulsed by the Russians. Of the Russian squadron, 5 battleships, a cruiser and 9 destroyers reach Port Arthur; *Tsesarevich* and 3 destroyers go to Tsingtao; the cruiser *Askold* and a destroyer go to Shanghai, the cruiser *Diana* to Saigon. These ships are interned. The small cruiser *Novik* goes east around Japan towards Vladivostok, and is forced to run aground at Sakhalin by Japanese cruisers. The Japanese fleet remains completely combat-ready. Russian casualties are 343 dead and wounded, Japanese 226. In Vladivostok,

the Russians have 3 armoured cruisers and a cruiser with which they wage a trade war in the Sea of Japan.

14 Aug 1904: Battle of the Japanese Sea (or Ulsan). The armoured cruisers *Rossiia*, *Gromoboi* and *Rurik*, under Rear Admiral Yessen, are steaming south to support the break-out of the First Pacific Squadron. At dawn on 14 August, they meet the Japanese armoured cruisers *Izumo*, *Azuma*, *Tokiwa* and *Iwade* and two cruisers, under Vice Admiral Kamimura. In a 4-hour fight, *Rurik* is sunk. The other two cruisers are not energetically pursued, but do not resume their trade raiding activities: from now on, the Japanese have undisputed command of the Yellow Sea.

Oct 1904: Since the outbreak of war, a second squadron for use in the Pacific has been in preparation in the Baltic, including several ships being overhauled. Construction work on 4 battleships and 4 cruisers is hurriedly completed and, in October, this 'Second Pacific Squadron' under Vice Admiral Rozhdestvensky leaves the Baltic for the Far East. The Russian ships that escaped to Port Arthur, after the Battle of the Yellow Sea, are repaired there, but do not attempt another break-out. Their guns are used as artillery support in the land battle, and their crews gradually absorbed into the land forces. Until December 1904, the fortress repels all Japanese assaults with loss.

6 Dec 1904: The Japanese capture 203 Metre Hill and, with artillery fire directed from there, they sink the battleships *Retvizan* and *Pobieda* that same day. *Poltava* is already aground, and *Peresviet* is now scuttled; *Sevastopol* moves to the outer roads, where she successfully repels Japanese torpedo-boat attacks for several days. She is scuttled in deep water before the fall of the fortress.

Dec 1904: Vice Admiral Rozhdestvensky reaches Madagascar with the Second Pacific Squadron.

2 Jan 1905: Port Arthur capitulates.

March 1905: Rozhdestvensky's squadron leaves Madagascar; off Indo-China, he awaits the arrival of a following squadron of coastal armoured ships.

End of May 1905: The combined squadrons approach the Korean coast. Togo, well informed of the Russian strength and movements, awaits them in the Korea Straits, off Tsushima Island.

27–28 May 1905: Battle of Tsushima. Relative strengths are as follows.

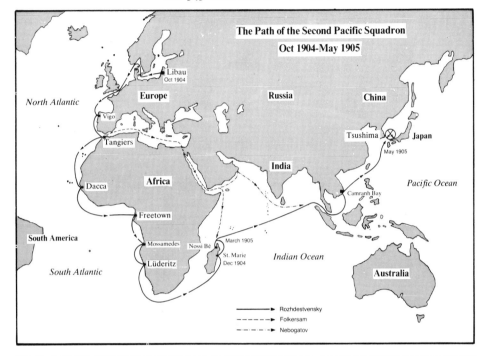

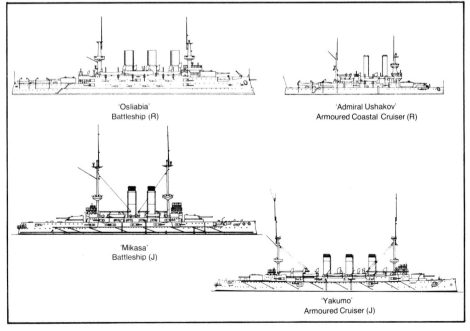

'Osliabia'
Battleship (R)

'Admiral Ushakov'
Armoured Coastal Cruiser (R)

'Mikasa'
Battleship (J)

'Yakumo'
Armoured Cruiser (J)

	JAPAN (Togo, *Mikasa*)	RUSSIA (Rozhdestvensky, *Knjaz Suvorov*)
Battleships	*Mikasa*	*Knjaz Suvorov*
	Shikishima	*Imperator Alexander III*
	Fuji	*Borodino*
	Asahi	*Orel*
		Osliabia
		Sysoi-Veliky
		Navarin
		Imperator Nikolai I
Armoured cruisers	*Nisshin*	*Admiral Nakhimov*
	Kasuga	3 armoured coast-
	Izumo	defence ships
	Azuma	
	Tokiwa	
	Yakumo	
	Asama	
	Iwade	
Old armoured cruisers	3	2
Cruisers	14	6+1 auxiliary cruiser
Destroyers	21	9
	+ many torpedo- boats, gunboats and auxiliary cruisers	+8 auxiliaries

27 May 1905: The Russian fleet is sighted by Japanese reconnaissance vessels, who inform their fleet.

5am: Rozhdestvensky forms line ahead on a north-easterly course.

1.40pm: As the Japanese fleet comes into view, the Russian auxiliaries are detached with a cruiser escort. Togo moves north-west of the Russians, heading ENE.

2.10pm: At 7,000 yards (6,400 metres), both sides open fire, the Japanese concentrating on the leading Russian ships.

2.30pm: *Osliabia* is badly hit, veers out of line, and capsizes half an hour later. The faster Japanese ships head off the Russian line, and force it to change course to SE.

3pm: *Suvorov* is disabled and set on fire. A destroyer takes the badly wounded Rozhdestvensky and part of his staff on board, and the ship is sunk at 7.30pm by Japanese destroyers with torpedoes. Led by *Imperator Alexander III*, the Russians again turn north. Togo follows, outflanks them, and turns them south again.

4pm: In fog and smoke, the fleets lose sight of each other. Simultaneous with this combat between the battleships, the opposing cruiser squadrons are grappling a little south of the main battle area. But, in the heavy seas, the accuracy of the cruisers' gunnery is not high. With the support of their 3rd Division (the armoured coast-defence ships), the Russians hold off the more numerous Japanese.

6pm: Rozhdestvensky is now unconscious: Rear Admiral Nebogatov, commander of the 3rd Division, assumes command of the Russian fleet.

6.10pm: The Russian fleet regroups and sets course for Vladivostok again.

6.20pm: The Japanese discover their prey to their north-west, and attack. The artillery fight is soon in full progress, and the Russian ships, some already badly damaged, receive new hits.

7pm: *Imperator Alexander III* sinks.

7.30pm: *Borodino* explodes. Togo now recalls his heavy units and hands the night attack over to his destroyers and torpedo-boats.

8.30pm to midnight: These encounter heavy resistance and suffer losses, but they do hit some Russian ships with their torpedoes. At 2am *Navarin* sinks; *Admiral Nakhimov* follows at 5am; *Sysoi-Veliky* sinks the next morning. The majority of the Russian ships still head north, but 3 cruisers and some other ships turn south and reach neutral ports, where they are interned.

28 May 1905: Nebogatov still has the battleships *Imperator Nikolai I* and *Orel*, the coastal armoured ships *Admiral Seniavin* and *Admiral Apraksin* as well as a cruiser with him.

10.30am: When he is sighted by the Japanese, Nebogatov hoists a white flag, and surrenders his completely operational ships to the enemy. Only the cruiser escapes, but is later run aground.

6pm: The slower coastal armoured ship *Admiral Ushakov* refuses to surrender and goes down fighting; the old armoured cruiser *Dimitry Donskoi* repulses repeated attacks from cruisers and destroyers (and is scuttled at 7am next day by her own crew).

Midday: The destroyer with Rozhdestvensky aboard is found by the Japanese, and surrenders on the orders of his Chief of Staff. Rozhdestvensky, badly wounded, becomes a prisoner of war. Only one cruiser and two destroyers manage to get through to Vladivostok. The Battle of Tsushima is one of the few decisive naval battles in history to be fought out to the bitter end. The heavy Russian losses are as follows: 8 battleships (6 are sunk, 2 captured); 3 coastal armoured ships (1 sunk, 2 captured); 3 armoured cruisers (all sunk); 5 cruisers (2 sunk, 3 interned); 7 destroyers (5 sunk, 1 interned, 1 captured); 4 transports (4 escape).

Russian casualties are 5,000 dead, 500 wounded and 6,000 prisoners; Japanese losses are 600 men dead and wounded, 3 torpedo-boats sunk, and 2 cruisers badly damaged. Of the battleships, only 3 have damage worth mentioning.

Sept 1905: Treaty of Portsmouth. Japan receives Port Arthur and South Sakhalin.

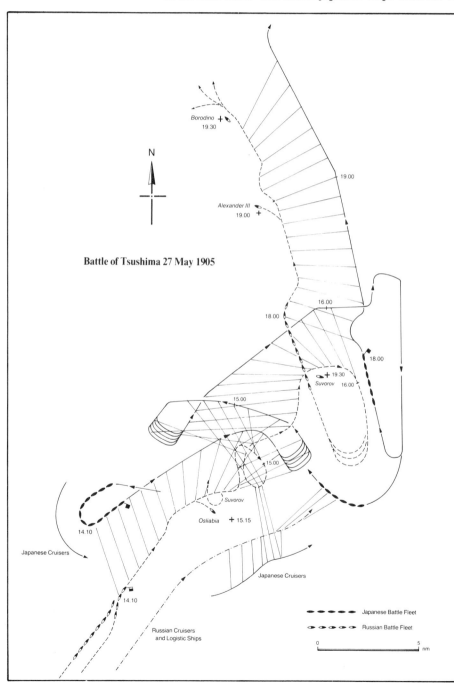

Battle of Tsushima 27 May 1905

Borodino
19.30

N

Alexander III
19.00

19.00

16.00

18.00

18.00

19.30
Suvorov   16.00

15.00

15.00

Suvorov

Osliabia   15.15

14.10

Japanese Cruisers

Japanese Cruisers

14.10

Russian Cruisers and Logistic Ships

Japanese Battle Fleet

Russian Battle Fleet

0   5
nm

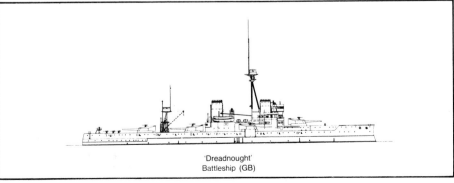

Battle of Tsushima 28 May 1905

2nd Day

Dimitry Donskoi

Isumrud

N

Nebogatov Capitulates
10.30

Korea

Adm. Ushakov
18.00

Japanese Battle Fleet

Pusan

Sysoi-Veliky
10.30

Navarin
02.00

Wlad. Monomach

Adm. Nakhimov
05.00

Honshu

Tsushima

27.5

Kure

Kyushu

Sasebo

'Dreadnought'
Battleship (GB)

During the first part of the Russo-Japanese War, the mine had demonstrated its potential, and special minelayers and minesweepers were now developed by the navies of the world. While destroyers and torpedo-boats had failed to live up to expectation, the Battle of Tsushima had shown battleships at their best. With quick-firing heavy artillery, ammunition of great explosive power, and proper fire control systems functioning, the close line ahead manoeuvring made possible concentrated gunnery of tremendous effect, at ranges of 4,000 to 8,000 yards (about 3,600-7,300 metres). On the larger scale, the voyage of the Second Pacific Squadron half-way round the world demonstrated the considerable problems involved in supplying a modern fleet far from its bases. The war also saw the first use of wireless, which kept Togo well informed about the movements of his opponents,

1903: The Wright brothers make the first flight by a powered heavier-than-air machine.

June 1905: Mutiny aboard the Russian battleship *Potemkin*.

1906: Launching of the first 'all-big-gun' ship, the British *Dreadnought*.

14 Nov 1910: Eugene Ely (USA) makes the first take-off with a wheeled aircraft from a warship, in Chesapeake Bay.

18 Jan 1911: Ely makes the first landing on the provisional flight deck of a warship.

1912–13: The First Balkan War

Greece, Serbia, Bulgaria and Montenegro push Turkey out of practically all her possessions in the Balkans. The small Greek fleet controls the Aegean and prevents Turkish troop reinforcements.

16 Dec 1912 and 18 Jan 1913: In two actions off the Dardanelles, Turkish attempts to push a fleet of 2 battleships, 2 cruisers and some torpedo-boats into the Aegean are repulsed by Greek forces (the modern armoured cruiser *Georgios Averoff* and 3 coastal armoured vessels).

6 Feb 1913: A Greek seaplane reconnoitres the Dardanelles (the first use of a seaplane in war).

Jan–May 1913: The Turkish cruiser *Hamidije* undertakes a successful raid in the eastern Mediterranean and Red Sea.

1914: Opening of the Panama Canal and completion of the widening of the Kiel Canal (linking the North Sea with the Baltic) for use by capital ships.

During the early years of the 20th century, commercial and political rivalries in Western Europe, augmented by unrest in the Balkans, created and maintained latent tensions between the Great Powers. This powder barrel was finally ignited on 28 June 1914, by the murder at Sarajevo of the Austrian heir apparent and his consort: ultimatums and mobilizations followed in rapid succession. The two sides consisted of the 'Central Powers'—Germany and Austria-Hungary, joined later by Turkey (1914), and Bulgaria (1915)—and the 'Entente' Powers: France, Great Britain, Russia and Serbia, joined later by Japan (1914), Italy (1915), Rumania (1916), and the United States and Greece (1917).

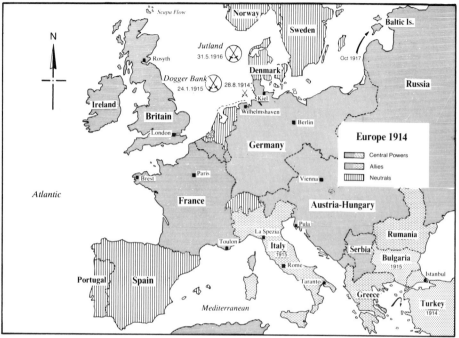

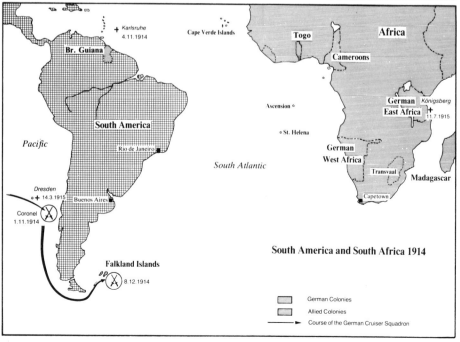

South America and South Africa 1914

	German Colonies
	Allied Colonies
→→	Course of the German Cruiser Squadron

The backbone of the fleets was now the dreadnought battleship, with big guns and strong armour, and the battlecruiser, also with big guns, but with armour sacrificed to attain higher speed. For some years, submarines had been in service with the navies: now they would begin to make a real impact on sea warfare. The strengths of the principal European fleets in 1914 were as follows.

	Britain	Germany	France	Italy	Austria	Russia
Dreadnoughts	21	15	4	4	3	–
Battlecruisers	9	5	–	–	–	–
Predreadnoughts	40	22	18	8	12	8
Arm'd cruisers	34	11	18	10	3	6
Cruisers	63	33	9	8	7	8
Destroyers and large torpedo-boats	250	90	80	30	70	100

For special duties, a great number of older warships, special ships and auxiliaries were also incorporated into the navies—first and foremost, the war at sea would be one of blockade and supply. On land, meanwhile, the momentum of the war was soon spent: after the initial German offensive, the fighting lapsed into static trench warfare in France and Russia and, in the Alps, the Italian attack ground to a halt; only on the Balkan Front did mobile warfare continue.

1914–18: THE FIRST WORLD WAR

1914–15: Elimination of Germany's commerce-raiders

At the start of the war, the British make efforts to destroy the German cruisers that are at large on the high seas: 2 armoured cruisers and 6 light cruisers, which threaten British trade routes. In the Indian Ocean, the light cruiser *Emden* carries out a successful campaign against British shipping, sinking 101,000 tons of merchant shipping. In the harbour of Penang, a French destroyer and a small Russian cruiser are destroyed, and the oil tanks in Madras set on fire.

20 Sept 1914: The German cruiser *Königsberg* sinks the small British cruiser *Pegasus* in Zanzibar harbour. From the beginning of Nov, *Königsberg* is blockaded by the British in the Rufiji delta.

Oct 1914: A German cruiser squadron, under Vice Admiral Graf Spee, sails from the Far East through the south seas to Easter Island, there to rendezvous with the cruisers of the American station. Rear Admiral Cradock, with an inferior force, seeks out the German squadron.

1 Nov 1914: Battle of Coronel. The British squadron finds Spee off the Chilean coast; although hopelessly outnumbered, Cradock does not hesitate to engage.

	GERMANY	BRITAIN
Armoured cruisers	*Scharnhorst*	*Good Hope*
	Gneisenau	*Monmouth*
Cruisers	3	1
Auxiliary cruisers	–	1

In heavy seas, only the guns of the armoured cruisers are effective and, in a bitter struggle in the twilight from 7–8pm, both of the old British armoured cruisers are shot into silence. The British flagship sinks after an hour, and *Monmouth* is then sunk by a torpedo from a German cruiser. There are no survivors. The German ships are practically undamaged. The other two British ships, meanwhile, escape in the darkness.

4 Nov 1914: The light cruiser *Karlsruhe* sinks in the Caribbean after an internal explosion.

9 Nov 1914: The Australian cruiser *Sydney* surprises *Emden* in the Cocos Islands and destroys her.

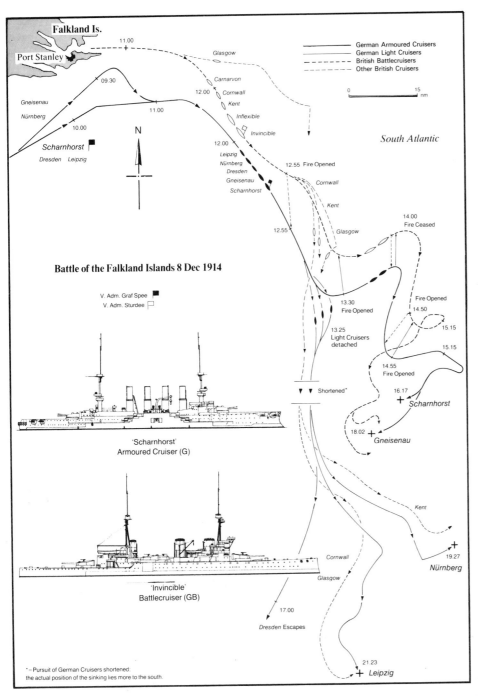

Falkland Is.

Port Stanley

11.00

Glasgow

09.30

12.00 Carnarvon

Cornwall

11.00 Kent

Inflexible

10.00 Invincible

Scharnhorst

Dresden Leipzig

Gneisenau
Nürnberg

N

12.00

Leipzig
Nürnberg
Dresden
Gneisenau
Scharnhorst

12.55 Fire Opened

Cornwall

12.55

Kent

Glasgow

South Atlantic

German Armoured Cruisers
German Light Cruisers
British Battlecruisers
Other British Cruisers

0   15
                nm

14.00
Fire Ceased

Battle of the Falkland Islands 8 Dec 1914

V. Adm. Graf Spee
V. Adm. Sturdee

Fire Opened

13.30
Fire Opened

14.50

15.15

13.25
Light Cruisers
detached

15.15

14.55
Fire Opened

▼ ▼ Shortened*

16.17
+ Scharnhorst

18.02 +
     Gneisenau

'Scharnhorst'
Armoured Cruiser (G)

Kent

'Invincible'
Battlecruiser (GB)

Cornwall

Glasgow

+
19.27
Nürnberg

17.00

Dresden Escapes

21.23
+ Leipzig

* = Pursuit of German Cruisers shortened:
the actual position of the sinking lies more to the south.

8 Dec 1914: Battle of the Falkland Islands. To reinforce British naval strength in the South Atlantic, 2 battlecruisers are detached from the Home Fleet to the Falkland Islands. The day after their arrival in Port Stanley, the German cruiser squadron attacks the harbour, thinking it undefended.

10am: The Germans detect the presence of the battlecruisers and turn away; the British pursue. Relative strengths of the opposing squadrons are as follows.

	BRITAIN (Sturdee, *Invincible*)	GERMANY (Graf Spee, *Scharnhorst*)
Battlecruisers	*Invincible* *Inflexible*	
Armoured cruisers	*Carnarvon* *Kent* *Cornwall*	*Scharnhorst* *Gneisenau*
Cruisers	2	
Auxiliary cruisers	1	

12.55pm: The battlecruisers open fire.

1.20pm: Escape is impossible: Graf Spee dismisses the smaller cruisers, while Sturdee, using the greater speed of his battlecruisers, conducts the fight against the German ships out of range of their guns.

4.17pm: *Scharnhorst* sinks with all hands.

6.02pm: *Gneisenau* sinks. The British cruisers pursue the remaining German cruisers.

7.27pm: *Kent* sinks *Nürnberg* after a long chase.

8.30pm: *Cornwall* and *Glasgow* catch *Leipzig*, which sinks at 11.23pm. Only one German cruiser, *Dresden*, escapes, and only 215 survivors are rescued. The British suffer only slight losses.

14 March 1915: *Kent* and *Glasgow* attack *Dresden* in neutral waters off the island of Mas-a-Fuera, west of Chile. She scuttles herself after a brief engagement.

11 July 1915: *Königsberg* is sunk by 2 British monitors.

From 1915 onwards, the German war against merchantmen was to be continued by U-boats and auxiliary cruisers only. Most successful of the latter was the raider Möwe, which captured 34 ships.

The War in the Mediterranean

4 Aug 1914: In the Mediterranean, the German battlecruiser *Goeben* and light cruiser *Breslau*, under Rear Admiral Souchon, bombard the Algerian harbours of Bône and Philippville. They then evade the British Mediterranean Squadron and, on 10 Aug, enter the Dardanelles. There the ships are handed over to Turkey and renamed *Yavuz Sultan Selim* and *Midilli*. Souchon becomes Commander-in-Chief of the Turkish Navy.

30 Oct 1914: The Turkish fleet bombards Sevastopol, Odessa, Feodosia and Novorossisk, and Turkey joins the Central Powers in the war.

3 Nov 1914: First bombardment of the Dardanelles by French and British naval forces.

19 Feb 1915: Opening of the main offensive on the Dardanelles by the British and French. Some 18 battleships and battlecruisers are employed at one time.

18 March 1915: The Dardanelles. After bombarding the external forts into silence, the battleships enter the Narrows. The French predreadnought *Bouvet* strikes a mine and explodes; the British battlecruiser *Inflexible* hits a mine, is damaged, and has to return to Malta. The British predreadnought battleships *Irresistible* and *Ocean* also run on to mines and sink. The attempt to break through with naval forces alone is abandoned.

25 April 1915: British and Australian troops land on the Gallipoli Peninsula, with naval support.

13 May 1915: The British predreadnought *Goliath* is sunk off the Dardanelles by a Turkish torpedo-boat.

24 May 1915: On the day Italy declares war on Austria-Hungary, the Austrian fleet bombards Ancona and other places on the eastern Italian coast. But, for the duration of the war, the Austrian fleet is effectively bottled up in the Adriatic.

25 May 1915: The German U-boat *U21* (Hersing) sinks the British predreadnought *Triumph* off the Dardanelles.

27 May 1915: *U21* sinks the British predreadnought *Majestic*.

8 Aug 1915: The British submarine *E21* sinks the Turkish battleship *Hairreddin Barbarousse* in the Dardanelles.

17 Aug 1915: A British seaplane, from the seaplane carrier *Ben-My-Chree*, carries out the first successful aerial torpedo attack, sinking a Turkish freighter (already damaged by a submarine) in the Dardanelles.

27 Sept 1915: The Italian predreadnought battleship *Benedetto Brin* explodes, after an Austrian sabotage attack in Brindisi harbour.

9 Jan 1916: The British evacuate their positions on Gallipoli.

27 April 1916: The British predreadnought battleship *Russell* sinks off Malta, after hitting a mine.

2 Aug 1916: The Italian battleship *Leonardo da Vinci* is destroyed, following an explosion (another Austrian sabotage attack) in Taranto harbour.

15 Sept 1916: Two Austrian seaplanes sink the French submarine *Foucault*, in the first successful bombing at sea.

26 Nov 1916: The German U-boat *U52* sinks the French predreadnought battleship *Suffren* off Lisbon.

11 Dec 1916: The Italian predreadnought *Regina Margherita* hits a German U-boat mine, and sinks off Valona.

27 Dec 1916: The German U-boat *UB47* sinks the French predreadnought battleship *Gaulois*.

4th Jan 1917: The Russian predreadnought battleship *Peresviet* sinks off Port Said, after striking a mine laid by a submarine. The ship had been bought back from the Japanese, and was on its way home from the Far East.

9 Jan 1917: The German U-boat *U32* sinks the British predreadnought *Cornwallis* east of Malta.

19 March 1917: The German U-boat *U64* sinks the French predreadnought battleship *Danton* in the western Mediterranean.

15 May 1917: Action in the Straits of Otranto. An Austrian squadron of 3 light cruisers and 2 destroyers attacks the Allied blockading forces in the Straits of Otranto. After destroying 14 armed trawlers, a destroyer and 2 merchantmen, the squadron turns back. They are pursued by Allied cruisers and destroyers, but manage to escape after a long chase.

10 Dec 1917: Italian motor torpedo-boats sink the Austrian predreadnought battleship *Wien* off Trieste.

20 Jan 1918: The Turkish ships with German crews, *Yavuz*

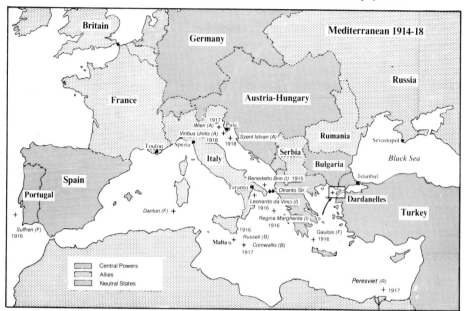

Mediterranean 1914-18

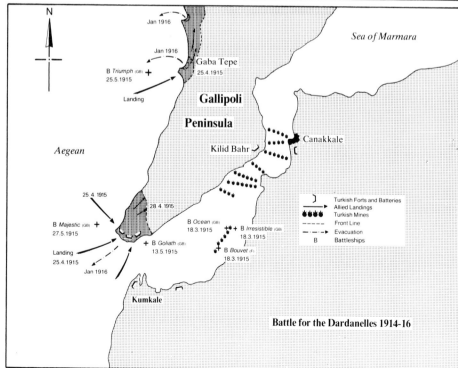

Battle for the Dardanelles 1914-16

Sultan Selim and *Midilli*, leave the Dardanelles to undertake a raid in the Aegean. Off Imbros, the battlecruiser sinks two British monitors. On the return journey, both vessels hit mines: *Midilli* sinks, and the battlecruiser runs aground. After several days of British air attacks, the vessel is refloated on 25 Jan, and returns to base.

10 June 1918: Italian motor torpedo-boats sink the Austrian dreadnought *Szent Istvan*.

1 Nov 1918: One day after the handover of the Austrian fleet to the new Yugoslavian state, Italian frogmen sink the dreadnought *Viribus Unitis*.

On the outbreak of war, Britain at once began to blockade the German coast. The Grand Fleet was stationed at Scapa Flow in the Orkneys, the Channel Fleet at Portsmouth; in south-east England there were only light forces. Since Russia held her Baltic Fleet back for the whole war, Germany was now able to concentrate her High Seas Fleet in the North Sea.

The War in the North Sea and the Baltic

28 Aug 1914: Action off Heligoland Bight. A British fleet under Rear Admiral Beatty attacks German ships in the Bight. The British force consists of the battlecruisers *Lion*, *Queen Mary*, *Princess Royal*, *Invincible* and *New Zealand*, 8 cruisers and a number of destroyers. In misty weather at dawn, British cruisers and destroyers attack the German outpost destroyers and sink one. Gradually, smaller German cruisers arrive and join the fight. The British light cruiser *Arethusa* and some destroyers are badly damaged, but, just in time, Beatty's battlecruisers arrive. Within a few minutes, the German light cruisers *Mainz*, *Köln* and *Ariadne* are sunk. The German battlecruisers, which leave port in the afternoon, arrive too late to take part.

5 Sept 1914: Off St. Abb's Head, the German U-boat *U21* (Hersing) sinks the British cruiser *Pathfinder*, in the first successful U-boat attack in history.

22 Sept 1914: The German U-boat *U9* (Weddingen) sinks the British armoured cruisers *Aboukir*, *Cressy* and *Hogue* in the Hoofden shallows within the space of one hour. This is one of the greatest naval disasters of the war.

27 Oct 1914: The British dreadnought *Audacious* sinks, after hitting a mine laid in the northern Irish Sea by the auxiliary cruiser *Berlin*.

3 Nov 1914: German battlecruisers bombard the English coast at Great Yarmouth.

16 Dec 1914: Renewed bombardment of the eastern English coast by German battlecruisers, this time at Hartlepool, Scarborough and Whitby, achieves minor material success, but has a considerable effect on morale. An attempted interception of the German ships by British battleships fails.

25 Dec 1914: Seven British seaplanes take off from their carriers, *Engadine*, *Riviera* and *Express*, to attack the German airship hangers at Nordholz, near Cuxhaven. This is the first offensive use of ship-based aircraft.

1 Jan 1915: The German U-boat *U24* sinks the British predreadnought *Formidable* in the English Channel.

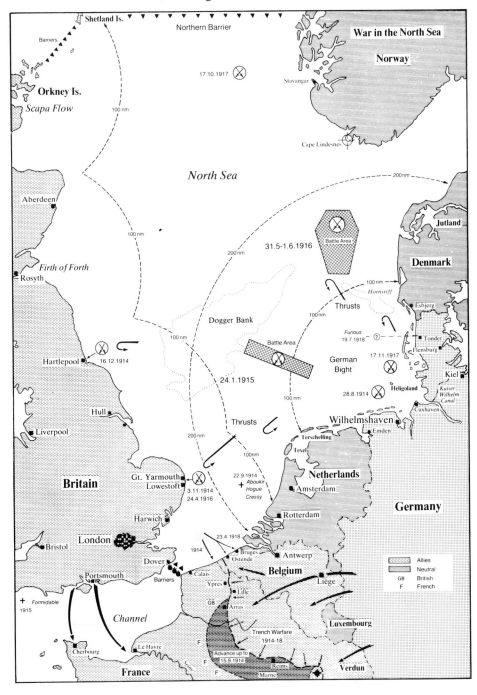

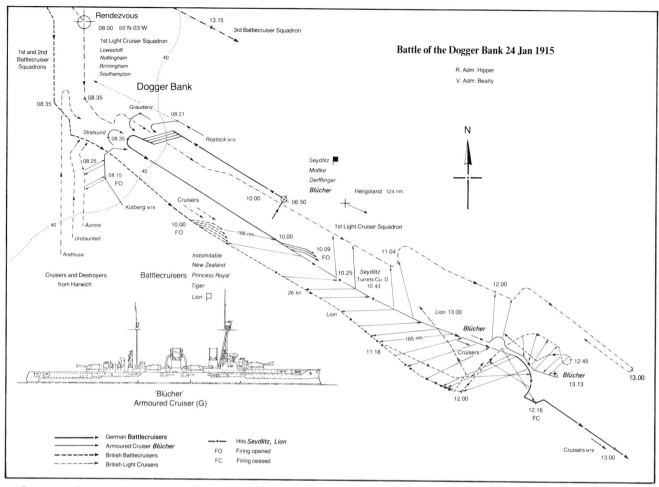

Battle of the Dogger Bank 24 Jan 1915

R. Adm. Hipper
V. Adm. Beatty

Rendezvous
08.00 55°N-03°W

3rd Battlecruiser Squadron

1st Light Cruiser Squadron
Lowestoft
Nottingham
Birmingham
Southampton

1st and 2nd
Battlecruiser
Squadrons

Dogger Bank

Graudenz

Stralsund

Rostock MTB

Kolberg MTB

Aurora

Undaunted

Arethusa

Cruisers and Destroyers
from Harwich

Battlecruisers

Cruisers

Indomitable
New Zealand
Princess Royal
Tiger
Lion

Seydlitz
Moltke
Derfflinger
Blücher

Heligoland 124 nm

1st Light Cruiser Squadron

Seydlitz
Turrets Cu. D
10.43

Lion

Lion 13.00

Blücher

Cruisers

Blücher
13.13

Cruisers MTB
13.00

'Blücher'
Armoured Cruiser (G)

	German **Battlecruisers**
	Armoured Cruiser *Blücher*
	British Battlecruisers
	British Light Cruisers
	Hits *Seydlitz*, *Lion*
FO	Firing opened
FC	Firing ceased

24 Jan 1915: Battle of Dogger Bank. German battlecruisers under Rear Admiral Hipper raid the Dogger Bank, to attack British trawlers and patrol craft. The British have known the German naval code for some time (and knew of the German raids in 1915 and 1916), so that Beatty, commander of the British battlecruiser force, is able to surprise the German ships.

	BRITAIN (Beatty, *Lion*)	GERMANY (Hipper, *Seydlitz*)
Battlecruisers	*Lion*	*Seydlitz*
	Princess Royal	*Derfflinger*
	Tiger	*Moltke*
	New Zealand	
	Indomitable	
Armoured cruisers	–	*Blücher*
Light cruisers	7	4
Destroyers	33	18

Recognizing the superior British strength, the Germans try to escape to the south-east, but are slowly overtaken by the faster British battlecruisers. At 10am the British open fire at a range of 18,000 yards (16,500 metres). The last German ship, *Blücher*, is soon hit, and gradually falls astern. *Seydlitz* is also badly hit, and both of her rear turrets knocked out of action. German fire is mainly concentrated on the leading British ship, *Lion*, which, after being hit a number of times, veers from the line, out of control. The momentum of the chase is thus lost, and the British ships content themselves with finishing off *Blücher*; the other German ships escape. This battle is the first between dreadnoughts and, for the first time, hits are scored in action at ranges of over 15,000 yards (16,500 metres).

18 Feb 1915: Germany declares British waters to be a war zone.

6 Jan 1916: The British predreadnought battleship *King Edward VII* sinks west of Scapa Flow, after hitting a mine laid by the German auxiliary cruiser *Möwe*.

24 Jan 1916: Vice Admiral Scheer becomes commander of the German High Seas Fleet.

24–25 April 1916: Battlecruisers under Rear Admiral Boedicker bombard the English coast at Lowestoft and Great Yarmouth; the rest of the High Seas Fleet is at hand to support them.

30 May 1916: The Grand Fleet under Admiral Jellicoe moves out to intercept the Germans in the Skagerrak.

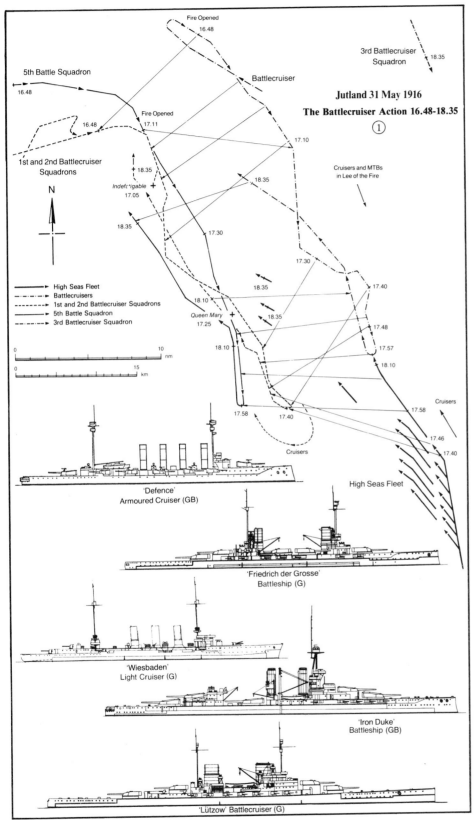

Jutland 31 May 1916

The Battlecruiser Action 16.48-18.35

①

N

| High Seas Fleet |
| Battlecruisers |
| 1st and 2nd Battlecruiser Squadrons |
| 5th Battle Squadron |
| 3rd Battlecruiser Squadron |

'Defence'
Armoured Cruiser (GB)

'Friedrich der Grosse'
Battleship (G)

'Wiesbaden'
Light Cruiser (G)

'Iron Duke'
Battleship (GB)

'Lützow' Battlecruiser (G)

31 May 1916: Battle of Jutland. Opposing fleet strengths in this battle are as follows.

BRITISH GRAND FLEET (Jellicoe, *Iron Duke*)
The Battlecruiser Force (Beatty, *Lion*):

Battlecruisers	*Lion*	*Tiger*
	Princess Royal	*New Zealand*
	Queen Mary	*Indefatigable*
Battleships	*Barham*	*Warspite*
	Valiant	*Malaya*

+ 1 seaplane carrier, 14 light cruisers, 27 destroyers.

The Main Battle Fleet (Jellicoe, *Iron Duke*):

Battleships	*Iron Duke*	*King George V*	*Marlborough*
	Royal Oak	*Ajax*	*Revenge*
	Superb	*Centurion*	*Hercules*
	Canada	*Erin*	*Agincourt*
	Benbow	*Orion*	*Colossus*
	Bellerophon	*Monarch*	*Collingwood*
	Temeraire	*Conqueror*	*Neptune*
	Vanguard	*Thunderer*	*St. Vincent*
Battlecruisers	*Invincible*	*Inflexible*	*Indomitable*
Armoured cruisers	*Minotaur*	*Hampshire*	*Cochrane*
	Shannon	*Defence*	*Warrior*
	Black Prince	*Duke of Edinburgh*	

+ 12 light cruisers, 50 destroyers, 1 minelayer.

GERMAN HIGH SEAS FLEET (Scheer, *Friedrich der Grosse*)
The Scouting Force (Hipper, *Lützow*):

Battlecruisers	*Lützow*	*Moltke*
	Derfflinger	*Von der Tann*
	Seydlitz	

+ 5 light cruisers, 30 destroyers.

The Main Battle Fleet (Scheer, *Friedrich der Grosse*):

Battleships	*Friedrich der Grosse*	*Ostfriesland*
	König	*Thüringen*
	Grosser Kurfurst	*Helgoland*
	Kronprinz	*Oldenburg*
	Markgraf	*Posen*
	Kaiser	*Rheinland*
	Kaiserin	*Nassau*
	Prinzregent Luitpold	*Westfalen*
Predreadnoughts	*Deutschland*	*Hannover*
	Hessen	*Schlesien*
	Pommern	*Schleswig-Holstein*

+ 6 light cruisers, 31 destroyers.

In sum, the line-up is as follows.

	BRITAIN	GERMANY
Dreadnoughts	28	16
Predreadnoughts	–	6
Battlecruisers	9	5
Armoured cruisers	8	–
Light cruisers	26	11
Destroyers	77	61
Total tonnage	1,250,000	660,000
Total crews	60,000	45,000

31 May, 1am: The German battlecruisers leave harbour.
2.20am: The German main fleet leaves harbour.
2.20pm: Advanced cruisers of the opposing fleets sight one another, and the first shots are exchanged.
3.10pm: The British seaplane carrier *Engadine* sends off a reconnaissance aircraft (the first to be involved in a naval battle).
3.30pm: Hipper, steering SE, tries to lure the British on to his main fleet. Both battle lines steer parallel courses, the British to the west.
3.48pm: *Lützow* opens fire; the British reply after 3 minutes. Engaged are 6 British battlecruisers against 5 German.
4.05pm: *Indefatigable* explodes, battered by *Von der Tann*.
4.11pm: Beatty's 4 battleships have now caught up, and enter the fight from the north.

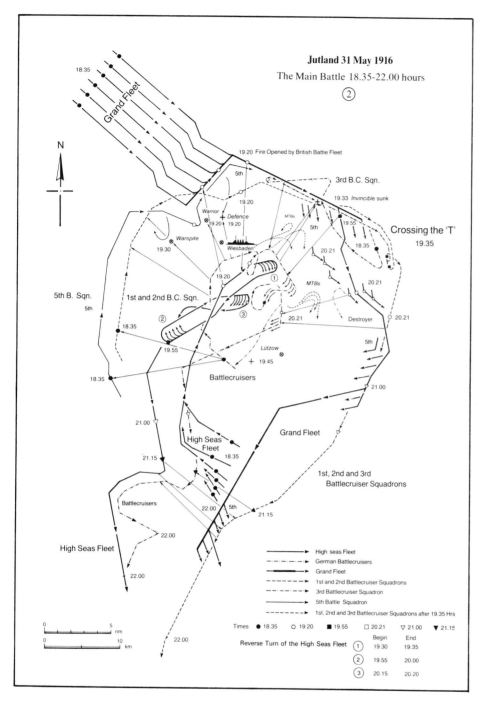

Jutland 31 May 1916

The Main Battle 18.35–22.00 hours

②

Grand Fleet

N

18.35

19.20 Fire Opened by British Battle Fleet

5th

3rd B.C. Sqn.

19.20

19.33 *Invincible* sunk

Warrior

+ *Defence*
19.20 19.20

MTBs

5th

19.55

Crossing the 'T'
19.35

⊗ *Warspite*
19.30

⊗ *Wiesbaden*

18.35

20.21

5th B. Sqn.

5th

1st and 2nd B.C. Sqn.

19.20

①

MTBs

20.21

18.35

②

③

20.21

Destroyer

20.21

19.55

Lützow ⊗

5th

19.55

+ 19.45

18.35

Battlecruisers

21.00

21.00

Grand Fleet

High Seas
Fleet

21.15

18.35

1st, 2nd and 3rd
Battlecruiser Squadrons

Battlecruisers

22.00   5th

21.15

22.00

High Seas Fleet

22.00

	High seas Fleet
	German Battlecruisers
	Grand Fleet
	1st and 2nd Battlecruiser Squadrons
	3rd Battlecruiser Squadron
	5th Battle Squadron
	1st, 2nd and 3rd Battlecruiser Squadrons after 19.35 Hrs

Times ● 18.35 ○ 19.20 ■ 19.55 □ 20.21 ▽ 21.00 ▼ 21.15

Reverse Turn of the High Seas Fleet	Begin	End
①	19.30	19.35
②	19.55	20.00
③	20.15	20.20

0 — 5 nm

0 — 10 km

4.25pm: Under fire from *Derfflinger* and *Seydlitz*, *Queen Mary* explodes.

After 4.20pm: Destroyer combat between the fleets. *Seydlitz* is hit by a torpedo, but can fight on.

4.46pm: The German main body appears and, 15 minutes later, the leading ships open fire. Beatty turns north with his ships, and the German battlecruisers follow suit at the head of their own main body. Beatty overhauls the Germans, and outflanks them on an easterly course, but the weather closes in and prevents continuous action.

5.55pm: The battlecruisers and light forces of the Grand Fleet enter the battle from the north-east. The small German cruiser *Wiesbaden* lies a wreck between the opposing lines, as the leading German ships gradually turn east.

6.10pm: The British battleship force enters the fight.

6.20pm: Under the fire of the leading German ships, the armoured cruiser *Defence* explodes, and *Warrior* becomes a wreck (and sinks next day).

6.30pm: The British battleship *Warspite*, her rudder jammed, leaves the battle line badly damaged. Scheer turns the German fleet about, to avoid being surrounded.

6.33pm: *Invincible* explodes, under fire from *Derfflinger* and *Lützow*. But only slowly can the German ships withdraw from the British fire.

6.45pm: *Lützow*, badly damaged, leaves the battle line and sinks the following night; *Marlborough* is hit by a torpedo, probably from *Wiesbaden*.

6.55pm: The Germans turn again towards the British.

7.15pm: A destroyer attack causes the British to turn away for a while; Scheer also turns away, and the battle between the main fleets is now ended.

8.15pm: The fleets again, but briefly, exchange fire.

9pm: Jellicoe turns south, so that next morning he may renew the battle about Hornsriff in the German Bight. He places his destroyers as rearguard, behind the bigger vessels.

9.10pm: Scheer sends his destroyers in on a night attack, but they steam too far north and cannot find the British fleet. Scheer makes for Hornsriff, and sails straight through the British cruisers and destroyers.

10.23pm: The light cruiser *Frauenlob* sinks, after being hit by shells and torpedoes from British cruisers.

1 June, 1.30am: Continuous British destroyer attacks (5 destroyers are sunk in the process). While taking evasive action, the light cruiser *Elbing* is rammed by one of the German battleships, and sinks two hours later.

2.10am: The light cruiser *Rostock* is hit by a torpedo, and sinks at 4.30am.

2.20am: The British armoured cruiser *Black Prince* sinks under fire.

4.10am: The British 12th Destroyer Flotilla carries out the last torpedo attack of the battle; as dawn breaks, the old battleship *Pommern* is hit and explodes.

5am: As the Germans are out of sight, Jellicoe turns north and scours the area of the battle for survivors and damaged ships. Later that day, the British fleet re-enters its harbours.

7.20am: The German battleship *Ostfriesland* hits a mine, but is only lightly damaged. At midday, the German fleet re-enters its harbours. The losses of the battle are as follows. British, 14 ships (155,000 tons), 6,090 men dead; German, 11 ships (61,000 tons), 2,550 dead. The German fleet has proved itself to be not only equal to the Royal Navy in many points, but even superior (steadiness, gunnery, night fighting). In material terms, the battle is a German victory, but it has no effect on the overall state of the war: a complete victory by the German Navy lies outside the realms of the possible. Scheer thus recommends that the U-boats should now take over the lead in prosecuting the sea war.

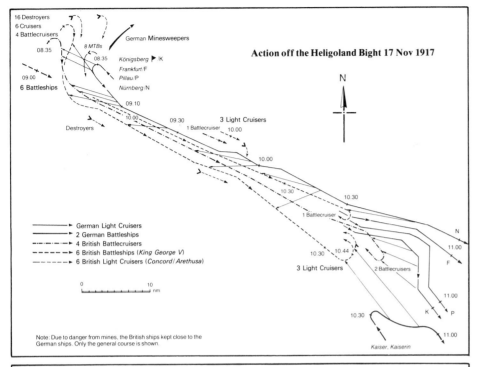

Action off the Heligoland Bight 17 Nov 1917

16 Destroyers
6 Cruisers
4 Battlecruisers

08.35

8 MTBs
German Minesweepers

08.35
Königsberg /K
Frankfurt /F
Pillau /P
Nürnberg /N

09.00
6 Battleships

09.10

09.30
10.00

Destroyers

3 Light Cruisers
1 Battlecruiser 10.00

N

10.00

1 Battlecruiser

10.30

N

10.30   10.44

11.00

3 Light Cruisers   2 Battlecruisers

F

10.30

11.00

K   P

11.00

Kaiser, Kaiserin

———► German Light Cruisers
———► 2 German Battleships
–·–·–► 4 British Battlecruisers
– – –► 6 British Battleships (*King George V*)
········► 6 British Light Cruisers (*Concord/Arethusa*)

0   10
| | | | | | | | | | |
                    nm

Note: Due to danger from mines, the British ships kept close to the
German ships. Only the general course is shown.

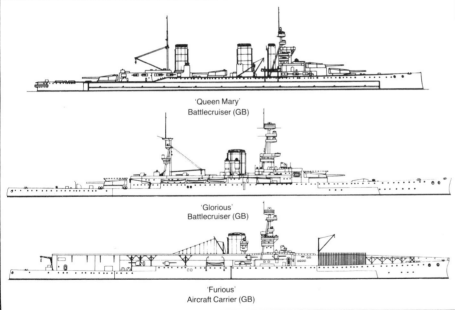

'Queen Mary'
Battlecruiser (GB)

'Glorious'
Battlecruiser (GB)

'Furious'
Aircraft Carrier (GB)

27 Sept 1917: The Russian destroyer *Ochotnik* sinks off Zerel (on the Sworbe Peninsula), after hitting a mine laid by a German aircraft. This is the first successful use of aerial minelaying.

11–19 Oct 1917: Landing Operations on the Baltic Islands. In the first large-scale German amphibious operations, troops under Lieutenant General von Kathen are landed on Osel and Dagö. Naval units under Vice Admiral Schmidt include the battlecruiser *Moltke*, 10 battleships, 9 light cruisers, 52 destroyers, minesweepers, auxiliaries and 19 transports for the troops.

17 Oct: Action between the battleships *König* and *Kronprinz*, in the Bay of Riga, with the old Russian battleships *Slava* and *Grazdhanin* (the old *Tsesarevich*) and the cruiser *Bajan*. *Slava* runs aground, badly damaged, and becomes a total loss.

17 Oct: The light cruisers *Brummer* and *Bremse* attack a British convoy running from Bergen to Britain. After sinking the 2 escorting destroyers, they sink 9 of the 12 freighters: only 3 escape.

17 Nov 1917: Action off Heligoland Bight. To protect minesweepers, German light cruisers are deployed with larger units in support, north-west of Heligoland. As in August 1914, the British try to surprise the German forces. The clash involves 4 German light cruisers plus the battleships *Kaiser* and *Kaiserin* and, on the British side, several light cruisers and the battlecruisers *Courageous*, *Glorious* and *Repulse*. In bad weather, the British succeed in catching the German cruisers unawares: these are chased south-east for almost 2 hours, until the German battleships appear. Only a few hits are scored in the bad visibility.

23 April 1918: Attack on Zeebrugge and Ostende. A bold attempt by the British to close the entrances to the German U-boat and torpedo-boat bases with blockships is a partial success, but the entrances are blocked for only a short while.

19 July 1918: Air Attack on Tondern. Seven land aircraft take off from the British aircraft carrier *Furious* to attack the German airship base in Tondern. Airships *L54* and *L60* are destroyed, in the first successful operation of land aircraft from an aircraft carrier.

9 Nov 1918: The British predreadnought *Britannia* is sunk by *U50* off Cape Trafalgar.

During the first year of the war, considerable uncertainty existed over the true potential of the submarine: the implications in international law of waging unrestricted war on merchantmen were to prove both controversial and complex.

The Submarine War

Feb 1915: After the German declaration of a war zone, Germany opens a submarine campaign against merchantmen. And, from June 1915, U-boats attack merchant shipping in the Mediterranean from bases in the Adriatic.

18 Sept 1915: The U-boat war is called off, following United States protests over the sinking of the liners *Lusitania* (7 May 1915) and *Arabic* (19 Aug 1915). Americans are among those killed on both ships.

1 Aug 1914 to 30 Sept 1915: 431 ships, totalling 792,000 tons, are sunk. In the Mediterranean, unlimited U-boat war is carried on; in the Atlantic, ships are halted and searched before being sunk.

23 Feb 1916: Resumption of unlimited U-boat war in the Atlantic war zone around the British Isles.

24 April 1916: The United States protests again, after the sinking of *Sussex* (24 Mar 1916), and the U-boat trade war is again abandoned.

1 Oct 1915 to 30 April 1916: 359 ships, totalling 900,000 tons,

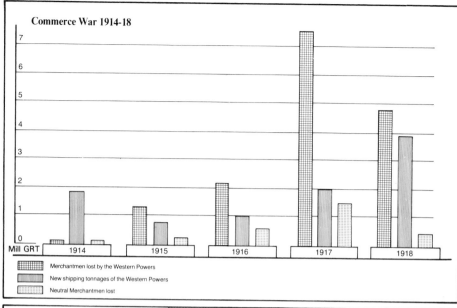

Commerce War 1914-18

Mill GRT — 1914, 1915, 1916, 1917, 1918

- Merchantmen lost by the Western Powers
- New shipping tonnages of the Western Powers
- Neutral Merchantmen lost

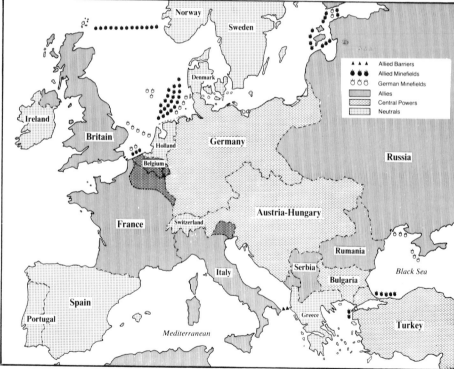

Norway, Sweden, Denmark, Ireland, Britain, Holland, Belgium, Germany, France, Switzerland, Russia, Austria-Hungary, Italy, Serbia, Rumania, Bulgaria, Spain, Portugal, Greece, Turkey, Mediterranean, Black Sea

- ▲▲▲ Allied Barriers
- Allied Minefields
- German Minefields
- Allies
- Central Powers
- Neutrals

are sunk. The U-boats are now employed on operations which lead, among other things, to the Battle of Jutland. Vice Admiral Scheer then recommends resumption of the U-boat war on a 'search then sink' basis.

1 May 1916 to 31 Jan 1917: First operations of U-boats off the American coast; 1,152 ships, totalling 2,100,000 tons, are sunk. Despite the danger of the United States' entry into the war, unlimited U-boat war on merchantmen is now declared.

6 April 1917: The United States declares war on Germany.

In 1916, the results of the increased U-boat construction programme had begun to tell, as new boats entered service. In 1917, the U-boat seemed about to bring Britain to the brink of defeat, and Germany commenced a submarine offensive off the east coast of America on 7 June. Operating from bases in Germany, Flanders and the Adriatic, 127 U-boats were now in service at any one time during 1917; and, of these boats, a third were always in the combat zones. In this year, the climax of the U-boat war, 2,566 ships were sunk—a total of 5,750,000 tons.

But, in September of the same year, the British adoption of the convoy system began to bear fruit: U-boat successes started to fall, and United States aid began to tell in the overall struggle.

1918: The American expeditionary army of over 1 million men is brought to Europe, practically without loss.

21 Oct 1918: End of U-boat commerce raiding. Since 1 Jan 1918, 1,046 ships (2,650,000 tons) have been sunk. The most successful submarine commanders of the First World War were as follows.

	SHIPS	TONS
Kapitanleutnant Lothar von Arnauld de la Periere (G)	194	454,000
Kapitanleutnant Dr. Walter Forstmann (G)	146	384,000
Kapitanleutnant Max Valentiner (G)	140	310,000
Kapitanleutnant Otto Steinbrink (G)	202	232,000

11 Nov 1918: Armistice ends the First World War. In accordance with the terms of the Armistice, the most modern German ships are sent to Scapa Flow to be interned: 11 battleships, 5 battlecruisers, 8 light cruisers, 50 destroyers and all U-boats.

21 June 1919: The commander of the delivery force, Rear-Admiral Reuter, allows the ships to be scuttled by their own crews.

1919: The Central Powers are forced to accept a dictated peace. Germany loses eastern areas to Poland, Alsace-Lorraine to France, and her colonies; she is also subject to rigorous armaments limitations and reparations payments. The Austro-Hungarian Navy is shared between the victors. 'German Austria' loses her coastline to Yugoslavia and ceases to be a sea power.

Turkey is confined to Asia Minor, but retains control over the Bosporus and Dardanelles, with a small 'bridgehead' in Europe; The Narrows themselves are placed under international control. Following the Revolution in 1917, Russia vanishes as a sea power for some time. By the terms of the Treaty of Versailles, the strength of the German fleet is limited to:

6 battleships with 11in (28cm) guns; 10,000 tons max.
6 cruisers with 6 in (15cm) guns; 6,000 tons max.
12 torpedo-boats of 800 tons max.

Aircraft carriers, aeroplanes and U-boats are forbidden.

Jutland had seen the first (and almost the only) large-scale clash between modern dreadnought battleships—the results of half a century of development, which had turned them into large, stable gun platforms, with fire control systems that enabled combat to be joined at ranges of up to 22,000 yards (20,000 metres). The future of naval warfare, however, lay in two new directions.

The submarine had introduced problems both legal and technical. As counter measures to the undersea menace, depth-charges and mines had proved effective, and mines had also played a special role as an extension of the blockade. In the English Channel and in the Straits of Otranto (in the Adriatic), mines had been used in combination with nets; and, with the entry of the United States into the war, the Allies attempted to seal off the North Sea, from Scotland to Norway, with a huge minefield designed to prevent U-boats getting out into the Atlantic. The result was that, from 1917 onwards, naval activity in the North Sea (as in the Baltic) was largely confined to the laying and clearing of mines.

The other new weapon, the aeroplane, had played but a modest role during the First World War—aircraft were not yet technically mature. British experiments with wheeled aircraft showed the future path, but, as an offensive weapon, it was the airship that had initially fulfilled expectations. In the longer term, however, the airship's limited manoeuvrability doomed it as a weapon of war.

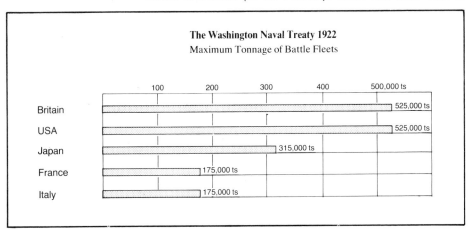

The Washington Naval Treaty 1922
Maximum Tonnage of Battle Fleets

Britain — 525,000 ts
USA — 525,000 ts
Japan — 315,000 ts
France — 175,000 ts
Italy — 175,000 ts

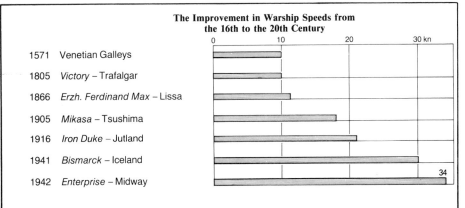

The Improvement in Warship Speeds from the 16th to the 20th Century

1571 Venetian Galleys
1805 *Victory* – Trafalgar
1866 *Erzh. Ferdinand Max* – Lissa
1905 *Mikasa* – Tsushima
1916 *Iron Duke* – Jutland
1941 *Bismarck* – Iceland
1942 *Enterprise* – Midway — 34

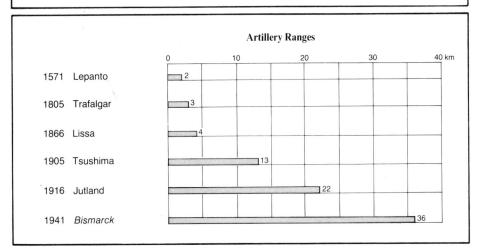

Artillery Ranges

1571 Lepanto — 2
1805 Trafalgar — 3
1866 Lissa — 4
1905 Tsushima — 13
1916 Jutland — 22
1941 *Bismarck* — 36

NAVAL EVENTS BETWEEN THE WORLD WARS

18 Aug 1919: In the Russian Civil War, British coastal motor boats (CMBs) attack the Red Fleet in Kronstadt harbour. At dawn, the battleships *Andrei Pervozvanni* and *Petropavlovsk* are hit and sink in shallow water. At the same time, aircraft from the aircraft carrier *Vindictive* bomb the harbour.

1922: **The Washington Naval Treaty.** In order to reduce the mammoth costs of building new warships, a treaty is signed by the 5 leading sea powers. This limits maximum fleet tonnages as follows. Great Britain and the United States, 525,000 tons each; Japan, 315,000 tons; France and Italy, 175,000 tons each.
The individual ship classes are limited as follows.

  Battleships   35,000 tons, with 16in (40.6cm) guns.
  Cruisers   10,000 tons, with 8in (20.3cm) guns.
  Aircraft carriers 27,000 tons, with 8in (20.3cm) guns.

Japan's gains from the First World War (the German South Sea colonies) make her the leading power in the Pacific, and she thus begins to come into conflict with the United States and Great Britain. Britain terminates her alliance with Japan in 1922.

1930: The London Naval Conference. Japan tries in vain to have her maximum permitted fleet strength improved from the ratio 5:5:3 (USA:GB:Japan).

1934: Japan renounces the Washington Naval Treaty.

1935: The London Naval Treaty between Great Britain and Germany. The size of the German fleet is limited to 35% of that of the Royal Navy (with parity in submarines). But, when the Washington Naval Treaty expires, a naval arms race begins between the leading sea powers.

1936-39: The Spanish Civil War
The rival forces have the following naval strengths.
  Republicans: the battleship *Jaime I*, 3 light cruisers, 14 destroyers, plus submarines.
  Nationalists: the battleship *España*, 2 light cruisers, 1 destroyer.
Within a year, the Nationalists have completed their 2 heavy cruisers and, in 1937, they buy 4 destroyers and 2 submarines from Italy.

29 Sept 1936: In a clash in the Straits of Gibraltar, a Republican destroyer is lost.

30 April 1937: The battleship *España* hits a mine and sinks off Santander.

6 March 1938: Three Republican destroyers sink the cruiser *Baleares* with torpedoes, in a night attack.

5 March 1939: The remaining Republican naval units (3 cruisers, 8 destroyers and 1 submarine) are all but inoperable, due to a lack of trained officers and men; they make their way to neutral Tunis, where they are interned. The Nationalists meanwhile blockade the Republican-held coastline, but their paucity of ships limits the blockade's effectiveness.

Second World War
Europe

Surface Units
1940-41

Allies
Axis
Neutrals
Axis Supporters
Areas under German occupation

A – Ark Royal 14.11.1941
B – Barham 25.11.1941
E – Eagle 11.8.1942
R – Roma 9.9.1943

Bear Is.

PQ17 2-10.7.1942

+ Scharnhorst 26.12.1943

Glorious 8.6.1940

Lofoten 9.4.1940

Narvik

Murmansk

Iceland

+ Rawalpindi 23.11.1939

Trondheim

Sweden

Finland

Archangelsk

Front 1942

USSR

Faeroes

Shetland Is.

Norway

Helsinki

Orkney Is. Scapa Flow + Royal Oak 15.10.1939

Oslo

Stockholm

Leningrad

SC7 and HX79 17-20.10.1940

RAF

Moscow

USSR

Ireland

Britain

London

Berlin 1939

Warsaw

Poland

Front 1942

Courageous + 17.9.1939

Germany

+ Bismarck 27.5.1941

Brest

Paris

France

Slovakia

Hungary

Rumania

Rostov

U-boats 1940-43

Genoa

Toulon

Italy

Yugoslavia

Bulgaria

Istanbul

Spain

Rome

Naples

Taranto

Greece

Turkey

Portugal

Madrid

Lisbon

C. Teulada 27.11.1940

Algiers 8.11.1942

Pt. Stilo 9.7.1940

C. Matapan 28.3.1941

Crete

Syria

Iraq

Casablanca

Oran 8.11.1942

Malta

Syrte 17.12.1941

Palestine

Transjordan

Morocco

Algeria

Libya

Alexandria

Egypt

Saudi Arabia

Canary Is.

The result of expansionist policies pursued by Germany and Japan in the late 1930s was a war involving practically all the major countries of the world—and encompassing all the oceans of the world. Main protagonists were the 'Axis' powers, Germany, Italy and Japan on one side, and the alliance of France, Great Britain, the United States and the USSR on the other. War was precipitated by Germany's occupation of Czechoslovakia, in flat contradiction of the Munich Agreement, and of Poland in 1939; Japan had, meanwhile, attacked China in 1937 and, 2 years later, America's termination of her trade agreement with Japan prompted Japan to move closer to the Rome–Berlin Axis.

At the outbreak of war, modern war ships could be classified generally as follows.

Battleships	35–40,000 tons with 15–16in (38–40·6cm) guns	
Aircraft carriers	17–27,000 tons with 40–90 aircraft	
Cruisers	6–10,000 tons with 6–8in (15–20cm) guns	
Destroyers	About 2,000 tons with 8–12 torpedo tubes	
Submarines	500–1,000 tons with 4–8 torpedo tubes	

Many warships that had seen service in the First World War also took part in the Second, some having been modernized; new units gradually came into service as the war progressed. Fleet strengths of the three naval powers at war in 1939 were as follows.

	GREAT BRITAIN	FRANCE	GERMANY
Battleships	15	7	2
Aircraft carriers	7	1	–
Heavy cruisers	15	7	4
Light cruisers	49	11	6
Destroyers	184	58	22
Submarines	57	71	56

1939-45: THE SECOND WORLD WAR

1 Sept 1939: Germany and the USSR invade Poland. In 3 weeks, the country is conquered and divided up.

3 Sept 1939: Britain and France declare war on Germany. At first, there are no large-scale land operations.

1939-42: The War in the Atlantic

17 Sept 1939: *U29* (Schuhart) sinks the British aircraft carrier *Courageous* in the Western Approaches.

14 Oct 1939: *U47* (Prien) penetrates the British naval base at Scapa Flow, and sinks the battleship *Royal Oak*.

21–27 Nov 1939: First foray of the German battlecruisers *Gneisenau* and *Scharnhorst* into the waters around Iceland, during which the British auxiliary cruiser *Rawalpindi* is sunk protecting its convoy.

13 Dec 1939: Battle of the River Plate. After a 3-month commerce raiding campaign in the South Atlantic, the German 'pocket' battleship *Graf Spee* is intercepted by 3 British cruisers under Commodore Harwood. *Exeter* is badly shot about, *Ajax* and *Achilles* damaged, but the German ship is also damaged, and runs into the neutral harbour of Montevideo.

17 Dec 1939: With but 3 days allowed for repairs, the Germans fear that a much-supplemented British force now awaits them. *Graf Spee* is scuttled in the Roads of Montevideo by her crew.

1939-40: Britain and France plan to occupy naval bases in northern Scandinavia, in order to cut off supplies of iron ore to Germany. The excuse for these operations is aid to Finland in her winter campaign against Russia.

8 April 1940: Britain mines Norwegian territorial waters.

9 April 1940: Germany occupies Denmark and Norway. German troops under General von Falkenhorst are landed at vital points in these countries. There is no resistance offered

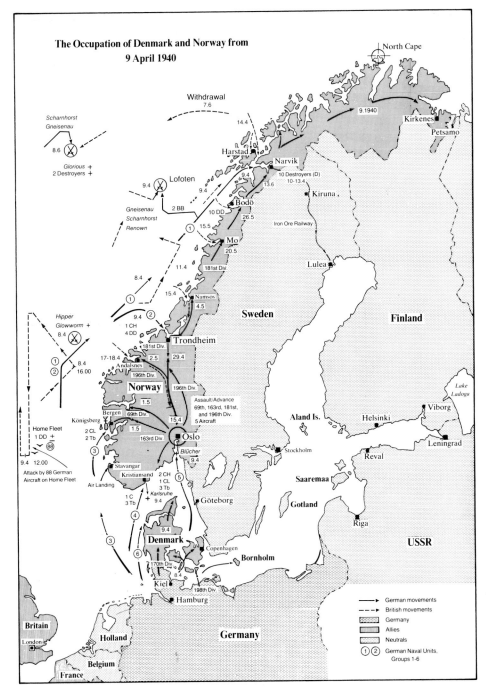

The Occupation of Denmark and Norway from 9 April 1940

Scharnhorst
Gneisenau

8.6 ⊗

Glorious +
2 Destroyers +

Withdrawal
7.6

14.4

9.1940

North Cape

Kirkenes

Petsamo

Harstad

Narvik

9.4 10 Destroyers (D)
10–13.4.

13.6

Gneisenau
Scharnhorst
Renown

2 BB

10 DD

Lofoten

9.4

9.4

Kiruna

Bodö

26.5

1 15.5

Mo
20.5

Iron Ore Railway

Lulea

11.4

181st Div.

8.4

15.4

1

Namsos
4.5

Sweden

Finland

9.4 2

1 CH
4 DD

181st Div.

Trondheim

2 5

29.4

Hipper
Glowworm +
8.4 ⊗

17–18.4

Andalsnes
196th Div.

Norway

196th Div.

1
2

8.4
16.00

196th Div.

1.5

Assault/Advance
69th, 163rd, 181st,
and 196th Div.
5 Aircraft

Aland Is.

Lake
Ladoga

Viborg

Königsberg

Bergen
2 CL
2 Tb

69th Div.

15.4

1.5

Helsinki

Home Fleet
1 DD ✛

88

163rd Div.

Oslo

Blücher
9.4

Stockholm

Reval

Leningrad

9.4 12.00

Attack by 88 German
Aircraft on Home Fleet

Stavangar

Kristiansand

2 CH
1 CL
3 Tb

Karlsruhe
9.4

5

Saaremaa

Göteborg

Gotland

1 C
3 Tb

4

Riga

3

Denmark

Copenhagen

Bornholm

USSR

6

170th Div.

9.4

8.4

Kiel

198th Div.

Hamburg

German movements
British movements
Germans
Allies
Neutrals
① ② German Naval Units. Groups 1–6

Britain

London

Holland

Germany

Belgium

France

---

in Denmark, but heavy fighting in Norway.

9 April 1940: 10 destroyers land mountain troops in Narvik; the Norwegian armoured coastal defence ships *Eidsfold* and *Norge* resist, and are sunk with torpedoes. In Trondheim, the heavy cruiser *Hipper* and 4 destroyers land troops, covered by the battlecruisers *Scharnhorst* and *Gneisenau*. In Bergen, the light cruisers *Köln* and *Königsberg*, with MTBs and auxiliaries, land troops; and in Kristiansand, the light cruiser *Karlsruhe* and MTBs land troops. The heavy cruisers *Blücher* and *Lützow*, the light cruiser *Emden* and MTBs enter Oslo fjord, where *Blücher* is sunk by artillery and torpedoes from the Dröbakenge battery. *Scharnhorst* and *Gneisenau* skirmish briefly with the British battlecruiser *Renown*.

The Luftwaffe attacks the British fleet south-west of Bergen, lightly damaging the battleship *Rodney* and the cruisers *Devonshire*, *Southampton* and *Glasgow* and sinking a destroyer.

10 April 1940: First destroyer action in Narvik Fjord. In a surprise attack, British destroyers sink 2 German destroyers and some freighters in Narvik harbour. Two British destroyers sink in the fighting with the other ships. British naval dive-bombers sink *Königsberg* at Bergen, in the first sinking of a large warship by naval aircraft.

13 April 1940: Second destroyer action in Narvik Fjord. The British battleship *Warspite* and 9 destroyers sink the remaining 8 German destroyers there. The crews of these ships are later valuable in reinforcing the land defences of the place.

Mid-April 1940: British landings at Narvik and Trondheim.

10 May: The German offensive in France begins to force the Allies to evacuate their positions in Norway.

28 May to 4 June 1940: Operation 'Dynamo', the evacuation by the British fleet of troops trapped in Dunkirk. In 8 days, 338,226 men are taken off in 848 craft of all types, and brought to Britain. The cost is 9 destroyers and a great number of smaller vessels, mostly sunk by air attack. Almost all army equipment has to be abandoned in France, but the essential personnel cadre for the reconstruction of a wartime army is saved.

4–10 June 1940: Offensive by the German Fleet. Admiral Marschall attacks the British evacuation fleet off Norway with the battlecruisers *Scharnhorst* and *Gneisenau*, the heavy cruiser *Hipper* and 4 destroyers. They sink the aircraft carrier *Glorious* and 2 destroyers, one of which, *Acasta*, scores a torpedo hit on *Scharnhorst*.

13 June 1940: Fifteen aircraft from *Ark Royal* attack *Scharnhorst* at Trondheim. But, for the loss of 8 aircraft, they score only one hit (and this bomb does not explode).

10 June 1940: Italy enters the war.

June 1940: With the fall of France, Germany controls the whole coastline of Europe from North Cape to the Bay of Biscay.

4 July 1940: Attacking a British convoy in the Channel, German dive-bombers sink 5 ships and badly damage 9 others.

July-Sept 1940: Germany prepares for a landing on the English coast (Operation 'Sea Lion'). But, as control of neither the air nor the sea can be achieved in the Channel, the operation is initially postponed indefinitely, and later cancelled altogether.

Oct 1940 to Nov 1941: German battleships and cruisers operate as commerce raiders in the Atlantic and the Indian Ocean, carefully avoiding combat with British naval forces. *Scharnhorst* and *Gneisenau* then enter Brest.

1–7 May 1941: Germany mounts heavy air raids on Liverpool. Eighteen merchantmen (35,000 tons) are sunk, and 25 others badly damaged.

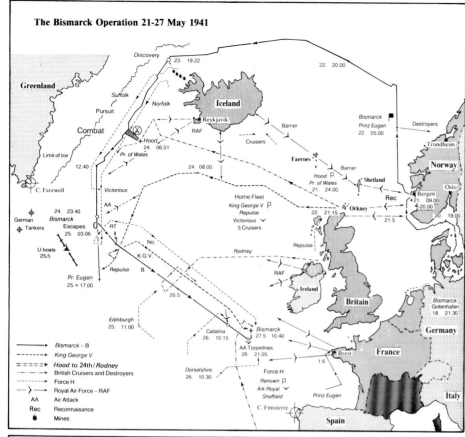

The Bismarck Operation 21-27 May 1941

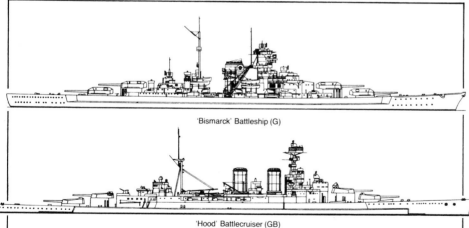

'Bismarck' Battleship (G)

'Hood' Battlecruiser (GB)

18–27 May 1941: The Bismarck Operation ('Rhine Exercise'). Encouraged by the successful operations in the winter of 1940–41, Germany sends the new battleship *Bismarck* and the heavy cruiser *Prinz Eugen*, under command of Admiral Lütjens, to raid commerce in the Atlantic.

18 May: Both ships leave Gotenhafen. Heading for a passage to the north of Iceland, they make a halt in Korsfjord, south of Bergen.

21 May: Here they are sighted by British reconnaissance aircraft, and counter measures are at once set in motion: north and south of Iceland, cruisers are sent on patrol to watch for the German ships; the battlecruiser *Hood* and the battleship *Prince of Wales*, under Vice Admiral Holland, leave Scapa Flow to reinforce the cruisers.

22 May: Admiral Tovey (Commander of the Home Fleet) goes to sea with the battleship *King George V*, the battlecruiser *Repulse*, the aircraft carrier *Victorious* and other light forces.

23 May: The heavy cruiser *Suffolk* sights the German ships in the Denmark Strait, between Iceland and Greenland, and her sister ship, *Norfolk*, makes contact soon afterwards. With the help of their modern radar, they shadow the German ships and give constant location reports.

24 May, early: Holland intercepts the German ships. In the ensuing fight, *Hood* blows up after 5 minutes, having been hit by shells from *Bismarck* and *Prinz Eugen*. A few minutes later *Prince of Wales*, hit four times by *Bismarck* and three times by *Prinz Eugen*, has to break off the fight. *Bismarck* is hit twice, and the resultant fuel leak causes Lütjens to abandon his sortie and make for Brest. The German ships proceed south while *Prince of Wales* and the other 2 cruisers follow them out of range. That evening, Lütjens sends *Prinz Eugen* off to raid commerce and, during the night, *Bismarck* is attacked by aircraft from *Victorious*. However, their torpedo hits have little effect.

25/26 May: Shortly after 3am, the British lose contact with *Bismarck*. Vice Admiral Somerville, with the British Force H (battlecruiser *Renown*, aircraft carrier *Ark Royal* and 2 cruisers), leaves Gibraltar in order to cut *Bismarck* off from France.

26 May: The German ship is sighted by a Coastal Command flying-boat. That evening, torpedo-bombers from *Ark Royal* score 2 hits in the twilight: one destroys the battleship's starboard rudder, rendering *Bismarck* uncontrollable. During the night, British destroyers carry out torpedo attacks under heavy fire, but score no hits.

27 May: Next morning, Tovey attacks with the battleships *King George V* and *Rodney*, and 2 cruisers. At the opening of the fight, *Bismarck* is badly hit and, after 90 minutes, she is a floating ruin: after several torpedo hits (and, possibly, the opening of the scuttles by her crew) she sinks, with her colours still flying.

1 June: *Prinz Eugen* has engine trouble and runs into Brest.

During the Bismarck *operation, the two German ships had been hunted by a total of 7 battleships, 2 aircraft carriers and 12 cruisers, and had been in direct combat, at one time or another, with the following units: the battleships* Hood, Prince of Wales, King George V, *and* Rodney; *the heavy cruisers* Suffolk, Norfolk *and* Devonshire; *the aircraft carriers* Victorious, *and* Ark Royal; *and 5 destroyers. As a follow-up, the Royal Navy mounted a concerted search for German supply ships in the North Atlantic, sinking most of them and, thereby, rendering operations by enemy surface units practically impossible. The German lack of aircraft carriers and the surveillance made possible by airborne radar would make attempts to break out into the Atlantic too grave a risk.*

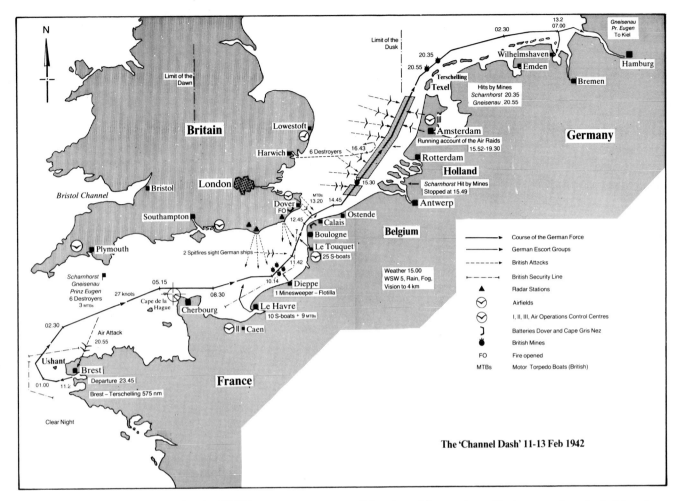

The map contains the following labels:

N

Limit of the Dusk

13.2 07.00

Gneisenau Pr. Eugen To Kiel

02.30

Wilhelmshaven

20.35

20.55

Emden

Hamburg

Terschelling

Bremen

Texel

Hits by Mines
Scharnhorst 20.35
Gneisenau 20.55

Amsterdam

Germany

Limit of the Dawn

Britain

Lowestoft

Running account of the Air Raids
15.52-19.30

Harwich

6 Destroyers

16.43

Rotterdam

Holland

London

15.30

Scharnhorst Hit by Mines
Stopped at 15.49

Bristol

Bristol Channel

MTBs
13.20   14.45

Dover
FO

Antwerp

Southampton

12.45

Ostende

Calais

Belgium

Boulogne

Le Touquet

Course of the German Force

Plymouth

2 Spitfires sight German ships

25 S-boats

German Escort Groups

11.42

Weather 15.00
WSW 5, Rain, Fog,
Vision to 4 km

British Attacks

British Security Line

10.14

Radar Stations

Scharnhorst
Gneisenau
Prinz Eugen
6 Destroyers
3 MTBs

05.15

Dieppe

Airfields

27 knots

08.30

1 Minesweeper – Flotilla

I, II, III, Air Operations Control Centres

Cape de la
Hague

Cherbourg

Le Havre

10 S-boats + 9 MTBs

Batteries Dover and Cape Gris Nez

02.30

British Mines

Air Attack
20.55

Caen

FO   Fire opened

Ushant

MTBs   Motor Torpedo Boats (British)

Brest

01.00   11.2

Departure 23.45

France

Brest – Terschelling 575 nm

Clear Night

The 'Channel Dash' 11-13 Feb 1942

22 June 1941: Germany Attacks the USSR

The numerical strength of the Soviet navy is 3 battleships (2 in the Baltic), 6 cruisers (2 in the Baltic), and 61 destroyers (23 in the Baltic). The Soviet Baltic Fleet, however, makes no offensive move. The rapid German advance results in the main naval bases at Kronstadt and Leningrad being surrounded by the autumn, and the Gulf of Finland is closed by minefields.

22–25 July 1941: Aircraft from the carriers *Victorious* and *Furious* attack Petsamo and Kirkenes with little effect; 15 aircraft are lost to AA fire.

28–29 Aug 1941: During the evacuation of the surrounded naval base of Reval, the Russians lose 24 ships (52,000 tons), 5 destroyers and a number of smaller vessels to German air attack and minelaying operations.

21–24 Sept 1941: German dive-bombers attack the Russian ships at Kronstadt; 2 destroyers capsize, and the battleships *Marat* and *Oktyabrskaya Revolutsia* and a number of other ships are damaged, some badly.

12 Feb 1942: The 'Channel dash'. The battlecruisers *Scharnhorst* and *Gneisenau* and the heavy cruiser *Prinz Eugen*, under Vice Admiral Ciliax, leave Brest escorted by numerous destroyers, MTBs, minesweepers and aircraft of Luftflotte 3. The ships are detected by the British shortly after passing through the Straits of Dover, and the coastal batteries open fire too late. Subsequent attacks by MTBs, destroyers and torpedo-carrying aircraft are beaten off.

Scharnhorst hits 2 mines, *Gneisenau* 1, but the bold undertaking is a success, due to meticulous planning, rigorous air cover, extreme secrecy and the divided control and multiplicity of British commands charged with protecting the Channel.

As in the First World War, Germany took full advantage of the fact that Great Britain was dependent for her survival upon the importation of food and raw materials, and embarked again upon a campaign aimed at strangling Britain's maritime communications. Submarines would provide the principal weapon in this struggle, but the German Air Force (Luftwaffe), surface naval units and mines would also be used.

During the first year of the war, political considerations tempered U-boat activity: neutrality was respected, and victims were searched before being sunk. Only in 1941 were sufficient U-boats available for a truly effective campaign against British commerce;

but, in the spring of 1940, U-boats were able to support the landings in Norway.

1939-43: The Convoy War and the Battle of the Atlantic

1940: In order to keep up attacks on British merchant shipping, even during the Norwegian operation, Germany sends the first wave of auxiliary cruisers into the Atlantic (armed and camouflaged merchant ships). From mid-April, *Atlantis*, *Orion*, *Pinguin*, *Widder* and *Thor* are employed successfully against Britain's trade routes and in August, the auxiliary cruiser *Komet* passes north of Siberia to raid commerce in the Pacific. In spite of their limited numbers during the first years of the war, the U-boats score their first great successes in 1940.

29 Aug to 2 Sept 1940: 6 U-boats sink 10 ships (40,000 tons) from convoys HX66, OB205 and OA204.

Sept 1940: 5 U-boats sink 12 ships (73,000 tons) of convoy HX72 from Halifax.

17-20 Oct 1940: Convoy battle in the North Channel. 9 U-boats attack convoys SC7 and HX79 (79 ships in all). In a 4-day battle, they sink 32 ships (a total of 155,000 tons) without loss to themselves. They break off the action when all their torpedoes have been fired.

23 Oct 1940: 2 U-boats sink 12 ships (48,000 tons) from convoys SC11 and OB244.

Oct 1940 to Mar 41: The battlecruisers *Scharnhorst* and *Gneisenau* and the heavy cruiser *Hipper* in the Atlantic, and the heavy cruiser *Scheer* in the Atlantic and the Indian Ocean, operate against Allied commerce. In all, they catch 49 ships (271,000 tons), of which the majority are sunk.

Dec 1940: U-boats sink 9 ships (53,000 tons) from convoy HX90.

8-11 Feb 1941: Convoy battle off Cape St. Vincent. *U37* sights convoy HG53, and sinks 2 ships. Her reports attract 5 long-range bombers, which sink 5 further ships. *U37* then sinks her third ship, and leads in the cruiser *Hipper*, which sinks some stragglers. On the last day, *Hipper* attacks convoy SLS64, and sinks 7 ships.

2-4 April 1941: 9 ships (50,000 tons) of convoy SC26 are sunk by 6 U-boats.

19-22 May 1941: Convoy HX126 is attacked by 9 U-boats, and loses 9 ships (54,000 tons).

20-29 June 1941: 15 U-boats attack convoys HX133 and OB336, and sink 9 ships (50,000 tons). The strong escort sinks 2 U-boats, and turns the rest away.

9-19 Sept 1941: Convoy SC42 (70 ships) is attacked by 15 U-boats; 18 ships (73,000 tons) are sunk, and 2 U-boats are destroyed by the convoy escort.

19-27 Sept 1941: U-boats sink 10 out of 25 merchantmen in convoy HG73, off Cape St. Vincent.

21-24 Sept 1941: 3 U-boats sink 7 ships (33,000 tons) out of 11 freighters in convoy SL87.

Sept 1941: The United States Navy begins escorting convoys as far as the Mid-Ocean Meeting Point.

15-18 Oct 1941: 9 U-boats attack convoy SC48. Of 39 ships, 9 (47,000 tons) are sunk, plus 2 of the escort vessels. US Navy destroyers form part of the escort.

14-23 Dec 1941: Convoy battle off Portugal. Convoy HG76 (32 ships with a strong escort, under Commander J. F. Walker) sails from Gibraltar to Britain. Cover is provided by 9 escorts, 3 destroyers, and Britain's first escort carrier, *Audacity*. 12 U-boats attack, but with the aid of the carrier's aircraft, the escort sinks 5 U-boats; only 3 merchantmen, plus *Audacity* and a destroyer, are sunk.

7 Dec 1941: The United States enters the war. The U-boat campaign can now be extended to the American coast.

13 Jan 1942: Suddenly, Operation 'Paukenschlag' (Kettledrum beat') begins, and the U-boats attack American shipping.

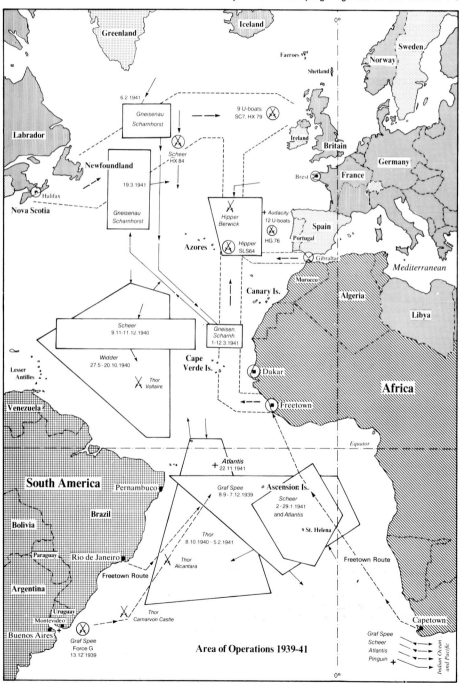

Area of Operations 1939-41

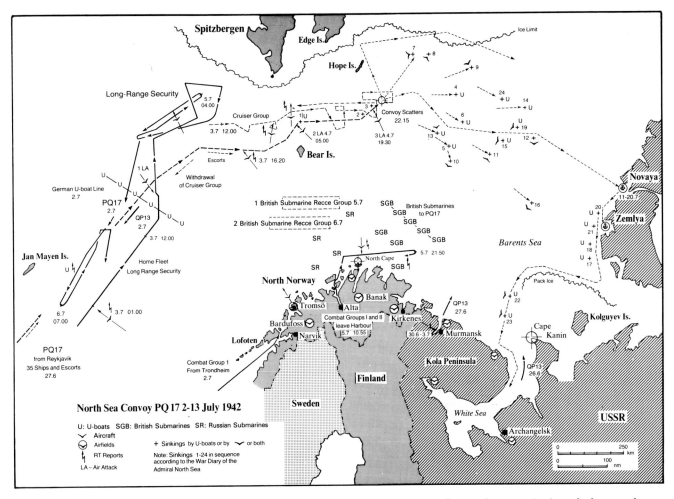

North Sea Convoy PQ 17 2–13 July 1942

U: U-boats   SGB: British Submarines   SR: Russian Submarines

⌄ Aircraft
◉ Airfields   + Sinkings by U-boats or by ⌄ or both
⚓ RT Reports   Note: Sinkings 1–24 in sequence
LA – Air Attack   according to the War Diary of the
                        Admiral North Sea

Against weak escorts, they achieve large kills initially, despite their limited numbers. From Jan to March 1942, they sink 1,200,000 tons of shipping.

21–25 Feb 1942: 6 U-boats sink 8 merchantmen (55,000 tons) from convoy ONS67, without loss to themselves.

12–13 May: 2 U-boats sink 7 ships (36,000 tons) of convoy ONS92.

From the winter of 1941/42 the Allies began sending convoys to Russia. These convoys, code-named 'PQ', were constantly threatened by German aircraft, U-boats and surface units.

2–13 July 1942: North Sea Convoy PQ17. This convoy to Russia includes 34 merchantmen, 3 rescue ships and 13 escort vessels. A close-support force of 4 cruisers and 3 destroyers accompanies the convoy, and long-range protection is provided by the Home Fleet under Admiral Tovey, with 2 battleships, 1 aircraft carrier, 2 cruisers and 14 destroyers.

2 July: First Luftwaffe attack on the convoy.

4 July: The British Admiralty receives news that the German North Sea Combat Group (battleship *Tirpitz*, cruisers *Scheer*, *Lützow* and *Hipper*) has put to sea in the direction of the North Cape. The Admiralty orders the convoy's long-range escort to sail west, and the convoy to disperse. The Home Fleet turns about at Bear Island: up to this point, the convoy has lost only 3 ships to air attack. Meanwhile, the

German Combat Group also turns back, as it does not know the position of the Home Fleet.

5–10 July: The convoy now suffers heavy losses by U-boat and Luftwaffe attack. 23 merchantmen and 1 rescue ship (144,000 tons total) are sunk, with two-thirds of the convoy's cargo. German losses are 5 aircraft.

12–15 July 1942: 3 U-boats sink 6 ships (38,000 tons) from convoy OS33.

3–11 Aug 1942: Convoy SC94, with 36 merchantmen, is attacked by 17 U-boats. 11 ships (53,000 tons) are sunk, for the German loss of 2 U-boats.

10–14 Sept 1942: Convoy ON127 (32 merchantmen and 6 escorts) is attacked by 13 U-boats, who sink 7 merchantmen (50,000 tons) and 1 destroyer, without loss.

12–18 Sept 1942: North Sea Convoy PQ18. 41 merchantmen and 21 escort ships (including an aircraft carrier) set out. 10 merchantmen are sunk by air attack, 3 by U-boats; the convoy escorts sink 3 U-boats and destroy 40 aircraft.

12–14 Oct 1942: Atlantic convoy SC104 loses 8 ships to U-boat attack (*U221* gets 5 of these). 3 U-boats are sunk.

27–29 Oct 1942: 4 U-boats sink 6 ships (52,000 tons) from convoy HX212.

27–31 Oct 1942: Convoy SL125 (37 merchantmen and 4 escorts) is attacked by 10 U-boats off Morocco. 11 ships (72,000 tons) are sunk, without U-boat loss. This operation attracts all U-boats west of Gibraltar: simultaneously, the troop transports for the Allied landings in North Africa pass unseen and unscathed.

1–6 Nov 1942: Convoy SC107 (42 merchantmen) is attacked by 13 U-boats in the western North Atlantic. It loses 15 ships (83,000 tons), while the escorts sink 2 U-boats.

24–31 Dec 1942: 20 U-boats are sent against convoy ONS154 (45 merchantmen); 14 ships (70,000 tons) are sunk.

8–11 Jan 1943: The first tanker convoy from Trinidad to North Africa, TM1 (9 tankers), loses 7 ships to U-boat attack (56,000 tons).

4–9 Feb 1943: Convoy SC118 (61 merchantmen) is attacked in the North Atlantic by 20 U-boats. 11 ships (60,000 tons) are sunk, and 3 U-boats are destroyed by the escorts.

21–25 Feb 1943: Convoy ON166 (49 merchantmen) is attacked by a large U-boat pack in the North Atlantic. 10 boats actually get into range, and 14 ships (88,000 tons) are sunk, for the loss of 1 U-boat.

6–11 March 1943: 27 U-boats attack convoy SC121 (59 merchantmen) in the North Atlantic. 12 ships (56,000 tons) are sunk, for no U-boat losses.

16–20 March 1943: Convoys HX229 and SC122. The greatest convoy battle of the war. Convoy SC122 leaves New York on 5 March, consisting of over 50 merchantmen; it is followed by the faster HX229 (40 ships), which leaves New York on 8 March and should overtake SC122 on 20th.

16 March: The attacks of up to 40 U-boats begin on HX229. On 16 and 17 March, the convoy loses 10 ships.

17 March: SC122, still ahead, is also attacked. The convoys separate, and the combat zone spreads over a large area. Up to 20 March, 21 ships (141,000 tons) are sunk for the loss of 1 U-boat. This is the climax of the U-boat war.

4–7 April 1943: 15 U-boats sink 6 ships (41,000 tons) of Convoy HX231, for the loss of 2 U-boats.

30 April to 1 May 1943: *U515* (Henke) sinks 7 ships (43,000 tons) with 9 torpedoes in a convoy off Freetown.

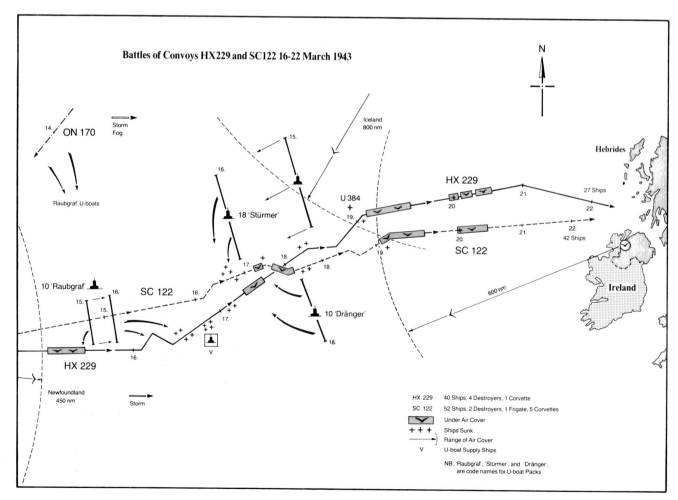

Battles of Convoys HX229 and SC122 16-22 March 1943

N

ON 170

Storm Fog

'Raubgraf' U-boats

Iceland 800 nm

Hebrides

18 'Stürmer'

U 384

HX 229

27 Ships

10 'Raubgraf'

SC 122

SC 122

10 'Dränger'

42 Ships

Ireland

600 nm

HX 229

Newfoundland 450 nm

Storm

HX 229   40 Ships, 4 Destroyers, 1 Corvette

SC 122   52 Ships, 2 Destroyers, 1 Frigate, 5 Corvettes

Under Air Cover

+ + +   Ships Sunk

Range of Air Cover

V   U-boat Supply Ships

NB: 'Raubgraf', 'Stürmer', and 'Dränger', are code names for U-boat Packs

On 10 June 1940, Italy opened hostilities, and the Mediterranean once more became a theatre of war. But, despite its considerable strength (6 battleships, 7 heavy cruisers, 14 light cruisers, 59 destroyers and 108 submarines), the Italian fleet was not active.

1940-42: The War in the Mediterranean

14 June 1940: French cruisers and destroyers bombard Genoa and Vado.

22 June 1940: The Vichy government of France concludes an armistice with the Axis powers. At this time, the French fleet is mainly in its North African bases, although a small proportion is in Alexandria and England, while an aircraft carrier and 2 cruisers are in the West Indies.

3 July 1940: The British seize the French ships within their sphere of power (2 battleships and a number of smaller ships). The Alexandria squadron is neutralized.

3 July 1940: Battle of Mers El-Kebir (Oran). In this harbour are the French battlecruisers *Dunkerque*, *Strasbourg*, the old battleships *Provence* and *Bretagne*, 11 destroyers, 5 submarines and the aircraft support ship *Commandante Teste*. The British Force H, under Vice Admiral Somerville, appears with the battlecruiser *Hood*, the battleships *Valiant* and *Resolution*, the aircraft carrier *Ark Royal*, 2 cruisers and 11 destroyers. The French commander, Admiral Gensoul, rejects the British ultimatum to hand over the fleet, as it contravenes the armistice conditions. The British battleships open fire, and *Ark Royal*'s aircraft also attack. After 15 minutes, the British break off the attack: *Bretagne* has exploded, *Dunkerque* and *Provence* are damaged; only *Strasbourg* escapes to Toulon with 6 destroyers. The British ships suffer no loss or damage.

4 July 1940: The French ships at Alexandria are demilitarized, by agreement between Cunningham and Admiral Godfroy.

5 July 1940: Torpedo-bombers from the aircraft carrier *Eagle* sink an Italian destroyer and an Italian freighter at Tobruk.

8 July 1940: A British task force consisting of the aircraft carrier *Hermes* and 2 heavy cruisers attacks Dakar, and damages the Vichy French battleship *Richelieu*.

9 July 1940: Battle of Punta Stilo (Calabria). The first clash between the British Mediterranean Fleet and Italian battleships takes place while the British are covering the passage of 2 convoys from Malta to Alexandria. Vice Admiral A. B. Cunningham commands the battleships *Warspite*, *Malaya* and *Royal Sovereign*, the aircraft carrier *Eagle*, 5 light cruisers and 16 destroyers. The Italians are meanwhile escorting a convoy from Naples to Benghazi. Squadron Admiral Campioni has the battleships *Guilio Cesare* and *Conte di Cavour*, 7 heavy cruisers, 12 light cruisers and 24 destroyers. South of Crete, the British are attacked by Italian high-altitude bombers, which hit a cruiser, but, despite this, the British are able to bring the already-withdrawing Italians to battle. As *Royal Sovereign* and *Malaya* are too slow to join the fight, the British try to slow down the Italian battleships with carrier-borne aircraft from *Eagle*, but

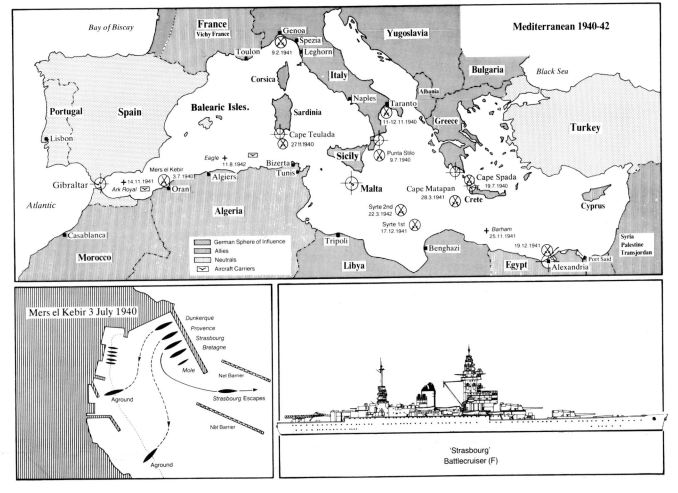

Mers el Kebir 3 July 1940

'Strasbourg'
Battlecruiser (F)

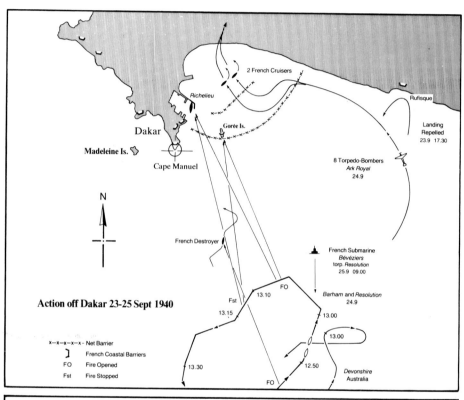

2 French Cruisers

Richelieu

Rufisque

Landing
Repelled
23.9 17.30

Dakar

Gorée Is.

Madeleine Is.

Cape Manuel

8 Torpedo-Bombers
Ark Royal
24.9

N

French Destroyer

French Submarine
Bévéziers
torp. Resolution
25.9 09.00

Action off Dakar 23-25 Sept 1940

FO
13.10

Fst

Barham and Resolution
24.9

13.15

13.00

x—x—x—x—x- Net Barrier

] French Coastal Barriers

FO   Fire Opened

Fst   Fire Stopped

13.00

13.30

12.50

FO

Devonshire
Australia

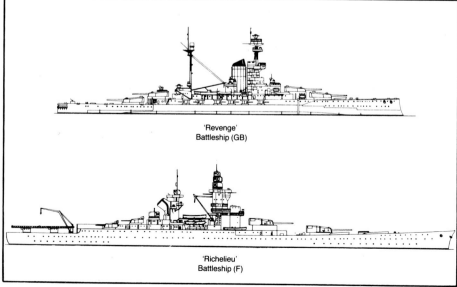

'Revenge'
Battleship (GB)

'Richelieu'
Battleship (F)

do not succeed. In a long-range artillery duel lasting 105 minutes, *Guilio Cesare* is hit by a 15in shell from *Warspite*. Campioni lays a smokescreen, and runs to the west behind his destroyers. 25 miles (40 kilometres) from the Calabrian coast, the British break off the chase. Air attacks by Italian high-altitude bombers score only near-misses on *Eagle*, but cause her to fall out of the operation against Taranto.

19 July 1940: Action off Cape Spada. The Italian light cruisers *Bartolomeo Colleoni* and *Giovanni della Bande Nere* meet the British light cruiser *Sydney* and 5 destroyers near Crete. A direct hit puts *Colleoni's* boiler room out of action, the cruiser loses way, and is sunk. *Bande Nere* scores hits on *Sydney*, but is damaged herself and limps off to Benghazi.

20 July 1940: Torpedo-bombers from *Eagle* sink 2 Italian destroyers and a freighter off Tobruk.

16 Sept 1940: Aircraft from the British aircraft carrier *Illustrious* attack Benghazi, and sink 2 Italian destroyers.

23–25 Sept 1940: Action at Dakar. The British are keen to take control of the French colonies and, among other projects, they try to land troops at Dakar. These consist of 4,200 British and 2,700 Free French, under General de Gaulle. Vice Admiral J. H. D. Cunningham's supporting forces are the battleships *Barham* and *Resolution*, the aircraft carrier *Ark Royal*, heavy cruisers *Devonshire*, *Cumberland* and *Australia*, and 6 destroyers. The Vichy French on Dakar, under Governor Boisson, have some medium coastal batteries, the battleship *Richelieu* (but unfit to put to sea), the cruisers *Georges Leygues* and *Montcalm*, 2 destroyers and 3 submarines.

23 Sept 1940: In the early morning, the Vichy French refuse an ultimatum to hand over their ships, and the coastal batteries open fire. The submarine *Persée* is sunk while trying to torpedo a cruiser; the destroyer *Audacieux* is bombarded into a wreck by *Australia*. On the British side, the cruiser *Cumberland* is badly hit, and 2 destroyers are damaged. In the afternoon, another British ultimatum is rejected, and an attempted landing at Rufisque (east of Dakar) by de Gaulle's troops is defeated.

24 Sept 1940: Next morning, the British bombard Dakar, and are answered in lively fashion by *Richelieu*, the cruisers and the coastal batteries. The Vichy French submarine *Ajax* is sunk by depth-charges, but the other French ships are almost untouched by the fire. *Barham* is hit 4 times.

25 Sept 1940: The last Vichy French submarine, *Bévéziers*, hits *Resolution* with a torpedo. As the French ships are still firing heavily, the British abandon the operation and withdraw.

11–12 Oct 1940: The British light cruiser *Ajax* meets an Italian flotilla of 4 destroyers and 3 MTBs off the Tunisian coast. In a spirited fight in brilliant moonlight, a destroyer and 2 torpedo-boats are sunk.

28 Oct 1940: Italy attacks Greece from Albania. This requires considerable Italian naval forces in the southern Adriatic.

11-12 Nov 1940: British attack on Taranto. The British Mediterranean fleet, under A. B. Cunningham, leaves Alexandria on 6 Nov. The actual attack is to be made by aircraft from *Illustrious*, which, with 4 cruisers and 4 destroyers as escorts, leaves the main fleet in the southern Ionian Sea. The carrier now approaches for a night attack. At 9 pm, 170 nautical miles from the target, *Illustrious* flies off aircraft carrying torpedoes, flares and high-explosive bombs. The torpedoes are adjusted to run in the shallow harbour waters just deep enough to hit the target ships below the armoured belt. Apart from the smaller warships in the harbour, there are 6 battleships, and 3 heavy cruisers. In spite of heavy anti-aircraft fire, the aircraft score 5 hits with torpedoes: 3 on the battleship *Littorio* (which sinks), and one each on *Conte di Cavour* and *Caio Duilio* (which also sinks). *Conte di Cavour* is so badly damaged that she remains out of service until the end of the war and vital fuel storage tanks at Taranto are destroyed. British losses are 2 aircraft to AA fire.

27 Nov 1940: Battle of Cape Teulada (Sardinia). The British Force H under Vice Admiral Somerville is to escort 3 fast freighters bound from Gibraltar to Alexandria. The Italians, under Squadron Admiral Campioni, try to intercept and destroy them.

	BRITAIN	ITALY
Battlecruiser	*Renown*	
Battleships	*Ramillies*	*Vittorio Veneto*
		Guilio Cesare
Aircraft carrier	*Ark Royal*	–
Cruisers	5	6
Destroyers	14	14

The Italians are detected south of Sardinia by British aircraft, and Somerville at once moves towards them. The cruiser groups clash first, and the slower *Ramillies* falls behind. When *Renown* enters the battle, the Italian cruisers fall back on to their battleships, which also join the fight shortly. *Ark Royal*'s aircraft fly unsuccessful sorties against the Italian battleships, but, as the Italians have no air cover, Campioni breaks off the fight. One Italian destroyer is badly damaged, while the British cruiser *Berwick* receives a serious hit.

17 Dec 1940: Aircraft from the British carrier *Illustrious* attack Rhodes.

18 Dec 1940: The battleships *Warspite* and *Valiant* bombard the Albanian harbour of Valona.

Jan 1941: In North Africa, the British capture all of Cyrenaica. Germany now sends General Rommel with the 'Afrikakorps' to Tripoli. To protect the troop transports, Fliegerkorps X (X Air Corps) is transferred to Sicily, with strong bomber forces.

10-11 Jan 1941: Convoy Operation 'Excess'. The British send another 4 fast merchantmen from Gibraltar, 1 to Malta, 3 to the Piraeus; Force H covers them to the Straits of Sicily and, from there on, they are escorted by the cruisers *Southampton*, *Gloucester* and *Bonaventure*, with 5 destroyers. South of Malta, the Mediterranean Fleet, with the battleships *Warspite* and *Valiant* and the carrier *Illustrious*, assume the long-range escort duty.

10 Jan: In the afternoon, Fliegerkorps X attacks from Sicily. Within a short time, *Illustrious* is hit by 6 bombs, and can only limp back to Malta with difficulty. *Warspite* is also hit.

11 Jan: Fliegerkorps X attacks the escorting British cruisers. *Gloucester* and *Southampton* are hit, the latter so badly that she has to be abandoned. But the 4 merchantmen reach their destinations.

9 Feb 1941: Bombardment of Genoa and Leghorn. Force H (Vice Admiral Somerville) leaves Gibraltar to raid the Gulf of Genoa. It consists of the battleship *Malaya*, the battlecruiser *Renown*, aircraft carrier *Ark Royal*, a cruiser and 10 destroyers. The battleships shell Genoa, and the carrier aircraft bomb Leghorn and drop mines off La Spezia. An Italian attempt to intercept the British, with the battleships *Vittorio Veneto*, *Guilio Cesare*, *Andrea Doria*, 3 cruisers and 10 destroyers, fails.

25 March 1941: Italian two-man torpedo-boats sink a large tanker in Suda Bay, Crete, and next day damage the heavy cruiser *York* so badly that she has to be run aground (where she is later destroyed by the Luftwaffe).

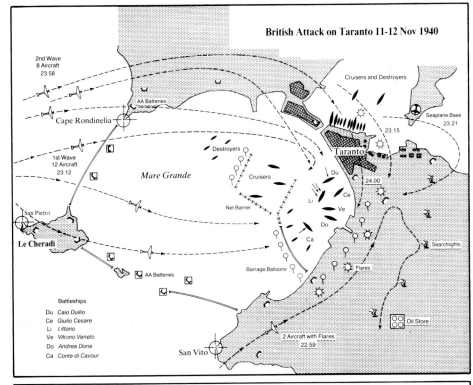

British Attack on Taranto 11-12 Nov 1940

2nd Wave
8 Aircraft
23.58

AA Batteries

Cape Rondinelia

1st Wave
12 Aircraft
23.12

Mare Grande

San Pietro

Le Cheradi

AA Batteries

Destroyers

Cruisers

Net Barrier

Cruisers and Destroyers

Seaplane Base
23.21

23.15

Taranto

Du
24.00
Ce
Li
Ve
Do
Ca

Searchlights

Barrage Balloons

Flares

Oil Store

2 Aircraft with Flares
22.59

San Vito

Battleships
Du   *Caio Duilio*
Ce   *Giulio Cesare*
Li   *Littorio*
Ve   *Vittorio Veneto*
Do   *Andrea Doria*
Ca   *Conte di Cavour*

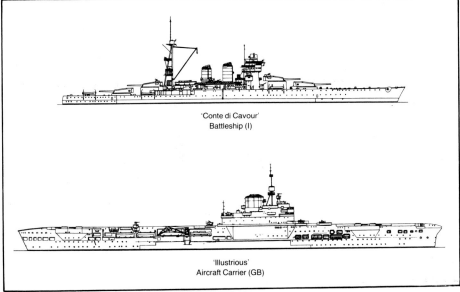

'Conte di Cavour'
Battleship (I)

'Illustrious'
Aircraft Carrier (GB)

28 March 1941: Battle of Cape Matapan. The Italian fleet moves into the waters south of Crete, to attack British Greece-bound convoys. They are detected by a British reconnaissance aircraft, and the Mediterranean fleet leaves Alexandria to rendezvous with a cruiser force from Crete. Relative fleet strengths are as follows.

	ITALY (Iachino, *Vittorio Veneto*)		BRITAIN (A. B. Cunningham, *Warspite*)
Battleships	*Vittorio Veneto*		*Warspite*
			Valiant
			Malaya
Aircraft carriers	–		*Formidable*
Cruisers	*Trento*	*Trieste*	*Orion*
	Bolzano	*Zara*	*Ajax*
	Fiume	*Pola*	*Perth*
	Guiseppe Garibaldi		*Gloucester*
	Duca degli Abruzzi		
Destroyers	14		13

Morning: The Italians sight the British cruisers, and try to trap them between their own cruisers and their battleship. But, when *Formidable*'s aircraft attack, the Italians break off the battle, as they have no air cover, and make for Taranto. The Italian ships are faster than the British, so Cunningham tries to slow them down with air attacks, using aircraft from *Formidable* and from Crete.

Afternoon: Carrier aircraft score a torpedo hit on *Vittorio Veneto*, stopping her for 15 minutes, after which she is able to proceed at a reduced speed of 19 knots. Later, *Pola* is hit by a torpedo, and also loses way.

8.30pm: Iachino thinks the British are far away, and sends *Zara* and *Fiume* back to help *Pola*: but the cruisers run straight into the guns of the British battleships, and are shot to ruins in a few minutes. Two Italian destroyers are also sunk, and *Pola* is destroyed with torpedoes from British destroyers in the early hours of 29th. Cunningham now regroups his forces, and sets off after the Italian fleet again. But, by morning, Iachino is out of his reach. As at Cape Teulada, the lack of Italian carrier-borne aircraft has proved decisive.

6/7 April 1941: German troops attack Yugoslavia and Greece. Bombers hit a British ammunition ship in Piraeus harbour, and the resultant explosion sinks 10 other ships (42,000 tons) and a great number of coastal and harbour craft, and renders the port virtually useless.

15/16 April 1941: Night action with an Italian Tripoli convoy. The Italian convoy, of 5 freighters with 3 destroyer escorts bound for North Africa, is detected by British aircraft. Four British destroyers from Malta intercept the convoy and, after a bitter fight, silence the 3 Italian destroyers and sink the freighters. The British lose one destroyer torpedoed.

21 April 1941: Bombardment of Tripoli. The Mediterranean fleet under Admiral Cunningham, with the battleships *Warspite*, *Barham* and *Malaya* and the aircraft carrier

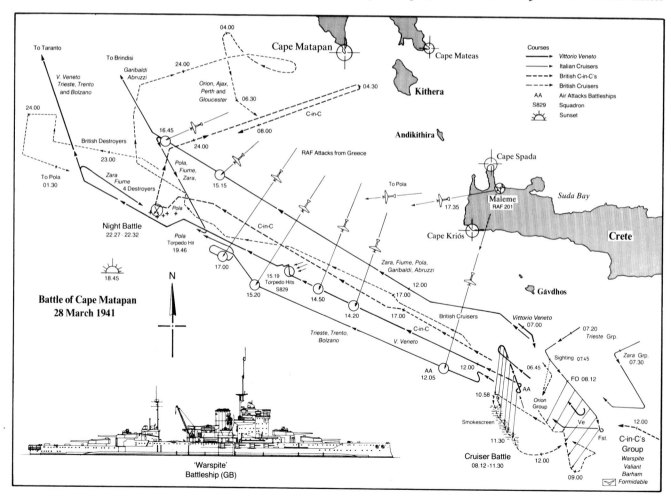

Battle of Cape Matapan
28 March 1941

'Warspite'
Battleship (GB)

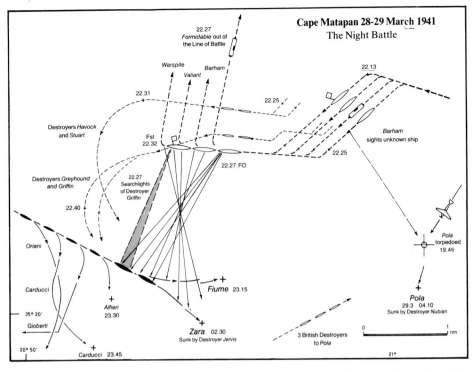

Cape Matapan 28-29 March 1941
The Night Battle

22.27
Formidable out of
the Line of Battle

22.31

Warspite
Valiant
Barham

Destroyers *Havock*
and *Stuart*

Fst
22.32

22.25

Barham
sights unknown ship

22.13

22.25

Barham

Destroyers *Greyhound*
and *Griffin*

22.27 FO

22.27
Searchlights
of Destroyer
Griffin

Pola
torpedoed
19.46

22.40

Oriani

Fiume 23.15

Pola
29.3 04.10
Sunk by Destroyer *Nubian*

Carducci

35° 20'

Alfieri
23.30

Gioberti

0   1
nm

20° 50'

Carducci 23.45

Zara 02.30
Sunk by Destroyer *Jervis*

3 British Destroyers
to *Pola*

21°

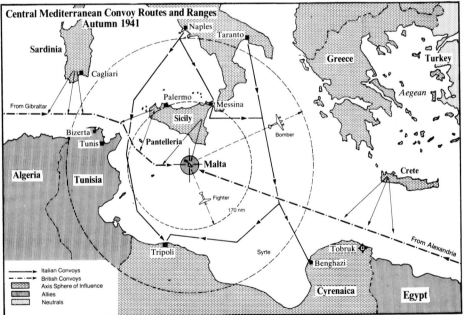

Central Mediterranean Convoy Routes and Ranges
Autumn 1941

Sardinia

Naples

Taranto

Cagliari

Greece

Turkey

From Gibraltar

Palermo

Messina

Sicily

Aegean

Bizerta

Pantelleria

Bomber

Tunis

Malta

Algeria

Tunisia

Crete

Fighter

170 nm

From Alexandria

Tripoli

Syrte

Tobruk

Benghazi

Italian Convoys
British Convoys
Axis Sphere of Influence
Allies
Neutrals

Cyrenaica

Egypt

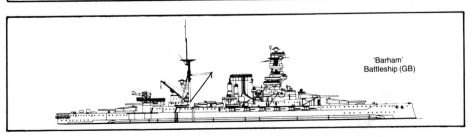

'Barham'
Battleship (GB)

Formidable, attacks Tripoli harbour for an hour. The coastal batteries reply late and ineffectively, and the harbour suffers serious damage.

23 April 1941: The Greek Army capitulates. The British withdraw their expeditionary force from the Morea to Crete.

23 April 1941: German dive-bombers sink the old Greek battleship *Kilkis* in Salamis Bay.

20 May 1941: German airborne landings on Crete (Operation 'Merkur'). The Royal Navy attempts to disrupt the German sea logistics, and throws itself fully into the task despite air attacks.

21/22 May: Overnight, Rear Admiral Glennie, with the cruisers *Dido*, *Orion*, *Ajax* and 4 destroyers, succeeds in destroying a German convoy of coastal motor vessels filled with German troops bound for Crete.

22 May: Heavy German air attacks on British naval units. The cruisers *Gloucester* and *Fiji* are sunk, together with a destroyer. The battleship *Warspite* and the cruisers *Naiad* and *Carlisle* are damaged.

26 May: Rear Admiral Pridham-Wippell tries to ease the pressure by attacking Italian airfields in the Dodecanese. His force consists of the battleships *Queen Elizabeth* and *Barham*, the aircraft carrier *Formidable* and 9 destroyers. Due to lack of aircraft, however, the attack is ineffective. Luftwaffe counterattacks score hits on one of the battleships and the aircraft carrier.

End of May: In spite of heavy Luftwaffe attacks, the Royal Navy evacuates 17,000 men from Crete.

7 June 1941: British and Free French troops attack Syria, in face of desperate Vichy French resistance to their superior invaders. The light Vichy French naval forces manage to maintain themselves in partially successful actions until the cease-fire on 14 July.

9 Nov 1941: British reconnaissance aircraft detect an Italian convoy en route to Tripoli. That evening, Force K (2 cruisers and 2 destroyers) leaves Malta. With the help of radar, the convoy is found and, in a surprise attack, all 7 freighters and 1 of the 6 escorting destroyers are sunk' The escort force of 2 heavy cruisers and 4 destroyers is not involved, and the British suffer no loss.

Autumn 1941: The Axis logistic system to North Africa is now practically stopped. From Nov, energetic measures are taken to hold the Royal Navy based on Malta in check: Fliegerkorps II is transferred to Sicily, and U-boats and MTBs are also employed.

13 Nov 1941: U-boat *U81* (Guggenberger) torpedoes the aircraft carrier *Ark Royal*, which sinks next day.

25 Nov 1941: U-boat *U331* (Tiesenhausen) sinks the battleship *Barham* off the coast of Cyrenaica. She is the first British battleship to be lost at sea in the Second World War.

12/13 Dec 1941: Action off Cape Bon. The Italian light cruisers *Albericoda Barbiano* and *Alberto di Giussano* are under way from Palermo to Tripoli: during the night, they meet 3 British and 1 Dutch destroyer off the Tunisian coast. In a brilliant night action, both Italian ships are hit by torpedoes from destroyers attacking from the dark coastal flank, and they sink in a short time.

17 Dec 1941: First Battle of Syrte. The Italian fleet under Admiral Iachino, with the battleships *Littorio*, *Caio Duilio*, *Andrea Doria* and *Guilio Cesare*, 5 cruisers and 20 destroyers, escorts a convoy to Tripoli. On the way, they meet British naval units under Rear Admiral Vian, with 5 cruisers and 20 destroyers escorting a freighter to Malta. After a brief, long-range artillery duel, Iachino breaks off the indecisive fight as evening falls.

18 Dec 1941: British Force K runs into an Italian minefield off Tripoli; the cruiser *Neptune* sinks, *Aurora* and *Penelope* are damaged; and a destroyer also sinks.

19 Dec 1941: Italian attack on Alexandria. The submarine *Scire* transports 3 two-man 'human torpedoes' (Maiales) to the harbour entrance, and the Italian frogmen succeed in placing their explosive charges under the battleships *Queen Elizabeth* and *Valiant* and a tanker. The resultant explosions cause damage to all 3 ships, and the battleships are out of action for months.

22 March 1942: Second Battle of Syrte. The British try to get an urgent convoy of 4 freighters from Alexandria to beleaguered Malta. Covering forces under Rear Admiral Vian are 4 cruisers and 10 destroyers and, from Malta, a cruiser and a destroyer. The Italians commit strong forces to destroy the convoy: under Admiral Iachino are the battleship *Littorio*, 3 cruisers and 10 destroyers. As soon as he sights the Italians, Vian releases the convoy with a light escort, and heads for the enemy, laying a smokescreen, behind which he launches a determined torpedo attack. The SSE wind drives the smoke on to the Italians, who do not attack for fear of the torpedoes. Several attempts to outflank the British force with *Littorio* to the west fail and, after 3 hours, Iachino breaks off the fight. Two British destroyers have been badly hit, but are brought home safely; 2 Italian destroyers sink in a storm on the way back to port. The convoy, meanwhile, has been held up so long that it only approaches Malta after dawn next day: Fliegerkorps II attacks and sinks 2 of the freighters off the island, and the other 2 are destroyed in Valetta harbour.

April 1942: Heavy air attacks by Fliegerkorps II on Malta. 3 destroyers, 3 submarines and several other ships are sunk, and the harbour rendered almost unusable for the British fleet.

11 May 1942: The Luftwaffe sink 3 out of 4 British destroyers making a sortie against an Axis Benghazi-bound convoy.

12-16 June 1942: Convoy Operations 'Harpoon' and 'Vigorous'. The British try to send 2 convoys to Malta, one from Gibraltar, one from Alexandria. After heavy fighting with Axis light surface units, U-boats and aircraft, the Alexandria convoy is recalled, with the loss of 2 freighters. The Italian fleet, which is at sea, is not engaged, but is attacked by land-based aircraft. The Gibraltar convoy loses 4 out of 6 freighters, but the other 2 get through to Malta. British escort forces lose the cruiser *Hermione* and 5 destroyers, and three cruisers are damaged. The Italians lose the cruiser *Trento*, while the battleship *Littorio* receives hits from bombs and torpedoes.

10-15 Aug 1942: Convoy Operation 'Pedestal'. The British try to bring a 14-freighter convoy (including the tanker *Ohio*) to Malta from the west, with a strong escorting force, under Vice Admiral Syfret, consisting of the aircraft carriers *Indomitable*, *Eagle*, *Victorious* and *Furious* (which flies off fighters to supplement Malta's defences), the battleships *Nelson* and *Rodney*, 7 cruisers and 27 destroyers. Due to lack of fuel, the Italian fleet remains in harbour, but heavy Axis attacks by air, MTBs and U-boats cause the loss of

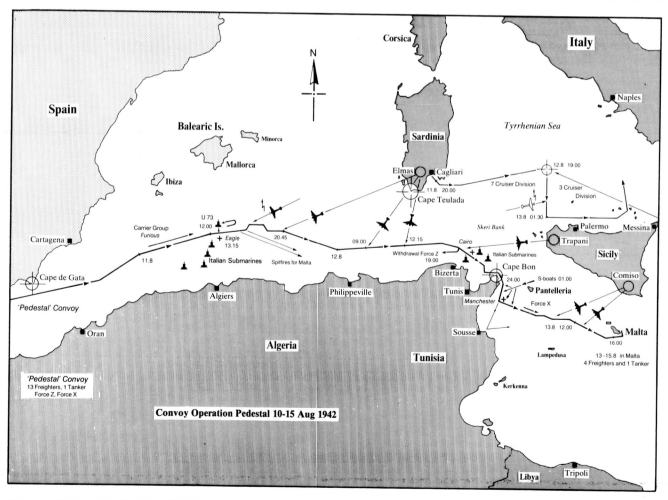

Convoy Operation Pedestal 10-15 Aug 1942

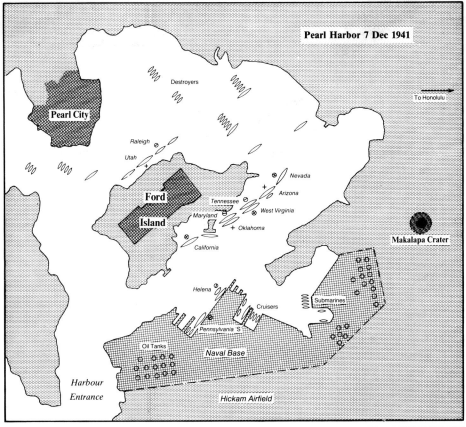

Pearl Harbor 7 Dec 1941

Destroyers

To Honolulu

Pearl City

Raleigh

Utah

Ford Island

Nevada

Arizona

Tennessee

West Virginia

Maryland

Oklahoma

California

Makalapa Crater

Helena

Cruisers

Submarines

Pennsylvania 'S'

Oil Tanks

Naval Base

Harbour Entrance

Hickam Airfield

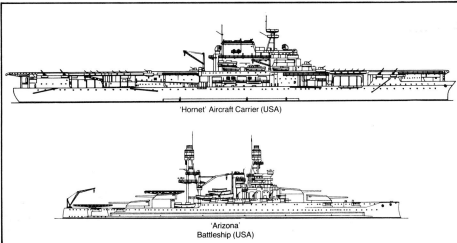

'Hornet' Aircraft Carrier (USA)

'Arizona' Battleship (USA)

In the Pacific, Japan aimed to start the war with a truly decisive blow. The drift to war with the United States had begun with the signing of a non-aggression pact with the USSR in 1941 which gave her a free hand in French Indo-China; in July of that year, the United States replied by blocking Japanese assets in America, stopping her imports of oil and iron and, at negotiations in Washington, insisting upon Japan's withdrawal from China. In October, General Tojo became Prime Minister, and war loomed ever nearer. At the beginning of Dec 1941, the naval balance of power in the Pacific Ocean was as follows.

	JAPAN	USA (Total)	USA (Pacific Fleet)
Battleships	10	17	9
Aircraft carriers	10	8	3
Heavy cruisers	18	18	12
Light cruisers	20	19	9
Destroyers	102	165	67
Submarines	64	106	28

Only a decisive blow—a pre-emptive strike—would alter the balance in Admiral Yamamoto's favour.

1941-42: The War in the Pacific

7 Dec 1941: Attack on Pearl Harbor. A Japanese task force under Vice Admiral Nagumo approaches the American naval base on Oahu from the north-west, through a bad weather zone. It consists of the aircraft carriers *Akagi, Kaga, Shokaku, Zuikaku, Hiryu* and *Soryu*, the battleships *Hiei, Kirishima,* 3 cruisers and 9 destroyers. It carries 423 aircraft. 275 nautical miles from Pearl Harbor, at dawn, the Japanese carrier aircraft take off in two waves: about 350 bombers, dive-bombers, torpedo-bombers and fighters are engaged. In Pearl Harbor are many of the ships of the US Pacific fleet: 8 battleships (*California, Tennessee, West Virginia, Maryland, Nevada, Oklahoma, Pennsylvania* and *Arizona*), 2 heavy and 5 light cruisers, and a great number of destroyers and auxiliaries. The 3 aircraft carriers, however, are not there. Despite the tense political climate, security precautions on Hawaii are inadequate, enabling the Japanese to achieve complete surprise (their actual declaration of war is delivered a few hours later). Part of the fighter and dive-bomber force attacks the army and navy aircraft on the various airfields on Oahu, and puts most of them out of action. The torpedo-bombers and the rest of the bombers concentrate on the battleships. The well adjusted torpedoes hit the ships in the outer ranks very badly, and hits with bombs are scored on all the battleships. *Arizona* explodes, *Oklahoma* capsizes, *West Virginia, Nevada* and *California* sink in shallow water on an even keel; the rest remain afloat. The target ship *Utah* capsizes; the cruisers *Helena* and *Raleigh* are hit by torpedoes; 2 destroyers explode. Meanwhile, 5 Japanese midget submarines trying to enter the harbour fail, and are sunk. As the Japanese attacks are concentrated on the capital ships and airfields, the harbour installations and logistic depots remain available for the future operations of the US Pacific fleet. Japanese losses are 5 midget submarines and 29 planes, and the task force escapes to the north-west without being detected. This bold attack puts the US battle fleet out of action for the beginning of the war, but all the ships are repaired and sent into action within the next months and years, except *Arizona* and *Oklahoma*.

Eagle, by *U73* (Rosenbaum), the cruisers *Manchester* and *Cairo* and a destroyer. The carriers *Indomitable* and *Victorious*, the cruisers *Nigeria* and *Kenya* are damaged. 9 freighters are sunk; 5, including some badly damaged, reach Malta and *Ohio*'s cargo of fuel enables air strikes to be flown against Rommel's supply lines.

1941-43: The Russian Black Sea Fleet supports land forces with tenacity and success by coastal bombardments, movement of troops and material and, above all, in the defence of Odessa (1941) and Sevastopol (1941-42).

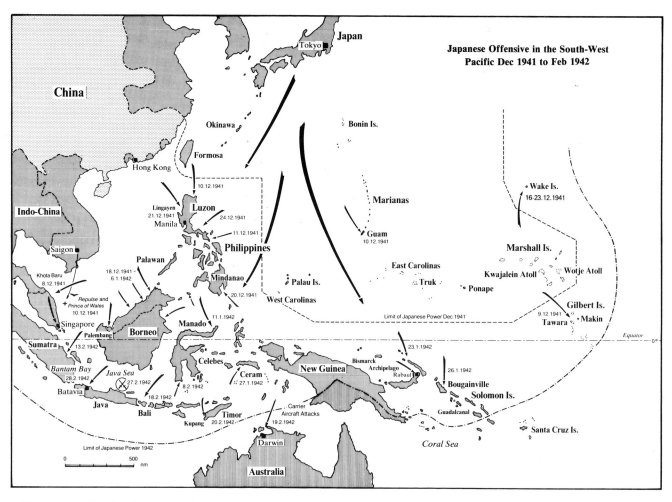

Japanese Offensive in the South-West Pacific Dec 1941 to Feb 1942

8 Dec 1941: The Japanese 'Southern Expeditionary Fleet' (Vice Admiral Ozawa) lands troops on the east coast of the Malayan Peninsula.

10 Dec 1941: The sinking of *Prince of Wales* and *Repulse*. A British battle group (battleship *Prince of Wales*, battle-cruiser *Repulse* and 4 destroyers under Rear Admiral Phillips) tries to attack a Japanese force off Kuantan. Japanese torpedo-bombers and bombers, flying from airfields around Saigon, attack in exemplary manner and sink both ships as they are returning to Singapore.

10 Dec 1941: Japanese troops under Vice Admiral Takahashi land on northern Luzon, covered by cruisers and destroyers.

11 Dec 1941: A Japanese attempted landing on Wake Island is repelled by USMC coastal artillery and aircraft, with the loss of 2 destroyers.

12 Dec 1941: Japanese landing on southern Luzon.

17 Dec 1941: Admiral Chester W. Nimitz is named Commander-in-Chief of the US Pacific fleet.

22 Dec 1941: The Japanese successfully land on Wake Island, covered by the aircraft carriers *Hiryu* and *Soryu*. The island is surrendered the following day.

21–24 Dec 1941: Large-scale Japanese landing in the Lingayen Gulf on Luzon. Fourteenth Army is landed by a fleet of 76 transports under Vice Admiral Takahashi. The escorting force, under Admiral Kondo, includes the battleships *Kongo* and *Haruna*, cruisers and destroyers. These landings take place within the range of Japanese land-based aircraft.

25 Dec 1941: The Japanese capture Hong Kong.

11 Jan 1942: Japanese landing at Menado on Celebes.

23 Jan 1942: Japanese landings in the Bismarck Archipelago (Rabaul, Kavieng), covered by the aircraft carriers *Akagi*, *Kaga*, *Shokaku* and *Zuikaku*.

Jan 1942: In Indonesia, an Allied combat group of British, Dutch and American ships is assembled under the Dutch Rear Admiral Doorman.

1 Feb 1942: 2 US task forces, centred around the aircraft carriers *Enterprise* and *Yorktown* with 5 cruisers and 10 destroyers, attack Japanese bases in the Marshall Islands with bombs and artillery in surprise raids. Material damage caused is slight, but, after the previous desperate months, this offensive works wonders for the moral of the US Navy.

4 Feb 1942: Rear Admiral Doorman, with 4 cruisers and 8 destroyers, attempts to attack a Japanese landing force in the Straits of Macassar. Japanese bombers hit the cruisers *Marblehead* (which is severely damaged) and *Houston*, and Doorman withdraws.

7–15 Feb 1942: The Japanese capture Singapore.

13 Feb 1942: The Japanese land at Palembang on Sumatra, covered by the aircraft carrier *Ryujo* and 5 cruisers.

18 Feb 1942: Japanese landing on Bali.

19 Feb 1942: The Japanese carrier fleet under Vice Admiral Nagumo (aircraft carriers *Akagi*, *Kaga*, *Hiryu* and *Soryu*, battleships *Hiei* and *Kirishima*, 3 cruisers and 9 destroyers) mounts a heavy air attack on Darwin, Australia. 11 freighters

and a US destroyer are sunk.

27 Feb 1942: Battle of the Java Sea. Doorman and his force meet a force of Japanese warships that had been escorting the Japanese Java-bound invasion fleet.

	ALLIES (Doorman)	JAPAN (Takagi)
Heavy cruisers	*Houston* (US)	*Nachi*
	Exeter (GB)	*Haguro*
Light cruisers	*De Ruyter* (NL)	*Jintsu*
	Java (NL)	*Naka*
	Perth (AUS)	
Destroyers	9	14

A long-range gunnery fight develops between the cruiser squadrons; *Exeter* is badly hit, and a Dutch destroyer is hit by a torpedo and explodes. In a destroyer duel around *Exeter* a British destroyer is sunk. The opponents sometimes lose sight of each other. Doorman tries several times to get around the Japanese warships and into the transports, but in vain. A British destroyer, meanwhile, sinks in a new mine-field. After 7 hours of intermittent, but savage, combat, *De Ruyter* and *Java* are hit by torpedoes and sink; Doorman dies with them, and the surviving Allied ships withdraw.

28 Feb 1942: Japanese landing in Bantam Bay, western Java. The landing fleet, under Vice Admiral Takahashi, takes the bulk of Sixteenth Army to the landing beaches on 56 transports. It is escorted by a force under Vice Admiral Kondo, with the battleships *Kongo, Hiei, Haruna, Kirishima*, the aircraft carriers *Akagi, Soryu, Hiryu, Shokaku* and *Zuikaku*, 3 cruisers and 8 destroyers operating to the south of Java. The cruisers *Houston* and *Perth* try to escape through the Sunda Strait; late that evening they run into the Japanese landing force, and sink 4 transports before being destroyed by the cruisers *Mikuma* and *Mogami* and several destroyers.

1 March 1942: The cruiser *Exeter* and 2 destroyers, meanwhile, attempt escape to the west, but are intercepted by 4 Japanese cruisers and sunk by them, and by aircraft from *Ryujo*. This eliminates Allied naval power in the East Indies.

9 March 1942: Capitulation of Allied forces on Java.

10 March 1942: Japanese landings at Lae and Salamaua on New Guinea. Aircraft from the US carriers *Lexington* and *Yorktown* mount a surprise attack, sinking one transport and damaging others.

5–9 April 1942: Japanese air attacks on Ceylon. The Japanese carrier fleet advances into the Indian Ocean, where the

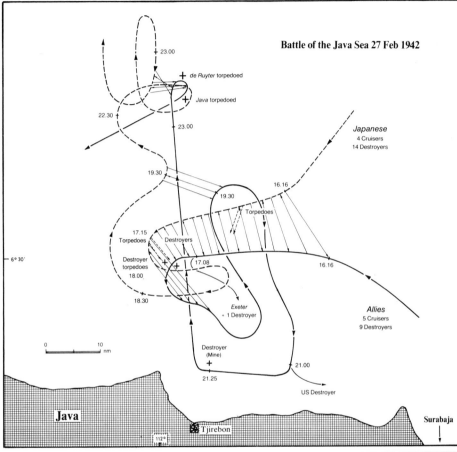

Battle of the Java Sea 27 Feb 1942

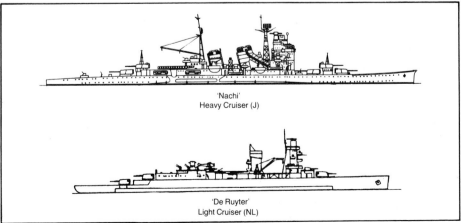

'Nachi'
Heavy Cruiser (J)

'De Ruyter'
Light Cruiser (NL)

British have concentrated strong naval forces after the Allied defeats in Indonesia. The Eastern Fleet under Vice Admiral Somerville comprises the carriers *Indomitable*, *Formidable* and *Hermes*, the battleships *Warspite*, *Resolution*, *Revenge*, *Ramillies* and *Royal Sovereign*, 7 cruisers and 16 destroyers. The Japanese carrier fleet under Vice Admiral Nagumo includes the carriers *Akagi*, *Shokaku*, *Zuikaku*, *Hiryu* and *Soryu*, the battleships *Kongo*, *Haruna*, *Hiei* and *Kirishima*, 4 cruisers and 8 destroyers. The Japanese fleet approaches Ceylon from the south-east, while the British fleet manoeuvres off the Maldives, south-west of Ceylon, keeping out of range of the Japanese carrier aircraft.

5 April: The Japanese attack Colombo harbour, and cause heavy damage to the harbour itself and to the ships lying there. South-west of Ceylon, Japanese reconnaissance planes sight the British cruisers *Cornwall and Dorsetshire* on their way to join the main fleet.

Midday: An attack by more than 50 carrier-based aircraft sinks both ships in a few minutes.

9 April: Japanese carrier aircraft attack the port of Trincomalee, on the east coast of Ceylon, with great effect. The aircraft carrier *Hermes* tries to escape to the south, but is intercepted and sunk by 80 bombers; a British destroyer is also sunk. At the same time, a Japanese cruiser force under Vice Admiral Ozawa attacks commerce in the Bay of Bengal. In all, at the beginning of April, the British lose one aircraft carrier, two heavy cruisers, a destroyer and 150,000 tons of shipping in the Indian Ocean. In the air, they lose 33 aircraft to 17 of the Japanese.

18 April 1942: US Army bombers, flying from the aircraft carrier *Hornet*, make the first air attack on Tokyo. The aircraft then fly on to China.

5-8 May 1942: British landing at Diego Suarez on Madagascar (which had been of strategic importance to the Axis powers). Naval forces under Rear Admiral Syfret (aircraft carriers *Indomitable* and *Illustrious*, battleship *Ramillies*, 2 cruisers and 11 destroyers) cover the landing against weak opposition.

As 1942 began, the Japanese planned further expansion. The first target would be Port Moresby, on southern New Guinea; bases would then be established by the eastern Solomon Islands, providing a stepping-stone to Midway Island, in the central Pacific. And, in the north, the empire would soon embrace the western Aleutians.

3-8 May 1942: **Battle of the Coral Sea.** The Japanese cover their thrust against Port Moresby with the light aircraft carrier *Shoho* and 4 cruisers, under Rear Admiral Goto. Off the Solomons is a carrier group under Vice Admiral Takagi, with the aircraft carriers *Zuikaku* and *Shokaku* (a total of 125 aircraft), 2 heavy cruisers and 6 destroyers. Admiral Nimitz (HQ, Pearl Harbor) concentrates 'Task Force 17' in the Coral Sea, under Rear Admiral Fletcher. It

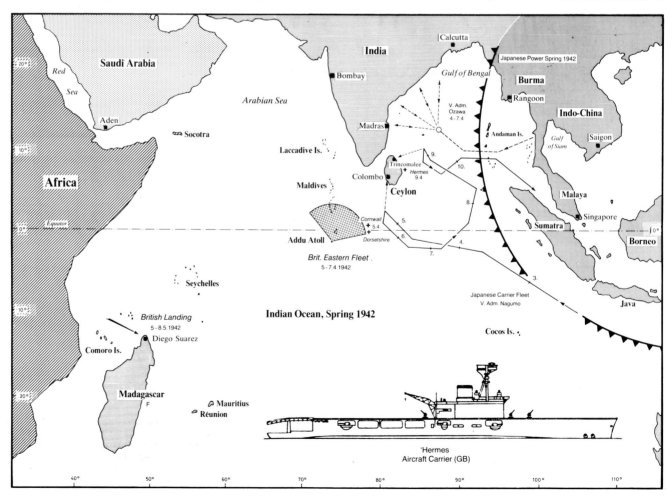

Indian Ocean, Spring 1942

'Hermes
Aircraft Carrier (GB)

includes the aircraft carriers *Yorktown* and *Lexington* (141 aircraft total), 5 cruisers and 9 destroyers. Also placed under Fletcher's command is the British Rear Admiral Crace with 3 cruisers and 2 destroyers. Two fleet supply tankers and 2 destroyers escort the carrier group.

3 May: The Japanese land unopposed on Tulagi and Guadalcanal in the eastern Solomon Islands.

4 May: Aircraft from *Yorktown* make a surprise attack on Japanese fleet units off Tulagi, and sink a destroyer and some smaller ships.

5 May: The US carrier force advances against the Japanese Port Moresby task force, and the Japanese carrier force enters the Coral Sea from the east.

6 May: Divided by only 70 nautical miles, the opposing forces refuel at sea without discovering each other's presence. US Army reconnaissance aircraft inform Fletcher of the location of the Japanese Port Moresby force.

7 May: Fletcher detaches the tanker *Neosho* with one destroyer to the south, and sets off north-west to attack the Japanese. Japanese reconnaissance planes locate the tanker and destroyer, and mistakenly report them as an aircraft carrier and a cruiser: Rear Admiral Takagi then sends 60 bombers after these ships, which are both destroyed in a few minutes. At the same time, aircraft from *Yorktown* and *Lexington* attack Rear Admiral Goto's force, concentrating on the small aircraft carrier *Shoho*, which is sunk very quickly. At this, the Japanese troop convoy is recalled. In the evening, the opposing task forces are so close to each other that 6 Japanese aircraft attempt landings on *Yorktown* in the dark.

8 May: Next morning, reconnaissance aircraft from both groups make sightings almost simultaneously, and air attacks made over a distance of about 200 miles (325 kilometres) go in at almost the same moment. The Japanese employ 90 aircraft, the Americans 78. As the Americans attack, the Japanese carrier *Zuikaku* finds refuge in a rain squall, but *Shokaku* is hit 3 times by bombs, and is forced to return to Truk. The torpedoes score no hits. Japanese flyers, meanwhile, carry out an exemplary torpedo attack on *Lexington* and score 2 hits; *Yorktown* is also hit, but remains serviceable. Some hours later, *Lexington* is ripped apart by the internal explosion of petrol vapour.

Although the Battle of the Coral Sea was, on paper at least, a material victory for the Japanese (reckoning the loss of Lexington *as a more severe blow than that of* Shoho*), the strategic victory lay with the Americans. The Japanese thrust towards Port Moresby had been stopped; and it was not reattempted.*

But the Coral Sea was also a battle of some significance in the development of naval warfare: for the first time, fleets had fought one another without direct visual contact. From now on, the aircraft carrier would begin to replace the battleship as the backbone of the fleet.

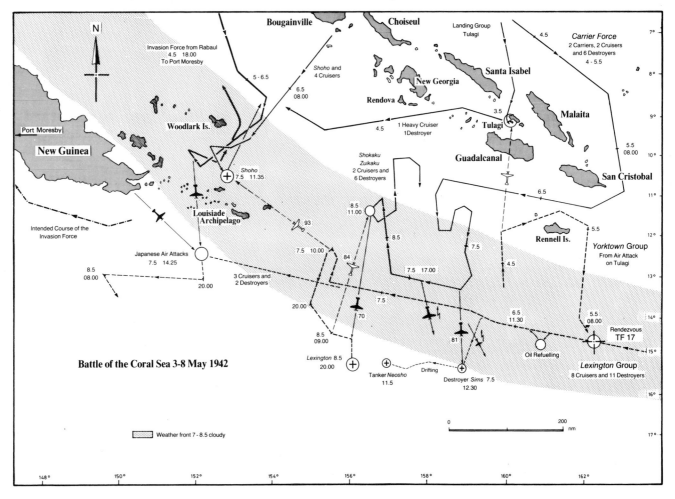

Battle of the Coral Sea 3-8 May 1942

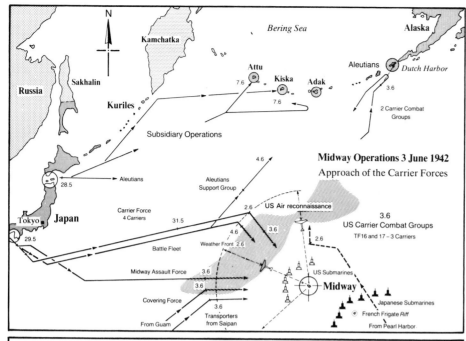

Midway Operations 3 June 1942
Approach of the Carrier Forces

US Carrier Combat Groups
TF16 and 17 – 3 Carriers

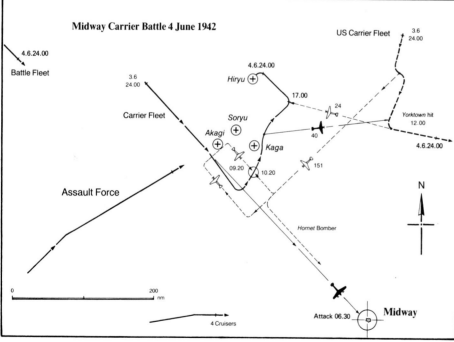

Midway Carrier Battle 4 June 1942

30 and 31 May 1942: Japanese midget submarines torpedo the British battleship *Ramillies* (putting her out of action for 12 months) and a tanker in the bay of Diego Suarez. A similar attack on Sydney harbour fails.

3–7 June 1942: Battle of Midway Island. The Americans learn of the Japanese plan to invade Midway Island at the beginning of June, and Admiral Nimitz concentrates all available naval forces for its defence. Two carrier forces are formed, as follows.

	TASK FORCE 16 (Spruance)	TASK FORCE 17 (Fletcher)
Aircraft carriers	*Enterprise* *Hornet*	*Yorktown*
Cruisers	6	2
Destroyers	9	6
Aircraft	Total of 230 in combined forces	

The Japanese guess that the US fleet will be used to defend Midway, so they bring up all available forces. Only the 2 carriers from the Coral Sea and the vessels detached for the raid on the Aleutians are missing. The Japanese fleet commander Yamamoto has the following forces:

CARRIER FLEET (Vice Admiral Nagumo):
Carriers *Akagi, Hiryu, Kaga, Soryu* (270 aircraft);
Battleships *Haruna, Kirishima*;
+ 3 cruisers, 12 destroyers.
BATTLE FLEET (Admiral Yamamoto):
Battleships *Yamato, Mutsu, Nagato, Ise, Hyuga, Fuso, Yamashiro*;
Light aircraft carrier *Hosho*;
+ 3 cruisers, 13 destroyers.
MIDWAY ASSAULT GROUP (Vice Admiral Kondo):
Battleships *Kongo, Hiei*;
Aircraft carrier *Zuiho*;
+ 10 cruisers, 21 destroyers, 12 transports with landing troops.
ALEUTIAN ASSAULT GROUP (Vice Admiral Hosogaya):
Light carriers *Ryujo* and *Junyo*; 90 aircraft;
+ 5 cruisers, 13 destroyers, 4 transports with troops. In addition to these groups, 15 submarines are positioned between Midway and Hawaii.

3 June: Aircraft of the Aleutian Assault Group attack Dutch Harbor, but with little effect, and do not distract American attention from their main target, Midway. Nimitz is informed of the approach of the Japanese fleets early on. In the afternoon, 'Flying Fortresses' from Midway fail in an attack on the Japanese landing fleet.

4 June: In the morning, over 100 carrier-borne Japanese aircraft fly off to destroy Midway's defences. Simultaneously, about 50 US Army and Navy aircraft from Midway attack the Japanese carrier fleet. They lose 17 planes without scoring

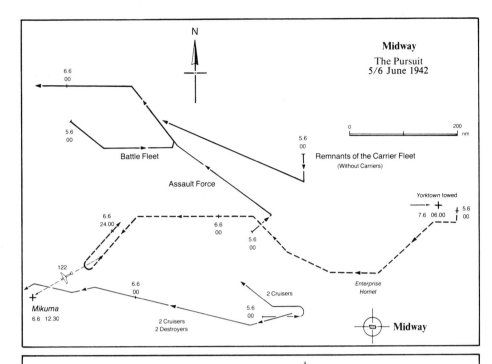

Midway
The Pursuit
5/6 June 1942

N

6.6
00

5.6
00

Battle Fleet

Assault Force

0   200
                 nm

5.6
00

Remnants of the Carrier Fleet
(Without Carriers)

Yorktown towed

7.6   06.00

5.6
00

6.6
24.00

6.6
00

5.6
00

6.6
00

2 Cruisers

Enterprise
Hornet

Midway

122

Mikuma
6.6   12.30

2 Cruisers
2 Destroyers

5.6
00

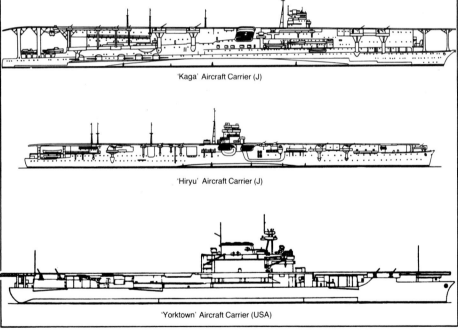

'Kaga' Aircraft Carrier (J)

'Hiryu' Aircraft Carrier (J)

'Yorktown' Aircraft Carrier (USA)

any hits, but damage on Midway from the Japanese attack is also slight. Nagumo plans a second attack on the island, and refuels his aircraft, unaware that he is about to be attacked.

9am: The US carrier force is sighted by a Japanese reconnaissance pilot, who reports their presence to Nagumo. But Nagumo has to await the return of aircraft from the attack on Midway before he can send of a second wave against the American fleet. As soon as Rear Admiral Spruance is aware of the location of the Japanese carriers, he sends his entire carrier-borne force at them, and they hit the Japanese just as they are turning their own aircraft around. Somewhat later, Rear Admiral Fletcher sends off half Yorktown's aircraft; in all 156 US planes attack. The 41 torpedo-bombers are at their targets first; 35 are shot down by Japanese fighters and ships' AA fire before being able to score a hit. Almost at the same time, the dive-bombers from Enterprise and Yorktown arrive on target, after a long diversion. The Japanese fighters are still engaged fighting off the torpedo-bombers and, within a few minutes, the American dive-bombers score vital hits on Kaga, Soryu and Akagi, the first two of which sink that afternoon. The Akagi remains afloat longer, but eventually also sinks. Hiryu, slightly ahead of her sister ships, is not discovered initially, and so escapes the attack.

11am: A bomb and torpedo attack wave takes off from Hiryu for Yorktown, which is hit by 3 bombs and 2 torpedoes and loses way, apparently doomed.

5pm: Dive-bombers from Enterprise and Hornet find Hiryu, and reduce her to a blazing wreck, which sinks next morning. Admiral Yamamoto, who is far to the west with his main fleet, and has not yet entered the fight, has to break off the operation after the loss of his 4 carriers. Rear Admiral Spruance takes up the chase with his 2 carriers.

5 June: 2 heavy cruisers of the Japanese Midway Assault Group collide and fall behind. Army bomber attacks are unsuccessful, but Navy dive-bombers from Midway score one hit.

6 June: Carrier aircraft from Enterprise and Hornet attack the 2 cruisers; Mikuma sinks after several bad hits, while Mogami and 2 destroyers escape badly damaged.

7 June: The Americans make great efforts to save Yorktown, which is still afloat, but torpedoes from the Japanese submarine I168 (Tanabe) hit the carrier and a destroyer, and both ships sink. This same day, Japanese troops land on the Aleutian Islands of Attu and Kiska.

Midway can now be seen as the turning point in the Pacific war, for the Japanese had lost 4 aircraft carriers, 1 cruiser, 250 aircraft, and 3,500 dead, including many pilots who would be irreplaceable. And, with the loss of 4 carriers, the Japanese were forced on to the strategic defensive. Against an American war machine that was rapidly gathering momentum, they would never be able to make good their losses in time to regain the initiative.

1942–44: The War in the Mediterranean

8 Nov 1942: Operation 'Torch' (the Allied landing in north-west Africa). To open a second front, the Allies land forces in French Morocco and Algeria. Allied Naval Commander is Admiral A. B. Cunningham; Supreme Commander is General Eisenhower. Western Task Force comes from the United States under Rear Admiral Hewitt: with 23 transports, he lands over 34,000 men under Major General Patton (US), at Fédala, Mehdia and Safi, both sides of Casablanca. Covering forces consist of the battleships *Massachusetts*, *Texas* and *New York*, the light aircraft carrier *Ranger*, 4 escort carriers, 7 cruisers and 38 destroyers. The French naval forces in Casablanca, under Rear Admiral de Lafond, try to get at the US landing force with the cruiser *Primauguet* and 6 destroyers, but in a long fight with the escort vessels, the French ships are either sunk or driven ashore. The uncompleted battleship *Jean Bart*, lying in the harbour, is badly damaged by fire from *Massachusetts* and air attack. On 11 Nov, French resistance in the Casablanca area ends.

Centre Task Force under Commodore Troubridge (GB) lands at Oran; the 39,000 troops under Major General Fredendall (US) are landed with 19 landing craft and 28 transports; direct support is given by 2 escort carriers, 3 cruisers and 13 destroyers. A break-out attempt by several French destroyers is beaten back and, on 10 Nov, French resistance in the Oran area is broken. Eastern Task Force, under Rear Admiral Sir Harold Burrough (GB), lands 33,000 troops at Algiers under Major General Ryder (US), using 17 landing craft and 16 transports. Covering forces include the aircraft carrier *Argus*, an escort carrier, 3 cruisers and 16 destroyers. In Algiers is the French headquarters under Admiral Darlan. British destroyers attempt to enter the harbour, but are driven off by French coastal artillery and ships' guns. But, in view of the Allied superiority, Darlan orders resistance in Algiers to cease on 8 Nov; fighting in Oran ends the next day. Meanwhile, to guard the flank of these Mediterranean landings against the possibility of intervention by the Italian fleet, the reinforced Force H under Vice Admiral Syfret (GB) is deployed in the western Mediterranean. It includes the battleships *Duke of York*, *Nelson* and *Rodney*, the battlecruiser *Renown*, the aircraft carriers *Victorious*, *Formidable* and *Furious*, 3 cruisers and 17 destroyers. As a consequence of the Allied invasion of North Africa, German forces now occupy Vichy France.

27 Nov 1942: When the Germans occupy Toulon, the Commander-in-Chief of the French Navy, Admiral de Laborde, scuttles his ships lying there. They include the battleships *Strasbourg*, *Dunkerque* and *Provence*, 7 cruisers and 30 destroyers. 3 submarines escape.

2 Dec 1942: British Force Q (3 cruisers and 2 destroyers) attacks an Italian convoy sailing for Tunis; all 4 freighters and an escorting destroyer are sunk.

4 Dec 1942: The US Air Force attacks the Italian fleet in Naples harbour. 1 cruiser is sunk, 2 others and 4 destroyers

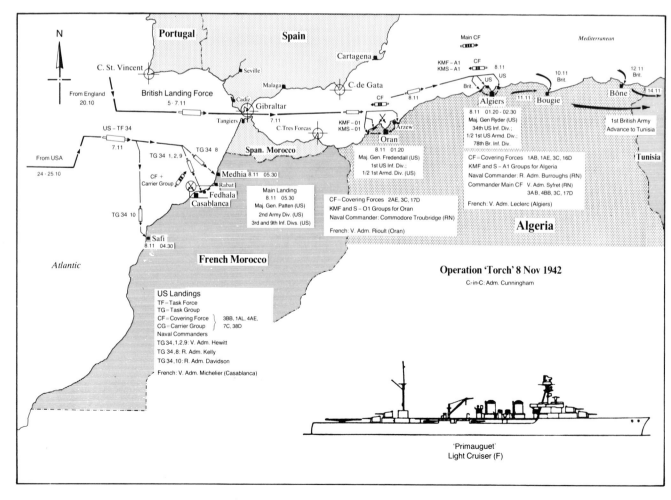

Operation 'Torch' 8 Nov 1942

C-in-C: Adm. Cunningham

'Primauguet'
Light Cruiser (F)

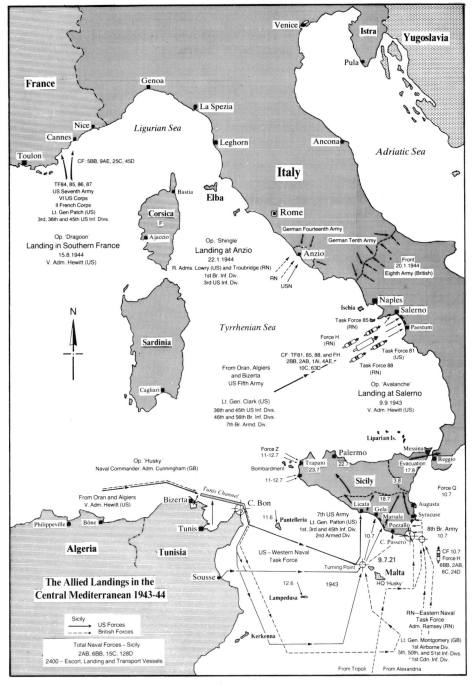

The Allied Landings in the Central Mediterranean 1943-44

10 July 1943: **Allied landing on Sicily** (Operation 'Husky'). Under supreme command of General Eisenhower, 180,000 men are concentrated. The Naval commander is Admiral A. B. Cunningham (GB). An American Western Naval Task Force, under Vice Admiral Hewitt, lands the US Seventh Army (Lieutenant General Patton) on the south coast of Sicily, while the British Eastern Naval Task Force (Admiral Ramsay) lands the British Eighth Army (Lieutenant General Montgomery) on the south-eastern point of the island. 580 warships and about 2,000 landing craft are used, including the new Landing Ship Tank (LST). The covering force is Force H under Vice Admiral Willis (GB), with the battleships *King George V*, *Howe*, *Nelson*, *Rodney*, *Warspite* and *Valiant*, the carriers *Indomitable* and *Formidable*, 6 cruisers and 24 destroyers. A counterattack by a German armoured division is repulsed by the ship's guns of the landing fleet.

17 Aug 1943: Axis forces evacuate Sicily.

3 Sept 1943: The Allies land at Calabria in the Straits of Messina.

9 Sept 1943: Following Mussolini's overthrow, Badoglio's government concludes an armistice with the Allies. The Italian fleet, of 6 battleships, 8 cruisers, 31 destroyers and torpedo-boats, sails from its bases at La Spezia, Genoa, Castellamare and Taranto to Malta, to be interned. (On the way there, the new battleship *Roma* is sunk by the Luftwaffe, using a wireless-controlled bomb; *Italia* is also damaged.) From now on, the Allied forces in the Mediterranean have no naval opposition.

9 Sept 1943: **Allied landing at Salerno** (Operation 'Avalanche'). Vice Admiral Hewitt lands the US Fifth Army (Lieutenant General Clark) with a fleet that includes one light aircraft carrier, 4 escort carriers, 11 cruisers and 43 destroyers. Force H (Vice Admiral Willis) covers the landing with the battleships *Nelson* and *Rodney* and the carriers *Illustrious* and *Formidable*. The battleships *Warspite*, *Valiant*, *Howe* and *King George V*, meanwhile, escort the Italian fleet into Malta, and cover a landing at Taranto, after which the first two ships join in the battle about the Salerno bridgehead. The German Luftwaffe attacks, and damages some of the ships (*Warspite*, cruisers *Savannah*, *Uganda* and *Philadelphia*).

2–3 Dec 1943: Night air raid on Bari. A Luftwaffe assault on this Allied transit harbour sinks 16 freighters and badly damages 8 others. Among the ships sunk is one loaded with gas shells which cause great loss of life. This is the heaviest Allied loss in one air raid since Pearl Harbor.

22 Jan 1944: **Allied landing at Anzio** (Operation 'Shingle'). In order to by-pass the now static front-line north of Naples, the Allies land a corps south of Rome. The landing fleet is commanded by Rear Admiral Lowry (US) and Rear Admiral Troubridge (GB). 4 cruisers and a number of destroyers provide covering fire. The cruiser *Spartan* is sunk by air attack on 29th, the cruiser *Penelope* by U-boat torpedo on 18 Feb. It is 4 months before the Allies can break out of the bridgehead.

15 Aug 1944: **Allied landing in southern France** (Operation 'Dragoon'). A fleet under Vice Admiral Hewitt lands Lieutenant General Patch's US Seventh Army (US VI Corps and French II Corps) between Cannes and Toulon. 500 landing and 200 escort vessels are supported by the battleships *Texas*, *Nevada*, *Arkansas*, *Ramillies* and *Lorraine*, 9 escort carriers, 25 cruisers and 45 destroyers. The landing meets little resistance and, in a few days, Toulon and Marseilles are in Allied hands.

Sept–Oct 1944: British naval forces in the Aegean (7 escort carriers, 7 cruisers, 19 destroyers and frigates, etc.) attack the German evacuation routes out of Greece. The last German naval units in the Aegean are destroyed.

are damaged.

10 April 1943: US bombers sink the Italian cruiser *Trieste* and badly damage the heavy cruiser *Gorizia*, in the Sardinian harbour of La Maddalena.

By the beginning of May 1943, the resupply of the Axis African army has become impossible, due to Allied control of the air and sea. German and Italian forces in North Africa capitulate.

11–12 June 1943: Operation 'Corkscrew'. The islands of Pantelleria and Lampedusa capitulate, after British naval and air bombardment.

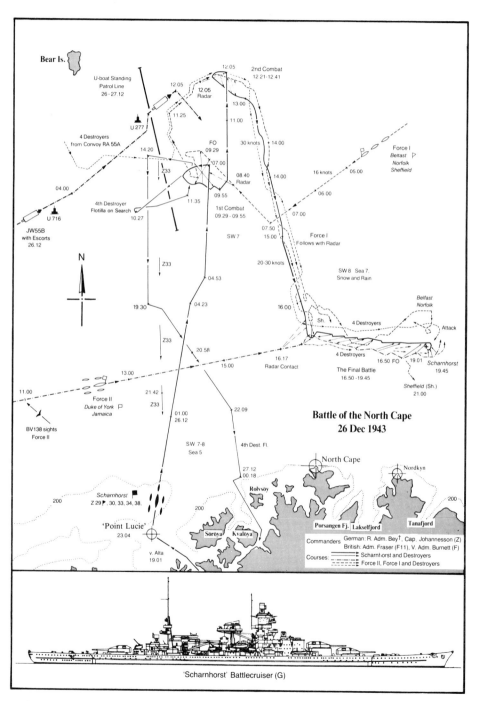

**Battle of the North Cape
26 Dec 1943**

Bear Is.

U-boat Standing
Patrol Line
26 - 27.12

4 Destroyers
from Convoy RA 55A

U 277

12.05

12.05 Radar

2nd Combat
12.21-12.41

13.00

11.25 11.00

14.00

30 knots 14.00

FO
09.29 07.00

08.40 Radar

Force I
Belfast
Norfolk
Sheffield

16 knots 05.00

06.00

07.00

Z33

14.20

04.00

U 716

JW55B
with Escorts
26.12

4th Destroyer
Flotilla on Search
10.27

11.35

1st Combat
09.29 - 09.55

SW 7

09.55

07.50
15.00

Force I
Follows with Radar

N

Z33

20-30 knots

SW 8 Sea 7.
Snow and Rain

04.53

04.23

16.00

Belfast
Norfolk

Z33

19.30

Sh

4 Destroyers

Attack

20.58

4 Destroyers

16.17
Radar Contact

16.50 FO

19.01

Scharnhorst
19.45

The Final Battle
16.50 -19.45

15.00

11.00

13.00

Force II
Duke of York
Jamaica

21.42

Z33

22.09

Sheffield (Sh.)
21.00

BV138 sights
Force II

01.00
26.12

200

200

SW 7-8
Sea 5

4th Dest. Fl.

North Cape

Nordkyn

27.12
00.18

Rolvsöy

Scharnhorst
Z 29, 30, 33, 34, 38.

200

200

200

'Point Lucie'
23.04

Söröya Kvalöya

Porsanger Fj. Lakselfjord

Tanafjord

Commanders German: R. Adm. Bey†, Cap. Johannesson (Z)
British: Adm. Fraser (F11), V. Adm. Burnett (F)

Courses: ——— Scharnhorst and Destroyers
----- Force II, Force I and Destroyers

v. Alta
19.01

'Scharnhorst' Battlecruiser (G)

In northern Norway, German naval units were strategically positioned so as to pose a continuous threat to Allied convoys bound for Russia.

1942–45: The War in northern European waters

6 March 1942: Vice Admiral Ciliax attempts to destroy convoy PQ12 with the battleship *Tirpitz* and 3 destroyers, but misses it in the bad weather. On the return journey, an attack by torpedo-carrying aircraft from *Victorious* is beaten off.

31 Dec 1942: Action off Bear Island. A German cruiser group under Vice Admiral Kummetz operates against the North Sea convoy JW51B. The heavy cruisers *Hipper* and *Lützow*, each with 3 destroyers, attack from north to south at noon, in poor light. The convoy is skilfully defended by 5 destroyers and when the British cruiser escort force (*Sheffield* and *Jamaica*, under Rear Admiral Burnett) joins the fight, Kummetz breaks off the struggle. *Hipper* is hit three times, and each side loses a destroyer.

22 Sept 1943: British midget submarines attack *Tirpitz* in Altenfjord, and put her out of action for 6 months.

4 Oct 1943: Allied carrier-borne aircraft attack German convoy traffic around Narvik, and sink about 40,000 tons of shipping.

26 Dec 1943: 'Battle of the North Cape'. The German battlecruiser *Scharnhorst*, under Rear Admiral Bey, leaves Altenfjord with 5 destroyers on 25 Dec to attack the North Sea convoy JW55B. This is escorted by 14 destroyers, and in close support, is a squadron under Vice Admiral Burnett with the cruisers *Belfast*, *Norfolk* and *Sheffield*. 200 miles (325 kilometres) sw is the long-range protection group under Admiral Fraser, with the battleship *Duke of York*, cruiser *Jamaica* and 4 destroyers.

9.30am: In heavy seas and bad visibility, Bey misses his prey becomes separated from his escorts, and tries to attack from the south with *Scharnhorst* alone. He meets Burnett's cruisers, turns away, and moves east to attack the convoy from the north-east.

Midday: Burnett's cruisers frustrate him again. In a 20-minute fight, each side scores 2 hits, and the battlecruiser makes off south at high speed, unaware of Fraser's approaching force.

4.50pm: With the aid of radar, the British cruisers follow out of sight, while Fraser now attacks from the south-west. *Scharnhorst* now comes under fire from both sides.

6.20pm: *Duke of York* scores several hits on *Scharnhorst* with radar-controlled gunfire, and then British destroyers attack with torpedoes, scoring several hits.

7.45pm: *Scharnhorst* loses way, and is battered by the British ships until she capsizes.

3 April 1944: Bombers from the carriers *Victorious* and *Furious* and 4 escort carriers attack *Tirpitz*, and put her out of action for a further 3 months.

12 Nov 1944: British bombers attack *Tirpitz* at Tromsö and, with five 4-ton bombs, cause the last active German battleship to capsize. The other German heavy surface units are now transferred to the Baltic for the rest of 1944, leaving the struggle against Allied North Sea convoys to be carried out by U-boats and the Luftwaffe alone.

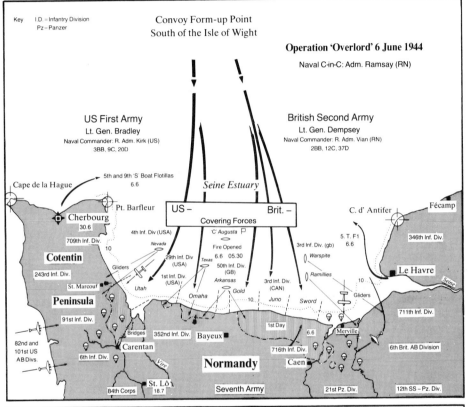

Key I.D. = Infantry Division
     Pz = Panzer

Convoy Form-up Point
South of the Isle of Wight

Operation 'Overlord' 6 June 1944

Naval C-in-C: Adm. Ramsay (RN)

US First Army
Lt. Gen. Bradley
Naval Commander: R. Adm. Kirk (US)
3BB, 9C, 20D

British Second Army
Lt. Gen. Dempsey
Naval Commander: R. Adm. Vian (RN)
2BB, 12C, 37D

5th and 9th 'S' Boat Flotillas
6.6

Seine Estuary

Cape de la Hague

Pt. Barfleur

Fécamp

Cherbourg
30.6

709th Inf. Div.

US —   Brit. —
Covering Forces

4th Inf. Div. (USA)

'C' Augusta

Fire Opened
6.6 05.30

Nevada

C. d' Antifer

346th Inf. Div.

Cotentin

243rd Inf. Div.

St. Marcouf

Gliders

Texas

29th Inf. Div.
(USA)

50th Inf. Div.
(GB)

1st Inf. Div.
(USA)

Arkansas

3rd Inf. Div. (gb)

Warspite

5. T. F1
6.6

Ramillies

Le Havre

Peninsula

91st Inf. Div.

Utah

Omaha

Gold

10.

Juno

Sword

Gliders

Seine

711th Inf. Div.

82nd and
101st US
AB Divs.

Bridges

352nd Inf. Div.

Bayeux

1st Day

6.6

Merville

6th Brit. AB Division

6th Inf. Div.

Carentan

Vire

716th Inf. Div.

Caen

Normandy

21st Pz. Div.

12th SS – Pz. Div.

St. Lô
18.7

84th Corps

Seventh Army

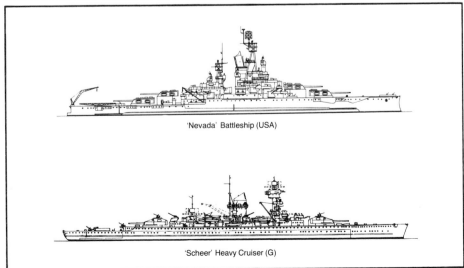

'Nevada' Battleship (USA)

'Scheer' Heavy Cruiser (G)

---

6 June 1944: Operation 'Overlord' (the Allied landing in Normandy). To put the 5 divisions of the first wave ashore between Cherbourg and Caen, the Allies concentrate the largest landing fleet in the European theatre of war. Supreme Allied Commander is General Eisenhower, and commander of the Allied naval forces is Admiral Ramsay. The British land in the east, their landing fleet commanded by Rear Admiral Vian; the bombardment group consists of the battleships *Warspite* and *Ramillies*, 12 cruisers and 37 destroyers. The Americans land to the west, their landing fleet commanded by Rear Admiral Kirk; fire support here is given by the battleships *Nevada*, *Texas* and *Arkansas*, 9 cruisers and 20 destroyers. In overall reserve are the battleships *Nelson* and *Rodney* and 3 cruisers. Allied air forces total 12,800 aircraft, and they have absolute control of the air over France. On the German side, few light surface naval units and no Luftwaffe units worth mentioning are available. The invasion thus succeeds at the first attempt. During the first nights, however, German destroyers and MTBs attack the invasion fleet from east and west and in a series of combats, 1 British and 2 German destroyers are sunk. Counterattacks against the Allied bridgehead by German ground forces are smashed by naval artillery and air attack. Apart from a number of landing craft and 4 destroyers sunk by mines, coastal artillery and air attack, the only Allied naval losses are 3 cruisers damaged and 1 cruiser put out of action by a German 'human torpedo'. U-boats cannot get at the fleet, due to alert defence by escorts of the landing force, and they suffer heavy losses.

14/15 June: 325 British bombers attack the port of Le Havre, and destroy practically all German light surface units there.

15/16 June: 300 British bombers attack the port of Boulogne, and destroy almost all the German minesweepers there.

25/26 June: The German 28cm (11in) coastal artillery battery 'Hamburg' near Cherbourg duels with the battleships *Nevada*, *Texas* and *Arkansas*, and cruisers and destroyers. One hit each is scored on *Texas* and a destroyer.

30 June 1944: Cherbourg is captured by the Allies. With the fall of Caen (9 July) and St. Lô (18 July), and the breakthrough at Avranches (25 July), the role of the Allied fleet as floating support artillery is ended. German naval surface units in the west have by now either been destroyed or have withdrawn into the North Sea, and German U-boats can now only operate from Norway.

From Aug 1944, German naval units support their land forces with artillery fire against Soviet advances in the Baltic. The cruisers *Scheer*, *Lützow* and *Hipper* go into action for the last time off the coasts of Courland and East Prussia. Most heavy naval units are destroyed in Allied air attacks on German harbours from March 1945 onwards; only the cruisers *Prinz Eugen*, *Nürnberg* and *Leipzig* are still serviceable at the end of the war.

1945: In the last months of the war, over 1,500,000 refugees are evacuated from Germany's eastern provinces by the German Navy.

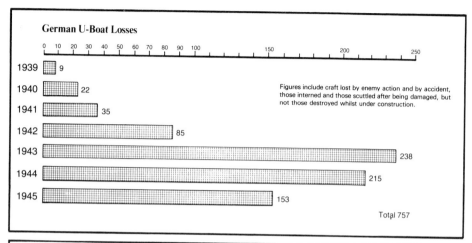

German U-Boat Losses

Year	Losses
1939	9
1940	22
1941	35
1942	85
1943	238
1944	215
1945	153

Figures include craft lost by enemy action and by accident, those interned and those scuttled after being damaged, but not those destroyed whilst under construction.

Total 757

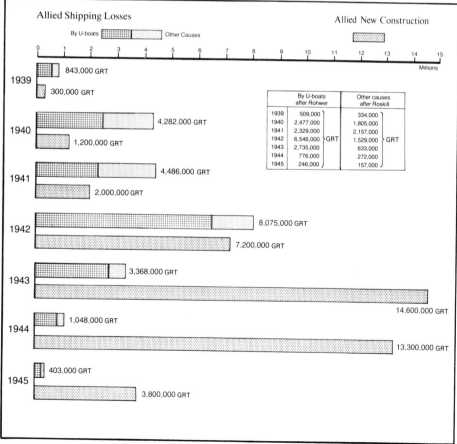

Allied Shipping Losses   **Allied New Construction**

By U-boats / Other Causes

	By U-boats	Other causes
	after Rohwer	after Roskill
1939	509,000	334,000
1940	2,477,000	1,805,000
1941	2,329,000	2,157,000
1942	6,546,000 GRT	1,529,000 GRT
1943	2,735,000	633,000
1944	776,000	272,000
1945	246,000	157,000

1939: 843,000 GRT / 300,000 GRT

1940: 4,282,000 GRT / 1,200,000 GRT

1941: 4,486,000 GRT / 2,000,000 GRT

1942: 8,075,000 GRT / 7,200,000 GRT

1943: 3,368,000 GRT / 14,600,000 GRT

1944: 1,048,000 GRT / 13,300,000 GRT

1945: 403,000 GRT / 3,800,000 GRT

1943–45: The Convoy War and 'The Battle of the Atlantic'

Spring 1943: The convoy system and new defensive measures against U-boats begin to take effect. Air surveillance by long-range aircraft covers almost the entire North Atlantic and apart from the normal convoy escorts, special U-boat hunting groups are formed. Escort carriers, which come into service in great numbers in the spring of 1943, accompany each group. The radar equipment in the escort vessels and in the patrol aircraft is improved. Depth-charge salvo launchers ('Hedgehogs') are mounted in ships' bows, to avoid disruption of the locating devices.

4–6 May 1943: Convoy ONS5 is heavily guarded. When 30 U-boats attack, they sink 12 ships (56,000 tons), but lose 7 of their own number.

9–13 May 1943: The remaining U-boats now attack the double convoy HX237–SC129. The escort carrier *Biter* gives air cover, and only 5 freighters are lost at a cost of 5 U-boats.

13–20 May 1943: For 5 days, a U-boat pack vainly attacks convoy SC130. The escort force sinks 5 U-boats.

The Battle of the Atlantic had now swung in favour of the Allies. During May 1943, Germany had lost 41 U-boats (about half of these to air attack, the remainder to convoy escorts); attacks on convoys in the North Atlantic were now abandoned.

July 1943: The Allies mount a heavy air offensive against U-boats in the Bay of Biscay, and sink 16 craft either setting out on or returning from operations. In July, newly built Allied shipping tonnage exceeds losses by U-boat action, for the first time since the start of the U-boat war.

September: The U-boats renew their attacks on Atlantic convoys, but now they are equipped with better AA defences, search receiver equipment, and acoustic torpedoes (Zaunköning).

19–23 Sept 1943: Convoys ONS18 and ON202 (69 merchantmen) are escorted by 19 vessels. 19 U-boats sink 6 ships (36,000 tons) and 3 escorts; only 2 U-boats are lost.

15–20 Oct 1943: Convoys ON206 and ONS20. In a 5-day battle, the U-boats can sink but 1 ship, while 6 U-boats are destroyed, 4 by air attack.

29 March to 3 April 1944: Arctic convoy JW58. 16 U-boats attack the strongly protected convoy without success, and lose 4 of their own number.

By the end of 1943, Germany had finally lost the Battle of the Atlantic. Throughout this year and the next, Allied coastal aircraft and anti-submarine groups achieved considerable success against the small groups of U-boats that remained in the Atlantic. The most successful U-boat commanders of the Second World War were as follows.

	SHIPS	TONS
Korvettenkapitan Otto Kretschmer	44	267,000
Korvettenkapitan Wolfgang Luth	43	226,000
Korvettenkapitan Erich Topp	34	194,000

In the Pacific, meanwhile, American submarines had literally been wiping out the Japanese merchant marine. Not only had the Japanese failed to develop effective counter measures to the submarine menace, but they used their own submarine fleet almost exclusively against Allied warships, not mounting any significant campaign against Allied commerce.

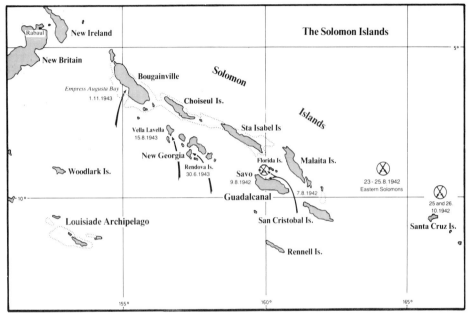

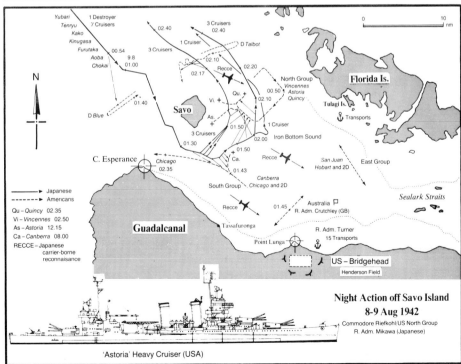

Night Action off Savo Island
8-9 Aug 1942
Commodore Riefkohl/US North Group
R. Adm. Mikawa (Japanese)

'Astoria' Heavy Cruiser (USA)

1942-45: The War in the Pacific
After the Battle of Midway, the Americans take the initiative in the Pacific.

7 Aug 1942: Landings on Guadalcanal and Tulagi. The building of Japanese air and naval bases on Guadalcanal is seen as a threat to US-Australian communications, so an amphibious force with 19 transports, under Rear Admiral Turner, lands the US 1st Marine Division on Guadalcanal and the adjacent Tulagi, against light resistance. Covering fire is provided by a support force under Rear Admiral Crutchley (GB), consisting of 8 cruisers and 15 destroyers, while air support comes from the carriers *Saratoga*, *Enterprise* and *Wasp*, with the battleship *North Carolina*, 6 cruisers and 16 destroyers under Vice Admiral Fletcher (US). The airfield (only just completed) is captured on the first day (and renamed 'Henderson Field'): the heavy fighting of the next months revolves around it.

8/9 Aug 1942: Night action off Savo Island. To cover the Guadalcanal landing fleet, a cruiser group lies to the west, by Savo Island, on the night of 8 Aug. It consists of the cruisers *Astoria*, *Quincy*, *Vincennes*, *Chicago* and *Canberra* (AUS), and 6 destroyers. At midnight, Vice Admiral Mikawa attacks suddenly from the direction of Rabaul with 7 cruisers and a destroyer and, in a short fight, all the Allied cruisers are badly hit: 2 capsize, 2 sink next morning. Of the Japanese ships, only the flagship *Chokai* receives a few hits. Mikawa fails to attack the landing fleet, however, and withdraws; on his return journey, a US submarine sinks the cruiser *Kako*.

23-25 Aug 1942: Battle of the Solomon Islands. The Japanese send 4 transports with troops to reinforce their men on Guadalcanal. Air cover is provided by a carrier force under Vice Admiral Nagumo, with the carriers *Shokaku* and *Zuikaku* (131 planes), the battleships *Mutsu*, *Hiei* and *Kirishima*, 10 cruisers and 21 destroyers. There is also a diversionary force with the light carrier *Ryujo* (37 planes), 1 cruiser and 2 destroyers. The Americans have two carrier groups under Vice Admiral Fletcher, with the carriers *Enterprise* and *Saratoga* (176 planes), the battleship *North Carolina*, 4 cruisers and 11 destroyers.

23 Aug: US planes fail to find the Japanese.

24 Aug: Aircraft from *Saratoga* sink *Ryujo* with bombs and torpedoes. Simultaneously, Japanese carrier aircraft attack *Enterprise*. The torpedo-bombers are fought off; the dive-bombers score 3 hits, causing fires, but these are soon extinguished, and the carrier is soon capable of limited action again.

25 Aug: US bombers, from Guadalcanal and Esperitu Sanctu, attack the Japanese transports, sinking the largest of them and one of the escorting destroyers. A cruiser is also hit, and the Japanese abandon the operation. They have lost 1 carrier, 1 destroyer and 90 aircraft; the Americans lose 20 aircraft.

15 Sept 1942: The Japanese submarine *I19* (Narahara) sinks the carrier *Wasp* and a destroyer, and damages the battleship *North Carolina* south-east of Guadalcanal.

11/12 Oct 1942: Night action off Cape Esperance. The Japanese escort a troop transport convoy bound for Guadalcanal with a cruiser force under Rear Admiral Goto. 3 cruisers and 2 destroyers of this force are to bombard the American airfield on the island at the same time. An American force (Rear Admiral Scott, with 4 cruisers and 5 destroyers) intercepts the Japanese and achieves complete surprise with his improved radar. Goto is killed, his flagship *Aoba* badly damaged; the cruiser *Furutaka* is sunk, as is a destroyer. The Americans lose a destroyer and the cruiser *Boise* is damaged. The night bombardment has been frustrated, but the Japanese troops are landed.

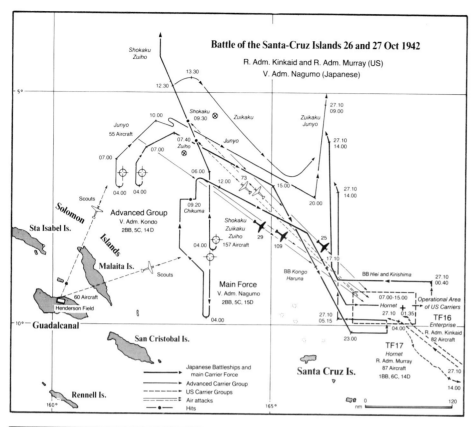

Battle of the Santa-Cruz Islands 26 and 27 Oct 1942

R. Adm. Kinkaid and R. Adm. Murray (US)
V. Adm. Nagumo (Japanese)

Shokaku
Zuiho

13.30
12.30

5°

Shokaku
09.30

Zuikaku

27.10
09.00

Zuikaku
Junyo

Junyo
55 Aircraft

10.00

07.40
Zuiho

Junyo

27.10
14.00

07.00
07.00

06.00
04.00   04.00

12.00   73

15.00

27.10
14.00

20.00

Solomon

Scouts

09.20
Chikuma

Advanced Group
V. Adm. Kondo
2BB, 5C, 14D

Islands

Sta Isabel Is.

04.00

Shokaku
Zuikaku
Zuiho
157 Aircraft   29   109   25

17.10

Malaita Is.

Scouts

BB *Kongo*
Haruna

BB *Hiei* and *Kirishima*

27.10
00.40

Main Force
V. Adm. Nagumo
2BB, 5C, 15D

07.00-15.00
Hornet

TF16
R. Adm. Kinkaid
82 Aircraft

**Operational Area
of US Carriers**

60 Aircraft
Henderson Field

04.00

27.10
05.15

27.10   01.35
Enterprise

10° **Guadalcanal**

23.00

04.00

San Cristobal Is.

TF17
Hornet
R. Adm. Murray
87 Aircraft
1BB, 6C, 14D

27.10
14.00

Japanese Battleships and main Carrier Force
Advanced Carrier Group
US Carrier Groups
Air attacks
Hits

Santa Cruz Is.

160°   165°   0   nm   120

Rennell Is.

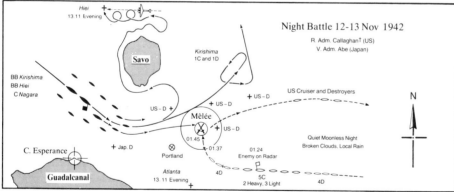

Hiei
13.11 Evening

Night Battle 12-13 Nov 1942
R. Adm. Callaghan† (US)
V. Adm. Abe (Japan)

Savo

Kirishima
1C and 1D

BB *Kirishima*
BB *Hiei*
C *Nagara*

US Cruiser and Destroyers

US–D

US–D   US–D

N

Mêlée

Jap. D

01.45   US–D

Quiet Moonless Night
Broken Clouds. Local Rain

C. Esperance

Portland   01.37   01.24   Enemy on Radar

Guadalcanal

Atlanta
13.11 Evening

4D   5C
2 Heavy, 3 Light   4D

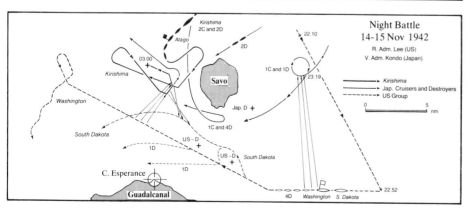

Kirishima
2C and 2D

Atago

22.10

**Night Battle
14-15 Nov 1942**
R. Adm. Lee (US)
V. Adm. Kondo (Japan)

03.00

2D

Kirishima

Savo

1C and 1D

23.19

Kirishima
Jap. Cruisers and Destroyers
US Group

Washington

Jap. D

0   nm   5

1C and 4D

South Dakota

US–D

South Dakota

1D

US–D

C. Esperance

1D

Guadalcanal

4D   *Washington* S. Dakota   22.52

26/27 Oct 1942: Battle of the Santa Cruz Islands. With their 'Henderson Field' air base on Guadalcanal, the Americans hold the air superiority in the eastern Solomon Islands. However, a premature report leads the Japanese Navy to believe that the Japanese army have captured the airfield, so their fleet comes up to cover the final subjugation of the island. Admiral Halsey can oppose them with only 2 carrier groups. Relative strengths are as follows.

JAPAN	Van (Kondo)	Main body (Nagumo)
Aircraft carriers	*Junyo*	*Shokaku*
		Zuikaku
		Zuiho
Battleships	*Kongo*	*Hiei*
	Haruna	*Kirishima*
Cruisers	5	5
Destroyers	14	15
Aircraft	55	157

USA
Two carrier groups (Vice Admirals Kinkaid and Murray)

Aircraft carriers	*Enterprise* } 171 aircraft
	Hornet
Battleship	*South Dakota*

+ 6 cruisers, 14 destroyers. A further 60 aircraft are available at 'Henderson Field'.

26 Oct early: US reconnaissance aircraft score a serious hit on *Zuiho* with a bomb. Both fleets now attack. *Shokaku* is hit by 5 bombs, and put out of action for several months. The first wave of Japanese aircraft concentrates on *Hornet*, which is hit by many bombs and 2 torpedoes. The second wave attacks *Enterprise*, and scores 3 bomb hits, nevertheless, the carrier remains operational. *South Dakota* and the cruiser *San Juan* are each hit by a bomb. Most of the Japanese aircraft are shot down by the very effective American AA fire (26 by *South Dakota* alone).

Afternoon: A group of planes from *Junyo* and *Zuikaku* attack *Hornet*, and score 1 torpedo and 2 bomb hits. The carrier has to be abandoned, as the Americans withdraw south. Realizing that 'Henderson Field' cannot now be captured, the Japanese fleet abandons its thrust. 100 Japanese aircraft have been lost, to 70 American, and the remaining Japanese aircraft are insufficient to subdue the airfield.

12/13 Nov 1942: First Night Battle off Guadalcanal. The Japanese bombard 'Henderson Field' repeatedly with the heavy guns of their ships, and the Americans try to intercept one of these bombarding groups. Rear Admiral Callaghan faces the enemy with 5 cruisers and 8 destroyers off Guadalcanal: the Japanese, under Vice Admiral Abe, have the battleships *Hiei* and *Kirishima*, 1 cruiser and 11 destroyers. The two forces clash in the dark (much to their mutual surprise) and, in a close-quarters fight, both suffer heavy losses. The Americans lose Admirals Callaghan and Scott; the cruiser *Atlanta* and 4 destroyers are sunk, and the cruisers *Juneau* and *Portland* badly damaged. The Japanese lose 2 destroyers sunk, and the battleship *Hiei* is left drifting badly damaged.

13 Nov: *Hiei* is sunk by carrier- and shore-based aircraft; *Juneau*, damaged on 12th, is sunk by Japanese submarine *I126*.

13/14 Nov: That night, the Japanese navy again bombards 'Henderson Field', and destroys 20 aircraft. But, next morning, aircraft from *Enterprise* sink the cruiser *Kinugasa* as the Japanese sail away.

14 Nov: Aircraft from 'Henderson Field' sink 7 out of 11 transports in a Japanese convoy. The survivors carry on towards Guadalcanal with their reinforcements, expecting protection from a Japanese navy bombardment force. This force, under Vice Admiral Kondo, includes the battleship *Kirishima*, 4 cruisers and 9 destroyers. Rear Admiral Lee

awaits them with the battleships *Washington* and *South Dakota* and 4 destroyers.

14/15 Nov 1942: Second Night Battle off Guadalcanal. The Japanese open fire on *South Dakota*, and damage her badly. *Washington* comes up unobserved and, with the aid of radar, reduces *Kirishima* to a wreck in a surprise bombardment. The Japanese also lose a destroyer; the Americans lose 3 destroyers. But the bombardment is frustrated and the Japanese transports beach themselves, where they are destroyed by the Americans next morning.

30 Nov/1 Dec 1942: Night action off Tassafronga (or Lunga

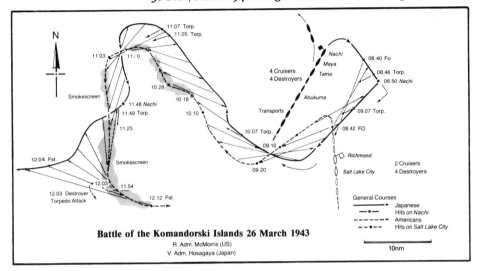

Battle of the Komandorski Islands 26 March 1943
R. Adm. McMorris (US)
V. Adm. Hosagaya (Japan)

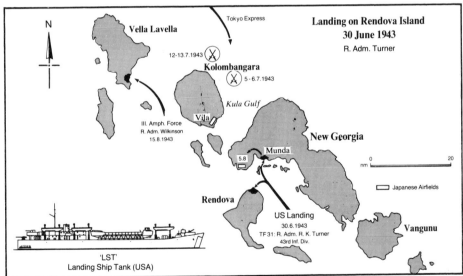

'LST'
Landing Ship Tank (USA)

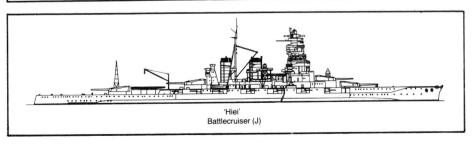

'Hiei'
Battlecruiser (J)

Point). With 8 destroyers under Rear Admiral Tanaka, the Japanese bring supplies to Guadalcanal. Rear Admiral Wright, with 5 cruisers and 6 destroyers, intercepts them. With the help of radar, the Americans open fire, and Tanaka's destroyers reply with a torpedo salvo, then turn away. A Japanese destroyer sinks, but torpedoes hit *New Orleans*, *Pensacola*, *Northampton* and *Minneapolis*. In spite of this success, however, the Japanese cannot maintain themselves on Guadalcanal, due to lack of logistic support.

29 Jan 1943: The US cruiser *Chicago* is sunk west of Guadalcanal by a Japanese torpedo-bomber, in the last Japanese victory in the waters around the Solomons.

At the beginning of Feb 1943, Rear Admiral Tanaka evacuates Japanese forces (12,000 men) from Guadalcanal, in a series of destroyer operations. Heavy weapons are abandoned.

From Sept 1942, Supreme Allied Commander in the 'Southwest Pacific Area' is the American General D. MacArthur. In New Guinea, his troops assume the offensive.

Jan 1943: The first airfields on the north coast of New Guinea are captured.

2–5 March 1943: Air-sea action in the Bismarck Sea. The Japanese send a convoy of 8 transports, escorted by destroyers, to reinforce their garrisons in New Guinea. US Army and Australian bombers attack the convoy, and sink all the transports and 4 destroyers. A whole Japanese division is lost.

26 March 1943: Battle off the Komandorski Islands. The Japanese escort a convoy to the Aleutians with a force of 4 cruisers and 4 destroyers, under Vice Admiral Hosagaya. The Americans attack, with 2 cruisers and 4 destroyers under Rear Admiral McMorris. In the last old-fashioned naval battle, line against line, the two fleets fight it out until their ammunition is exhausted. (This is an especially unusual action in the Pacific War, as neither aircraft nor submarines are involved.) The American cruiser *Salt Lake City* and a destroyer are damaged, the Japanese cruiser *Nachi* is damaged, and the Japanese convoy turns back, fearing American air attack.

April 1943: The Japanese Navy Air Force conducts an offensive against Guadalcanal, and suffers heavy losses.

18 April 1943: Fleet Admiral Yamamoto is shot down by American fighters while on an inspection flight over the western Solomon Islands. (The Americans had intercepted and decoded his entire timetable.) His successor as commander of the Japanese fleet is Admiral Koga.

11 May 1943: Recapture of Attu. An American task force under Rear Admiral Kinkaid lands the US 7th Division on the Aleutian Island of Attu. Naval forces are 3 battleships, an escort carrier, 7 cruisers, 21 destroyers and numerous transports. By the end of May, the 2,600 Japanese defenders have been destroyed.

Summer 1943: After a pause of some months, the Americans resume the offensive in the Solomons.

30 June 1943: Landing on Rendova Island (opposite the Japanese air base on New Georgia). The landing fleet under Rear Admiral Turner uses modern landing craft for the first time: the LST (Landing Ship Tank) for 20 tanks; the LCT (Landing Craft Tank) for 3 tanks, and LCI (Landing Craft Infantry) for 400 men. To guard against Japanese intervention, several combat groups are available, including 2 aircraft carriers, 3 escort carriers, 5 battleships and a number of cruisers and destroyers. The resupply of strongpoints leads to several naval actions.

5/6 July 1943: Night action in the Kula Gulf. An American battle group of 3 cruisers and 4 destroyers, under Rear Admiral Ainsworth, meets 10 Japanese destroyers under Rear Admiral Akiyama. 2 Japanese destroyers are sunk, but the US cruiser *Helena* is hit by a torpedo salvo, and sinks.

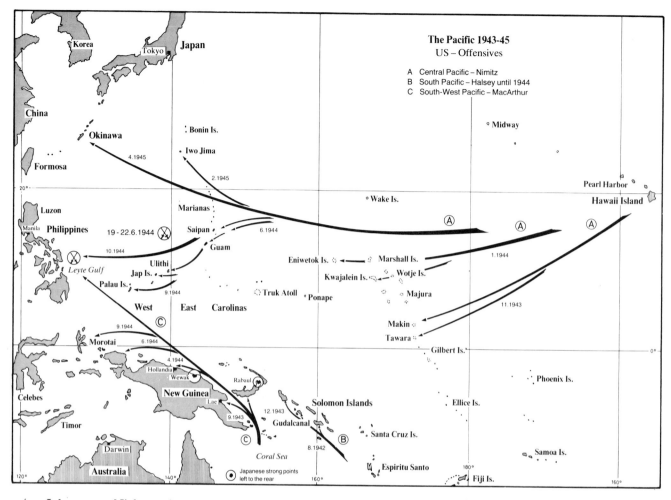

The Pacific 1943-45
US – Offensives

A Central Pacific – Nimitz
B South Pacific – Halsey until 1944
C South-West Pacific – MacArthur

Japanese strong points left to the rear

12/13 July 1943: Night action off Kolombangara. Rear Admiral Izaki brings a force of a cruiser and 9 destroyers, 4 with troops on board, for the Japanese strongpoint at Vila. They are intercepted off the north coast of Kolombangara by Rear Admiral Ainsworth, with 3 cruisers and 10 destroyers. The Japanese cruiser *Jintsu* blows up under gunfire, while Japanese destroyers fire torpedoes which hit all three Allied cruisers (*Honolulu*, *St. Louis* and the New Zealand *Leander*), and sink a destroyer.

5 Aug 1943: The Americans capture Munda, the target of their New Georgia offensive in the Solomons.

15 Aug 1943: After a 2-week bombardment, the US Navy lands 34,000 men on Kiska in the Aleutians. However, the island has been quietly evacuated by the Japanese a few days before the start of the bombardment.

15 Aug 1943: US landing on Vella Lavella. Avoiding the strongly fortified island of Kolombangara, the Americans land III Amphibious Force (Rear Admiral Wilkinson) on Vella Lavella, in the Solomons.

3 Sept 1943 onwards: US Landings on Lae and Salamaua. General MacArthur's VII Amphibious Force (Rear Admiral Barbey) lands near the Japanese strongpoint in the Gulf of Huon (New Guinea), and captures it shortly afterwards.

1 Nov 1943: US Landing in Empress Augusta Bay. Rear Admiral Wilkinson's III Amphibious Force lands the US 3rd Marine Division on the south coast of Bougainville (the most westerly of the Solomon Islands). The Japanese hold

out in the jungle on the island until the end of the war.

2 Nov 1943: Action in Empress Augusta Bay. A Japanese force of 2 heavy and 2 light cruisers and 6 destroyers, under Rear Admiral Omori, leaves Rabaul to mount a night attack on the American invasion force, which is covered by Rear Admiral Merrill's 4 cruisers and 8 destroyers. The Japanese are repelled by radar-controlled gunfire, and lose the cruiser *Sendai* and a destroyer. The cruiser *Haguro* is damaged. On the American side, only *Denver* receives hits, which fail to explode, and *Foote* is hit by a ship of her own division.

5 Nov 1943: US carrier attack on Rabaul. The Japanese reinforce their naval units in Rabaul, but 97 aircraft from the US carriers *Saratoga* and *Princeton*, under Rear Admiral Sherman, make a surprise attack and score hits on the cruisers *Maya*, *Takao*, *Mogami*, *Atago*, *Agano* and *Noshiro*. US losses are only 10 aircraft.

11 Nov 1943: The Americans repeat the air raid on Rabaul, with 185 planes from the carriers *Essex*, *Bunker Hill* and *Independence* under Rear Admiral Montgomery. The cruiser *Agano* is damaged, and a destroyer sunk. The Japanese mount an aerial counterattack from Rabaul, but are repulsed with heavy losses without scoring a hit. Attacks by the new Japanese carrier squadrons from Rabaul, on the US landing fleet off Bougainville, are also beaten off with a heavy loss of aircraft for the Japanese, but they do score 2 torpedo hits on American cruisers. From now on, Rabaul is too insecure to serve as a Japanese naval base.

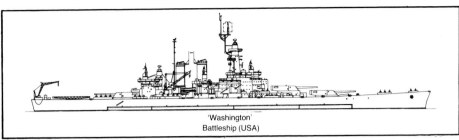

'Washington'
Battleship (USA)

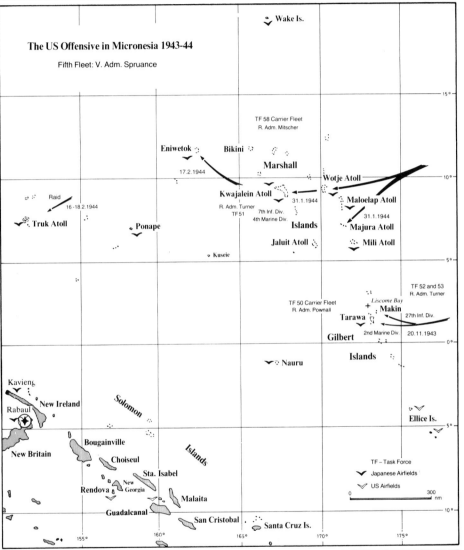

The US Offensive in Micronesia 1943-44

Fifth Fleet: V. Adm. Spruance

Wake Is.

TF 58 Carrier Fleet
R. Adm. Mitscher

Eniwetok   Bikini

17.2.1944   Marshall

Wotje Atoll

Kwajalein Atoll   Maloelap Atoll
R. Adm. Turner   31.1.1944
TF 51   7th Inf. Div.
4th Marine Div.   31.1.1944

Raid   Majura Atoll
16-18.2.1944   Islands

Truk Atoll   Ponape   Mili Atoll

Jaluit Atoll

Kuseie

TF 52 and 53
R. Adm. Turner

TF 50 Carrier Fleet   Liscome Bay
R. Adm. Pownall   Makin
Tarawa   27th Inf. Div.

Gilbert   2nd Marine Div.   20.11.1943

Islands

Nauru

Kavieng

New Ireland   Ellice Is.

Rabaul

Solomon

New Britain   Bougainville

Choiseul   Islands

Sta. Isabel   TF – Task Force

New   Japanese Airfields
Rendova   Georgia   US Airfields
Malaita   0   300
                                    nm

Guadalcanal

San Cristobal

Santa Cruz Is.

155°   160°   165°   170°   175°

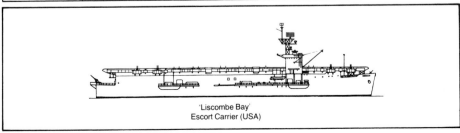

'Liscombe Bay'
Escort Carrier (USA)

During 1943, new warships had been entering service with the US Navy in ever-increasing numbers, especially aircraft carriers, which were by now capable of carrying some 90 aircraft each; light aircraft carriers could hold 40–50 aircraft. New battleships, cruisers, destroyers, landing craft and a vast number of auxiliaries now equipped the United States forces for an offensive through the islands of the central ocean, starting with the Gilbert Islands.

Nov 1943: US landing on the Gilbert Islands. Overall Commander is Vice Admiral Spruance, and the carrier force is commanded by Rear Admiral Pownall. This is the first operation to be undertaken by the newly formed Fifth Fleet. Forces engaged are as follows.

AIRCRAFT CARRIERS	LIGHT CARRIERS	BATTLESHIPS
Yorktown	*Princeton*	*South Dakota*
Lexington	*Independence*	*Washington*
Enterprise	*Monterey*	*Massachusetts*
Essex	*Belleau Wood*	*North Carolina*
Bunker Hill	*Cowpens*	*Indiana*
Saratoga		

+ 6 cruisers and 21 destroyers.

From 19 Nov 1943: With its 700 aircraft, this fleet attacks all Japanese airfields in range of Tarawa and Makin (the chosen landing points), putting the Japanese air force in the eastern Marshall Islands and in the Gilbert Islands out of action at the time of the landings.

20 Nov 1943: The US 2nd Marine Division and parts of the US 27th Infantry Division land on the islands of Tarawa and Makin, strongly defended by 4,500 Japanese under Rear Admiral Shibasaki. The landing fleet (Rear Admiral Turner) includes 20 troop and supply carriers, as well as 2 new dock landing ships. The troops receive air and artillery support from 8 escort carriers (216 aircraft), the battleships *Idaho, New Mexico, Colorado, Pennsylvania, Mississippi, Tennessee* and *Maryland*, 6 heavy and 2 light cruisers, and 38 destroyers. After heavy fighting, Makin is captured that same day; Tarawa falls 3 days later.

20 Nov 1943: In the Gilbert Islands, the light carrier *Independence* is hit by a torpedo from a Japanese bomber.

24 Nov 1943: The Japanese submarine *I175* sinks the escort carrier *Liscombe Bay* (again, in the Gilbert Islands).

4 Dec 1943: 2 of the 4 US carrier groups attack Kwajalein Atoll. In their withdrawal, the Japanese score an aerial torpedo hit on the new *Lexington*.

15 Dec 1943: US landing at Arawe. Troops of General MacArthur's 'Southwest Pacific Area' command land on the south coast of New Britain.

26 Dec 1943: US landing at Cape Gloucester. The US 1st Marine Division lands on the western tip of New Britain.

2 Jan 1944: US landings at Saidor on New Guinea, opposite New Britain. Strong Japanese forces in Sio (east New Guinea) are thus cut off.

29 Jan to 6 Feb 1944: A US carrier fleet (Task Force 58, Vice Admiral Mitscher) attacks Japanese airfields in the Marshall Islands to cover American landing operations. It consists of the carriers *Enterprise, Yorktown, Essex, Intrepid, Bunker Hill* and *Saratoga*, the light carriers *Belleau Wood, Princeton, Langley, Cowpens, Monterey* and *Cabot* (730 aircraft in all), the battleships *Washington, Massachusetts, North Carolina, Indiana, South Dakota, Alabama, New Jersey* and *Iowa*, 3 heavy and 3 light cruisers, and 36 destroyers.

31 Jan 1944: US landing on Kwajalein (Marshall Islands). Fifth Fleet (Vice Admiral Spruance) puts ashore the 4th Marine and 7th Infantry Divisions. The landing fleet has almost 100 transports and landing craft; the support fleet consists of 8 escort carriers (190 aircraft), the battleships *Pennsylvania, New Mexico, Mississippi, Tennessee, Idaho,*

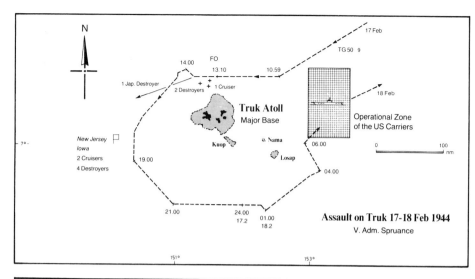

Assault on Truk 17-18 Feb 1944
V. Adm. Spruance

N

Truk Atoll
Major Base

FO
14.00   13.10   10.59   17 Feb

TG 50 9

1 Jap. Destroyer
2 Destroyers   1 Cruiser

18 Feb

Operational Zone
of the US Carriers

New Jersey
Iowa
2 Cruisers
4 Destroyers

Kuop   Nama   Losap

19.00   06.00   18 Feb

0   100
nm

21.00   24.00   01.00   04.00
17.2   18.2

151°   153°

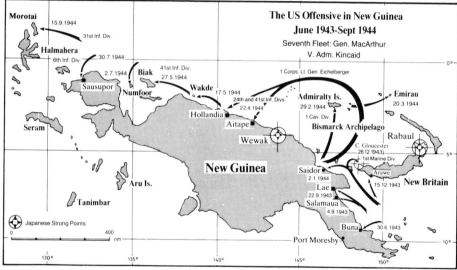

The US Offensive in New Guinea
June 1943-Sept 1944
Seventh Fleet: Gen. MacArthur
V. Adm. Kincaid

Morotai   15.9.1944   31st Inf. Div.
Halmahera   30.7.1944   6th Inf. Div.
2.7.1944   Biak   41st Inf. Div.   27.5.1944
Sausupor   Numfoor   Wakde   17.5.1944   1 Corps. Lt. Gen. Eichelberger
Seram   24th and 41st Inf. Divs.   22.4.1944   Admiralty Is.   29.2.1944   Emirau   20.3.1944
Hollandia   Aitape   1 Cav. Div.
Wewak   Bismarck Archipelago   Rabaul
New Guinea   C. Gloucester   26.12.1943   5°
Saidor   1st Marine Div.
2.1.1944   Arawe
Aru Is.   Lae   15.12.1943   New Britain
22.9.1943
Tanimbar   Salamaua
4.9.1943
Japanese Strong Points   Buna   30.6.1943
0   400   Port Moresby   10°
nm
130°   135°   140°   145°   150°

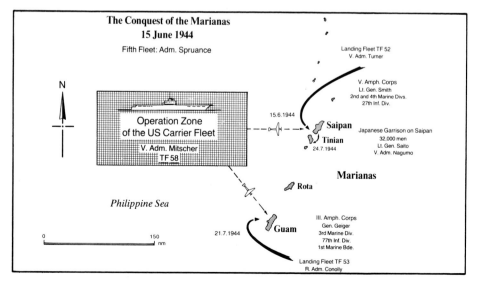

The Conquest of the Marianas
15 June 1944
Fifth Fleet: Adm. Spruance

N

Operation Zone
of the US Carrier Fleet
V. Adm. Mitscher
TF 58

Landing Fleet TF 52
V. Adm. Turner

V. Amph. Corps
Lt. Gen. Smith
2nd and 4th Marine Divs.
27th Inf. Div.

15.6.1944   Saipan
Tinian   Japanese Garrison on Saipan
24.7.1944   32,000 men
Lt. Gen. Saito
V. Adm. Nagumo

Marianas

Philippine Sea

Rota

21.7.1944   Guam   III. Amph. Corps
Gen. Geiger
3rd Marine Div.
77th Inf. Div.
1st Marine Bde.

0   150
nm

Landing Fleet TF 53
R. Adm. Conolly

Colorado and *Maryland*, 9 cruisers and 45 destroyers. The target atoll (the islands of Roi, Namur and Kwajalein) is subjected to a preliminary bombardment by the battleships and, despite desperate Japanese resistance by 8,600 men under Rear Admiral Akiyama, Kwajalein is in American hands a week later. At the same time, the unoccupied atoll of Majuru is seized to provide a good fleet anchorage.

15 Feb 1944: III Amphibious Force (Rear Admiral Wilkinson) lands the 3rd (New Zealand) Division on Green Island, east of New Britain.

17-18 Feb 1944: Assault on Truk. In order to pre-empt Japanese naval and air attacks, part of Fifth Fleet attacks the large Japanese base on Truk Island, in the Caroline Islands. Vice Admiral Spruance leads the assault with the carriers *Essex, Enterprise, Yorktown, Intrepid* and *Bunker Hill*, the light carriers *Belleau Wood, Cabot, Monterey* and *Cowpens*, the battleships *New Jersey, Iowa, North Carolina, Massachusetts, South Dakota* and *Alabama*, 10 cruisers and 29 destroyers. In the harbour are only Japanese light surface units; the cruiser *Naka* is sunk by carrier aircraft, the auxiliary training cruiser *Katori* and 2 destroyers are sunk by the battleships. The Japanese also lose 26 merchantmen and 300 of their 365 planes. 25 American planes are lost. In a counterattack by 7 Japanese torpedo-bombers, a hit is scored on *Intrepid*. Truk, like Rabaul, has been neutralized.

17 Feb 1944: US landing on Eniwetok. The unused reserves of the Kwajalein operation (27th Infantry Division) are transferred and used in a landing on the most westerly atoll of the Marshall Islands. In 4 days, the 3,400 Japanese defenders are defeated.

23 Feb 1944: Two US carrier groups attack Saipan, Tinian and Rota in the Marianas.

29 Feb 1944: US landing in the Admiralty Islands. The 1st Cavalry Division of the 'Southwest Pacific Area' command (MacArthur) lands on several islands off the north coast of New Guinea. The aim is to capture Manus, with its deep harbour, for use as a naval base. By 30 March, and in the face of sometimes desperate resistance, the operation is completed.

20 March 1944: US landing on Emirau (Bismarck Archipelago). The ring is now closed around the Japanese fortress of Rabaul, and MacArthur can now carry out a long hop to the west, in order to get around the Japanese strongpoint of Wewak on New Guinea.

14th April 1944: An ammunition ship explodes in Bombay harbour, destroying 20 ships (100,000 tons), 11 of which are total losses. The fire in the dock area burns for 14 days.

19 April 1944: Aircraft from the carrier *Illustrious* (GB) and *Saratoga* (US) attack Sabang on Sumatra.

22 April 1944: US landing at Hollandia. As preparation, a carrier fleet (Vice Admiral Mitscher) attacks the Palau islands on 30 and 31 March, the Japanese air force suffering further heavy blows, and the Americans losing but 25 aircraft. At the time of the landing itself, the fleet gives air cover over New Guinea, and keeps the Japanese bases in check. The landing fleet (Seventh Fleet, Vice Admiral Kinkaid) lands the 24th and 41st Infantry Divisions in face of slight resistance. They are supported by 8 escort carriers and 5 cruisers.

29-30 April 1944: In preparation for the assault on the Marianas, the carrier fleet attacks Truk again; the Japanese lose 90 aircraft, the Americans 26. MacArthur now makes further small hops to the west.

17 May 1944: US landings on Wakde. 124 miles (200 kilometres) west of Hollandia, an airfield is established on the island.

27 May 1944: US landing on Biak. The landing fleet (Rear Admiral Fechteler) puts the 41st Infantry Division ashore on this island off the north-west coast of New Guinea. The landing is successful, but almost a month is needed to root

out the well dug-in defence. The island of Noemfoor and the airfield of Sansapor on western New Guinea are captured in July 1944.

19-31 May 1944: The US destroyer escort *England* sinks 6 Japanese submarines in 12 days, a record for a single ship in the Second World War.

Now the Americans were poised to tackle the Japanese inner defences: the Marianas would bring their long-range bombers within striking distance of the Philippines and Japan itself. But the defensive garrisons of these islands, commanded by Lieutenant General Saito, would make them tough nuts to crack.

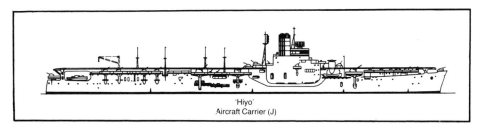

'Hiyo'
Aircraft Carrier (J)

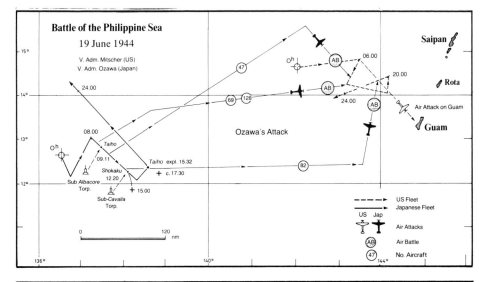

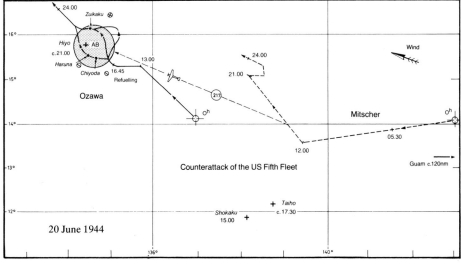

11-17 June 1944: The carrier fleet (Task Force 58, Vice Admiral Mitscher) is divided into four combat groups, and attacks the Marianas to destroy the Japanese air force. Japanese counterattacks are unsuccessful.

15-16 June 1944: Two combat groups attack the Bonin Islands, half way to Japan, in order to intercept reinforcements from there. In the ensuing struggle, the Japanese lose 300 aircraft, the Americans 22.

15 June 1944: US landing on Saipan (Marianas). The island is defended by 22,700 troops and 6,700 sailors. US landing fleet (Task Force 52, Vice Admiral Turner) lands V Amphibious Corps (Lieutenant General H. M. Smith) with the US 2nd and 4th Marine Divisions; the 27th Infantry Division is in reserve. The landing fleet totals 550 ships of all types. Covering forces consist of 8 escort carriers with 170 planes, the battleships *Tennessee, California, Maryland, Colorado, Pennsylvania, New Mexico* and *Idaho*, 11 cruisers and 50 destroyers. Aboard 4 escort carriers, with the logistic support units, are reserve aircraft for the assault carriers. Underwater demolition teams of frogmen are sent in, but find no obstacles. Japanese resistance on Saipan is particularly tough, as they expect their fleet to intervene.

19-20 June 1944: Battle of the Philippine Sea ('The Marianas Turkey Shoot'). Relative fleet strengths are as follows.

	US FIFTH FLEET (Spruance) Carrier Fleet (Mitscher)		JAPAN (Ozawa)
Aircraft carriers	*Hornet*		*Taiho*
	Yorktown		*Shokaku*
	Bunker Hill		*Zuikaku*
	Enterprise		*Junyo*
	Wasp		*Hiyo*
	Lexington		
	Essex		
Light carriers	*Cabot*	*Langley*	*Ryuho*
	Cowpens	*Bataan*	*Chitose*
	Belleau Wood	*Monterey*	*Chiyoda*
	San Jacinto	*Princeton*	*Zuiho*
Aircraft total	890		430
Battleships	*Iowa*		*Yamato*
	New Jersey		*Musashi*
	Washington		*Haruna*
	North Carolina		*Kongo*
	South Dakota		*Nagato*
	Alabama		
	Indiana		
Heavy cruisers	8		11
Light cruisers	13		2
Destroyers	67		28
Total crews	Almost 100,000		40,000

The Japanese fleet concentrates east of the Philippines, in order to relieve Saipan, while the US fleet takes position west of the Marianas to cover the landing fleet. Both sides send submarines into the Philippine Sea, but only American submarines come into action. Ozawa tries to get the American fleet between his ships and the air force in the Marianas, so as to attack them from both sides. His carrier aircraft can then refuel and replenish at the land bases on Guam and Rota, and attack the Americans again on their flight back to the carrier.

18 June, afternoon: Japanese aircraft sight the American carrier fleet.

19 June, early: As Mitscher does not know the exact location of the Japanese fleet, he has the majority of his 450 fighters prepared for take-off.

10am-3pm: The first Japanese attacks come from Guam, but they are intercepted by fighters before they can reach the American fleet. This is followed by an attack in four waves by Japanese carrier-borne aircraft. Mostly caught by the fighters, and the remainder decimated by the ships' AA fire.

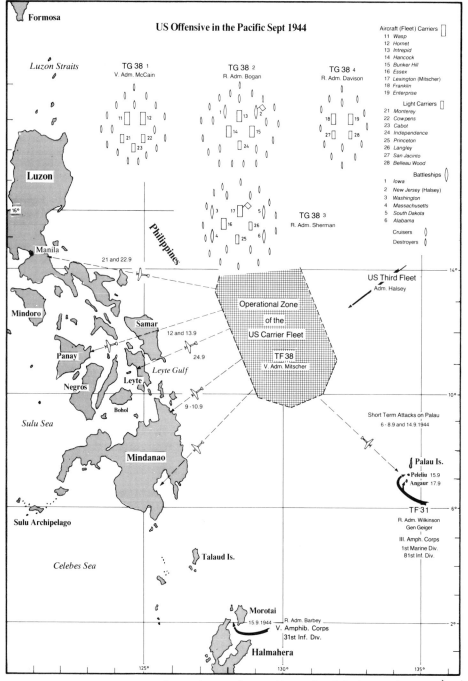

US Offensive in the Pacific Sept 1944

Formosa

Luzon Straits

TG 38 1
V. Adm. McCain

TG 38 2
R. Adm. Bogan

TG 38 4
R. Adm. Davison

Aircraft (Fleet) Carriers	
11	Wasp
12	Hornet
13	Intrepid
14	Hancock
15	Bunker Hill
16	Essex
17	Lexington (Mitscher)
18	Franklin
19	Enterprise

Light Carriers	
21	Monterey
22	Cowpens
23	Cabot
24	Independence
25	Princeton
26	Langley
27	San Jacinto
28	Belleau Wood

Battleships	
1	Iowa
2	New Jersey (Halsey)
3	Washington
4	Massachusetts
5	South Dakota
6	Alabama

Cruisers

Destroyers

Luzon

Manila

Philippines

TG 38 3
R. Adm. Sherman

21 and 22.9

12 and 13.9

24.9

9-10.9

Mindoro

Samar

Panay

Leyte Gulf

Leyte

Negros

Bohol

Sulu Sea

Mindanao

US Third Fleet
Adm. Halsey

Operational Zone
of the
US Carrier Fleet

TF 38
V. Adm. Mitscher

Short Term Attacks on Palau
6 - 8.9 and 14.9.1944

Palau Is.

Peleliu 15.9
Angaur 17.9

TF 31
R. Adm. Wilkinson
Gen Geiger
III. Amph. Corps
1st Marine Div.
81st Inf. Div.

Sulu Archipelago

Celebes Sea

Talaud Is.

Morotai
15.9.1944

R. Adm. Barbey
V. Amphib. Corps
31st Inf. Div.

Halmahera

only about 100 Japanese aircraft return to their carriers.

19/20 June: During the night, Ozawa steers slowly WNW. Mitscher leaves behind the carrier group that is lowest on fuel to hold Guam in check, and advances west with the other three.

20 June: It is not until the afternoon that Mitscher's scout aircraft sight the enemy and although the Japanese are at the limit of his aircraft's range, Mitscher at once sends off a full 'deck load' (217 aircraft) to the attack. Ozawa has only 35 fighters to oppose them.

6.40pm: In a dusk attack, the American aircraft sink the carrier *Hiyo* and 2 tankers; the carriers *Zuikaku* and *Chiyoda*, the battleship *Haruna* and a cruiser are damaged. Ozawa has now lost almost all his aircraft, and orders a withdrawal. The Americans lose only 20 aircraft in the attack, but on the return flight many of them run out of fuel, and 80 crash-land in the sea or on the carrier decks. Most of the crews are saved by the rescue services, and only 49 flyers are killed. Mitscher's proposal to continue the pursuit with part of his force is, meanwhile, rejected by Spruance.

The Battle of the Philippine Sea was another body-blow for the Japanese: 3 aircraft carriers, 400 naval aircraft and 50 aircraft from Guam had perished. Japan's carrier-borne air power was thus practically annihilated.
The Americans, meanwhile, had lost 130 aircraft and 76 aircrew. Spruance, cautiously rejecting Mitscher's proposal for a pursuit, now turned his attention to securing the Saipan invasion fleet.

24 June 1944: After the Battle of the Philippine Sea, 3 carrier groups sail for Eniwetok to replenish, but the 4th Carrier Group (Rear Admiral Clark) makes one further advance prior to this, and makes strikes against Iwo Jima and the Pagan Islands.

9 July 1944: Organized Japanese resistance on Saipan ends.

21 July 1944: Landing on Guam. Task Force 53 (Rear Admiral Conolly) lands III Amphibious Corps on Guam, supported by some of the battleships and escort carriers employed at Saipan. Vice Admiral Mitscher's Task Force 58 attacks Japanese bases within range of the Marianas at the same time. After several weeks, Japanese resistance on Guam is broken, and the island is developed into a major US western Pacific base. (The landing on Guam represents the first use of close ground-support of an amphibious landing by carrier-borne aircraft.)

24 July 1944: Landing on Tinian. Task Force 52 lands V Amphibious Corps; long-range fire support is given by the fleet and by army heavy artillery on Saipan. The Japanese defenders are wiped out in only a few days.

25 July 1944: In the Indian Ocean, aircraft from the British carriers *Victorious* and *Illustrious* attack Sabang on Sumatra. Escorting surface ships bombard the dock areas.

4-5 Aug 1944: Two carrier groups, under Vice Admiral Mitscher, attack Bonin Island, destroying 25 aircraft and a convoy of 5 destroyers and 7 transports.

24 Aug 1944: In the Indian Ocean, the British aircraft carriers *Victorious* and *Indomitable* send their aircraft to attack Padang on Sumatra and, the same day, attacks on the airfield at Sabang are followed by bombardment by the British Eastern Fleet.

Sept 1944: Admiral Halsey is now placed in command of the fast US naval force, Third Fleet. In order to weaken the Japanese air force further and to prepare for the next landings, he undertakes the following actions.

31 Aug to 2 Sept: A carrier group attacks the Bonin Islands.

7-10 Sept: The entire carrier-borne aircraft of Task Force 38 (Mitscher) attacks the southern Philippines, striking at airfields and naval installations. Resistance is light.

They only manage one hit on *South Dakota* and near misses on *Indiana*, *Bunker Hill* and a cruiser. Some of these Japanese aircraft fly on to Guam, and are destroyed by American aircraft as they land there.

9.11am: After the Japanese aircraft have taken off, 2 US submarines attack their carrier fleet: *Albacore* (Blanchard) scores a torpedo hit on *Taiho*, petrol fumes from a burst pipe fill the whole vessel and, after 6 hours, a gigantic explosion destroys the Japanese flagship.

12.20pm: The submarine *Cavalla* (Kossler) scores 3 torpedo hits on *Shokaku*, and she sinks after 3 hours. In the afternoon,

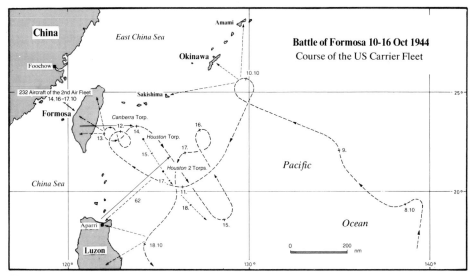

Battle of Formosa 10-16 Oct 1944
Course of the US Carrier Fleet

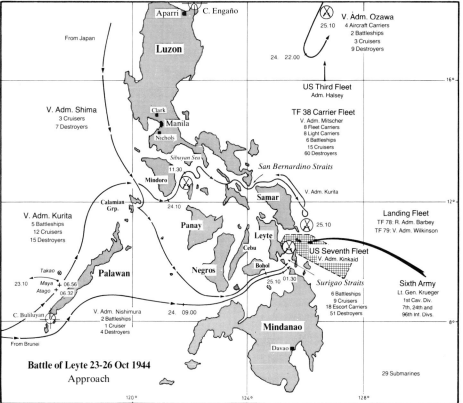

Battle of Leyte 23-26 Oct 1944
Approach

12-13 Sept: Attacks on the central Philippines, mainly against Visayas and Manila area. The fleet then redeploys to support the next landings.

15 Sept 1944: Landing on Morotai. MacArthur's VII Amphibious Force lands the 31st Infantry Division on this weakly defended island; its capture brings the eastern Sunda Islands within range of the US Air Force.

15-23 Sept 1944: Landing on the Palau Islands. Rear Admiral Wilkinson's Task Force 31 lands III Amphibious Corps; the supporting fleet includes 12 escort carriers, the battleships *Pennsylvania, Tennessee, Maryland, West Virginia* and

Mississippi, 8 cruisers and 27 destroyers. The 1st Marine Division lands on Peleliu against light resistance, but the Japanese hold out on a ridge in the centre of the island for 2 months. The 8th Infantry Division is put down on the weakly defended island of Angaur, and the undefended atoll of Ulithi is occupied and developed into a naval base.

21-22 Sept: The carrier fleet (Task Force 38) attacks Manila Harbour. 3 destroyers and over 20 freighters are sunk, and harbour installations and airfields badly hit.

24 Sept 1944: Air sorties are flown against Japanese shipping and positions in the central Philippines.
All these attacks destroy 1,200 Japanese aircraft and sink 13 ships, at a cost of 72 aircraft. As the air defences in the central Philippines are weaker than expected, the assault on the islands is brought forward from Dec to Oct, and the landing and support vessels of the Central Pacific Command (Admiral Nimitz) are placed under General MacArthur's command. Halsey's Third Fleet operates independently.

10-16 Oct 1944: Battle of Formosa. On the first day, Halsey attacks Okinawa with 340 aircraft. Then, after a short diversionary attack on northern Luzon, the fleet makes a thrust at Formosa. Here the Japanese have the strong 2nd Air Fleet (Vice Admiral Fukudoma).

12 Oct: Aircraft from the 17 carriers of Task Force 38 attack Formosa; in a hard fought air battle, the Americans lose 43 aircraft, the Japanese 160.

13 Oct: The American aircraft attack airfields and port facilities. In a counterattack on the US fleet, the Japanese score a torpedo hit on the cruiser *Canberra*.

14 Oct: More attacks are flown against Formosa and northern Luzon; Japanese air counterattacks score only one torpedo hit on the cruiser *Houston*.

15 Oct: Heavy air battles over northern Luzon, between the withdrawing Third Fleet and the Japanese 1st Air Fleet (Vice Admiral Terouka). The Japanese score a further torpedo hit on *Houston*. In 7 days the Japanese lose 600 aircraft, the Americans 90.

17-19 Oct 1944: In the Indian Ocean, aircraft from the British carriers *Victorious, Illustrious* and *Indomitable* attack Nicobar Islands.

20 Oct 1944: US landing on Leyte. General MacArthur's landing fleet is commanded by Vice Admiral Kinkaid (Seventh Fleet). It includes 300 transports and landing ships, which put Sixth Army (Lieutenant General Krueger) ashore at Tacloban on Leyte. The first wave ashore consists of the 1st Cavalry Division, the 7th, 24th and 96th Infantry Divisions. Fire support is once more given by the old battleships, cruisers and destroyers under Rear Admiral Oldendorf. Halsey's Third Fleet keeps the Japanese air force on Luzon and the central Philippines busy, but the Japanese succeed in hitting the cruiser *Honolulu* with a torpedo and the cruiser *Australia* (AUS) with a bomb.

23-26 Oct 1944: Battle of Leyte Gulf. The loss of the Philippines would finally cut the Japanese off from their south Asian sources of raw materials, and they therefore commit their fleet to the struggle completely. The result is the greatest battle in naval history. It consists of four parts:

24 Oct: Air-sea battle in the Sibuyan Sea.

25 Oct: Night battle in the Surigao Straits.

25 Oct: Battle off Samar.

25 Oct: Air-sea battle off Cape Engano.

At the news of the US landing on Leyte, the whole Japanese fleet puts to sea. From the north, Ozawa's carrier fleet attacks: with his 116 aircraft, his task is to lure the main American fleet (Third Fleet) to the north, thus opening the way for the Japanese battle fleet (Vice Admiral Kurita) to attack from the west. From the south come two battle groups under Vice Admirals Shima and Nishimura. 14 submarines are also

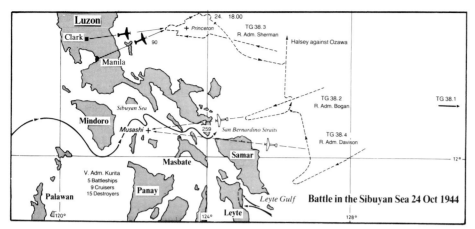

Battle in the Sibuyan Sea 24 Oct 1944

Luzon · Clark · Manila · Mindoro · *Sibuyan Sea* · Palawan · Panay · Masbate · Samar · Panaon · Leyte · *Leyte Gulf* · *Musashi* · San Bernardino Straits · *Princeton* · TG 38.3 R. Adm. Sherman · Halsey against Ozawa · TG 38.2 R. Adm. Bogan · TG 38.4 R. Adm. Davison · TG 38.1

V. Adm. Kurita
5 Battleships
9 Cruisers
15 Destroyers

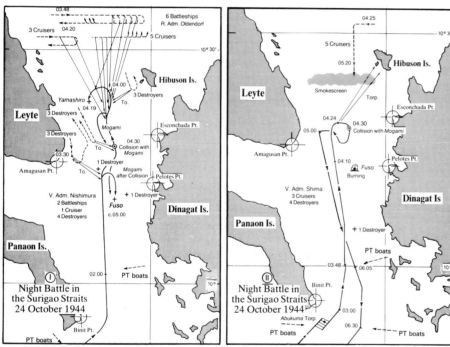

Night Battle in the Surigao Straits 24 October 1944

Leyte · Hibuson Is. · *Yamashiro* · *Mogami* · Esconchada Pt. · Pelotes Pt. · Amagusan Pt. · Dinagat Is. · Panaon Is. · *Fuso* · 3 Cruisers · 5 Cruisers · 6 Battleships R. Adm. Oldendorf · 3 Destroyers · Mogami after Collision · Collision with Mogami · 1 Destroyer · V. Adm. Nishimura 2 Battleships 1 Cruiser 4 Destroyers · PT boats · Binit Pt.

Night Battle in the Surigao Straits 24 October 1944

Leyte · Hibuson Is. · Esconchada Pt. · Amagusan Pt. · Pelotes Pt. · *Fuso* Burning · Collision with Mogami · Smokescreen · Torp. · 5 Cruisers · V. Adm. Shima 3 Cruisers 4 Destroyers · Dinagat Is · Panaon Is. · PT boats · *Abukuma* Torp. · Binit Pt.

brought into the area. The Third US Fleet is operating in 4 approximately equal battle groups; a logistic supply fleet (11 escort carriers with replacement aircraft, 33 tankers, 10 ocean-going tugs, 6 ammunition ships and 40 escort destroyers) gives it the capability of operating at sea for long periods. The opposing fleets at the Battle of Leyte Gulf are as follows.

USA

Third Fleet (Halsey)
Carrier Fleet (Mitscher)
Aircraft carriers *Wasp, Hornet, Lexington, Hancock, Intrepid, Essex, Franklin, Enterprise*
Light carriers *Cowpens, Cabot, Independence, Princeton, Langley, San Jacinto, Belleau Wood, Monterey*
Aircraft total about 1,000
Battleships *New Jersey, Iowa, Massachusetts, South Dakota,*
Washington, Alabama
6 heavy cruisers
9 light cruisers
60 destroyers

Seventh Fleet (Kinkaid)
Support Force (Oldendorf)
Battleships *Mississippi, Maryland, West Virginia, Tennessee, California, Pennsylvania*
4 heavy cruisers
5 light cruisers
30 destroyers
Carrier Group (Sprague)
18 escort carriers
Aircraft total 400
21 destroyers

+ 29 submarines
Total tonnage 1,330,000
Total crews 140,000

JAPAN

Northern Force (Ozawa)
Aircraft carrier *Zuikaku*
Light carriers *Zuiho, Chitose, Chiyoda*
Aircraft total 116
Battleships *Hyuga, Ise*
3 light cruisers
9 destroyers

Centre Force (Kurita)
Battleships *Yamato, Musashi, Nagato, Kongo, Haruna*
10 heavy cruisers
2 light cruisers
15 destroyers

Southern Force (Shima/Nishimura)
Battleships *Fuso, Yamashiro*
3 heavy cruisers
1 light cruiser
11 destroyers

300 aircraft available on Luzon

+ 14 submarines
Total tonnage 730,000
Total crews 43,000

23 Oct: The US submarines *Dace* and *Darter* discover Kurita's fleet north of Palawan, and succeed in torpedoing 3 heavy cruisers; Kurita's flagship (*Atago*) and *Maya* sink rapidly. In pursuing the damaged *Takao*, *Darter* runs on to a reef and has to be abandoned. The rest of the Japanese fleet proceeds on course and, next morning, is in the Sibuyan Sea.

24 Oct 1944: Battle in the Sibuyan Sea. In the morning, the Japanese aircraft from Luzon attack the northernmost US carrier group, but Ozawa's carrier planes fail to find it, and fly on to Luzon; most of them are intercepted and destroyed en route. Only the light carrier *Princeton* receives a bomb hit, but a subsequent explosion in the vessel also damages the cruiser *Birmingham* which is alongside the stricken carrier to aid her. The carrier sinks. Two other US carrier groups attack Kurita's battle fleet in the Sibuyan Sea, in 4 waves throughout the day. The battleship *Musashi* sinks after being hit by 11 torpedoes and 19 bombs; the heavy cruiser *Myoko* has to turn back after a torpedo hit; the battleships *Yamato* and *Nagato* are hit by bombs, but are still fit for combat. During these attacks Kurita temporarily reverses course, and this causes Halsey to consider the Japanese battle fleet as defeated. He therefore moves north with the carrier groups 38.2, 38.3 and 38.4, in order to attack Ozawa's carrier group next day. (Carrier group 38.1 is replenishing its fuel stocks.) Kurita, however, returns and, at midnight, passes through the San Bernardino Straits unopposed. As Kinkaid believes the Straits to be guarded by Halsey, he concentrates his support forces off the Surigao Straits to await the Japanese Southern Force, which has already been attacked that day by carrier aircraft, but with little success.

24/25 Oct 1944: Night battle in the Surigao Straits. The heavy units of Seventh Fleet Support Force, under Rear Admiral Oldendorf, stand in line ahead across the Surigao Straits, the battleships in the centre, the cruisers on both flanks, destroyers and PT boats advanced into the Straits, awaiting Shima and Nishimura.

2am: After a non-effective PT boat attack, the US destroyers score some torpedo hits: the battleship *Fuso* lies sinking together with 3 Japanese destroyers.

4.20am: *Yamashiro* runs straight into the fire of the whole American battle line, in the last artillery action fought between battleships. Under the radar-controlled fire of battleships and cruisers, she sinks with all hands, including Admiral Nishimura. The cruiser *Mogami* is able to limp away badly damaged. The remaining ships of the Japanese

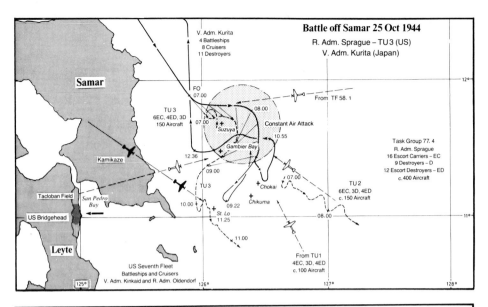

Battle off Samar 25 Oct 1944
R. Adm. Sprague – TU 3 (US)
V. Adm. Kurita (Japan)

V. Adm. Kurita
4 Battleships
8 Cruisers
11 Destroyers

Samar

TU 3
6EC, 4ED, 3D
150 Aircraft

FO
07.00

From TF 58. 1

Suzuya

Constant Air Attack

Gambier Bay

Kamikaze

Task Group 77. 4
R. Adm. Sprague
16 Escort Carriers – EC
9 Destroyers – D
12 Escort Destroyers – ED
c. 400 Aircraft

Chokai

Chikuma

TU 2
6EC, 3D, 4ED
c. 150 Aircraft

Tacloban Field
San Pedro
Bay
US Bridgehead

St. Lo
11.25

Leyte

US Seventh Fleet
Battleships and Cruisers
V. Adm. Kinkaid and R. Adm. Oldendorf

From TU1
4EC, 3D, 4ED
c. 100 Aircraft

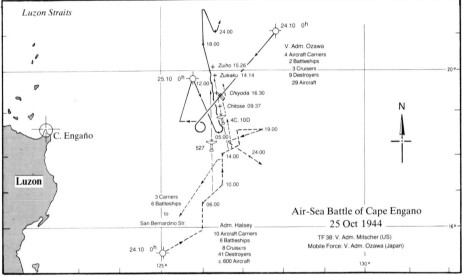

Luzon Straits

V. Adm. Ozawa
4 Aircraft Carriers
2 Battleships
3 Cruisers
9 Destroyers
29 Aircraft

Zuiho 15.26
Zuikaku 14.14
Chiyoda 16.30
Chitose 09.37

4C. 10D

N

C. Engaño

527

Luzon

3 Carriers
6 Battleships
to
San Bernardino Str.

Adm. Halsey
10 Aircraft Carriers
6 Battleships
8 Cruisers
41 Destroyers
c. 600 Aircraft

Air-Sea Battle of Cape Engano
25 Oct 1944

TF 38: V. Adm. Mitscher (US)
Mobile Force: V. Adm. Ozawa (Japan)

Southern Force turn away, but, in so doing, *Nachi* collides with the damaged *Mogami*. The light cruiser *Abukuma*, which had been hit by an MTB torpedo, is sunk next day by US Army aircraft; next day also, *Mogami* is sent to the bottom by carrier aircraft from Seventh Fleet. Of the Japanese Southern Forces, only 2 heavy cruisers and some destroyers eventually escape.

6.45am: In the north meanwhile, a US reconnaissance aircraft sights Kurita's battle fleet east of Samar.

25 Oct 1944: Battle of Samar. At 6.58am, Kurita opens fire on the northernmost group of escort carriers of Seventh Fleet. These fly-off their aircraft, and steam away south, finding protection in rain showers and smokescreens. Despite this, however, their position is hopeless: in the following chase, *Gambier Bay* is sunk and *Fenshaw Bay*, *Kalinin Bay* and *White Plains* are damaged.

9.20am: US destroyers carry out torpedo attacks to slow down the Japanese, during which 3 of the US destroyers are sunk; but they do manage to hit the heavy cruiser *Kumano*. The aircraft of the three escort carrier groups also attack the

Japanese with bombs and torpedoes. Kurita now sights the second escort carrier group ahead, mistakes it for Halsey's Third Fleet, and breaks off the pursuit. At this moment the first planned 'kamikaze' (suicide) attacks are flown by Japanese pilots. Four aircraft attack the 2nd Escort Carrier Group: *Santee* and *Suwanee* are hit, and *Santee* is also hit by a torpedo from a Japanese submarine. While Kurita cruises indecisively east of Samar, further kamikaze attacks are made. The carrier *St. Lô* sinks after being hit, and the carriers *Kalinin Bay* and *Kitkun Bay* are also hit. Kurita then learns that the major part of the US landing fleet (his main target) has already left Leyte Gulf, and that the Japanese Southern Force has been destroyed. He suspects that Halsey's Third Fleet is at hand, and does not know that kamikaze attacks have destroyed several carriers.

Midday: Without knowing of the support the kamikazes are bringing him, Kurita orders a withdrawal. The heavy cruisers *Chokai*, *Chikuma* and *Suzuya* are so badly damaged that they have to be abandoned and scuttled. The cruisers *Haguro* and *Tone* are also damaged.

25 Oct 1944: Battle off Cape Engano. Vice Admiral Halsey is informed of the location of Ozawa's carrier fleet on the afternoon of the 24th. He believes that Kurita is beaten in the Sibuyan Sea, and throws the entire Third Fleet (minus 1 carrier group) to the north, leaving the San Bernardino Straits unguarded.

8am: The first of a total of 6 waves of Mitscher's 527 aircraft take off to raid Ozawa's Northern Force off Cape Engano. The Japanese 20 defending fighters are soon destroyed. The light carrier *Chitose* sinks in the first attack and, during the following raids, the carriers *Zuikaku*, *Zuiho* and *Chiyoda* are also destroyed; the light cruiser *Tama* is damaged, and is later sunk by a submarine. The Japanese carrier fleet is thus destroyed. On hearing calls for help from Seventh Fleet off Leyte, Halsey breaks off the pursuit, but he is not able to catch Kurita before he passes through the Straits.

25–26 Oct: Kurita's fleet is attacked as it withdraws by aircraft of both US Third and Seventh Fleets, and he loses the light cruiser *Noshiro*. The cruiser *Kinu*, which is escorting a troop transport to Leyte, is also sunk.

In contrast to Spruance 4 months earlier, Halsey now strains with his whole fast fleet to destroy the Japanese carrier fleet and places Seventh Fleet in a precarious position. (Kurita's fleet remnants would be too battle-worn and low on ammunition to stand up to Oldendorf's fully replenished battleships and cruisers.)

Losses sustained during this epic battle were as follows.

	USA	JAPAN
Aircraft carriers	–	1
Light carriers	1	3
Escort carriers	2	–
Battleships	–	3
Heavy cruisers	–	6
Light cruisers	–	4
Destroyers	3	11
Total tonnage	35,000	300,000
Aircraft destroyed	100	150
Dead	1,500	10,000

Although part of the Japanese fleet had escaped, the battle was decisive: from now on, the United States had no serious naval opposition in Pacific waters.

27 Oct to 27 Nov 1944: Third Fleet operates east of the Philippines, in support of the American land forces on Leyte, until the end of Nov. In this period 800 Japanese aircraft are shot down, and one of their troop convoys bound for Leyte is destroyed. The cruisers *Nachi*, *Kumano* and

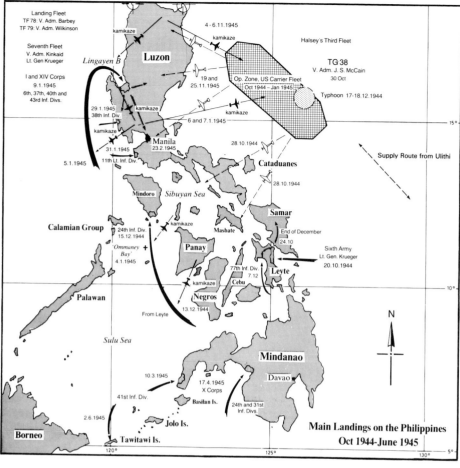

Main Landings on the Philippines
Oct 1944–June 1945

Landing Fleet
TF 78: V. Adm. Barbey
TF 79: V. Adm. Wilkinson

Seventh Fleet
V. Adm. Kinkaid
Lt. Gen Krueger

I and XIV Corps
9.1.1945
6th, 37th, 40th and
43rd Inf. Divs.

Luzon

kamikaze

4 - 6.11.1945

kamikaze

Halsey's Third Fleet

TG 38
V. Adm. J. S. McCain
30 Oct

Op. Zone, US Carrier Fleet
Oct 1944 – Jan 1945

Lingayen B

19 and
25.11.1945

Typhoon 17-18.12.1944

29.1.1945
38th Inf. Div.

kamikaze

6 and 7.1.1945

Manila
23.2.1945

28.10.1944

kamikaze

Supply Route from Ulithi

31.1.1945
11th Lt. Inf. Div.

5.1.1945

Cataduanes

28.10.1944

Mindoro

Sibuyan Sea

Samar

Calamian Group

24th Inf. Div.
15.12.1944

kamikaze

Masbate

End of December
24.10

'Ommaney
Bay'
4.1.1945

Panay

Leyte

Sixth Army
Lt. Gen. Krueger
20.10.1944

Palawan

77th Inf. Div.
7.12

Cebu

kamikaze

Negros

13.12.1944

From Leyte

Sulu Sea

N

Mindanao

Davao

10.3.1945

17.4.1945
X Corps

41st Inf. Div.

Basilan Is.

24th and 31st
Inf. Divs.

2.6.1945

Jolo Is.

Borneo

Tawitawi Is.

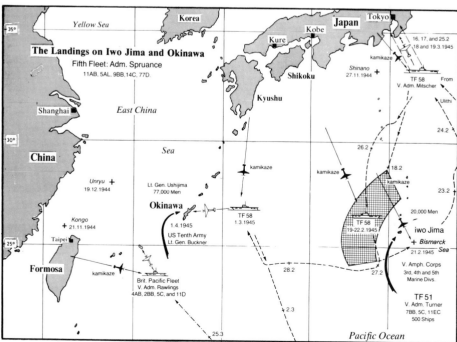

The Landings on Iwo Jima and Okinawa
Fifth Fleet: Adm. Spruance
11AB, 5AL, 9BB, 14C, 77D.

Yellow Sea

Korea

Japan

Tokyo

Kobe

Kure

Japan

16, 17, and 25.2
18 and 19.3.1945

kamikaze

Shanghai

Shikoku

Kyushu

Shinano
27.11.1944

TF 58
From
V. Adm. Mitscher

Ulithi

East China

24.2

China

Sea

26.2

kamikaze

18.2

Unryu
19.12.1944

Lt. Gen. Ushijima
77,000 Men

kamikaze

23.2

Okinawa

20,000 Men

Kongo
21.11.1944

1.4.1945
US Tenth Army
Lt. Gen. Buckner

TF 58
1.3.1945

TF 58
19-22.2.1945

iwo Jima

Taipei

Bismarck
21.2.1945

Sea

Formosa

kamikaze

28.2

27.2

V. Amph. Corps
3rd, 4th and 5th
Marine Divs.

Brit. Pacific Fleet
V. Adm. Rawlings
4AB, 2BB, 5C, and 11D

TF 51
V. Adm. Turner
7BB, 5C, 11EC
500 Ships

25.3

Pacific Ocean

Kiso, 13 destroyers and a number of troop transports are sunk. Third Fleet loses 170 planes, and the light cruiser *Reno* is torpedoed. Kamikaze pilots sink a destroyer and hit the aircraft carriers *Intrepid*, *Franklin*, *Lexington*, *Essex* and *Hancock*, as well as the light carriers *Cabot* and *Belleau Wood*.

21 Nov 1944: The US submarine *Sealion* (Reich) sinks the battleship *Kongo*.

27 Nov 1944: The US submarine *Archerfish* (Enright) sinks the new aircraft carrier *Shinano*.

15 Dec 1944: US landing on Mindoro. Supported by 3 battleships, 7 cruisers and 6 escort carriers, the Americans land on this island south of Manila.

18 Dec 1944: 'Halsey's Typhoon'. While supporting the landing on Mindoro with air attacks on Luzon, Third Fleet is hit by a heavy typhoon; 3 destroyers sink, 3 light carriers are damaged, and 146 aircraft are lost overboard or smashed.

19 Dec 1944: The US submarine *Redfish* (McGregor) sinks the new Japanese aircraft carrier *Unryu*.

4 Jan 1945: In the Indian Ocean, aircraft from the British carriers *Indomitable*, *Victorious*, *Illustrious* and *Indefatigable* attack the oil refineries in north-eastern Sumatra.

9 Jan 1945: US landing on Luzon. Halsey's Third Fleet attacks airfields in Luzon again. MacArthur then lands I and XIV Army Corps (4 infantry divisions in the first wave) in Lingayen Gulf, with the aid of Kinkaid's Seventh Fleet, of 600 vessels. Close support is given by the battleships *Mississippi*, *West Virginia*, *New Mexico*, *California*, *Pennsylvania* and *Colorado*, 11 cruisers and 18 escort carriers. The Japanese fly kamikaze missions against the landing fleet, and the escort carrier *Ommaney Bay* is sunk, and the battleships *New Mexico* and *California*, 4 cruisers and 3 escort carriers damaged. Aircraft of the 1st Navy Air Fleet (Vice Admiral Onishi) hit *Mississippi* from Luzon, but by 12 Jan US Third Fleet has destroyed all Japanese mainland air forces.

10–21 Jan 1945: After defeating the Japanese air force on Luzon and Formosa, Halsey advances into the South China Sea. Harbours and shipping from Formosa to Saigon are attacked by carrier aircraft which meet little resistance. Over 200,000 tons of shipping is sunk. In kamikaze counter-attacks, meanwhile, *Ticonderoga* and *Langley* are hit.

24 and 29 Jan 1945: In the Indian Ocean, aircraft from the British carriers *Indomitable*, *Illustrious*, *Indefatigable* and *Victorious* carry out an effective strike on the oil refinery at Palembang, Sumatra.

At the end of Jan 1945, Amphibious Groups 8 and 9 land two US divisions north and south of Manila Bay and, by mid-Feb, the Bataan Peninsula and the rocky island of Corregidor are in American hands again.

Spring 1945: In a series of coastal landings, the Americans recapture most of the southern Philippines.

16–17 Feb 1945: A fast carrier fleet (Task Force 58, under Vice Admiral Mitscher, with 16 carriers, 9 battleships, 14 cruisers and 77 destroyers) launches the first large-scale US Navy air attack on Japan. 500 Japanese aircraft are destroyed at a cost of 88 of the attackers.

19 Feb 1945: US landing on Iwo Jima. Since autumn 1944, long-range bombers have been attacking Japan from bases in the Marianas. In order to be able to give these bombers fighter protection, Iwo Jima (about half way between the bases and their targets) is attacked. Admiral Spruance's Fifth Fleet carries out the landings, and Mitscher supplies long-range support with the carriers of Task Force 58. The landing fleet (Task Force 51) is commanded by Vice Admiral Turner: it comprises 500 ships, and carries V Amphibious Corps (Lieutenant General Smith) with the 3rd, 4th and 5th Marine Divisions. For direct support, Task Force 51 has 7 battleships, 5 cruisers and 11 escort carriers. The well-defended island is garrisoned by 20,000 Japanese under

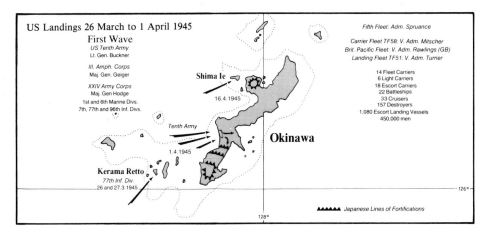

US Landings 26 March to 1 April 1945
First Wave
US Tenth Army
Lt. Gen. Buckner
III. Amph. Corps
Maj. Gen. Geiger
XXIV Army Corps
Maj. Gen Hodge
1st and 6th Marine Divs.
7th, 77th and 96th Inf. Divs.

Shima Ie
16.4.1945

Tenth Army

Okinawa

1.4.1945

Kerama Retto
77th Inf. Div.
26 and 27.3.1945

Fifth Fleet: Adm. Spruance

Carrier Fleet TF58: V. Adm. Mitscher
Brit. Pacific Fleet: V. Adm. Rawlings (GB)
Landing Fleet TF51: V. Adm. Turner

14 Fleet Carriers
6 Light Carriers
18 Escort Carriers
22 Battleships
33 Cruisers
157 Destroyers
1,080 Escort Landing Vessels
450,000 men

▲▲▲▲▲ Japanese Lines of Fortifications

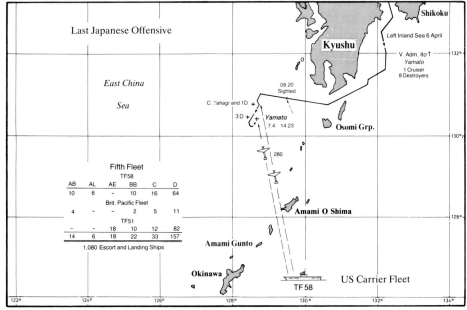

Last Japanese Offensive

Shikoku

Kyushu

Left Inland Sea 6 April

V. Adm. Ito †
Yamato
1 Cruiser
8 Destroyers

East China
Sea

08.20
Sighted

C. Yahagi and 1D

3 D   Yamato
7.4 14.23

Osomi Grp.

280

Fifth Fleet
TF58

AB	AL	AE	BB	C	D
10	6	–	10	16	64

Brit. Pacific Fleet

| 4 | – | – | 2 | 5 | 11 |

TF51

| – | – | 18 | 10 | 12 | 82 |
| 14 | 6 | 18 | 22 | 33 | 157 |

1,080 Escort and Landing Ships

Amami O Shima

Amami Gunto

Okinawa

TF 58   US Carrier Fleet

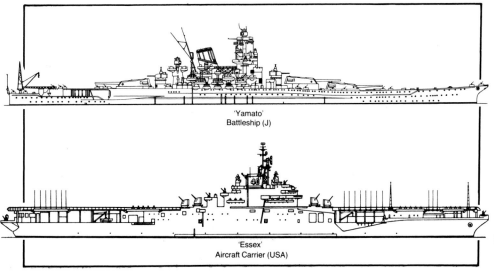

'Yamato'
Battleship (J)

'Essex'
Aircraft Carrier (USA)

Lieutenant General Kuribayashi.

21 Feb: Kamikaze attacks on the US fleet off Iwo Jima. The escort carrier *Bismarck Sea* is sunk; the carrier *Saratoga* is hit six times, but can be saved. After a month, Japanese resistance on the island is broken, but American losses are 23,000 dead and wounded.

18-19 March 1945: In preparation for the next big landing, the carrier fleets attack Japan again and hit airfields and naval bases on the Inland Sea. The ships involved are the fleet carriers *Hornet, Bennington, Enterprise, Franklin, Essex, Bunker Hill, Hancock, Yorktown, Intrepid* and *Wasp*, the light carriers *Belleau Wood, San Jacinto, Bataan, Langley, Independence* and *Cabot* with a total of 1,200 aircraft; the battleships *Massachusetts, Indiana, North Carolina, Washington, South Dakota, Wisconsin, New Jersey, Missouri*, the battlecruisers *Alaska* and *Guam*, 16 cruisers and 64 destroyers. The Japanese 5th Air Fleet (Vice Admiral Ugaki) counter-attacks, hitting the carriers *Franklin, Wasp, Enterprise, Intrepid* and *Yorktown. Franklin* suffers 1,000 casualties.

10 March 1945: Amphibious Group 6 lands the 41st Infantry Division at Zamboanga on the south-western tip of Mindanao.

1 April 1945: US landing on Okinawa. This large island is defended by 77,000 men under Lieutenant General Ushijima; a further 10,000 naval personnel are also on the island. They await the American landing in well-prepared positions on the southern part of the island. Leading the American forces involved is Admiral Spruance, with Fifth Fleet. The carrier fleet (Task Force 58, Vice Admiral Mitscher) secures and supports the operation, and it is reinforced by the British Pacific Fleet under Vice Admiral Rawlings (aircraft carriers *Indomitable, Victorious, Illustrious, Indefatigable* with 220 aircraft; the battleships *King George V* and *Howe*, and 5 cruisers). The landing fleet (Task Force 51, under Vice-Admiral Turner) has 430 transports and large landing ships, the battleships *New Mexico, Maryland, Arkansas, Colorado, Tennessee, Nevada, Idaho, West Virginia, Texas* and *New York*, 13 cruisers, 18 escort carriers and 540 aircraft. Fifth Fleet also has a logistic supply group of tankers, aircraft transports, supply ships, workshop vessels and ocean-going tugs. At the end of March, the 77th Infantry Division lands on the scantily defended Kerama Islands, and builds a naval base there.

1 April: The US Tenth Army (Lieutenant General Buckner), with four divisions in the first wave, lands on the west coast of Okinawa, against resistance that is initially light. Later, there are hard battles fought in the southern part of the island.

6 April 1945: The Japanese begin a kamikaze offensive against the US Fleet off Okinawa. At the same time, a Japanese battle group (battleship *Yamato*, 1 cruiser and 8 destroyers) put to sea, destination Okinawa.

7 April 1945: 280 US aircraft sink *Yamato*, the cruiser and 4 destroyers; the rest escape. The kamikaze offensive, which lasts for 6 weeks, causes the Americans considerable loss: 26 ships are sunk (none bigger than a destroyer) and 164 damaged. The latter include the carriers *Intrepid, Enterprise* and *Bunker Hill*, the battleships *Maryland, Tennessee* and *New Mexico*. Among the British ships, the carriers *Indefatigable, Formidable* and *Victorious* are hit. About 2,000 suicide pilots are employed in these attacks.

11 April 1945: In the Indian Ocean, the British Eastern fleet, including the battleships *Queen Elizabeth* and *Richelieu* (F), 2 escort carriers, 2 cruisers and 5 destroyers, bombards Sabang on Sumatra.

17 April 1945: Amphibious Group 8 lands the 24th and 31st Infantry Divisions on the west coast of Mindanao.

15-16 May 1945: A British destroyer flotilla sinks the Japanese heavy cruiser *Haguro* in the Malacca Straits, in a classic night torpedo attack.

27 May 1945: Admiral Halsey takes over from Spruance the command of the fast fleet in the Pacific, which is now called 'Third Fleet' once more. Vice Admiral McCain takes over from Mitscher as commander of the carrier fleet (Task Force 58, which now becomes Task Force 38).

June 1945: Japanese resistance on Okinawa is broken; but the conquest costs the Americans 48,000 dead and wounded.

14–18 July 1945: The US carrier fleet flies heavy attacks on Japan; main targets are airfields, harbours and sea-borne traffic. US battleships bombard coastal industrial targets for the first time.

24–30 July 1945: Halsey's Third Fleet continues its attacks on Japan, in preparation for a landing. Priority targets are the Japanese naval bases on the Inland Sea. Almost all surviving major naval units of the Japanese fleet are destroyed (including the new aircraft carrier *Amagi* and the battleships *Ise*, *Hyuga* and *Haruna*).

6 and 9 Aug 1945: Atomic bombs, dropped on Hiroshima and Nagasaki, speed the capitulation of Japan.

9–14 Aug 1945: Third Fleet makes its last attack on Japan.

8/9 May 1945: End of the war in Europe.

2 Sept 1945: End of the war in the Pacific. After their capitulation, Germany and Japan have to hand over the remnants of their fleets; Italy is permitted to maintain a small fleet, but is forbidden to build battleships and aircraft carriers.

During the course of the Second World War, naval warfare had changed drastically. The age of the battleship had ended and, instead of heavy artillery, carrier-borne aircraft were now the decisive factor. Battleships and cruisers had clashed but rarely and, by the end of the war, had largely been relegated to the role of floating artillery support for combined operations. It was the aircraft carrier that had played the dominant role: in combat groups fighting great battles in the Pacific; escorting transports through the Mediterranean; hunting U-boats in the Atlantic; and supporting landings in all the theatres of the war. In the early years of the war, submarines had again proved themselves a potent strategic weapon, but the development of effective counter measures—the convoy system, U-boat hunting groups, air surveillance, new locating methods and improved depth-charges—had, in the end, defeated them. Revolutionary new German submarines, with high underwater speed and endurance, arrived too late to reverse the balance. Electronic and technological innovations had also made their mark on naval warfare: the introduction of radar made it possible to search large areas of sea (even at night and in bad visibility) and, from 1942, the British and the Americans could produce accurate artillery fire at night, with the use of radar. Mines, too, had developed from simple contact devices into magnetic, pressure and acoustic types, making necessary ever-increasing systems for mine clearance.

Combined land–sea operations, especially in the Pacific, made new demands, resulting in the development of special landing craft, which enabled tanks and wheeled vehicles to be discharged directly on to beaches. And, in a war that spanned the globe, large fleets operating independently of shore bases for long periods required entire fleets of logistic resupply vessels—tankers, ammunition ships, aircraft transports, workshop ships, ocean-going tugs and hospital ships.

The conversion from coal to oil fuel made possible refuelling at sea (and even under way), leading to a great increase in the operational radius of warships, and a consequent increase in the scope and scale of naval campaigns. The two most significant developments of the Second World War, however—nuclear power and the rocket as a weapon system—reserved their impact for the post-war world.

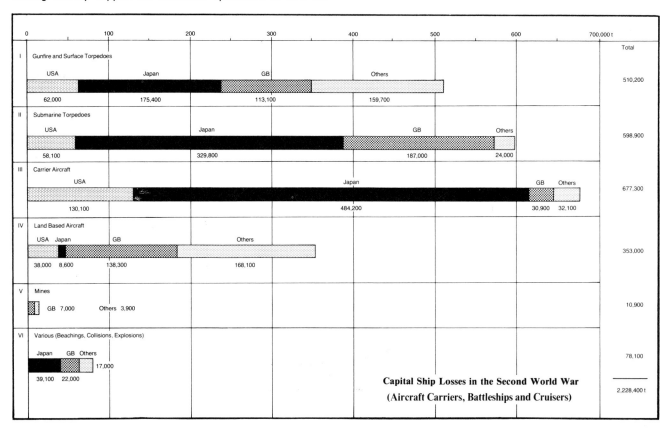

Capital Ship Losses in the Second World War
(Aircraft Carriers, Battleships and Cruisers)

The Nuclear Age

Illustration by Geoff Hunt

1 July 1946: The United States carries out an experimental atomic explosion above the surface of the sea at Bikini Atoll.

25 July 1946: The United States tests an underwater atomic detonation at Bikini Atoll. Among the 90 test ships of all types are the carriers *Saratoga* and *Independence*, the battleships *Arkansas*, *Nevada*, *New York*, *Pennsylvania* and *Nagato* (ex-Japanese), and the ex-German cruiser *Prinz Eugen*. Much is learned in the fields of naval construction and tactics, from this experiment.

1950-53: The Korean War

North Korean troops attack South Korea, which requests United Nations military aid. After condemning the invasion, troops from 15 UN nations enter the war on the side of South Korea, under American leadership.

25 June 1950: Start of the communist offensive.

15 Sept 1950: Landing at Inchon. The Allied counterattack begins, as the US Seventh Fleet (Vice Admiral Struble) lands the reinforced US 1st Marine Division behind the North Korean lines. In an almost perfect amphibious operation, the division is put ashore by 200 ships and landing craft. Covering forces include the carriers *Boxer* (US), *Philippine Sea* (US), *Valley Forge* (US) and *Triumph* (GB), 2 escort carriers, 7 cruisers, 34 destroyers and a great number of frigates and minesweepers. The landing forces the North Koreans into a headlong withdrawal.

25 Oct 1950: Landing at Wonsan. Magnetic mines so delay the landing fleet that the town falls to the South Korean ground forces, which advance from the south.

24 Dec 1950: Evacuation of Hungnam. Under an umbrella of naval gunfire, the UN troops are evacuated in the face of the Chinese forces.

27 July 1953: An armistice is signed, after much fighting and the intervention of Red China in the war.

Naval warfare in the Korean War generally followed the style of the Second World War: however, jet aircraft made their first sorties from aircraft carriers, and helicopters were, for the first time, used on a large scale. North Korea, with no navy, was naturally vulnerable to sea-borne landings, and her attempts to defend herself with mines and improvized units was effective enough to cause some difficulties to the UN forces.

1954: Completion of the first nuclear-powered warship, the US submarine *Nautilus*.

Oct 1956: The Suez Campaign. Strong British and French forces land in the Canal Zone against Egyptian opposition. 45 Commando Royal Marines (600 men) are put ashore from the carriers *Ocean* (GB) and *Theseus* (GB) in 90 minutes, by means of helicopters. Also involved in the action are the carriers *Eagle* (GB), *Albion* (GB), *Bulwark* (GB), *Arromanches* (F), and *Lafayette* (F), and the battleship *Jean Bart* (F), 3 cruisers and about 100 other warships.

1958: The US nuclear submarine *Nautilus* makes the first journey under the Polar ice cap, from Pacific to North Atlantic.

1959: Completion of the first US nuclear submarine armed with Intercontinental Ballistic Missiles (ICBMs), *George Washington*.

1960: The US nuclear submarine *Triton* makes the first underwater circumnavigation of the globe at an average speed of 18 knots.

1961: Completion of the nuclear-powered aircraft carrier USS *Enterprise*.

12 April 1961: First manned spaceship orbits the earth (Yuri Gagarin, USSR).

Oct 1962: The Cuba Crisis. In late summer, the USSR begins to assemble ICBMs in Cuba. By a rigidly applied naval blockade ('quarantine'), the United States forces the Soviet Union to dismantle the rocket bases.

1964: A nuclear-powered United States battle group (aircraft carrier *Enterprise*, cruisers *Long Beach* and *Bainbridge*) circumnavigate the globe in 64 days without replenishing fuel. Their average speed is 22 knots.

1964-73: The Vietnamese War

2 Aug 1964: In the 'Gulf of Tongking incident', the US destroyer *Maddox* is mistakenly attacked by North Vietnamese MTBs.

5 Aug: Retaliatory strikes against North Vietnamese MTB bases are carried out by aircraft from the carriers *Ticonderoga*

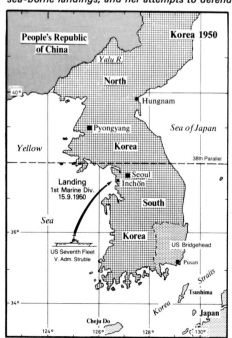

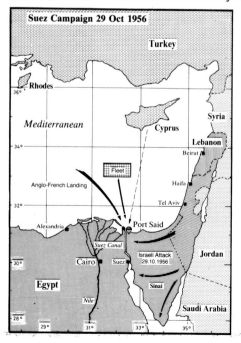

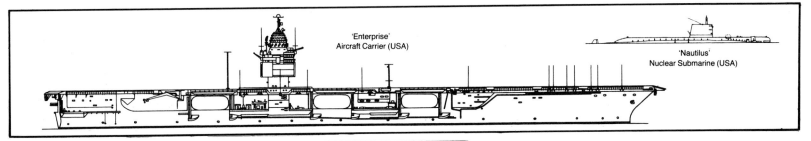

'Enterprise'
Aircraft Carrier (USA)

'Nautilus'
Nuclear Submarine (USA)

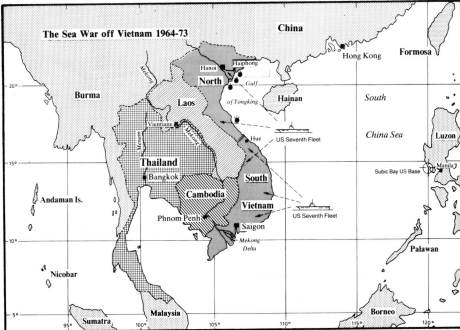

The Sea War off Vietnam 1964-73

China

Burma

North

Laos

Mekong

Hanoi

Haiphong

Gulf

Hong Kong

Formosa

of Tongking

Hainan

Vientiane

Menam

Mekong

Thailand

Bangkok

Hué

US Seventh Fleet

South

China Sea

Luzon

Manila

Subic Bay US Base

Andaman Is.

Cambodia

Phnom Penh

South

Vietnam

US Seventh Fleet

Saigon

Mekong
Delta

Palawan

Nicobar

Malaysia

Borneo

Sumatra

and *Constellation*.

7 Feb 1965: The first large-scale air attack of the war is made by aircraft from the US Seventh Fleet, against ground targets in North Vietnam. From now on, Seventh Fleet affords considerable air support to US ground operations (but with considerable political implications). On average, 3-4 carriers are constantly in use.

Autumn 1968: After having been refitted, the battleship *New Jersey* is employed as a floating artillery battery for coastal fire support until March 1969. This is the last use of the heavy guns of battleships in war.

Oct 1968: Cessation of United States air attacks on North Vietnam.

21-22 Nov 1970: After a long pause, retaliatory air raids on North Vietnam are made from the carriers *Ranger* and *Hancock*.

April 1972: In answer to the communist Spring offensive, the Americans again bomb North Vietnam.

15 April 1972: Carrier aircraft and B-52 bombers attack Haiphong; several Soviet freighters in the harbour are damaged.

11 May 1972: North Vietnamese harbours are mined, and the coast closely blockaded by Seventh Fleet.

Oct 1972: The carriers *Midway*, *America*, *Saratoga*, *Kitty Hawk*, *Oriskany* and *Enterprise* are all in action at the same time with Seventh Fleet.

28 Jan 1973: Signing of the armistice. American troops leave Vietnam.

The American naval blockade had been a considerable factor in bringing North Vietnam to the negotiating table, but, apart from this, naval units played but a restricted role in the war. Cruisers and destroyers (and, for a short period, a battleship) provided coastal fire support, and naval units helped guide carrier-borne aircraft to intercept enemy MIG fighters and rescue shot-down pilots. Two innovations were the use of surface-to-air missiles by both sides, and the successful employment of hovercraft in action on Vietnamese inland waterways.

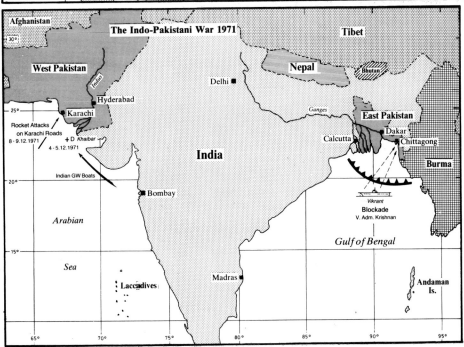

Afghanistan

The Indo-Pakistani War 1971

Tibet

West Pakistan

Indus

Delhi

Nepal

Bhutan

Hyderabad

Karachi

Rocket Attacks
on Karachi Roads
8 - 9.12.1971

D *Khaibar*

4 - 5.12.1971

Indian GW Boats

India

Ganges

East Pakistan

Calcutta

Dakar

Chittagong

Burma

Bombay

Vikrant
Blockade
V. Adm. Krishnan

Arabian

Sea

Gulf of Bengal

Laccadives

Madras

Andaman
Is.

June 1967: Arab-Israeli War. One consequence of this is that the Suez Canal is blocked resulting in the construction of mammoth tankers for the transport of oil around Africa, from the Middle East to Europe.

21 Oct 1967: First successful use of surface-to-surface missiles (SSM) against ships. Egyptian MTBS, armed with Russian missiles, sink the Israeli destroyer *Elath* off Port Said.

1968: First manned flight to the moon, by a United States space craft.

1969: First man lands on the moon, Commander Neil Armstrong (US), in *Apollo 11*.

1971: The Indo-Pakistani War

India's eastern naval command under Vice Admiral Krishnan completely isolates East Pakistan, by blockading the Bay of Bengal. 8 foreign merchantmen are caught.

4 Dec onwards: Aircraft from the carrier *Vikrant* attack

Chittagong and Cox's Bazaar.

4/5 Dec: Night action at Karachi. MTBs equipped with rockets from the Indian western naval command (Vice Admiral Kohli) sink the Pakistani destroyer *Khaibar* and a minesweeper.

8/9 Dec: In a night attack on Karachi Roads, Indian rocket-equipped MTBs sink 3 merchantmen and set a tanker ablaze.

9 Dec: The Pakistani submarine *Hangor* sinks the Indian frigate *Khukri* in the Arabian Sea. Land forces in East Pakistan are forced to capitulate after a few weeks, due to India's complete control of the air and sea.

Oct 1973: The Arab–Israeli 'Yom-Kippur' War. This war sees the first clash between Fast Patrol Boats (FPBs), 300-ton boats equipped with guided weapons.

April 1975: On the last day before the communists take over power in Saigon, the US Seventh Fleet evacuates 15,000 Americans and South Vietnamese by helicopter.

May 1975: The 'Mayaguez incident'. Aircraft from *Coral Sea* sink 3 Cambodian FPBs, which have captured the US freighter *Mayaguez* in the Gulf of Siam. Next day, both ship and crew are freed by US marines, in a helicopter-borne operation.

Today, the centuries-old concepts concerning the freedom of the seas are increasingly being questioned, and nations are laying claim to sovereignty over waters up to 200 miles (325 kilometres) from their shores. This thorny question, together with those concerning the commercial exploitation of minerals in the continental shelves, fishing rights and the protection of the sea against pollution, provided the UN Maritime Law Conferences of 1958, 1960 and 1974–77 with problems that are yet to be solved. Such disagreements—which concern a medium that covers more than two-thirds of the Earth's surface—lends greater emphasis than ever before to naval strength.

Appendix 1: The Ship Catalogue of the Iliad (Homer), the oldest surviving written naval order of battle

This famous document lists the 29 contingents, drawn from various tribes, together with the number of ships carrying them, that took part in the siege of Troy. Recent research has thrown new light upon it as a work of historical significance, and the latest estimated dates for the fall of that city are as follows:

Eratosthenes (275–195BC)	1184/83BC
C. W. Blegen (*The Cambridge Ancient History*, II, 2, p. 163)	c. 1250BC
F. H. Stubbins (ibid., II, 2, p. 343)	c. 1200BC

If the 'storm of the sea peoples' destroyed the Mycenaean civilization about 1200BC, the Trojan expedition would have been mounted shortly before, placing it in the second half of the 13th century BC.

The number of ships sent by the tribes of Thessaly—230—seems too high, since the character of that particular coast and the weather conditions prevalent thereabouts have never been conducive to maritime pursuits. Apart from this, the greatest number of ships are attributed to the inland tribes (nos. 19, 20, 21). The grand total of 1,116 vessels listed might have been capable of transporting some 100,000 men, but such a figure is almost certainly far too high. The total cited would include many ships of relatively small size, so the number of men can be reduced considerably, probably to below 50,000. It may be assumed that in the larger vessels each oar would have been pulled by 2 men (and thus, 2 men × 25 oars × 2 sides of the ship = 100 crew).

COUNTRY/TRIBE/CITY	SHIPS	LEADER/REMARKS
1. Mycenae, Corinth, Sicyon	100	Agamemnon, Commander-in-Chief
2. Tiryns, Epidaurus, Asine, Aegina, Argos	80	Diomedes
3. Lacedaemonians from Sparta	60	Menelaeus
4. Pylos, Cyparissiae, inc. Alphaios	50	Nestor
5. Arcadia with Orchomenos, Tegea	60	Provided by Mycenae
6. Epeirans from Elis	10	
7. Dulichion (Leucas), Echinades Is.	40	
8. Ithaca, Cephallenia, Zacynthus	12	Odysseus
9. Aetolia	40	
10. Boeotia	50	Each 120 men
11. Orchomenus (Boeotia)	30	
12. Phocaeans	40	
13. Locria	40	
14. Euboea (Chalcis, Eretria, Histiaea)	40	Elphenor
15. Pelasgian Argos (Valley of the Sperchins), land of the Achaeans, Helenes and Myrmidians	50	Achilles
16. Phylace, Parrhasos, Itonus, Antron	40	
17. Perae, Boebe, Glaphira, Iolkus	11	
18. Methone, Thaumakia, Meliboea, Olizon	7	
19. Tricca, Ithome, Ochalia	30	Each 50 men — Tribes from Thessaly
20. Ormenus, Asterion, Mount Titanus	40	
21. Argissa, Elon, Orthe, Olooson	40	
22. Cyphos	22	
23. Magnetes	40	
24. Attica (inc. Athens)	50	Menestheus
25. Salamis	12	Ajax
26. Crete (Cnossos, Phaestus, Miletus)	80	Idomeneus
27. Rhodes	9	Tlepolemus
28. Syme	3	
29. Calydna, Carpathos, Cos, Casos (inc. s Sporades)	30	

Appendix 2: Attempted points table of the great naval battles

N = Numbers involved (1–4 points); S = Strategic significance (0–2 points); T = Tactical execution (0–2 points); P = Political significance (0–1 point).

DATE	BATTLE	N	T	S	P	TOTAL	DATE	BATTLE	N	T	S	P	TOTAL
494BC	Lade	1	1	1	1	4	306BC	Salamis (Cyprus)	2	2	1	1	6
480BC	Artemisium	2	1	1	–	4	260BC	Mylae	2	2	1	–	5
480BC	Salamis	3	1	2	1	7	256BC	Ecnomus	3	2	1	–	6
479BC	Mycale	1	2	1	–	4	249BC	Drepanum	2	2	–	–	4
466BC	Eurymedon	1	1	1	–	3	241BC	Aegates Is.	2	2	2	1	7
449BC	Salamis (Cyprus)	1	1	1	1	4	36BC	Naulochus	3	2	1	–	6
433BC	Sybota	1	1	1	–	3	31BC	Actium	3	2	1	1	7
429BC	Naupactus	1	1	1	–	3	323	Hellespont	2	1	–	–	3
413BC	Syracuse	1	2	1	1	5	551	Sena Gallica	1	2	–	–	3
410BC	Cyzicus	1	2	–	–	3	655	Battle of the Masts	1	1	1	–	3
407BC	Notium	1	1	1	–	3	698	Carthage	1	1	1	–	3
406BC	Arginusae	1	1	1	–	3	718	Constantinople	1	2	1	–	4
405BC	Aegospotami	1	2	1	–	4	747	Ceramea (Cyprus)	1	2	1	1	5
394BC	Cnidus	1	2	1	–	4	888	Milazzo	1	1	1	–	3

DATE	BATTLE	N	T	S	P	TOTAL
964	'Destructive'	1	2	–	–	3
1217	Dover	1	2	–	–	3
1340	Sluys	2	2	1	–	5
1372	La Rochelle	1	2	1	–	4
1380	Chioggia	1	1	1	–	3
1571	Lepanto	3	2	–	1	6
1588	The Armada	2	1	2	1	6
1639	The Downs	1	2	1	–	4
1652	Kentish Knock	2	1	1	–	4
1652	Dungeness	1	1	1	–	3
1653	Portland	2	2	1	–	5
1653	Gabbard Bank	2	2	1	–	5
1653	Scheveningen	2	2	1	–	5
1658	Sound	1	2	1	–	4
1665	Lowestoft	2	1	1	–	4
1666	Four Days Fight	2	2	1	–	5
1666	St. James's Day	2	2	1	–	5
1672	Sole Bay	2	1	1	–	4
1673	Schooneveldt I	2	1	–	–	3
1673	Schooneveldt II	2	1	–	–	3
1673	Texel	2	1	2	1	6
1676	Palermo	1	2	1	–	4
1677	Kjöge Bay	1	2	1	–	4
1690	Beachy Head	3	1	1	–	5
1692	La Hogue	3	2	2	–	7
1704	Malaga	2	1	1	–	4
1718	Cape Passaro	1	2	1	–	4
1744	Toulon	2	1	–	–	3
1756	Minorca	1	1	1	–	3
1759	Lagos Bay	1	2	1	–	4
1759	Quiberon Bay	2	2	2	–	6
1779	Grenada	2	1	–	–	3
1780	Cape St. Vincent	1	2	1	–	4
1780	Martinique	2	1	–	–	3
1781	Chesapeake Bay	2	–	2	1	5
1782	The Saints	3	2	1	–	6
1790	Tendra	2	1	1	–	4
1790	Svensksund	1	1	1	1	4
1794	Glorious 1st June	2	2	1	–	5
1797	Cape St. Vincent	2	1	1	–	4
1797	Camperdown	1	2	1	–	4
1798	Nile	1	2	2	1	6
1801	Copenhagen	1	2	1	1	5
1805	Cape Finisterre	1	1	1	–	3
1805	Trafalgar	3	2	2	–	7
1827	Navarino Bay	1	2	1	1	5
1864	Mobile Bay	1	1	1	–	3
1866	Lissa	2	1	1	–	4
1894	Yalu River	1	1	1	–	3
1898	Santiago	1	2	1	–	4
1904	Yellow Sea	2	1	1	–	4
1905	Tsushima	2	2	1	1	6
1914	Falklands	1	2	1	–	4
1915	Dogger Bank	2	1	–	–	3
1916	Jutland	4	2	1	–	7
1940	SC7/HX79	1	2	–	–	3
1941	Cape Matapan	1	1	1	–	3
1941	Pearl Harbor	2	2	1	1	6

DATE	BATTLE	N	T	S	P	TOTAL
1942	Coral Sea	1	1	1	–	3
1942	Midway	3	1	2	–	6
1942	PQ17	1	2	–	–	3
1942	Pedestal	2	1	–	–	3
1942	Solomons	2	1	1	–	4
1942	Santa Cruz Is.	2	1	1	–	4
1942	Guadalcanal	2	2	1	–	5
1943	HX229/SC122	2	2	–	–	4
1944	Philippine Sea	4	1	1	–	6
1944	Leyte Gulf	4	2	2	–	8

N = Numbers involved (1–4 points); S = Strategic significance (0–2 points); T = Tactical execution (0–2 points); P = Political significance (0–1 point).

The greatest naval battles in points order

DATE	BATTLE	TONNAGE[1]	CREW[2]	N	T	S	P	TOTAL
1944	Leyte Gulf	2,060	183	4	2	2	–	8
480BC	Salamis	200	200[2]	3	1	2	1	7
241BC	Aegates Is.	110	110[2]	2	2	2	1	7
31BC	Actium	180	160[2]	3	2	1	1	7
1692	La Hogue	220	60	3	2	2	–	7
1805	Trafalgar	150	50	3	2	2	–	7
1916	Jutland	1,910	105	4	2	1	–	7
306BC	Salamis (Cyprus)	70	70[2]	2	2	1	1	6
256BC	Ecnomus	160	180[2]	3	2	1	–	6
36BC	Naulochus	210	170[2]	3	2	1	–	6
1571	Lepanto	230	160[2]	3	2	–	1	6
1588	The Armada	115	45	2	1	2	1	6
1673	Texel	160	52	2	1	2	1	6
1759	Quiberon Bay	115	31	2	2	2	–	6
1782	The Saints	150	45	3	2	1	–	6
1798	Nile	60	24	1	2	2	1	6
1905	Tsushima	380	22	2	2	1	1	6
1941	Pearl Harbor	650	50	2	1	2	1	6
1942	Midway	1,050	80	3	1	2	–	6
1944	Philippine Sea	1,470	140	4	1	1	–	6
413BC	Syracuse	40	60[2]	1	2	1	1	5
260BC	Mylae	70	70[2]	2	2	1	–	5
747	Ceramea (Cyprus)	?	?	1	2	1	1	5
1340	Sluys	100	60[2]	2	2	1	–	5
1653	Portland	60	17	2	2	1	–	5
1653	Gabbard Bank	110	29	2	2	1	–	5
1653	Scheveningen	110	30	2	2	1	–	5
1666	Four Days Fight	120	33	2	1	1	–	5
1666	St. James's Day	120	35	2	2	1	–	5
1690	Beachy Head	210	51	3	1	1	–	5
1781	Chesapeake Bay	100	28	2	–	2	1	5
1794	Glorious 1st June	130	41	2	2	1	–	5
1801	Copenhagen	60	20	1	2	1	1	5
1827	Navarino Bay	90	30	1	2	1	1	5
1942	Guadalcanal	540	44	2	2	1	–	5

[1] In thousands of tons; [2]in thousands of men. Note that, at the time of the galley fleets, a large proportion of the crews consisted of the rowers (mainly slaves or convicts); these elements vanish in the later sail and steam eras. Dates are AD unless otherwise indicated.

Appendix 3: The world's naval powers (by numbers of ships), 1859–1977

1859	SHIPS OF THE LINE		FRIGATES		CORVETTES		COAST DEFENCE SHIPS	PADDLE-STEAMERS, SMALL SHIPS	AUXILIARIES
	Screw	Sail	Screw	Sail	Screw	Sail			
Great Britain	36	32	19	55	14	71	21	370	87
France	33	14	15	28	9	15	5	197	59
Russia	7	12	11	7	12	7	–	45	57
Sweden	2	5	–	5	3	5	–	70	21
USA	–	6	7	11	–	–	–	42	7
Netherlands	–	5	3	12	5	5	4	34	18
Denmark	–	4	3	5	2	4	1	21	20
Turkey	–	7	–	6	–	4	–	7	25
Austria-Hungary	1	–	3	4	2	3	–	60	11

1882	ARMOURED SHIPS	COASTAL ARMOURED SHIPS	ARMOURED GUNBOATS	CRUISERS, FRIGATES, CORVETTES	GUNBOATS	TORPEDO-BOATS	AUXILIARIES
Great Britain	41	16	3	69	114	100	57
France	38	9	–	50	63	60	42
Russia	15	15	2	22	21	110	19
Germany	12	1	11	18	17	11	14
Italy	12	2	1	8	15	16	13
Austria	11	–	–	13	7	12	20
Spain	5	3	–	20	64	3	8
Turkey	7	8	–	7	30	–	16

1908	BATTLESHIPS	ARMOURED COAST DEFENCE SHIPS	ARMOURED CRUISERS	CRUISERS	GUNBOATS	DESTROYERS, MTBS	SUBMARINES	AUXILIARIES
Great Britain	53	–	37	84	31	202	54	31
France	22	–	21	23	13	308	46	15
Germany	24	8	8	30	15	128	2	20
USA	25	5	15	20	17	46	12	32
Japan	13	2	12	17	5	74	7	4
Russia	10	2	4	8	13	173	26	33
Italy	10	–	6	8	5	51	7	24
Austria	9	2	3	5	–	33	2	20

1927	BATTLESHIPS	AIRCRAFT CARRIERS	CRUISERS	DESTROYERS	MTBS, GUNBOATS, ETC.	SUBMARINES	AUXILIARIES
Great Britain	20	5	53	176	136	56	99
USA	18	3	32	295	148	120	64
Japan	10	3	32	83	43	43	37
France	9	1	13	68	158	60	33
Italy	5	–	13	73	126	44	42
Spain	2	–	6	8	19	16	7
Brazil	2	–	3	11	6	3	2
Sweden	–	–	2	15	19	16	15

(Note: Many of the numerous ships in the USSR Navy were not fit to sail.)

1938	BATTLESHIPS	AIRCRAFT CARRIERS	CRUISERS	DESTROYERS	MTBS, GUNBOATS	SUBMARINES	SMALL SHIPS	AUXILIARIES
Great Britain	15	7	62	175	37	56	209	130
USA	15	5	34	221	43	90	118	100
Japan	10	6	36	83	41	61	40	40
France	7	1	19	60	21	76	58	52
Italy	4	–	24	74	63	96	120	60
USSR	3	–	6	20	25	160	180	40
Germany	2	–	9	17	32	43	66	70

1952	AIRCRAFT CARRIERS	BATTLESHIPS	CRUISERS	DESTROYERS	SUBMARINES	SMALL VESSELS	AMPHIBIANS	AUXILIARIES
USA	102	15	72	385	207	850	530	850
Great Britain	15	5	24	119	55	650	86	135
USSR	–	3	15	90	400	400	120	60
France	3	2	6	11	13	270	50	34
Argentina	–	2	5	15	3	18	29	30
Italy	–	2	4	6	–	150	30	30
Spain	–	–	5	18	6	60	–	9
Brazil	–	1	2	9	3	36	–	16

1966	AIRCRAFT CARRIERS	CRUISERS	DESTROYERS, FRIGATES	NUCLEAR SUBMARINES	CONVENTIONAL SUBMARINES	SMALL WARSHIPS	AMPHIBIANS	AUXILIARIES
USA	50	69	370	72	137	537	383	560
USSR	–	21	120	30	340	900	100	220
Great Britain	7	10	68	3	44	208	34	187
France	3	4	18	–	23	153	21	68
Netherlands	1	2	14	–	6	85	2	19
Italy	–	3	8	–	7	120	29	36
Japan	–	–	21	–	6	243	10	8
Argentina	1	3	11	–	2	13	10	33
Brazil	1	2	16	–	4	22	–	29
Australia	2	–	15	–	1	19	4	8
India	1	2	8	–	–	31	3	6

1977	AIRCRAFT CARRIERS	CRUISERS	FRIGATES, DESTROYERS	NUCLEAR SUBMARINES	CONVENTIONAL SUBMARINES	LESSER UNITS	AMPHIBIANS	AUXILIARIES
USA	20	36	185	110	14	186	223	320
USSR	1	33	150	140	260	960	150	400
Great Britain	1	10	57	14	18	58	13	192
France	2	7	41	4	21	110	21	77
Italy	–	3	19	–	10	70	22	32
Japan	–	–	47	–	16	206	8	34
Spain	1	1	26	–	9	60	16	37
Brazil	1	1	17	–	10	24	2	23
China	–	–	16	1	60	690	50	20
Germany (West)	–	–	17	–	24	77	50	109

Naval Strengths and Global Disposition of the Superpowers, 1976

USA	Atlantic (2nd Fleet)	5 aircraft carriers	68 surface warships	
	Mediterranean (6th Fleet)	2 aircraft carriers	16 surface warships	
	Eastern Pacific (3rd Fleet)	4 aircraft carriers	59 surface warships	1 amphibian group
	Western Pacific (7th Fleet)	2 aircraft carriers	18 surface warships	1 amphibian group
USSR	Northern Fleet	126 submarines	51 surface warships	
	Baltic Fleet	12 submarines	47 surface warships	
	Black Sea Fleet	19 submarines	59 surface warships	
	Mediterranean Squadron			
	Pacific Fleet	74 submarines	57 surface warships	
China	Northern Fleet	150 warships		
	Eastern Fleet	400 warships		
	Southern Fleet	150 small warships		

Appendix 4: The world's naval powers (by tonnages), 1882–1974

1882	TOTAL TONNAGE	WARSHIPS/AUXILIARIES	ARMOURED SHIPS	ARMOURED COASTAL SHIPS	ARMOURED GUNBOATS	CRUISERS, FRIGATES, CORVETTES	GUNBOATS	TORPEDO-BOATS	AUXILIARIES
Great Britain	676,000	586,000 90,000	41	16	3	69	114	100	57
France	522,000	410,000 112,000	38	9	–	50	63	60	42
Germany	172,000	157,000 15,000	12	1	11	18	17	11	14
Russia	166,000	149,000 17,000	15	15	2	22	21	110	19
Italy	147,000	130,000 17,000	12	2	1	8	15	16	13
USA	145,000	140,000 5,000	–	20	–	36	3	–	5
Spain	120,000	105,000 15,000	5	3	–	20	64	3	8
Turkey	115,000	97,000 18,000	7	8	–	7	30	–	16
Austria-Hungary	99,000	84,000 15,000	11	–	–	13	7	12	20

1908	TOTAL TONNAGE	WARSHIPS/AUXILIARIES	BATTLESHIPS	COASTAL ARMOURED SHIPS	ARMOURED CRUISERS	CRUISERS	GUNBOATS	DESTROYERS, MTBS	SUBMARINES	AUXILIARIES
Great Britain	1,930,000	1,800,000 130,000	53	–	37	84	31	202	54	31
USA	770,000	700,000 70,000	25	5	15	20	17	46	12	32
France	650,000	600,000 50,000	22	–	21	23	13	308	46	15
Germany	610,000	570,000 40,000	24	8	8	30	15	128	2	20
Japan	420,000	400,000 20,000	13	2	12	17	5	74	7	4
Russia	420,000	290,000 130,000	10	2	4	8	13	173	26	33
Italy	290,000	200,000 90,000	10	–	6	8	5	51	7	24
Austria-Hungary	170,000	130,000 40,000	9	2	3	5	–	33	2	20

1938	TOTAL TONNAGE	WARSHIPS/ AUXILIARIES	BATTLESHIPS	AIRCRAFT CARRIERS	CRUISERS	DESTROYERS	MTBS/ GUNBOATS	SUBMARINES	SMALL SHIPS	AUXILIARIES
Great Britain	2,140,000	1,450,000 690,000	15	7	62	175	37	56	209	130
USA	1,830,000	1,430,000 400,000	15	5	34	221	43	90	118	100
Japan	1,360,000	1,100,000 260,000	10	6	36	83	41	61	40	40
France	670,000	600,000 70,000	7	1	19	60	21	76	58	52
Italy	650,000	490,000 160,000	4	–	24	74	63	96	120	60
USSR	400,000	250,000 150,000	3	–	6	20	25	160	180	40
Germany	320,000	240,000 80,000	2	–	9	17	32	43	66	70
Argentina	140,000	126,000 14,000	2	–	3	16	–	3	14	12

1952	TOTAL TONNAGE	WARSHIPS/ AUXILIARIES	BATTLESHIPS	AIRCRAFT CARRIERS	CRUISERS	DESTROYERS	SUBMARINES	SMALL SHIPS	AMPHIBIANS	AUXILIARIES
USA	9,000,000	4,690,000 4,310,000	15	102	72	385	207	850	530	850
Great Britain	2,200,000	1,300,000 900,000	5	15	24	119	55	650	86	135
USSR	1,300,000	1,000,000 300,000	3	–	15	90	400	400	120	60
France	370,000	290,000 80,000	2	3	6	11	13	270	50	34
Italy	260,000	150,000 110,000	2	–	4	6	–	150	30	30
Argentina	230,000	130,000 100,000	2	–	5	15	3	18	29	30
Spain	150,000	120,000 30,000	–	–	5	18	6	60	–	9
Brazil	115,000	74,000 41,000	1	–	2	9	3	36	–	16
Australia	110,000	100,000 10,000	–	1	3	10	–	47	3	3
Turkey	110,000	70,000 40,000	1	–	–	10	11	70	–	17

1974	TOTAL TONNAGE	WARSHIPS, LANDING SHIPS, AUXILIARIES	AIRCRAFT CARRIERS	CRUISERS	DESTROYERS, FRIGATES	NUCLEAR SUBMARINES	CONVENTIONAL SUBMARINES	CORVETTES	AMPHIBIANS	AUXILIARIES
USA	5,590,000	2,820,000 2,770,000	20	40	250	107	24	235	242	370
USSR	3,580,000	2,100,000 1,480,000	–	33	150	120	270	930	160	330
Great Britain	1,050,000	370,000 680,000	1	11	64	12	22	76	17	178
France	410,000	160,000 250,000	2	5	45	3	20	111	20	84
Germany (West)	255,000	87,000 168,000	–	–	17	–	28	109	50	107
Japan	220,000	185,000 35,000	–	–	44	–	14	228	11	25
China	210,000	156,000 54,000	–	–	18	–	40	600	50	10
Italy	178,000	100,000 78,000	–	3	19	–	10	85	32	43
Spain	163,000	105,000 58,000	1	1	28	–	6	54	17	30
India	135,000	73,000 62,000	1	1	16	–	4	43	1	14
Brazil	134,000	87,000 47,000	1	1	20	–	6	26	2	16
Netherlands	100,000	78,000 22,000	–	1	16	–	6	63	–	20

(Note: Obsolete vessels, hulks and small harbour and wharf vessels are not included. For the United States and Japan, coastguard vessels are included. River craft are excluded. From 1908, gunboats and small, unarmoured cruisers are counted together. In 1977, all warships of over 5,000 tons displacement are counted as cruisers (including US frigates, British County class destroyers and French frigates).

Appendix 5: Major warships sunk by mines, 1864–1941

DATE	LOCATION	SHIP/NATIONALITY	TONNAGE	MINES LAID BY
The American Civil War, 1861–65:				
5 Aug 1864	Bay of Mobile	Monitor *Tecumseh* (US)	2,100	Confederate States
15 Jan 1865	Charleston Harbor	Monitor *Patapsco* (US)	1,900	Confederate States
28 March 1865	Bay of Mobile	Monitor *Milwaukee* (US)	1,300	Confederate States
29 March 1865	Bay of Mobile	Monitor *Osage* (US)	600	Confederate States
The War between Paraguay and the Triple Alliance (Brazil, Argentina, Uruguay), 1864–70:				
2 Sept 1866	Rio Parana	Armoured ship *Rio de Janeiro* (BZ)	1,500	Paraguay
The Russo-Japanese War, 1904–05:				
12 Feb 1904	Off Port Arthur	Cruiser *Bojarin* (R)	3,200	Russia
12 April 1904	Off Port Arthur	Battleship *Petropavlovsk* (R)	11,400	Japan
15 May 1904	Off Port Arthur	Battleship *Yashima* (J)	12,320	Russia
15 May 1904	Off Port Arthur	Battleship *Hatsuse* (J)	15,300	Russia
18 Sept 1904	W of Port Arthur	Armoured gunboat *Heien* (J)	2,150	Russia
30 Nov 1904	W of Port Arthur	Cruiser *Saien* (J)	2,440	Russia
13 Dec 1904	S of Port Arthur	Cruiser *Takasago* (J)	4,160	Russia
The First World War, 1914–18:				
6 Aug 1914	Hoofden	Cruiser *Amphion* (GB)	3,440	Germany
27 Oct 1914	N of Ireland	Battleship *Audacious* (GB)	23,000	Germany
4 Nov 1914	Off Wilhelmshaven	Armoured cruiser *Yorck* (G)	10,300	Germany
17 Nov 1914	W of Memel	Armoured cruiser *Friedrich Karl* (G)	9,900	Russia
18 March 1915	Dardanelles	Battleship *Bouvet* (F)	12,000	Turkey
18 March 1915	Dardanelles	Battleship *Irresistible* (GB)	15,000	Turkey
18 March 1915	Dardanelles	Battleship *Ocean* (GB)	12,950	Turkey
3 April 1915	Off Odessa	Cruiser *Medjidiye* (T)	3,200	Russia
17 Dec 1915	Off Windau (Coeurland)	Cruiser *Bremen* (G)	4,750	Russia
6 Jan 1916	N of Scotland	Battleship *King Edward VII* (GB)	16,350	Germany
11 Feb 1916	Off Harwich	Cruiser *Arethusa* (GB)	3,520	Germany
17 April 1916	Off Malta	Battleship *Russell* (GB)	14,000	Germany
5 June 1916	Off Orkney Islands	Armoured cruiser *Hampshire* (GB)	10,850	Germany
11 Dec 1916	Off Albania	Battleship *Regina Margherita* (I)	13,450	Germany
4 Jan 1917	Off Port Said	Battleship *Peresviet* (R)	12,700	Germany
27 June 1917	Off Brest	Armoured cruiser *Kleber* (F)	7,700	Germany
19 July 1917	Off New York	Armoured cruiser *San Diego* (US)	13,680	Germany
20 Jan 1918	Dardanelles	Cruiser *Breslau* (G)	5,600	Great Britain
The Spanish Civil War, 1936–39:				
30 April 1937	Off Santander	Battleship *España* (Nationalists)	15,000	Republicans
The Second World War, 1939–45:				
29 Sept 1941	Bay of Finland	Armoured cruiser *Ilmarinen* (FINLAND)	3,900	USSR
19 Dec 1941	Off Tripoli (Libya)	Cruiser *Neptune* (GB)	7,000	Italy/Germany

(Note: The capital ships of the Second World War were heavily protected below the waterline, so that conventional mines could damage them, but rarely sink them.)

Appendix 6: Major warships sunk by submarines

DATE	LOCATION	SHIP/NATIONALITY	TONNAGE	SUBMARINE	COMMANDER
The First World War, 1914–18:					
5 Sept 1914	Firth of Forth	Cruiser *Pathfinder* (GB)	2,940	*U21*	Hersing (G)
13 Sept 1914	Off Heligoland	Cruiser *Hela* (G)	4,280	*E9*	Horton (GB)
22 Sept 1914	Hoofden	Armoured cruisers *Aboukir, Cressy* and *Hogue* (GB)	Each 12,000	*U9*	Weddingen (G)
11 Oct 1914	Off Gulf of Finland	Armoured cruiser *Pallada* (R)	7,780	*U26*	von Berckheim (G)
15 Oct 1914	N North Sea	Armoured cruiser *Hawke* (GB)	7,350	*U9*	Weddingen (G)
13 Dec 1914	Sea of Marmara	Battleship *Messudieh* (T)	9,250	*B11*	Holbrook (GB)
1 Jan 1915	W English Channel	Battleship *Formidable* (GB)	15,000	*U24*	Schneider (G)
27 April 1915	N Ionian Sea	Armoured cruiser *Léon Gambetta* (F)	12,500	*U5*	von Trapp (A)
25 May 1915	Dardanelles	Battleship *Triumph* (GB)	12,000	*U21*	Hersing (G)
27 May 1915	Dardanelles	Battleship *Majestic* (GB)	14,900	*U21*	Hersing (G)
7 July 1915	Off Venice	Armoured cruiser *Amalfi* (I)	9,400	*UB14*	Heimburg (G)
28 July 1915	SW of Cattaro	Armoured cruiser *Guiseppe Garibaldi* (I)	7,350	*U4*	Singule (A)
8 Aug 1915	Sea of Marmara	Battleship *Heireddin Barbarousse* (T)	10,670	*E11*	Nasmith (GB)
23 Oct 1915	W of Libau (Coeurland)	Armoured cruiser *Prinz Adalbert* (G)	9,900	*E8*	Goodhart (GB)
7 Nov 1915	NE of Rügen	Cruiser *Undine* (G)	4,650	*E19*	Cromie (GB)
8 Feb 1916	Off Beirut	Armoured cruiser *Amiral Charner* (F)	4,700	*U21*	Hersing (G)
18 Aug 1916	W North Sea	Cruiser *Falmouth* (GB)	5,250	*U63*	Schultze (G)
19 Aug 1916	W North Sea	Cruiser *Nottingham* (GB)	5,440	*U52*	Walther (G)
26 Nov 1916	Off Lisbon	Battleship *Suffren* (F)	12,700	*U52*	Walther (G)
27 Dec 1916	NW of Crete	Battleship *Gaulois* (F)	11,200	*UB47*	Steinbauer (G)
9 Jan 1917	E of Malta	Battleship *Cornwallis* (GB)	14,000	*U 32*	Hartwig (G)
19 March 1917	S of Sardinia	Battleship *Danton* (F)	18,300	*U64*	Moraht (G)
2 Oct 1917	N of Ireland	Armoured cruiser *Drake* (GB)	14,100	*U79*	Rohrbeck (G)

DATE	LOCATION	SHIP/NATIONALITY	TONNAGE	SUBMARINE	COMMANDER
14 Dec 1917	Gulf of Patras	Armoured cruiser *Châteaurenault* (F)	8,000	*UC38*	Wendlandt (G)
7 Aug 1918	North Atlantic	Armoured cruiser *Dupetit Thouars* (F)	9,500	*U62*	Hashagen (G)
9 Nov 1918	w of Gibraltar	Battleship *Britannia* (GB)	16,350	*UB50*	Kukat (G)

The Second World War, 1939–45:

DATE	LOCATION	SHIP/NATIONALITY	TONNAGE	SUBMARINE	COMMANDER
17 Sept 1939	w of Ireland	Aircraft carrier *Courageous* (GB)	18,600	*U29*	Schuhart (G)
14 Oct 1939	Scapa Flow	Battleship *Royal Oak* (GB)	29,150	*U47*	Prien (G)
10 April 1940	Skagerrak	Cruiser *Karlsruhe* (G)	6,500	*Truant*	Hutchinson (GB)
12 June 1940	N of Tobruk	Cruiser *Calypso* (GB)	4,120	*Bagnolini*	Tosoni-Pittoni (I)
25 Feb 1941	SE of Tunis	Cruiser *Armando Diaz* (I)	5,350	*Upright*	Norman (GB)
31 March 1941	NE of Sollum	Cruiser *Bonaventure* (GB)	5,750	*Ambra*	Arillo (I)
14 Nov 1941	N of Algiers	Aircraft carrier *Ark Royal* (GB)	22,000	*U81*	Guggenberger (G)
24 Nov 1941	NE of Pernambuco	Cruiser *Dunedin* (GB)	4,850	*U124*	Mohr (G)
25 Nov 1941	NE of Sollum	Battleship *Barham* (GB)	31,100	*U331*	Tiesenhausen (G)
14 Dec 1941	NW of Alexandria	Cruiser *Galatea* (GB)	5,250	*U557*	Paulshen (G)
21 Dec 1941	w of Portugal	Aircraft carrier *Audacity* (GB)	5,500	*U751*	Bigalk (G)
11 March 1942	s of Crete	Cruiser *Naiad* (GB)	5,750	*U565*	Jebsen (G)
1 April 1942	N of Sicily	Cruiser *Bande Nere* (I)	5,200	*Urge*	Tomkinson (GB)
2 May 1942	N of Kola Peninsula	Cruiser *Edinburgh* (GB)	10,000	*U456*	Teichert (G)
7 June 1942	NE of Midway Is.	Aircraft carrier *Yorktown* (US)	20,000	*I.168*	Tanabe (J)
15 June 1942	Ionian Sea	Cruiser *Trento* (I)	10,500	*Umbra*	Maydon (GB)
16 June 1942	s of Crete	Cruiser *Hermione* (GB)	5,750	*U205*	Reschke (G)
10 Aug 1942	Off Rabaul	Cruiser *Kako* (J)	8,850	*S.44*	Moore (US)
11 Aug 1942	N of Algiers	Aircraft carrier *Eagle* (GB)	22,600	*U73*	Rosenbaum (G)
12 Aug 1942	Off Bizerta	Cruiser *Cairo* (GB)	4,200	*Axum*	Ferrini (I)
15 Sept 1942	s of Solomon Is.	Aircraft carrier *Wasp* (US)	14,700	*I.19*	Narahara (J)
13 Nov 1942	s of Solomon Is.	Cruiser *Juneau* (US)	6,000	*I.26*	Yokota (J)
15 Nov 1942	w of Gibraltar	Aircraft carrier *Avenger* (GB)	8,200	*U155*	Piening (G)
18 Dec 1942	NE of New Guinea	Cruiser *Tenryu* (J)	3,250	*Albacore*	Lake (US)
24 Nov 1943	Off Gilbert Is.	Aircraft carrier *Liscombe Bay* (US)	7,800	*I.175*	Tabata (J)
4 Dec 1943	s of Japan	Aircraft carrier *Chuyo* (J)	15,600	*Sailfish*	Ward (US)
11 Jan 1944	w of Sumatra	Cruiser *Kuma* (J)	5,700	*Tally Ho*	Bennington (US)
16 Feb 1944	N of Truk	Cruiser *Agano* (J)	6,650	*Skate*	Gruner (US)
18 Feb 1944	w of Anzio	Cruiser *Penelope* (GB)	5,250	*U410*	Fenski (G)
13 March 1944	s of Japan	Cruiser *Tatsuta* (J)	3,250	*Sandlance*	Garrison (US)
27 April 1944	Off Palau Is.	Cruiser *Yubari* (J)	2,900	*Bluegill*	Barr (US)
29 May 1944	North Atlantic	Aircraft carrier *Block Island* (US)	9,800	*U549*	Krankenhagen (G)
19 June 1944	Philippine Sea	Aircraft carrier *Shokaku* (J)	25,680	*Cavalla*	Kossler (US)
19 June 1944	Philippine Sea	Aircraft carrier *Taiho* (J)	29,300	*Albacore*	Blanchard (US)
19 July 1944	s of Hong Kong	Cruiser *Ohi* (J)	5,700	*Flasher*	Whitaker (US)
7 Aug 1944	s of Japan	Cruiser *Nagara* (J)	5,700	*Croaker*	Lee (US)
18 Aug 1944	E of Philippines	Cruiser *Natori* (J)	5,700	*Hardhead*	McMaster (US)
18 Aug 1944	N of Luzon	Aircraft carrier *Tayo* (J)	15,600	*Rasher*	Munson (US)
19 Sept 1944	SE of Hong Kong	Aircraft carrier *Unyo* (J)	15,600	*Barb*	Fluckey (US)
23 Oct 1944	w of Philippines	Cruiser *Atago* (J)	13,400	*Darter*	McClintock (US)
23 Oct 1944	w of Philippines	Cruiser *Maya* (J)	13,400	*Dace*	Claggett (US)
25 Oct 1944	NE of Luzon	Cruiser *Tama* (J)	5,700	*Jallao*	Icenhower (US)
17 Nov 1944	NE of Shanghai	Aircraft carrier *Shinyo* (J)	17,500	*Spadefish*	Underwood (US)
21 Nov 1944	Off Formosa	Battleship *Kongo* (J)	32,150	*Sealion*	Reich (US)
29 Nov 1944	SE of Japan	Aircraft carrier *Shinano* (J)	62,000	*Archerfish*	Enright (US)
19 Dec 1944	sw of Shanghai	Aircraft carrier *Unryo* (J)	17,150	*Redfish*	McGregor (US)
7 April 1945	Java Sea	Cruiser *Isuzu* (J)	5,700	*Charr/Gabilan*	Boyle/Parham (US)
8 June 1945	SE of Sumatra	Cruiser *Ashigara* (J)	13,000	*Trenchant*	Hezlet (GB)
29 July 1945	E of Philippines	Cruiser *Indianapolis* (US)	9,800	*I.58*	Hashimoto (J)

(Note: Sinkings in which submarines played the predominant role are shown as well as pure submarine actions. Sources: German Naval Archives, *Der Krieg zur See 1914–1918*; Hans Sokol, *Österreich-Ungarns Seekrieg 1914–1918*; and Rohwer/Hummelchen, *Chronik des Seekriegs 1939–1945.*)

Appendix 7: Sinking rates of the U-boats of the Central Powers in the commerce war, 1914–1918

DATE	HIGH SEAS FLEET	MARINE-CORPS	MEDITERRANEAN GERMAN U-BOATS	AUSTRO-HUNGARIAN U-BOATS	BASED AT CONSTANTINOPLE	BALTIC	U-BOAT/CRUISER GROUPS	TOTALS
August	–	–	–	–	–	–	–	–
September	–	–	–	–	–	–	–	–
October	866	–	–	–	–	–	–	866
November	2,084	–	–	13	–	–	–	2,097
December	419	–	–	–	–	–	–	419
1914 total	3,369	–	–	13	–	–	–	3,382
January	17,577	–	–	–	–	–	–	17,577
February	22,785	–	–	–	–	–	–	22,785
March	89,517	–	–	21	–	–	–	89,538
April	30,926	9,713	–	–	–	849	–	41,488

DATE	HIGH SEAS FLEET	MARINE-CORPS	MEDITERRANEAN GERMAN U-BOATS	AUSTRO-HUNGARIAN U-BOATS	BASED AT CONSTANTINOPLE	BALTIC	U-BOAT/CRUISER GROUPS	TOTALS
May	107,515	–	–	–	19,380	–	–	126,895
June	101,211	14,080	–	–	–	–	–	115,291
July	85,732	6,998	–	–	5,275	–	–	98,005
August	155,637	7,709	4,067	1,074	11,154	4,205	–	183,846
September	75,881	793	53,363	–	6,011	–	–	136,048
October	–	19,866	63,848	–	2,350	–	–	86,064
November	–	14,091	152,882	25	350	200	–	167,548
December	14,001	17,045	76,693	180	–	–	–	107,919
1915 total	700,782	90,295	350,853	1,300	44,520	5,254	–	1,193,004
January	–	17,172	32,438	43	–	–	–	49,653
February	–	47,711	47,379	475	–	–	–	95,565
March	66,287	68,424	20,475	271	5,350	–	–	160,807
April	93,524	37,775	56,008	–	–	–	–	187,307
May	25,891	21,398	72,092	2,238	–	–	–	121,619
June	2,259	18,389	67,125	11,424	5,420	–	–	104,617
July	9,713	10,958	86,432	–	3,453	172	–	110,728
August	19,621	7,929	129,368	188	2,666	3,561	–	163,333
September	36,613	86,808	105,742	4,309	731	1,679	–	235,882
October	127,719	84,487	125,152	4,299	3,041	964	–	345,662
November	71,480	87,608	166,130	–	116	1,355	–	326,689
December	55,638	115,492	136,717	–	–	–	–	307,847
1916 total	508,745	604,151	1,045,058	23,247	20,777	7,731	–	2,209,709
January	165,494	84,356	78,541	–	–	–	–	328,391
February	280,602	134,140	105,670	–	–	–	–	520,412
March	316,852	185,728	61,917	–	–	–	–	564,497
April	447,913	156,472	254,911	23,127	251	787	–	883,461
May	244,984	195,098	170,626	13,376	–	5,608	–	629,692
June	356,054	143,054	164,299	6,894	14,500	5,276	13,542	703,619
July	309,095	128,912	90,334	11,764	–	413	26,760	567,278
August	249,991	129,788	79,549	35,201	40	–	13,004	507,573
September	124,620	116,942	111,241	–	799	–	13,004	353,602
October	177,482	115,699	144,603	12,667	2,175	1,426	25,157	479,209
November	84,737	99,579	104,479	4,300	1,201	–	12,603	306,899
December	138,159	117,621	148,331	–	–	–	7,655	411,766
1917 total	2,895,983	1,607,389	1,514,501	107,329	18,966	13,510	98,721	6,256,399
January	114,094	57,280	103,738	26,020	12,408	–	8,110	321,650
February	147,174	65,461	83,957	–	161	–	38,449	335,202
March	11,650	99,395	110,456	17,331	2,891	–	44,354	386,077
April	93,556	90,606	75,866	40	4,221	–	35,820	300,109
May	113,211	39,277	112,693	9,159	97	–	31,280	305,717
June	96,260	58,931	58,248	–	–	–	55,066	268,505
July	119,471	53,612	76,629	217	–	–	31,108	281,037
August	115,248	48,658	65,377	2,209	3,904	–	76,993	312,389
September	82,063	35,725	35,856	5,004	1,833	–	16,495	176,976
October	52,095	9,815	28,007	–	7,315	–	19,005	116,237
November	–	–	10,233	–	–	–	–	10,233
December	–	–	–	–	–	–	–	
1918 total	1,044,822	558,760	761,060	59,890	32,830	–	356,680	2,814,132
Totals	5,153,701	2,860,595	3,671,472	191,869	117,093	26,495	455,401	12,476,626

(Note: The figures for German U-boat sinkings are based on data in the German naval work: *Der Krieg zur See 1914–1918, Der Handelskrieg mit U-Booten*, V, *Annex 3*. The successes of the Austro-Hungarian U-boats are extracted from the manuscript of Wladimir Aichelburg's *Österreich-Ungarns U-Boote, eine Dokumentation 1976*, which is in the process of publication.)

Appendix 8: Allied shipping losses in the Second World War

	NORTH SEA, ATLANTIC	BARENTS SEA	BALTIC	BLACK SEA	MEDITERRANEAN	INDIAN OCEAN	PACIFIC	TOTALS
September	178,620	–	–	–	–	–	–	178,620
October	156,156	–	–	–	–	–	–	156,156
November	72,721	–	–	–	–	–	–	72,721
December	101,823	–	–	–	–	–	–	101,823
1939	509,320	–	–	–	–	–	–	509,320
January	169,630	–	–	–	–	–	–	169,630
February	182,369	–	–	–	–	–	–	182,369
March	69,826	–	–	–	–	–	–	69,826

	NORTH SEA, ATLANTIC	BARENTS SEA	BALTIC	BLACK SEA	MEDITERRANEAN	INDIAN OCEAN	PACIFIC	TOTALS
April	30,927	–	–	–	–	–	–	30,927
May	61,635	–	–	–	–	–	–	61,635
June	356,937	–	–	–	8,029	8,215	–	373,181
July	197,878	–	–	–	4,097	–	–	201,975
August	287,571	–	–	–	1,044	–	–	288,615
September	294,707	–	–	–	–	4,008	–	298,715
October	361,459	–	–	–	–	–	–	361,459
November	181,595	–	–	–	–	–	–	181,595
December	257,129	–	–	–	–	–	–	257,129
1940	2,451,663	–	–	–	13,170	12,223	–	2,477,056
January	117,336	–	–	–	–	–	–	117,336
February	237,194	–	–	–	–	–	–	237,194
March	239,271	–	–	–	–	–	–	239,271
April	260,337	–	–	–	–	–	–	260,337
May	363,073	–	–	–	–	–	–	363,073
June	322,012	–	–	–	3,805	–	–	325,817
July	99,916	558	4,100	–	–	–	–	104,574
August	80,542	633	–	–	–	–	–	81,175
September	212,123	–	–	–	3,525	–	–	215,648
October	161,960	3,487	–	–	1,966	–	–	167,413
November	63,677	–	–	1,975	10,820	5,757	–	82,229
December	56,967	–	–	–	34,084	3,404	40,666	135,121
1941	2,214,408	4,678	4,100	1,975	54,200	9,161	40,666	2,329,188
January	295,776	5,135	–	–	–	69,092	7,627	377,630
February	424,255	–	–	–	–	41,305	4,799	470,359
March	491,818	11,507	–	–	4,189	28,752	–	536,266
April	388,280	18,816	–	–	8,131	32,404	–	447,631
May	588,521	12,344	–	–	15,900	–	11,821	628,586
June	628,074	–	–	–	10,651	74,678	16,978	730,381
July	348,673	102,296	–	–	6,294	28,818	30,045	516,126
August	537,461	6,845	–	–	33,897	5,237	533	583,973
September	415,234	40,511	–	–	813	28,852	–	485,410
October	427,292	163	–	–	–	172,539	13,691	613,685
November	534,039	36,541	–	–	86,152	160,633	–	817,365
December	287,550	–	–	–	27,617	23,692	–	338,859
1942	5,366,973	234,158	–	–	193,644	666,002	85,494	6,546,271
January	196,800	5,881	–	–	20,031	–	26,625	249,337
February	308,895	7,460	–	4,648	21,751	31,696	11,988	386,438
March	490,323	18,245	–	8,229	46,823	65,966	–	629,586
April	223,067	–	–	–	13,934	50,136	32,172	319,309
May	195,188	–	–	–	5,979	42,623	33,472	277,262
June	28,917	–	–	1,783	23,720	50,275	20,431	125,126
July	136,106	857	–	11,794	25,949	97,213	–	271,919
August	21,749	3,472	–	–	20,741	46,401	7,176	99,539
September	47,192	9,649	–	–	21,623	39,471	1,280	119,215
October	44,935	4,757	–	–	28,543	25,833	–	104,068
November	23,245	–	–	–	7,481	29,234	6,711	66,671
December	47,785	–	–	–	8,009	31,173	–	86,967
1943	1,764,202	50,321	–	26,454	244,584	510,021	139,855	2,735,437
January	14,535	21,530	–	–	–	56,213	–	92,278
February	7,048	–	–	–	21,706	64,169	–	92,923
March	34,500	7,062	–	–	29,231	74,900	–	145,693
April	35,310	7,176	–	–	7,210	5,277	–	54,973
May	17,276	–	–	–	7,147	–	–	24,423
June	21,665	–	–	1,850	–	22,587	–	46,102
July	38,395	–	–	–	–	30,176	–	68,571
August	35,259	5,885	–	–	–	50,310	–	91,454
September	23,303	14,395	–	–	–	13,092	–	50,790
October	–	–	1,650	–	–	–	7,176	8,826
November	14,995	–	–	–	–	14,025	11,316	40,336
December	51,338	1,556	–	–	–	–	7,180	60,074
1944	293,624	57,604	1,650	1,850	65,294	330,749	25,672	776,443
January	44,156	–	640	–	–	–	–	44,796
February	29,543	22,505	–	–	–	14,312	–	66,360
March	44,339	14,386	–	–	–	–	–	58,725
April	64,335	1,603	–	–	–	–	–	65,938

	NORTH SEA, ATLANTIC	BARENTS SEA	BALTIC	BLACK SEA	MEDITERRANEAN	INDIAN OCEAN	PACIFIC	TOTALS
May	10,319	–	–	–	–	–	–	10,319
June	–	–	–	–	–	–	–	–
July	–	–	–	–	–	–	–	–
August	–	–	–	–	–	–	–	–
1945	192,692	38,494	640	–	–	14,312	–	246,138
Totals	12,792,882	385,255	6,390	30,279	570,892	1,542,468	291,687	15,619,853

The figures are taken from J. Rohwer: *Die U-Boot-Erfolge der Achsenmächte 1939–1945*. The figures include all merchantmen and auxiliary Allied warships sunk or taken as prizes. Damaged ships and those laid up are only considered as total losses when they failed to reach an Allied harbour.

Appendix 9: Japanese merchant marine losses, 1941–1945 (ships of over 500 tons)
Based on the Joint Army–Navy Assessment Committee (JANAC)

DATE	SUBMARINES	CARRIER-BORNE AIRCRAFT	LAND-BASED NAVAL PLANES	ARMY AIR FORCE	MINES	SURFACE GUNFIRE	ACCIDENTS AND UNKNOWN CAUSES	TOTALS
December 1941	31,693	–	–	16,901	–	–	7,466	56,060
January	28,351	–	–	6,757	1,548	22,751	14,388	73,795
February	15,975	–	–	–	–	10,485	6,788	33,248
March	26,183	21,610	–	4,109	14,618	7,170	4,469	78,159
April	26,886	–	–	9,798	–	–	–	36,684
May	86,110	–	–	–	10,546	–	–	96,656
June	20,021	–	–	12,358	–	–	–	32,379
July	39,356	–	–	20,775	–	4,286	3,111	67,528
August	76,652	–	9,309	420*	–	–	5,950	92,331
September	39,389	–	–	7,190	–	–	–	46,579
October	118,920	–	25,546	5,863	–	3,311	11,187	164,827
November	35,358	–	77,607	24,510	–	10,438	11,079	158,992
December	48,271	–	548	9,591	–	–	13,377	71,787
1942 January	80,572	–	–	41,269	–	–	179	122,590
February	54,276	–	10,568	19,478	–	3,121	5,732	93,175
March	109,447	–	–	37,939	–	–	3,187	150,573
April	105,345	–	–	24,521	–	–	1,916	131,782
May	122,319	–	1,917	2,060	–	–	5,144	131,440
June	101,581	–	–	953	–	–	6,581	109,115
July	82,784	–	–	4,425	–	–	3,298	90,507
August	80,799	–	–	4,468	–	–	13,561	98,828
September	157,002	–	–	15,429	2,663	–	22,812	197,906
October	119,623	–	–	15,253	–	–	10,718	145,594
November	231,683	–	5,824	70,458	2,455	–	4,370	314,790
December	121,531	26,017	14,397	36,266	–	–	8,918	207,129
1943 January	240,840	6,738	55,184	22,823	2,428	3,535	8,103	339,651
February	256,797	186,725	8,207	40,983	5,307	–	21,540	519,559
March	106,529	86,812	2,655	13,224	–	–	16,546	225,766
April	95,242	1,775	2,230	21,942	–	2,722	5,985	129,846
May	264,713	992	–	9,626	–	–	1,891	277,222
June	195,020	65,146	966	7,753	–	8,742	7,577	285,204
July	212,907	9,486	–	7,865	2,284	–	9,110	241,652
August	245,348	22,918	6,659	13,610	1,018	–	4,546	294,099
September	181,363	213,250	8,095	3,258	13,411	–	4,772	424,149
October	328,843	131,308	12,256	23,627	5,964	–	12,947	514,945
November	220,476	120,373	8,627	37,350	2,350	–	2,232	391,408
December	103,836	8,217	4,158	54,996	–	–	20,669	191,876
1944 January	93,796	283,234	549	20,620	17,322	584	9,400	425,505
February	55,746	1,384	1,677	8,593	13,166	–	6,898	87,464
March	70,727	27,563	14,373	30,931	21,402	–	21,122	186,118
April	60,696	–	875	18,174	20,145	–	1,812	101,702
May	32,394	–	57,041	2,358	109,991	–	9,752	211,536
June	92,267	–	16,163	11,470	69,009	–	7,271	196,180
July	27,408	113,831	16,372	11,802	63,323	–	3,094	235,830
August 1945	14,559	1,805	1,715	22,884	18,462	–	–	59,425
Totals	4,859,634	1,329,184	363,518	774,680	397,412	77,145	308,386	8,141,591

(Note: At least 12% of the sinkings by Army Air Force are attributed to Allied Air Forces. At least 23% of the carrier-borne aircraft sinkings in July 1945 are attributed to the British Pacific fleet. Approximately 2% of the submarine sinkings are attributed to British and Dutch submarines. Sinkings due to more than one cause have been distributed among those variously responsible.) * = sinkings shared with submarines.

Select Bibliography

Albas, A. d', *Death of a Navy. Japanese Naval Action in World War II*, Devin-Adair, New York, 1957.

Almanach für die k.u.k. Kriegsmarine 1862-1918.

The American Neptune, Peabody Museum of Salem, Massachusetts, 1941 ff.

Anderson, R. C., *Naval Wars in the Baltic, 1522-1850*, Edwards, London, 1969.

Anderson, R. C., *Naval Wars in the Levant, 1559-1853*, University Press, Liverpool, 1952.

Archibald, E., *The Wooden Fighting Ship of the Royal Navy*, Blandford, London, 1968.

Attlmayr, F., *Der Krieg Osterreichs in der Adria 1866*, Gerold, Pula, Vienna, 1896.

Auphan, P., *The French Navy in World War II*, U.S. Naval Institute, Annapolis, 1959.

Auphan, P. and Mordal, *Unter der Trikolore*, Stalling, Oldenburg, 1964.

Bennett, G., *Naval Battles of World War II*, Batsford, London, 1975.

Bragadin, Marc Antonio, *The Italian Navy in World War II*, U.S. Naval Institute, Annapolis, 1957.

Breyer, S., *Battleships and Battlecruisers, 1905-1970*, Macdonald & Jane's, London, 1973. Translated from *Schlachtschiffe und Schlachtkreuzer, 1905-1970*, Lehmanns, Munich, 1970.

Burgess, R. F., *Ships beneath the Sea*, Hale, London, 1976.

Cagle, M. W. and Manson, F. A., *The Sea War in Korea*, U.S. Naval Institute, Annapolis, 1957.

Casson, L., *The Ancient Mariners*, Gollancz, London, 1960.

Clowes, Sir W. L., *Four Modern Naval Campaigns*, Unit Library, London, 1902.

Clowes, Sir W. L., *The Royal Navy*, 7 vols., Sampson Low, Marston, London, 1897/1903.

Corbett, J. S., *Naval Operations, 1914-18*, Longmans Green, London, 1920-31.

Dt. Marine Archiv, *Der Krieg zur See 1914-1918*, 22 vols., Mittler, Berlin/Frankfurt, 1922-1966.

DTV, *Atlas zur Weltgeschichte*, Dt. Taschenb. Vg., Munich, 1964.

Eikhoff, E., *Seekrieg und Seepolitik zwischen Islam und Abendland*, de Gruyter, Berlin, 1966.

Faber, G., *Piraten oder Staatengründer (Normannen vom Nordmeer bis Bosporus)*, Bertelsmann, Gütersloh, 1968.

Field, J. A., *A History of United States Naval Operations in Korea*, Govt. Printing Office, Washington, 1962.

Foss, M. *Marinekunde*, Union dt. Verl Ges., Stuttgart, 1909.

Frere-Cook, G. and Macksey, K., *The Guinness History of Sea Warfare*, Guinness Superlatives, Enfield (Mddx.), 1975.

Gröner, E., *Die dt. Kriegsschiffe, 1815-1945*, 2 vols., Lehmanns, Munich, 1966/68.

Hailey, F. and Lancelot, M., *Clear for Action*, Duell, Sloan & Pearce, New York, 1964.

James, W., *The Naval History of Great Britain*, 4th edition, 6 vols., R. Bentley, London, 1847.

Jane's Fighting Ships, Sampson Low, Marston, London, 1897 ff.

Jenkins, E. H., *A History of the French Navy*, Macdonald & Jane's, London, 1973.

Jurien de la Gravière, E., *Guerres Maritimes sous La République et L'Empire*, 2 vols., Charpentier, Paris, 1847.

Jurien de la Gravière, E., *Les Marins du 15me et 16me Siècles*, Plon, Paris, 1879.

Jurien de la Gravière, E., *Nelson und die Seekriege, 1798-1815*, Senf's Vg. Bh., Leipzig, 1870.

Kemp, P. K. (ed.), *The Oxford Companion to Ships and the Sea*, Oxford University Press, London, 1976.

Klepsch, P., *Die fremden Flotten im Zweiten Weltkrieg und ihr Schicksal*, Lehmanns, Munich, 1968.

Lewis, A., *Naval Power and Trade in the Mediterranean, 500-1100*, Princeton University Press, 1951.

Macintyre, D. and Bathe, B. W., *The Man-of-War*, Methuen, London, 1968. Translated to *Kriegsschiffe in 5000 Jahren*, Delius/Klasing, Bielefeld, 1968.

Mahan, A. T., *The Influence of Sea Power on History, 1660-1783*, Sampson Low, London, 1890.

Mahan, A. T., *The Influence of Sea Power upon the French Revolution and Empire, 1793-1812*, 3 vols., Sampson Low, London, 1892.

Mahan, A. T., *The Major Operations of the Navies in the War of American Independence*, Sampson Low, London, 1913.

Mahan, A. T., *Sea Power and its Relation to the War of 1812*, 2 vols., Sampson Low, London, 1905.

Mahan, A. T., *Der Einflub der Seemacht auf die Geschichte*, 2 vols., Mittler & Sohn, Berlin, 1896/99.

Maltzahn, K., *Der Seekrieg zwischen Russland und Japan, 1904-1905*, 3 vols., Mittler, Berlin, 1912-1914.

The Mariners Mirror, The Society for Nautical Research, Greenwich, 1911 ff.

Marine-Rundschau, Lehmanns, Munich, 1890 ff. (seit 1974).

Meurer, A., *Seekriegsgeschichte*, Hase u. Köhler, Leipzig, 1925.

Mordal, J., *Twenty-five Centuries of Sea Warfare*, Souvenir Press, London, 1965.

Morison, S. E., *History of U.S. Naval Operations in World War II*, 15 vols., Little, Brown, Boston, 1947/62.

Parkes, O., *British Battleships*, Seeley Service, London, 1956 repr. 1970.

Polmar, N., *Aircraft Carriers*, Macdonald, London, 1969.

Potter, E. B., Nimitz, C. and Rohwer, J., *Seemacht*, Bernard & Graefe, Munich, 1974.

Proceedings, U.S. Naval Institute, Annapolis, 1875 ff.

Rehder and Sander, *Die Verluste der Kriegsflotten, 1914-1918*, Lehmanns, Munich, 1969.

Reynolds, C. G., *Command of the Sea*, Hale, London, 1976; Morrow, New York, 1976.

Rodgers, W. L., *Greek and Roman Naval Warfare*, U.S. Naval Inst., Annapolis, 1939 repr. 1970.

Rodgers, W. L., *Naval Warfare under Oars*, U.S. Naval Inst., Annapolis, 1939 repr. 1970.

Röhr, A., *Handbuch der dt. Marinegesch*, Stalling, Oldenburg, 1963.

Rohwer, J., *Die U-Booterfolge der Achsenmachte, 1939-1945*, Lehmanns, Munich, 1968.

Rohwer, J. and Hummelchen, G., *Chronology of the War at Sea, 1939-1945*, 2 vols., Ian Allan, London, 1972/74. Translated from *Chronik des Seekrieges, 1939-1945*, Stalling, Oldenburg, 1968.

Roskill, S. W., *The War at Sea*, 3 vols. (in 4), HMSO, London, 1954/61.

Rost, G. A., *Vom Seewesen und Seehandel in der Antike*, B. R. Grüner, Amsterdam, 1968.

Ruge, F., *Sea Warfare, 1939-1945*, Cassell, London, 1957.

Sanderson, M., *Sea Battles*, David & Charles, Newton Abbot, 1975.

Shepard, A. N., *Sea Power in Ancient History*, Heinemann, London, 1925.

Sokol, H. H., *Osterreich-Ungarns Seekrieg, 1914-1918*, 4 vols., Kriegsarchiv, Vienna, 1933.

Starr, C. G., *The Roman Imperial Navy, 31BC-AD324*, 2nd edition, Heffer, Cambridge, 1960.

Stenzel, A., *Seekriegsgeschichte*, 7 vols., Hahn'sche Vg. Bh., Hanover, 1907-1921.

Tramond, J., *Manuel d'histoire Maritime de la France*, Challamel, Paris, 1916.

Treue, W., *Der Krimkrieg und die Entwicklung der mod. Flotten*, Musterschmidt, Göttingen, 1954.

U.S. Naval Hist. Div., *Civil War Naval Chronology, 1861-1865*, Govt. Printing Office, Washington, 1971.

Warner, O., *Nelson's Battles*, Batsford, London, 1965.

Warship International, Naval Records Club (later International Naval Research Organisation), Toledo, Ohio, 1964 ff.

Wilson, H. W., *Battleships in Action*, 2 vols., Sampson Low, London, 1926.

Wilson, H. W., *Ironclads in Action*, 2 vols., Sampson Low, London, 1896.

Index

Taranto, Battle off, 26; British attack on, 121
Taranto harbour, Austrian attacks on, 104
Tarawa Island, US landing on, 141
Tarentum (Taranto), Hannibal's capture of, 18
Tarentum, Treaty of, 20
Tariq, Arab general, 25
Tarragona, action off, 44
Tartessus (Tarshish), destruction of, 15
Task Forces, US: TF16, 130; TF17, 128, 130; TF31, 145; TF38, 144, 145, 150; TF51, 148, 149; TF52, 143, 144; TF53, 144; TF58, 141, 143, 144, 148, 149
Tasman, Abel, Dutch navigator, 70
Tassafronga, night action off, 139
Tchesme, see: Chesme, Battle of, 70
Tegetthoff, Commodore Wilhelm von, 92, 93
Telegraph cable, first submarine, 90; first transatlantic submarine, 91
Tendra, Battle of, 75
Tenth Army, US, 149
Terouka, Vice Admiral K., 145
Teulada, see: Cape Teulada, Battle of, 121, 122
Texel (Camperdown), Battle of the, 54
Thames estuary, Dutch blockade of, 52
Themistocles, 12
Thermoplae, Battle of, 19
Thessalonica, plunder of, 26
Third Coalition, War of the, 83
Third Fleet, US, 144, 145, 146, 147, 148, 150
Thirty Years War, 41, 44
Three Emperors' (Austerlitz), 'Battle of the, 85
Ticinus, Battle of, 17
Tientsin, Peace of, 94
Tiesenhausen, Commander von, 123
Tilsit, agreement of, 85
Ting Ju-ch'ang, Admiral, 94
Tinian, US attack on, 142; US landing on, 144
Tirpitz, 117, 134
Tissaphernes, Persian satrap of Lydia, 13, 14
Tobago, action off, 55
Tobruk, action off, 120
Togo, Admiral Heihachiro, 98, 99, 100, 101
Tojo, General Hideki, 125
Tokyo, first American air attack on, 128
Tondern, British air attack on, 109
Tongking, see: Gulf of Tongking incident, 152
Topp, Korvettenkapitan Erich, 136
Tordenskjold, Admiral, 64
Tordesillas, Treaty of, 40, 41
Torpedoes:
    acoustic, 136; aerial attack, first successful, 104; human (Maiales), 124, 135; self-propelled, first successful attack with, 94; 'spear', 92; Whitehead, 93
Torrington, Admiral Arthur Herbert, Lord, 58
Totila, Ostrogoth king, 23
Toucher, Commodore des, 72
Toulon, Allied capture of, 62; Battle of, 66; French Royalists surrender of, 78; German occupation of, 132
Toulouse, Admiral Comte de, 61, 62
Tours, Battle of, 26
Tourville, Count Anne Hilarion de, 58, 59, 60
Tovey, Admiral Sir John, 114, 117

Trafalgar, Battle of, 84
Trani, Battle off, 30
Trapani, Battle of, 31
Trasimenus, Battle of, Lake, 17
Trebbia, Battle of the, 17
Trincomalee, action off, 74; Japanese attack on, 128
Tripartite Naval War, 27
Tripoli, British bombardment of, 122, 123
Triton, 152
Trolle, Herlof, 34
Tromp, Cornelius, 50, 51, 52, 54, 56
Tromp, Admiral Martin Van, 43, 45, 46, 47
Trondheim, British landings at, 113
Troubridge, Rear Admiral Thomas H., 133
Truk Island, US assault on, 142
Tsushima, Battle of, 99, 100
Tulagi, US landing on, 137
Tunis, Genoese-Pisan capture of, 29; Turkish capture of, 35
Turin, Peace of, 32
Turkish-Egyptian War, 87
Turner, Vice Admiral Richmond Kelly, 137, 141, 143, 148, 149
Twelve Years Truce, 43
Tyre, siege and capture of, 14

U9, 105
U21, 105
U-boat attack, first successful, 105
U-boat Commanders, most successful First World War, 110; most successful Second World War, 136
U-boats, attacks by, 109, 110, 112, 116, 117, 118, 123, 124, 125, 133, 135, 136
Ugaki, Vice Admiral M., 149
Ulithi atoll, US occupation of, 145
Ulsan, see: Japanese Sea, Battle of the, 99
Uluch Ali, 36, 37
Umayyad dynasty, founding of, 24
United States, British recognition of, 74
UN Maritime Law Conferences, 154
Unryu, 148
Urban II, Pope, 29
Ushakov, Rear Admiral Fedor Fedorovich, 75
Ushant, Battle of, 71, 78
Ushijima, Lieutenant General M., 149
Utrecht, Peace of, 63

Vado, French bombardment of, 119
Valentiner, Kapitanleutnant Max, 110
Valona, British bombardment of, 121
Vandals, 23
Varangians, 28
Vasa, Gustav (later Gustav I of Sweden), 34
Velez Malaga, see: Malaga, Battle of, 62
Vella Lavella, US landing on, 140
Veneti tribe, Caesar's defeat of, 20
Venetian-Genoese Wars, 31, 32
Venetian-Levantine fleet, Genoese capture of, 31
Venetian-Turkish War, 65
Veniero, Sebastiano, 36
Verde, see: Cape Verde, 74
Verela (Wereloe), Peace of, 77
Versailles, Peace of, 74; Treaty of, 110
Vestal Virgins, 21
Vian, Rear Admiral Sir Philip, 123, 124, 135
Vichy French, 119, 120, 123, 132
Vicksburg, Unionist capture of, 92

Vienna, Congress of, 86
Vietnamese War, 152, 153
Vigo, Allied attack on, 61
Vikings settlement in Iceland, 28
Villaret-Joyeuse, Rear Admiral Louis, 79, 80
Villeneuve, Pierre Charles de, 81, 83, 84
Virginia (ex-*Merrimack*), 91
Visigoths, 25
Vitalienbruder ('Equal Sharers'), 34
Vitgeft, Admiral Wilhelm, 98
Vivonne, Count (Duc de Mortemart), 54, 55
Vlissingen, British capture of, 86
Voltaire, François, 67
Vries, Admiral de, 51
Vyborg, Swedish break-out from, 77

Wachtmeister, Admiral Hans, 64
Wagram, Battle of, 86
Wakde Island, US landings on, 142
Wake Island, Japanese capture of, 126
Walcheren expedition, the, 86
Waldemar IV, King of Denmark, 34
Walker, Commander J.F., 116
Wallis, Samuel, British sailor, 70
Warships, general classification of, 97, 112
Washington, George, 71
Washington Naval Treaty, 111
Wassenaer van Obdam, Jacob van, 49, 50
Waterloo, Battle of, 86
Watt, James, British engineer, 88
Weddingen, Kapitanleutnant Otto, 105
Weiheiwei, capitulation of, 95
Wereloe, see: Verela, Peace of, 77
West Indies, Franco-Dutch attacks in, 52; War in the, 72
Westminster, Treaty of, 48, 54
Westphalia, Peace of, 44
Wewak, Japanese strongpoint of, 142
Whitby, German bombardment of, 105
Whitehead, Robert, English engineer, 93
Wilkinson, Rear Admiral Theodore S., 140, 142, 145
Willaumez, Rear Admiral, 86
William I ('the Conqueror'), 28
William I of Orange (William the Silent), 41
William III of Orange, 53, 58
Willis, Vice Admiral Sir Algernon, 133
Wind, Jorgen, 44
Winter, Admiral Jan Willem de, 80
Wireless, first use of, 101
Wisby, 34
With, Witte de, 43, 46, 47
Witt, Jan de, 50, 53
Wittenberg, Hanseatic admiral, 34
Wolfe, General James, 69
Won Kyun, 38
Wonsan, South Koreans land at, 152
World War, First, 102–111; Second, 112–150
Wrangel, Count Carl Gustaf, 44, 49
Wright, Rear Admiral Carleton H., 139
Wright, Wilbur and Orville, 101

Xanthippos, Athenian admiral, 12
Xanthippos, Spartan general, 16
Xerxes I, King of Persia, 12

Yalu River, Battle of the, 94, 95
Yamamoto, Admiral Isoroku, 125, 130, 131, 139
Yazid, Arab prince, 25
Yessen, Rear Admiral, 99

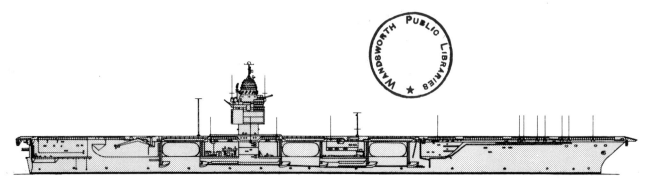